U2

THOMAS DUNNE BOOKS
St. Martin's Press New York

U2

The Definitive Biography

John Jobling

THOMAS DUNNE BOOKS.
An imprint of St. Martin's Press.

Printed in the United States of America. For information, address
St. Martin's Press, 175 Fifth Avenue, New York, N.Y. 10010.

www.thomasdunnebooks.com
www.stmartins.com

Photographs on title page spread:
Larry and Adam courtesy of Otto Kitsinger;
Bono courtesy of Steve Kalinsky;
Edge courtesy of Glenn Shambrook/Feedback 1993

Designed by Kathryn Parise

The Library of Congress Cataloging-in-Publication Data is available upon request.

ISBN 978-1-250-02789-4 (hardcover)
ISBN 978-1-250-02790-0 (e-book)

St. Martin's Press books may be purchased for educational, business, or promotional use. For information on bulk purchases, please contact Macmillan Corporate and Premium Sales Department at 1-800-221-7945, extension 5442, or write specialmarkets@macmillan.com.

First Edition: October 2014

10 9 8 7 6 5 4 3 2 1

In memory of my father,

John Robert Jobling

Contents

Introduction

U2 is rock-and-roll royalty. Born from the spirit of punk rock in 1976 in Dublin, Ireland, and fronted by the charismatic singer, entrepreneur, and political activist Bono, the band has won the hearts of fans and critics worldwide with their anthemic four-piece sound and professed ideals, and have sold more than 155 million albums in the process. And despite their advancing years, their popularity shows no sign of waning: their 360° Tour in 2009–11 played to more than 7 million people and was the highest-grossing trek ever, with takings of $736 million.

U2: The Definitive Biography is the first unauthorized biography of U2 to document and analyze their near-forty-year career objectively, going beyond the myth to present a fascinating warts-and-all portrait of the Irish rock band. Featuring previously unpublished photographs and original interviews with U2's closest friends and business associates, the book offers new information on their pre-contract days in Dublin when they begged and borrowed every last penny just to be heard; played to half-empty clubs, having been rejected by every major record label; and clashed with rival gangs in a hotbed of religious intolerance. It takes us deep inside their lives, exploring their intimate relationships, controversial business dealings, and complex spiritual beliefs, including their early involvement in an evangelical Christian group as Bono looked to fill the void left by the death of his mother when he was only fourteen years old, and the ongoing battle between their Christian values and worldly temptations. It also traces their evolution as musicians from raw post-punk champions to political crusaders, avant-gardists to all-conquering stadium rockers, and finally post-modern cyberpunks to revered rock veterans who have achieved unprecedented cross-generational success.

Furthermore, the book examines U2's humanitarian work, particularly Bono's role as spokesman and lobbyist for the poor and AIDS-stricken in Africa. A three-time Nobel Peace Prize nominee, the lead singer has crossed to the other side of the police barricades to become a major player respected by global corporate chieftains, world leaders, and U.S. Republicans and Democrats alike. At the White House, his ability to bend powerful political ears has caused him to become known affectionately as "the Pest." In doing so, Bono has altered the political power of celebrity. However, his work has also come under fire from both sides of the picket fence. Certain quarters of the media have branded him a political puppet, liberals have heavily criticized his association with power-hungry capitalists looking to sculpt the world in their own corporate vision, and his fellow campaigners have accused him of lending legitimacy to the G8's role in Africa rather than challenging it. Drawing on exclusive interviews with activists, analysts, and government officials, the book sheds new light on Bono's journey into the shady world of politics, in which the line between charity and personal gain can often become blurred.

U2

1

Into the Heart

Ireland in the 1970s was a grim and depressing sight, a far cry from the picturesque snowdrops, daffodils, and early-morning dew cited in the country's Eurovision-winning entry "All Kinds of Everything" at the dawn of the decade. Ireland was dreary, oppressive, and bereft of hope; ravaged by nationwide inflation, endless public-sector strikes, high unemployment, and high emigration. Dublin's north inner city was the epicenter of Ireland's crisis. There the buildings were dirty and decrepit, with over 70 percent of the old Georgian tenements without hot running water, according to historical data. You could literally smell the abject poverty. Speaking at the launch of Combat Poverty's twentieth anniversary in 2007, Father Peter McVerry recalled that the tough inner-city area of Summerhill, for example, was "crawling with rats—rats the size of little kittens and immune from every poison ever invented. Parents would tell you of waking up in the morning and finding a rat on the baby's cot. Some blocks of flats had to share an outside toilet and the children had to be washed in the local Sean McDermott Street swimming pool, as they had no baths or showers."

It was an era when the Catholic Church still exercised powerful influence on government policy and the lives of everyday people, particularly in terms of anything that concerned sexual morality. Sex before marriage was a sin and a social evil. Contraceptives were banned. Homosexuality was a crime. Divorce and abortion, also illegal. Even the slightest "morally dubious" reference found in the media, such as the imported feminist magazine *Spare Rib* showing women how to examine their breasts, was blue-penciled into oblivion as the Church and State sought to hold back the tide of liberalism surging in from Britain and America, and preserve and strengthen Catholic moral teaching in the Irish population, 90 percent of whom attended Mass every Sunday.

Meanwhile, the political struggle in the North was a continual presence in the news. Belfast was Baghdad. Walls and fences divided religious sects. Soldiers patrolled streets. People got tortured. Death piled upon death.

In this period of social and economic crisis and sexual repression, many young people turned to hard drugs in an effort to escape. Coke and heroin replaced acid and hash on Dublin's inner-city streets, and plunged entire neighborhoods further into darkness. And the authorities didn't seem to care; that is until the spread of heroin led to an upsurge in property crime in more-affluent areas as users searched for ways to finance their next fix.

Irish music struggled to find its voice amid the soul-destroying oppression in the South and the fatal bomb blasts in the North. There were very few venues or professional recording studios for the rock bands brave (or stupid) enough to make a noise, and no music press or rock radio existed for much of the decade. The smartly dressed show bands reigned supreme, and made a decent living performing their polite covers of contemporary pop hits and traditional country favorites. But their lack of ambition was crippling. Youth culture's only glimmer of light came from the outer world: *NME*, *Sounds*, pirate radio, and, at least in Dublin, the BBC, which broadcast *Top of the Pops* and *The Old Grey Whistle Test*. True, Ireland had whipped Thin Lizzy and Rory Gallagher into fighting shape, but they both had to move to London to get noticed.

Ireland was a cultural backwater that drowned anyone who stayed there for too long.

It was against this hopeless backdrop that a fourteen-year-old boy called Larry Mullen pinned a note on the bulletin board at Dublin's Mount Temple Comprehensive School looking for fellow students to form a rock-and-roll band. The note read: "Money wasted on a drum kit. Anyone done the same on guitars?"

■

Lawrence (Larry) Joseph Mullen was born on October 31, 1961, in Artane, on the north side of Dublin. His namesake father was a civil servant at the Department of Health and Environment, having previously considered a life in the priesthood, and his mother, Maureen, was a housewife. He was the middle child of three, and the Mullens' only son. Larry was a good-looking lad, but physically small and painfully shy around people he didn't know very well. At the age of nine, his parents thought it would be good for him to express himself through music and enrolled him in a piano course at the College of Music in Chatham Row, near St. Stephen's Green. His teacher was, in his own words, "a really nice lady," but within a few months she pulled him aside and told him that he was probably wasting his time learning the piano because his heart didn't seem to be in it. Larry agreed; he didn't practice much at home and hated studying the scales. But as he was leaving the college that day with his mother, he heard the sound of drums being played in an adjacent room. He immediately turned to her and said, "You hear that? That's what I want to do." His mother agreed to let him, but only if he paid for the lessons himself. So Larry washed cars and mowed lawns until he had saved enough money to attend a weekly class at the college under the tutelage of Joe Bonnie, a veteran of the Irish theater world who specialized in military-style drumming. Larry instantly fell in love with the instrument, but again demonstrated little interest in going through the rudiments of music theory. The little drummer boy was far more interested in doing his own thing, which was tapping along on a drum pad to the music he heard when tuning in to Radio Luxembourg on his pocket radio or watching *Top of the Pops,* specifically glam rockers The Glitter Band, Sweet, and David Bowie.

Tragedy befell the Mullen household when Larry's little sister, Mary, died in 1973. She was nine years old. Larry continued to attend the drum lessons, albeit halfheartedly and less frequently, until 1974 when Bonnie died of a heart attack and his more demanding daughter Monica inherited the class by default. Larry's father and older sister, Cecilia, rewarded him for sticking with the course for so long by buying him his first full drum kit (which was made by a Taiwanese toy company) for seventeen pounds.

In many ways, Larry and his old man had a typical Irish father-son relationship. His father was a tough man, a disciplinarian, and Larry, subconsciously or otherwise, challenged his authority at almost every turn. His father was well educated and hardworking, and he expected his son to follow in his footsteps. But Larry showed little interest in school or education in general. However, father and son had at least one common bond: Gaelic football. Both were supporters of the Dubs and regularly attended games together at Croke Park, and it was there Larry first saw the Christian Brothers–run Artane Boys' Band, dressed in their distinctive blue-and-scarlet uniforms, entertaining the spectators at halftime. Before long, his father had signed him up to the junior marching band, but Larry left after just three days when the Brother in charge ordered him to chop off his shoulder-length golden locks—Larry's pride and joy. Eventually, Larry settled on the Post Office Workers' Union Band, which was a more relaxed outfit and afforded him the opportunity to goof around with friends. He spent two blissful years with them, playing in towns up and down the country.

In the autumn of 1974, Larry joined Mount Temple Comprehensive School after failing the entrance exams to St. Paul's College and Chanel College. Mount Temple had opened its doors just two years earlier and held the distinction of being Dublin's first co-educational, multi-denominational school under Protestant management. It was considered a place that encouraged expression and individuality, free from the sexual, physical, and emotional abuse prevalent in the Catholic-run institutions. Here, it almost seemed as if the old world had died, and the new one was fighting to be born.

Larry was well liked at Mount Temple, especially among the young ladies in his year. "He was quiet but popular," recalls Janice Bearman, an ex-classmate. "I must admit I did not see the attraction, but two of my friends were very taken with him and you were aware that Larry had a lot of female admirers, though he was modest and did not seem to be aware of it. If he was, it did not go to his head." One such admirer was a chatty, blond-haired girl called Ann Acheson, and soon she and Larry were spotted holding hands in the schoolyard.

However, life at Mount Temple wasn't all blushing teenage girls and budding romance for Larry. Because he was quiet and short in stature, he was bullied by a number of older children. His bus ride home, for example, was often a bumpy one. Recalls a former pupil: "We used to get a bus from school that went up Malahide Road and he used to get off at the roundabout in Artane, the same as us. I feel quite embarrassed about it now, but we used to give him a clip over the head. He'd be sitting near the back and everyone who went by would just clatter the poor kid."

Bruised head aside, Larry relished the relative freedom of Mount Temple, which in turn sparked an improvement in his schoolwork. He became particularly adept at maths and art. But the drums remained his true passion. Always the drums. And in September 1976—at the suggestion of his father—he plucked up the courage to put out a call on the school notice board for guitarists to join a new band. "You are not going to get anywhere," Larry Senior told him, "if you continue playing on your own." Although no one paid much attention to his ad to begin with, Larry was determined. He had heard Mount Temple's new arrival Adam Clayton was a mean bass player, and approached him in the schoolyard. "I got so excited when I saw him," Larry said later, "because he had bushy blond hair, he was wearing tinted glasses and a really long afghan coat. He looked so cool and I just said, 'I want to be in a band with him!' "

■

Adam Charles Clayton was born on March 13, 1960, in his grandparents' home in the quaint English village of Chinnor in Oxfordshire. His father, Brian, was a pilot for the RAF, and his mother, Jo, was a rather glamorous-looking housewife and part-time air hostess. In 1964, the Clayton family—Brian, Jo, Adam, and his younger sister, Sarah Jane—upped sticks and moved to Nairobi when Brian landed a job with East African Airways. It was an incredible place to live: the heat, the smells, the servants. But within a year, the threat of ethnic violence amid a tribal conflict had become too great, and affluent white families were encouraged to leave. Brian promptly accepted an offer to work for the Irish airline Aer Lingus and the Claytons settled down in Malahide, a middle-class coastal town ten miles north of Dublin city. Another child, Sebastian, was born there.

Adam attended St. Andrew's National School until he was eight, after which his parents enrolled him at the preparatory school Castle Park in south Dublin, where he boarded through the week. But Adam hated every minute of it. He was chubby, bespectacled, and allergic to every sporting activity outside of cricket, and from day one, he exhibited a total lack of interest in the value systems of getting a good education or working hard in a nine-to-five job. Adam's defense mechanism was to be the class clown and push the boundaries of what was acceptable in an antiquated schooling system. He was a rebel, but a charming rebel. He spoke with a posh English accent and was invariably polite and well mannered. Nevertheless, he often found himself hauled in front of the principal for being disruptive. "What's going to happen to you?" the exasperated principal asked him one day. To which Adam replied: "Well, sir, I'm obviously going to be a comedian."

Pop music and television were frowned upon at Castle Park, but Adam found a small window of escapism in the Gramophone Society, which got together twice a week to listen to classical music. An outgoing teacher also played him the soundtracks from Andrew Lloyd Webber's rock opera *Jesus Christ Superstar* and David Greene's screen adaptation of *Godspell* on an old tape recorder. This inspired him to experiment with piano lessons, but he soon gave them up when he realized that he had neither the hand coordination nor the discipline to do the instrument justice.

At the age of thirteen, Adam was on the move again, to another boarding school in south Dublin, St. Columba's College. It was cold there, terribly cold. There was no heating throughout the old buildings, and the enormous dormitories housed around twenty-five to thirty shivering students. Adam shared a bunk bed with an English boy called John Leslie, and the two of them became close friends. "I think it [St. Columba's] was a shock to both our systems," recalls Leslie, "and we immediately hit it off. Adam was a much more outgoing character than I, and he was up to hijinks literally from the minute he hit the ground there. He was always up for a laugh in the nicest possible way. Never nasty."

Adam and Leslie fell in love with classic rock in a big way when Leslie's brother in England began to ply them with cassette tapes of bands like the Grateful Dead, The Who, and Crosby, Stills, Nash & Young. Later, Adam persuaded his father to bring him back sacks full of tapes whenever he was on pilot duty in Singapore. Then he would make copies and sell them to other students to fund the purchase of cigarettes and alcohol. "By the time Adam was fourteen or fifteen, he had the most enormous library of cassettes," says Leslie. "He was absolutely riveted by rock music really from as soon as he and I could get our hands on it."

Leslie had started playing guitar when he was around twelve, and spent hour after hour practicing in the music room to stave off the boredom of boarding school. Adam occasionally joined him on a secondhand acoustic guitar, and even took a few classical guitar lessons at the school. Eventually, Leslie sold him on the idea of picking up a bass guitar, saying that he thought it would be "quite good craic to make some noise together." It was then that Adam formed a cunning plan and presented it to his parents: buy me a bass and my grades will improve. His parents took the bait and handed him fifty pounds to obtain his weapon of choice. "I remember we went off down to McCullough Piggot's, which is a well-known music store in Dublin, but decided they were far too expensive," recalls Leslie. "We ended up in a tiny little guitar shop to the left of Dame Street where we spied a brown Ibanez bass copy and that's the one he got. Then we just messed about. I didn't really teach him. Adam was a typical rock-and-roll bass player right from when he started in that he wasn't that much interested about playing it. What he was interested in was having a good time, and that's what he did!"

Indeed. Adam grew his hair, wore hippie clothes, and skipped classes. He was regularly put in detention.

Soon the two friends roped in a young drummer called Paul Newenham and started fleshing out a rock musical Leslie had begun to write. "I suppose loosely speaking we were a band, the three of us together," says Leslie. "We rehearsed together in a place called the Concrete Sock, which was an old pig house in the farmyard that was attached to the school beyond the science block. That was our first attempt at playing with other people."

But, alas, the trio's bid to become the heirs to Andrew Lloyd Webber's musical throne was cut short in the summer of 1976 when St. Columba's asked Adam to leave due to his awful grades and taste for the absurd. The mood in the Clayton household was one of anger and shame. Not wanting to stick around for it, Adam agreed to visit Pakistan and Afghanistan for a couple of months with another St. Columba's castoff, George Petherbridge, whose father, John, was the Australian ambassador there. It was during this period that Adam discovered two other abiding fascinations: pretty women and drugs. "That summer was a wild and mind-expanding time, two months of sex and drugs and rock 'n' roll that determined that whatever I would do in future, it had to be creative," he told *The Observer* in 2011. "There was a lot of incense, patchouli oil, and smoking pipes with big lumps of black stuff in them, all the things you associate with the seventies and the hippie trail. I bought an afghan coat, heard Bob Marley for the first time and was drawn to the freedom in his music."

Upon his return, Adam, now sporting an Afro hairdo and the aforementioned tinted glasses and afghan coat, was sent to Mount Temple, where he prepared himself for an uncertain future. Yet again, he found school life intolerably dull and would do anything to alleviate the boredom. The more eccentric and antiestablishment, the better. He took to wearing a yellow hard hat and kilt as he strolled through the school corridors, drank coffee from a flask during lessons, and hung out with the dope smokers at lunchtime. Yet again, detention became like a second home to him.

Larry was two years behind Adam, but couldn't help but notice him. Everybody noticed Adam. Talking music in the schoolyard, Larry was impressed with his apparent rock-and-roll knowledge and invited him to swing by his house that Saturday and audition for his new band. Adam agreed, and soon was joined by Dave and Richard Evans.

■

David Howell Evans was born on August 8, 1961, in Barking, Essex, in East London, and was of Welsh parentage; his father, Garvin, and mother, Gwenda, both hailing from Llanelli, an old industrial town on the south coast of West Wales. His brother, Richard, was two years older than him. Dave's parents had moved to Malahide when he was twelve months old, and Garvin's employer, the electronics giant Plessey, offered the engineer the chance to run their new plant in Dublin. Dave's sister, Gillian, was born there a couple of years later. In his junior years, Dave attended St. Andrew's National School, where he briefly met Adam before the young maverick was wheeled off to prep school. He was a quiet, studious child, but equipped with a sly sense of humor. He claimed, years later, that being Protestant and Welsh-English in origin in a predominantly Catholic country made him feel like "a bit of a freak," and he spent much of his time indoors with his brother reading books and listening to music.

In fact, there was always music playing in the Evans household in some shape or form when Dave was growing up. Garvin had founded the Dublin Welsh Male Voice Choir in 1966 and played a bit of piano, while Gwenda, herself a member of the Malahide Musical Society and a veteran of numerous Welsh church choirs, often sang hymns to her three children before bedtime. It was Gwenda who first introduced Dave to the musical instrument that would become his calling card, when she gave him a toy Spanish guitar for his ninth birthday. Dave liked the shiny look of it and he and Richard spent many an hour fighting over it. Then, at the age of eleven, Dave vowed to follow in his father's footsteps by studying the piano, but called it quits two years later out of frustration. "I always had a good ear," he later told *Hot Press*. "I never used to read the music. I'd just figure it out. But that was no good because the idea was to read the dots and I could never get that together. It was like teaching arithmetic to somebody who already had a calculator."

Upon his arrival at Mount Temple, Dave found the clash of cultures tough going and retreated further into his shell, burying his head in textbooks and hiding out in the school library between classes. From the age of fourteen, he started to take a more serious interest in the guitar, fueled by his discovery of the Horslips (whom he later lost his concert virginity to in a darkened ballroom in Skerries), Rory Gallagher (his second concert experience), and Patti Smith's proto-punk opus *Horses*. When his mother bought him an old acoustic guitar at a local jumble sale for one pound, he began to practice on it religiously. His big brother taught him a few basic chords and he later joined a guitar class at school. Richard, an electronics enthusiast prone to performing wild experiments in the family garden shed, also attempted to build the two of them an electric guitar from scratch following a step-by-step guide in *Everyday Electronics* magazine. The result was essentially a crude yellow V-shaped plank of wood with strings, but for once, Dave had no trouble being heard. When his genial music teacher Albert Bradshaw suggested that he reply to Larry's ad, Dave agreed that it seemed like the next logical step, and he invited Richard along for the ride.

Last to arrive at the audition was Paul Hewson, a charismatic fireball with a God-shaped hole.

■

Paul David Hewson came kicking and screaming into this world on May 10, 1960, at the Rotunda Hospital in Dublin. He was the second child of Bob and Iris (their firstborn, Norman, arrived seven years earlier) and was raised at the semi-detached 10 Cedarwood Road, Glasnevin, sandwiched between Finglas and Ballymun on the north side of the city. Bob was a postal worker, a solid middle-class occupation at that time, while Iris was a stay-at-home mother. On the surface, they were a typical Irish middle-class couple; however, he was a Roman Catholic and she a Protestant, a rare and frequently forbidden arrangement in the highly sectarian Ireland. "My father was very cool about it, he was very evolved," Paul was to recall many years later. "He got a lot of flak and criticism for marrying a Protestant woman. He used to drive us to church [St. Canice's Church of Ireland on Church Street in Finglas] on a Sunday with my mother, drop us off, and then go to Mass [at St. Canice's Roman Catholic Church on Main Street]."

Bob was something else, all right; he was a tough, no-nonsense Dubliner who listened to opera music and conducted the stereo with Iris's knitting needles. The big regret in his life was that he hadn't learned the piano when he was younger, and yet he never encouraged either of his children to be musical or to pursue their own dreams. In fact, quite the opposite was true. "To dream is to be disappointed," he told them. It would be inviting to think that Paul's impulse to think big developed here—an act of rebellion, if you will.

Paul was by nature restless and unpredictable, the kind of kid who was impossible to tie down. He could be charming, thoughtful, and full of laughter, but there was also a lot of aggression and violence in his makeup. On his first day of school at the Protestant-run Glasnevin National School, aged four, he saw a boy bite the ear of his friend James Mahon and responded in kind by taking the culprit's head and banging it off an iron railing until a teacher intervened. Another time, after a row at home, his father caught him placing a banana skin in the hallway and quietly sniggering to himself. "People used to—and family still sort of—put up the cross whenever I come in," he later joked to *Rolling Stone*. "They used to call me the Antichrist."

That same year, Paul befriended Derek Rowen, who lived across the road from him at 5 Cedarwood Road with his father Robert and nine siblings. Paul and Derek literally did everything together, whether it was taking turns on the swing in Paul's back garden, exploring the surrounding fields, or painting in the evenings under the watchful eye of Bob Hewson, himself a willing slave to the canvas. "You're good," Bob would say to Derek. "You've got talent." But he never said the same to his own son. "He used to think there was a future for [Derek], but never for me," Paul would later lament. "That was always the way—same with music, same with anything."

Derek was brought up Plymouth Brethren, with his father, a strict disciplinarian, forcing his children to attend Brethren Sunday school and midweek meetings held at the Merrion Hall in the city center. Paul sometimes tagged along and was both fascinated and frightened by the various Old Testament fundamentalists that spoke constantly of the Scriptures and warned the youngsters about the fires of hell. Between this and attending St. Canice's Church of Ireland every week with his mother, Paul developed a strong foundation of Christian faith from which to build upon.

Around the age of seven, Paul became enamored with the world of television and developed a taste for the theatrical. He would reenact scenes from his favorite shows—*Batman, Skippy the Bush Kangaroo,* and, later, *Hawaii Five-O*—in his living room and the schoolyard. Anything to get attention. One day, he acquired a Batman costume and vowed to rid Glasnevin's streets of crime. However, the big boys made fun of him and pulled the mask over his eyes so that he couldn't see where he was going. He never donned the iconic cape and cowl again. Paul was often living in a world of his own, lost in the power of storytelling. Even back then, he seemed to understand the value and importance of legend. Years later, he would tell the world that he grew up in the heart of Ballymun, which was one of Dublin's most deprived areas, a concrete jungle full of haggard junkies and dealers, as well as feral children riding bareback on ponies and horses. "Bono says that he's from Ballymun because there's more cred, but actually he's from Glasnevin/Finglas," says Dave Robinson, former president of Island Records. "He's very good, he's changed a lot of the little historical facts to suit the U2 story, and that's the sign of a great promotion man."

Paul's interest in music was piqued by seeing Tom Jones perform on a Saturday-night variety show in 1969. The gold-chained, big-voiced Welshman was thrusting his hips and sweating like an animal, causing the middle-aged housewives in the studio to scream and go weak at the knees. It was almost pornographic. "I'm thinking, what is this? Because this is changing the temperature of the room," Paul later told *Rolling Stone*. Then, in 1971, he watched the Scottish pop group Middle of the Road mime along to their UK chart hit "Chirpy Chirpy Cheep Cheep" on *Top of the Pops*. This also made an impression on him. "I thought, Wow! This is what pop music is all about. You just sing like that and you get paid for it." The first record Paul bought was John Lennon's idealistic utopian carol "Happy Xmas (War is Over)," the second Alice Cooper's "Hello Hooray," a pop star's confession that he needs his audience as much as they need him. Soon he would pinch records from his brother's private collection, including David Bowie, Kenny Rogers, Rory Gallagher, Led Zeppelin, and The Beatles.

However, music was yet to become a dominant force in his life. Around the age of twelve, he became obsessed with the game of chess after reading a book about its grand masters. "I found I was being pressured into organizing my thoughts and I wanted to be able to do that because I have a very competitive instinct," he recalled in *NME*. "I was too erratic as a persona and so I found a game like chess suited me because I was able to put everything from my mind and work with something abstract." He later claimed that he went on to compete in major international tournaments, although his father said this was an exaggeration—he merely beat the chairman of his local chess club one time.

Paul remained an erratic fantasist. He'd wake up one day and want to be a politician, the next a traveling salesman like his beloved uncle Jack. On one particular occasion, he wanted to be a thespian and ran away from home, only to return the same day when he found out there were no drama schools in the area. His headstrong and impetuous manner resulted in his dismissal from St. Patrick's Cathedral Choir School (where, incidentally, he studied campanology and assisted the elders in ringing the church bells, summoning the believers to their place of worship) when he was caught throwing dog excrement at his Spanish teacher in a nearby park in 1972, and he was off-loaded to Mount Temple.

There, Paul quickly established a reputation as an unabashed extrovert with a powerfully charged battery of energy and an insatiable curiosity for just about anyone or anything. He was always on the hunt for a good conversation, a willing audience, and he appeared to know everyone at the school by first name. He especially enjoyed the company of the opposite sex and acquired a group of female admirers known simply as "Paul's girls," led by meek bookworm Maeve O'Regan. In his second year, he went on the charm offensive to woo Alison Stewart, who was in the year below. The daughter of a small electrical business owner, Ali was the quintessential girl next door: smart, sweet, pretty, with short dark hair, brown eyes, skin as white and smooth as cream, and a soft, round figure. She was compulsively clad in a gingham dress and Wellington boots. Paul was truly smitten. "He worked very hard at being the heartthrob," Ali would recall in the *Evening Standard*. "He came up to me within the first day and asked, did I know where his class should be going? It was just an excuse to talk to me, and I thought, What an eejit. I remember that on the fourth day at school, I saw him walking across the courtyard and it was, bing. That is the guy for me."

However, Paul's world came crashing down on September 10, 1974, when his mother died of a brain hemorrhage after collapsing at her father's funeral. She was in her midforties. Norman Hewson later told *The Sunday Independent*: "She was on life support for three days, but there was nothing they could do about the brain hemorrhage, and the machine had to be turned off. It was tough for all of us, but hardest on my father." With three alpha males struggling to come to terms with their loss, it was nigh impossible to maintain the same level of standards in the household. Paul and Norman were constantly at each other's throats—especially when it came to carrying out their chores. "I was a bully," Norman admitted. "I gave him a hard time."

Paul wasn't particularly close to either of his parents, but in a strange way this only made it harder for him to let go of Iris. He told *Rolling*

Stone: "When it all went wrong—when my mother died—I felt a real resentment, because I actually had never got a chance to feel that unconditional love a mother has for a child. There was a feeling of that house pulled down on top of me, because after the death of my mother that house was no longer a home—it was just a house."

Paul's mental anguish also manifested itself at school. He was yelling insults, throwing chairs across the classroom, and turning over tables before storming out. One time, he even pinned a teacher up against a wall. Eventually, he was sent to the school's guidance counselor, Jack Heaslip, who nursed him through the darkest stages of the bereavement process. Paul began to question God's judgment and motives, and in 1976, he joined Mount Temple's Christian Union, a group of pupils who held Bible studies in a classroom during lunch hour. Sophie Shirley, the school's young religious teacher and a born-again Christian, presided over the meetings in an unofficial capacity. The eccentric Shirley played an important role in defining Paul and the other members' relationship with God. She portrayed Jesus as a kind of spiritually enlightened and morally robust hippie-cum-rock-superstar and showed them the moralistic film *The Cross and the Switchblade,* in which the lives of a pastor and a gang member are transformed by the power of God. She personally reassured Paul that He loved him and would never stop loving him, that His intentions were true and everything in the universe happens for a reason. "God's fingerprints are everywhere," she said. All he needed to do was look around and listen.

This was a monumental time for Paul, as it was also the year that he and Ali officially became an item (although they briefly broke up after six weeks, when Ali promised her best friend Jackie Stewart that she'd get him out of her system) and when he was exposed to the British rock band The Who on his brother's reel-to-reel tape recorder. The confessional lyrics of Bob Dylan and John Lennon had already struck a chord with the tortured teenager, but it was the dramatic power chords and rage of The Who's guitarist Pete Townshend that set his imagination on fire. It was a visceral and magical sound, where everything and anything seemed possible. Like being a lead guitarist. Consequently, on the advice of his closest friend at Mount Temple, Reggie Manuel, Paul went along to Larry's house to try out for the group. The fact that he could barely tune his brother's old acoustic guitar, let alone play it, was neither here nor there.

▪

And so it was, on Saturday, September 25, 1976, that a group of disparate teenagers crammed into Larry's kitchen at 60 Rosemount Avenue on the north side of Dublin with dreams of becoming a rock-and-roll band. The entire group consisted of Larry on his toy drum kit, David and Richard taking turns on their acoustic and homemade electric guitars, Adam on his brown Ibanez bass copy which he had plugged into a battered purple Marshall amp, and Paul on his brother's acoustic guitar, as well as two other Mount Temple pupils, Peter Martin and Ivan McCormick, whose involvement was always going to be short-lived (Martin was Larry's friend and hoped to be the manager. McCormick, meanwhile, was a spotty thirteen-year-old who was invited to the audition solely because he owned a rather jazzy-looking Fender Stratocaster copy). Much of the meeting was spent tuning up their respective instruments and discussing their favorite music: The Rolling Stones, Fleetwood Mac, Led Zeppelin, Thin Lizzy, T. Rex, etc. Something to emulate, even outshine. Then the evening concluded with a shambolic jam session in which the teenagers attempted to claw their way through The Stones' "Brown Sugar" and "Satisfaction." Soon they had a band name: Feedback. "That was really the name we gave ourselves because that was the predominant sound of our rehearsal, this squealing sound of feedback as we all tried to plug into the same amp," Dave was to recall. "We never made it to the end of a song. We'd always get about a minute and a half in and just the sheer strain would be too much."

Rehearsals continued in Mr. McKenzie's music room at Mount Temple on Wednesdays, which was a half day with optional activities in the afternoon, and Adam's grandmother's house on weekends. The adhesive that held Feedback together was their passion for music and a shared sense of humor and identity inextricably wrapped up with the larger appeal of being in a gang. But for the timid Larry, his days as leader of the pack were numbered pretty much from the get-go. Paul was an alpha male, and what he lacked in musical talent, he more than compensated for with his charisma, enthusiasm, and bravado. Abandoning his own acoustic guitar, he exhibited an almost shamanistic ability to conjure something resembling a melodic sound from the other youngsters' instruments. "He [Paul] was larger than life and the absolute ideal man to front the band, which I think is something that Adam recognized from literally the minute he met him," says John Leslie, who observed many of the rehearsals. Within weeks, Paul had dropped the idea of being a guitarist altogether and appointed himself the lead singer of the band. The fact that he couldn't sing was again irrelevant.

During practice it was clear that Dave was streets ahead of everybody else in terms of musicianship. Relieving the younger McCormick of his beloved Fender Stratocaster copy, Dave would dazzle the others with an array of Rory Gallagher guitar solos he had perfected over the years, and thus positioned himself to be the rational choice for lead guitarist. Richard, for his part, resisted various hints that he was a fifth wheel and declared himself the rhythm guitarist. Larry's status was never in doubt; he was responsible for bringing the teenagers together and could just about keep a beat. Adam, on the other hand, only pretended he could play bass. He had a persuasive "been there, done that" vibe all his own as he nonchalantly smoked his way through a packet of cigarettes and used buzzwords like gig, fret, and action. This justified his place in the final lineup.

The same, however, could not be said of McCormick and Martin, and after just six weeks, both were pushed out the door. McCormick's departure was particularly unceremonious. Adam called him at home one evening and told him that the band had landed a pub gig. He explained to him that he was too young to get into the venue and hoped there would be no hard feelings between them. McCormick was heartbroken and cried his eyes out. It was only later that he realized that his now-former bandmates were also too young for such a gig. He'd been well and truly shafted.

In truth, Feedback's live debut came at a talent contest held in Mount Temple's gymnasium on the last day of autumn term. Virtually all of the students in the school were in attendance, chatting among themselves between acts and eagerly awaiting the final bell. Feedback (minus brainiac Richard, who was at university) were the penultimate act and walked nervously onto the makeshift stage composed of classroom desks thrust together. As legend would have it, when Dave struck the first chord of Peter Frampton's "Show Me the Way," the young audience went wild and almost blew the gymnasium roof off. But that is all it is: legend concocted by the band and perpetrated by their Irish media disciples. In reality, Feedback's two-song set (which also included a cover of the Bay City Rollers' "Bye Bye Baby") was loud, sloppy, and barely recognizable. Most of the pupils either looked on in bemusement or covered their ears. "I just wanted it to end," laughs ex-pupil Janice Bearman. "There was another group that played which I preferred."

Nevertheless, Paul in particular devoured the few crumbs of applause friends felt duty-bound to toss their way, the ecstasy of acceptance and being the center of attention temporarily filling the emotional void left by the loss of his mother and his experiences with his emotionally distant father. He believed God had answered his prayers in the form of the band.

2

Street Mission

After the Mount Temple performance, Adam told his bandmates that he was going to get them gigs in real venues. He had contacts, he said. People who could help them get a foot in the door. For the others, Feedback was nothing more than a hobby. Something to do at night after school, and on weekends. For Paul, it was at best a form of therapy, and prompted a renewed focus on his Leaving Certificate Exam, which he would sit at the end of the school year. Then he was off to University College Dublin (UCD) to study for an arts degree. Dave was a year below Paul, but had plans to get a degree in natural sciences or medicine. Richard had already been awarded a government grant to pursue a bachelor of engineering degree at Trinity College Dublin. And Larry was toying with the idea of leaving school early and finding a full-time job. Nevertheless, Adam remained convinced that the band was the only viable career path. "If you're just another asshole from the suburbs, I think it's pretty understandable if one was offered a chance to take on the world and win, you'd go for it," he later reflected in an interview with Q. "I wasn't destined for greatness in any other area. I'd have ended up being some kind of bad landscape gardener or something."

Exploring and expanding their primitive sound in rehearsals, Feedback added two female backing singers to the lineup in the shape of Stella McCormick, Ivan's big sister, and her best friend Orla Dunne, who had been a part of Albert Bradshaw's singing group at Mount Temple, The Temple Singers, along with Paul. Soon after, Adam persuaded a bunch of students from rival school St. Fintan's to let the new-look band play at an upcoming gig on April 11, 1977 (Easter Monday), in their school hall. St. Fintan's was the local boys' school which the kids in Sutton and the surrounding areas attended, while Mount Temple was seen as a posh liberal school in comparison, so there was always a certain amount of antagonism between the two. Feedback practiced at Adam's house out in Malahide in the week leading up to the show, adding the Eagles' "Peaceful Easy Feeling," Neil Young's "Heart of Gold," David Bowie's "Suffragette City," Jimi Hendrix's reimagining of "Johnny B. Goode," and The Moody Blues' "Nights in White Satin" (with Dunne performing the flute solo, no less) to their repertoire. They were all pretty nervous. At one point, the two girls likened Paul's singing to a pet shop on fire and suggested to Dave that he take over as the lead vocalist.

The gig itself was a farce. Feedback was first on the bill, opening for St. Fintan's hard-rock outfit Rat Salad and headliners The Arthur Phybes Band. Prior to taking the stage, they got into a heated discussion with the former over which group was going to tackle "Johnny B. Goode." "There was a bit of a disagreement backstage as it was one of the only fast songs in their set," recalls former Rat Salad bassist Jack Dublin. "It was settled by agreeing to exchange some drum bits and pieces between Larry and our drummer Robert Campbell, and Rat Salad wouldn't play it. But we played it anyway!"

Feedback's performance was a disaster, according to Dublin. "They were absolutely dire," he says. "I don't think they actually played a song in time together." The low point came when the girls' microphones malfunctioned during "Nights in White Satin," which led Paul, acoustic guitar slung over his back, to kneel at the feet of Dunne and hold his microphone up toward her flute as if she were a guitar god busting out a face-melting solo. The effect looked as comical as it sounded. Backstage after the show, Dunne broke down into tears out of sheer embarrassment. It was agreed there and then that the addition of female backing singers had been a huge mistake. McCormick and Dunne were out. The five boys also eventually decided to distance themselves from the name Feedback and redubbed themselves The Hype, which was the stage name of Bowie's old backing band. (Incidentally, Adam would suffer another humiliating episode at St. Fintan's later that same month when standing in on bass for The Max Quad Band, bringing their rendition of Free's "All Right Now" to an abrupt halt due to his timing issues.)

The Hype continued to practice at Mount Temple as well as play the odd student gig, driven primarily by Adam's unwavering belief that they could carve a name for themselves on Ireland's third-world music scene and escape the mundane trappings of suburban life. Hope arrived in the summer of 1977 when—belatedly riding the explosion of punk rock in London—Niall Stokes launched Ireland's first proper mainstream music magazine, *Hot Press,* and rock DJ Dave Fanning fronted pirate station Radio Dublin. Fanning and *Hot Press* writer Bill Graham (two of only a handful of respected Irish journalists to embrace punk, especially in the context of British "dole-queue rock" which was rooted in economic and social inequality) combed the bars in Dublin, reviewing gigs, interviewing bands. Overnight middle-class and lower-middle-class brats with disposable incomes and a yearning to reject their parents' values stuck safety pins through their noses, mastered the art of gobbing, and formed bands inspired by punk's amateurism and sense of rebellion. It was, in the words of ex-Smiths front man Morrissey, a "musical movement without music."

The curious and free-spirited Adam experienced punk firsthand during his school holidays in London, soaking up its DIY ethic and drugs, and returned to Dublin with a batch of new tapes to inspire his bandmates. "I connected with it immediately," he recalled in *The Observer.* "Suddenly there was a line between people who listened to Led Zeppelin and people who listened to punk and I knew which side I was on."

The introduction of a serious rock media in Ireland had British record labels throwing a curious glance toward Dublin, but the influx of young bands made scoring a gig in a major venue twice as hard. Stuck in the wilderness of school gymnasiums and church halls, Adam called on a few established local musicians for advice on how to break into the burgeoning music scene on Grafton Street and Lower Baggot Street. Steve Averill, lead singer with The Radiators From Space and a graphic designer for a local ad agency, taught him the basics of free advertising, such as putting up flyers in shop windows, handing out cards at other bands' gigs, and calling into radio phone-ins. Adam went one step further, posting self-penned congratulatory fan mail to The Hype to *Hot Press* and *NME*, often under the pseudonym "Brian."

Averill advised him to keep in regular contact with the bars, remain a visible figure. Again, Adam took it to the extreme. Underage, he used a fake ID card to sidestep doormen, and once in the joint he talked to the management and staff like he would be the one doing the favor by letting his band play there. For most, it was hard not to warm to him, the brandy-drinking, cigar-smoking young hustler with impeccable manners and more than a hint of desperation behind his huge fogged-up glasses. Still, for all his hyping, there were no gigs available. "Come back later," he was told repeatedly.

John Leslie recalls: "Adam was very involved in the initial management of them, and perhaps he spent less time worrying about whether he could play and a lot more time about maneuvering them into a decent position where they could take it seriously as a career. Of course, later he would become one of the best rock bass players around."

Meanwhile, Paul had gone to UCD as planned. But just as he was settling into his new surroundings, it emerged that he had failed his Irish Leaving Cert, which was an obstacle one had to overcome to enter university. He was told that if he went back to Mount Temple for another year and demonstrated a degree of proficiency in Irish language then UCD would be more than happy to accommodate him again. He and his father protested, but to no avail. He returned to his old stomping ground with his tail tucked between his legs. The year would be a long one.

On the positive side, the fact that he was now studying only one subject gave Paul more free time to perfect his role as class clown. He caused a scene in the school corridor one morning when he showed up as Mount Temple's first punk, rocking purple drainpipe jeans with matching suit jacket, black Cuban heels, cropped hair, and a chain running from an earring to his bottom lip. Teachers and students gasped in horror at the sight of him, while Ali stormed off in a huff. But it was all a ruse to get attention: the tight-fitting '60s clothes had been dug out from the back of his brother Norman's wardrobe, and the apparent lip chain piercing was in fact a fake.

Away from his school life, Paul had become a founding member of Lypton Village, a surrealist street gang who took their inspiration from the British sketch comedy series *Monty Python's Flying Circus*. United in their discontent with the drabness and predictability of suburban life in Dublin, the teenage friends escaped into a world of humor, music, and literature. Paul, Derek Rowen, and Fionan Hanvey, a shy, androgynous Bowie fanatic who they had befriended at the age of twelve, roamed their neighborhood at night making fun of adult stereotypes and recruiting like-minded "outsiders" usually found playing among the trees in the grounds of the mental asylum up the road. "We grew up studying people on street corners, we laughed at the way they talked and at the expressions they made," Paul said later in *NME*. "We mocked the adult world and agreed we'd never grow up because all we saw was silliness."

Each member of Lypton Village was given a nickname that reflected their personality and the imaginary altered state they inhabited. It was here that Paul christened Derek "Guggi," and Guggi returned the favor by calling him "Steinhegvanhuysenolegbangbangbangbang." But Paul eventually rejected the moniker and instead nominated "Bono Vox of O'Connell Street," with Bono Vox being an alteration of "Bonavox," the Latin phrase for "good voice" (although he denied all knowledge of this) and the name of a hearing aid store just off the aforementioned street. He later shortened it to just "Bono." Dave Evans, a casual associate of the gang, was to be known henceforth as "the Edge" because of his sharp mind and the shape of his head. Other colorful nicknames included

"Gavin Friday" (Fionan Hanvey), "Strongman" (Trevor Rowen), "Dik" (Richard Evans), "Pod" (Anthony Murphy), "the Bottle of Milk" (Tommy McCann), "Dave-iD Busaras" (David Watson), and "the Cocker Spaniel" (Reggie Manuel). Adam and Larry, meanwhile, were dubbed "Mrs. Burns" and "Jamjar," respectively, although neither name stuck due to their non-member status.

Lypton Village was a nice distraction, but Bono kept his eye on the prize: UCD. Adam told him to forget about it. The Hype was the future. But like Edge, Dik, and Larry, Bono couldn't help but question his bass player's faith. That was until The Clash came to town to play at Trinity College Dublin in October. Bono recalled in *The Observer*: "Can't remember the set list, can't remember much about the music, to be honest. I just know that everything changed that night, and I'm sure it was not just for me. Year zero. The shock of the new, where everything reconfigured. . . . As I sat in the box room [at home] and stared out the window the next day, it was very clear. The world is more malleable than you think; reality is what you can get away with."

But first things first; The Hype would have to start composing their own material. Their gigs thus far had been comprised of cover versions, and badly received ones at that—bottle throwing was considered a rational response when they kicked into their rendition of Young's "Heart of Gold." Bono had previously tried his hand at writing a country rock song called "What's Going On," but, despite the band's eagerness to play it live a couple of times, it remained very much a work in progress. Their songwriting process was to be a messy and often confusing one, in which they relied on instinct and musical passion rather than a rigid formula to guide them through the creative swamp. As Edge later admitted in the *Los Angeles Times*, "[I]t became clear to us that we had no idea about songwriting technique. Our way into songwriting was to dream it up. We'd try to imagine how others might do the song, The Clash or Lennon or The Jam." Edge's go-to guitarist was Tom Verlaine of the New York post-punk band Television, and he spent the next twelve months closely emulating Verlaine's simple-but-dramatic rhythm/lead style until he stumbled upon his own variation of it. Bono also adopted a Verlaine-esque nasal whine, itself inspired by Patti Smith, while Larry and Adam just tried to keep in time. "Street Mission," which featured a rare Edge guitar solo, and "The Fool" were the result of this practice and were soon added to the band's set list, along with covers of the Sex Pistols' "Anarchy in the U.K.," Tom Robinson Band's "2-4-6-8 Motorway," and the Ramones' "Gimme Gimme Shock Treatment" and "Glad to See You Go."

Incidentally, the teenagers would have the Ramones' infectious brand of bubble-gum punk to thank for giving them their first big break on national television. Upon hearing that Albert Bradshaw was meeting a producer from RTÉ Television to discuss The Temple Singers appearing on the channel's flagship children's show *Youngline,* Bono told his old music teacher of his desire to audition for the program and practically begged him to bring his big-shot guest down to one of The Hype's rehearsals. The producer arrived in suit and tie, all business, and with the understanding that the young band before him wrote and performed all their own material. By the time they had kicked into their second song, his jaw had almost dropped to the floor in astonishment. He returned to his office at RTÉ HQ convinced that he had singlehandedly discovered the next big Irish act, and eager to boast about it to his colleagues. Little did he know that the teenagers had just passed off the only two Ramones songs they knew how to play as their own.

At the actual taping of the show—which took place on March 2, 1978, yet wasn't broadcast until three months later—The Hype (minus one Dik) dropped the Ramones covers in favor of a prerecorded version of "Street Mission." Their television debut had the uneasy feeling of jumping in at the deep end, with Edge warming to the cameras like a rabbit in headlights and Larry hiding his anxiety behind a smile that suggested he'd been raiding the medicine cabinet. Bono, meanwhile, moved like Mick Jagger, but struggled to master the basics, like lip-syncing in time with the playback. Only Adam looked relatively cool under the heat of the studio lights. Nevertheless, the experience gave them a small taste of show business and reinforced their belief that they were heading in the right direction.

The same could not be said of Adam's school grades. Just days after the *Youngline* breakthrough, the bassist's parents were summoned to the headmaster's office at Mount Temple where they were informed that their wayward son had contributed almost nothing in the two years he had been attending the school—if and when he bothered to attend. If Adam failed to change his ways, he wouldn't be eligible to sit for his Leaving Cert, let alone pass it. This was not what Brian and Jo wanted to hear. Adam had assured them both when they bought him the bass guitar that he would settle down and study hard. "All he ever seems to think about is this 'group' of his," Mr. Medlycott told them.

Adam was read the riot act back home, and things appeared to die down for a couple of weeks. That is, until he was caught streaking through the school's main corridor one lunch break. Enough was enough. In exchange for the Claytons removing their son from Mount Temple, Mr. Medlycott would give the boy a favorable reference that made no suggestion of expulsion. It read: "Adam Clayton, born 13.3:1960, was a pupil of this school from September 1976 to March 1978. He has worked well when stimulated. He has shown considerable initiative and organizing ability, especially in relation to his music 'group,' which has had considerable success. He is a pleasant, cheerful person, was popular and took part in the social life of the school. Because of his late arrival, he has not held a position of responsibility in the school but I have found him to be honest, truthful, and reliable, and am sure that in a suitable position he will be both conscientious and committed."

Jo Clayton was worried her son was heading for the life of a layabout and encouraged him to go out and look for a job. She gave him chores to do around the house so he could earn a little money in the meantime, like washing the dishes, cleaning the bathroom, mowing the lawn. Unknown to her, Adam was using the cash to buy drinks and the odd recreational spliff for his new acquaintances on the Dublin scene, where he spent much of his time hustling for gigs, more determined than ever to make The Hype work.

One night, Adam heard Thin Lizzy's Phil Lynott was in town and staying at The Clarence Hotel on Wellington Quay. He managed to get hold of Lynott's room number through a contact and, unable to curb his enthusiasm, rang him early the next morning for advice on The Hype's next step toward world domination. Lynott was courteous, but nobody's at their best while rubbing sleep from their eyes. He told Adam to cut a demo and send it to the record labels in London. Get a proper manager, someone who's not afraid to bust a few balls. And for god's sake, make allies before you make enemies.

A few days after their conversation, Adam and Larry were leafing through the *Evening Press* when they came across an article about the forthcoming Limerick Civic Week "Pop Group '78" competition co-sponsored by the newspaper and Harp Lager Guinness, in which the winning act got to record a demo with CBS Records free of charge as well as take home five hundred pounds in prize money. Adam threw the paper down, picked up the phone, and entered The Hype. Then he arranged a warm-up gig at the Project Arts Centre, an alternative theater housed in a converted factory on East Essex Street and a place for young and emerging artists from all fields to experiment and develop their craft.

At this stage, Adam had become worried about the band's name. "The Hype" seemed too obvious, lacked a certain kind of mystery. Steve Averill agreed. He told Adam to give him a couple of days to come up with a few alternatives, and one of the names he pitched was U2. It was the name of an American spy plane shot down over Soviet territory in 1960 that set in motion a pattern of extreme mistrust that culminated in the Cuban Missile Crisis. It was also the name of Eveready's most popular dry-cell battery. Or it could simply mean "you too." Adam loved it. Shortly thereafter, Bono and Edge were spotted strutting down the main corridor at Mount Temple wearing homemade U2 badges, eagerly awaiting the inevitable question: "What's all that about?"

On March 17, the newly christened U2 boarded a train heading southwest to participate in the two-day pop contest in Limerick, accompanied by most of Lypton Village. Adam immediately notified the officials of the band's name change, which they misheard as "U2 Malahide," and then took a seat with the others to eye up the competition.

They were one of thirty-six acts scattered around several local venues hoping to survive the preliminary stage, with fellow Dubliners Rockster and Athenry natives The Doves tipped as hot favorites. Still recovering from their gig at the Project Arts Centre the night before, Bono apologized in advance for his hoarse vocals as Edge launched into their three-song set: "Street Mission," "The TV Song" (which was a tribute to their heroes Television), and "Life on a Distant Planet." According to eyewitness accounts, the sound was a muddy mess and Bono was right about his voice, but it didn't matter. U2 progressed to the final eight anyway, where they caused a major upset by snatching victory from their rivals' hands.

"Not just my bandmates, but members of other bands in the concert were of the opinion that they were probably the worst band in the final!" recalls Francis Kennedy, who was a guitarist in The Doves. "They were younger than the rest of us and out of their depth. Bono had a mullet hairstyle and wore a tight double-breasted jacket with brass buttons and epaulettes and leather boots to his knees. All I remember was that he looked cocky but he didn't impress. Both the guitarist and the bassist sounded like beginners [with] poor tone and technique. We thought it was a mistake!"

The adjudicators for the final—held at the multipurpose fleapit the Savoy Cinema—included CBS Ireland's marketing manager, Jackie Hayden, and Billy Wall, head of light entertainment at RTÉ Television, the latter of whom U2 appeared to be on friendly terms with following their appearance on *Youngline*. For many of the contestants, the result reeked of nepotism. "All I know is that I saw Billy Wall coming into the band room at the interval," says Kennedy. "He ignored all the bands except U2, with whom he sat around a small table throughout the interval, chatting. To us, it was a snub—not that any of us wanted to chat with Mr. Wall, but it showed blatant favoritism on his part . . . we were just pawns in the launch of a Dublin band."

During the awards ceremony, Hayden personally pledged to give U2 some serious studio time, while Colm Clarke, Limerick area representative for Guinness, presented them with the check for five hundred pounds. "This means we can solve our money problems in a big way, particularly with regard to equipment," Bono told the one-hundred-strong audience, gripping the check as if his life depended on it. "Now we hope to be able to buy a van." Adam added: "No one in Dublin was interested in us and we came down here as a last resort."

Dik Evans, who neither played his guitar nor cheered from the sidelines in the Limerick victory, officially quit the group two days later to form the Virgin Prunes with Gavin Friday and Guggi. His former bandmates organized a farewell gig for him at the Presbyterian Church in Howth, performing a short set of covers as The Hype, with Dik on rhythm guitar. Then, after briefly stepping aside to let the Prunes make their live debut, they returned to the stage and closed the show with a set of original material as the prize-winning quartet U2. Given Dik's reduced involvement in recent months, his decision to jump ship came as a surprise to no one. "They [U2] became very intense about it and I wasn't, it was almost a generation gap type of gulf between us. I just didn't fit in, the attitude more than anything," he said later. "I never at any stage thought, 'Yeah, I want to be in a band and that's all,' whereas everyone else was starting to feel that way."

Around this time, Adam decided *Hot Press* writer Bill Graham could be of some use and bombarded him with phone calls inviting him to watch U2 play. Graham got calls like these from young wannabe rock stars every day at the office, but no one had ever taken to calling him at the Howth home he shared with his mother Eileen like Adam had. Graham hadn't seen U2 live, but he had read about their Limerick exploits, and this coupled with Adam's tenacity was enough for him to agree to meet them at the Green Dolphin restaurant in Raheny one April afternoon. Graham was twenty-seven years old, a world of backstabbing away from the fresh-faced teenagers. He was a warm, bighearted man; the antithesis of the circles he roamed. He was sharp as a whip, incredibly so, and possessed a deep knowledge of rock-and-roll and Irish-roots music. He liked U2 right off the bat. They asked practical questions about the Dublin scene, and exuded a genuine modesty and seriousness that separated them from the shortsighted posers he had the unfortunate pleasure of dealing with on a regular basis.

U2 invited Graham along to their upcoming recording session with Jackie Hayden at Dublin's Keystone Studios. It wasn't the most productive of evenings, as the band's inexperience in the studio was painfully obvious, while Larry was dragged off home early by his father because it was a school night. Regardless, Hayden was intrigued by their raw potential and offered them a contract on CBS's Irish division. But U2 politely declined. The contract paper read like a Japanese instruction manual and they weren't prepared to commit themselves to something they clearly knew nothing about. Graham was also titillated by what he saw and heard, and when he returned home later that night he sat down and wrote the first feature article on the band for *Hot Press,* simply titled "Yep! It's U2." (In what was an early sign of Bono's propensity to analyze every detail from every conceivable angle imaginable to the point of obsession, when the story first appeared in the magazine he took it upon himself to stake out a newsagent's in Grafton Street and find out what sort of people were interested in the band.)

Graham became a kind of father figure to U2 in those early days. He let them pick his brain, warned them of the excesses of rock and roll, and gave them the keys to his record collection. Lypton Village christened him "Burgundy" because of his claret lips. And like Phil Lynott, he stressed the importance of finding a full-time manager, especially if they wanted to break the local scene and beyond. When Adam asked Graham if he had anyone in mind, he replied: "Paul McGuinness."

■

Paul McGuinness was born in June 1951 in an army hospital in Rinteln, Germany, where his father, Philip, a flight lieutenant in the RAF, was stationed. His mother, Sheila, was a schoolteacher and a native of Kerry. McGuinness had spent much of his childhood in England and Malta as his father moved from base to base. He was homeschooled by his mother before being sent to Ireland at the age of ten to continue his education at a boarding school in Kildare, run by the Jesuits, where, according to the late economics editor for *The Irish Times* Paul Tansey, he acquired "the natural arrogance that is inculcated into students of Clongowes Wood [College]." Of chubby build, he was bullied at school and a friend, speaking to the same Irish paper, remembers him as moody and withdrawn at social events. However, this did not arrest his academic development: he directed two reasonably well-received plays, edited the school magazine, and won the gold medal for best debater.

Receiving honors in English, French, and Latin in his Leaving Cert, McGuinness then enrolled at Trinity College Dublin in 1968 to read philosophy and psychology. Trinity was a pretty cool place to be. There was a steady supply of dope to be smoked and a surprising amount of no-strings-attached sex to be had, regardless of the sense of immorality and illegality of it all; indeed, it was often joked that at least half of the forty-five hundred students at Trinity were on the pill for medical reasons. McGuinness's closest friends there included such future luminaries as Michael Colgan, director of the Gate Theatre in Dublin, who at one stage defeated him for the chairmanship of the Trinity Players drama group; Donnell Deeny, onetime member of the Arts Council of Northern Ireland; and a certain Bill Graham. He also met Kathy Gilfillan, whose fruitless campaign for the presidency of Trinity Students' Union he personally oversaw. He and Kathy later married in 1977.

McGuinness was, by all accounts, quite a poor stage actor. Yet he still stood out from his star-bright peer group, a fact attributed to the formidable work ethic and ruthless ambition he exhibited. He often confessed to friends that he would never be truly happy until he was rich.

In his third year at Trinity, McGuinness edited the college magazine, *TCD Miscellany,* which he used as a means to enact revenge on those who he felt had spited him in some way. In the words of another student, Chris de Burgh, the veteran pop balladeer, "Paul always used to draw these bizarre pictures of guys lying down with their tongues hanging out, and with nails through the tongues. Quite weird." One regular victim was Brendan Kennelly, the junior dean whose candor and playful compassion clashed with McGuinness's biting wit, just one symptom of "the arrogant and aggressive aspects of his nature" that in time many others would encounter (according to those close to him, such behavior may be a product of him overcompensating for shyness). But Kennelly would claim a small victory. At the end of the year, McGuinness received a letter from his archnemesis, regretfully informing him that he hadn't attended enough lectures to sit his final exams. McGuinness was sent packing.

Though he would earn enough money driving a taxi around London and working as a tour guide in Lourdes to return to Trinity and repeat his third year, he didn't stick around long enough to finish his degree. After landing the job of location manager on *Zardoz,* John Boorman's 1974 sci-fi film starring Sean Connery in a less-than-flattering red thong with matching suspenders, he opted to remain in the industry, largely as an assistant director on TV commercials.

By 1976, McGuinness was a regular patron of The Bailey, a popular pub on Dublin's Duke Street, where he would bump into a few of his old Trinity chums, including one by the name of Don Knox. Knox was then a member of the folk-rock group Spud, who had enjoyed some success in both Ireland and Sweden with their first two albums, *A Silk Purse* and *The Happy Handful,* as well as building a strong live reputation throughout Europe. One evening over drinks, Knox told McGuinness that Spud's three-year record contract with Polydor was up, and that they had begun to question their manager's vision for the band. Although he was not much of a music connoisseur, McGuinness had often shown an interest in becoming a rock-and-roll manager. He related the success of The Beatles and The Rolling Stones to their respective managers, Brian Epstein and Andrew Oldham, and had watched with envious eyes as Donnell Deeny's older brother, Michael, helped turn Horslips into a relatively successful Celtic rock export. More than ever, McGuinness thought band management a viable road to the wealth he coveted, and he offered his services to Knox and Spud.

But it wasn't exactly a match made in heaven. Knox recalls: "Whereas our previous manager had been getting all the dates and was acting as agent as well, Paul wasn't so hot at that, and the possibility of forging a link with Louis Walsh, then a young band agent, was explored. That didn't happen so we had to get an independent agent and immediately our costs went up. We felt that the band had a right to 50 percent of the turnover, but after expenses and commissions it was hard to do. Paul has said that our sights weren't set very high, but all I've wanted to do is play music and make a living out of it, where nobody's trying to be a star. I mean, there'd be an inherent difference between himself and myself; he sees music as an industry, and I see it as a gift."

To his credit, McGuinness organized the release of Spud's self-financed Irish single "Kitty," persuaded his journalist friend Bill Graham to write about the band in *Scene* magazine, and in the teeth of the punk revolution secured an album deal with the Swedish-based label Sonet Records. However, that latter deal turned out to be a double-edged sword, as Spud fell victim of British record company politics. "We were rather forced on Sonet UK by the Swedish company, and Rod Buckle [Sonet's managing director] wasn't at all happy with us being inflicted on him," says Knox. "He kind of buried us, really."

McGuinness and Spud parted company just twelve months into their business relationship, after he tried to push through plans for a new commercially oriented pop direction, which led to irreconcilable creative differences within the original lineup and eventually tore them apart. "There were a couple of guys who were writing stuff and I think maybe they saw his vision as being the way to go, to become pop stars and so on," recalls Knox, who was very much against the idea. "We'd already done one album with Sonet and we started to record the second one, but it ended up on the rocks. The writers left and I soldiered on without the manager because basically he'd been sidelined by the band. He was shafted, really. I suppose I was disloyal to him because I was trying to hang on to my living. I'd put years into the band." McGuinness's exit "wasn't really amicable, but it wasn't the opposite of that," adds Knox. "I reached a settlement with Paul, and I'm still welcome to his New Year's Day parties."

McGuinness returned to the film industry, but in the back of his mind he continued to believe that with the right band, one that was young, hungry, and had fewer fiscal obligations, he could realize his dream of making it rich. Managing Spud had been more bother than it was worth, he told Bill Graham one night over a bottle of wine. He explained that his management philosophy minimized the importance of Irish popularity, emphasizing that a weekly spot on Grafton Street did not make you a successful act. Yes, the money was decent, but the chances of ever making a comfortable living out of it were limited. The Grafton crowd would soon tire of seeing you week in, week out. McGuinness underlined the importance of finding and holding down an international audience. It would take time and money. What you earned you would have to pump straight back into the band for touring expenses, equipment, and so forth. But the audiences were there for the taking if you were willing to devote yourself to finding them. He just hadn't found that "baby band" yet.

Graham agreed with McGuinness 100 percent, so it came as little surprise that he recommended him to Adam. The U2 bassist promptly called McGuinness and arranged to meet him at his flat on Dublin's Waterloo Road in late April 1978, and brought along a tape of U2 rehearsing, which McGuinness played on his telephone answering machine (he didn't own a music player). McGuinness wasn't exactly blown away by what he heard, but agreed to see the band perform live out of respect for Graham. He put it off for as long as he could, however, until May 25, when U2 opened for The Gamblers at the Project Arts Centre. It was a case of killing two birds with one stone. His fifteen-year-old sister Katy managed The Gamblers, and big brother was there to make sure she got paid.

As for U2 in the flesh, McGuinness was surprised by their stage presence, especially Bono, who prowled it like a young Iggy Pop, minus the wrist cutting and blood. The punk-rock thing to do at the time was to hide behind your haircut or turn your back on the audience, but Bono appeared to be looking every one of them straight in the eye, foolishly and courageously, demanding their full attention. He was the ultimate exhibitionist. The music, which would certainly need a degree of polishing, possessed the energy of punk, yet the vibe of it was undeniably more positive. "They were brilliant, but very coarse," McGuinness told *Vanity Fair* in 2004. "In a way, they were doing exactly what they do now. Only badly."

After the show, McGuinness bought the U2 teenagers a round of orange juice in the pub next door. He shared with them his management philosophy, and was pleased to see it registering. He thought they seemed like good kids, if a little naïve. But they were enthusiastic and they asked the right questions. Bono in particular was a good listener and an even better talker. Intrigued by their raw potential and hunger, McGuinness agreed in principle to represent the band, although it wouldn't be until some months later that he fully committed himself to the U2 cause. His experience with Spud had taught him to err on the side of caution until he had a clearer picture of the group.

Bono said later of McGuinness: "He was in that tradition of public school managers of punk rock bands—The Rolling Stones had one. He was a dapper dresser. Barmen wouldn't argue with Paul, and later it was customs officials, record companies, agents. He had a slightly pompous air, but that came from a belief that this band was the best band on the planet. He's kind of an extraordinary man."

■

While McGuinness gradually eased into the U2 managerial position, Adam went about trying to increase funds and develop a local following, eventually gaining the band support slots with Modern Heirs, Revolver, and Brit pilgrims Advertising in the subsequent weeks. However, as far as identifying potential venues went, he wasn't exactly spoiled for choice. "There was a distinct lack of venues and the ones that were there left a lot to be desired," remembers Jack Dublin, then bass guitarist in Dublin punk outfit Rocky de Valera and the Gravediggers. "Smelly, dark, and incredibly dirty places, and in some cases downright dangerous. Dressing rooms usually smelled of piss, stale beer, and the worst B.O. imaginable. If you saw these venues on the inside during daylight you would probably run away screaming, having discovered some mutant animal or plant life living blissfully on the floors that when you stood still for too long stuck you to the spot. The Baggot Inn and Toners were side by side on Dublin's Baggot Street and were incredibly claustrophobic when full, but were the best pubs to play in the city center. The Baggot Inn being the more prestigious. The Celebrity Club was for bands with a larger following or the UK bands that toured Ireland, as was McGonagles."

Soon, Mount Temple would be off-limits to U2, as Bono, Edge, and Larry were about to leave the school for good and move on to pastures new. They bid farewell to the place that helped shape them at an open day event held in the teacher's car park shortly before their end-of-year exams, although few onlookers appreciated their efforts. "They were rubbish, to be honest," laughs ex–Mount Temple pupil Mark Evans. "It was on top of the boiler house roof and, I suppose, because it was the only real band in school everybody was out to watch them. But they were nothing special. In fact, most of the people I hung around with at that time didn't like the band and thought they were tossers. It was only as time went on people started to appreciate them."

Since they were left without a rehearsal room of their own, Bill O'Neill, the outgoing Presbyterian minister for Howth and Malahide, let U2 practice in the local church halls, although he confessed at the time that he "simply can't make heads or tails of their music." Edge's parents also gave the band permission to turn their garden shed into a makeshift rehearsal space, lining it with old carpets to keep the sound in. Now and again, the teenagers would come barreling out of the boiling-hot hut, coughing and gasping for oxygen. Edge's sister, Gillian, would cool them down by throwing buckets of cold water over them. Occasionally, she filled their rumbling bellies with food.

Furthermore, as none of U2 had passed their driving test yet, they relied on the kindness of friends and relatives to chauffeur them to and from gigs. "I took them around in an old van I had at that point—Crofton Airport Hotel, McGonagles, and The Baggot Inn, those sorts of places," remembers John Leslie. "But I wasn't with them for long because I was actually working over there in theater." In Leslie's absence, Gwenda Evans and Jo Clayton stepped up to the plate, cramming everyone and everything into Gwenda's battered old Beetle. One such good deed saw the mothers end up at the Top Hat Ballroom, where U2 opened for The Stranglers in front of twenty-five hundred punks baying for their decidedly un-punk blood (Bono would later claim that he liberated a bottle of wine from The Stranglers' own private stash after they didn't even extend U2 the courtesy of a sound check or dressing room). Eventually, younger and more socially acceptable roadies came forward, eager to attach themselves to the up-and-coming group.

Around this time, Edge was accepted into the natural sciences program at the College of Technology, Kevin Street, but asked his parents if he could take a year off from school to focus on the band. Gwenda and Garvin allowed him to do so, with the understanding that if U2 had failed to secure a record deal by the end of that school year, then he would go off to college. Bono reached a similar agreement with his father.

There was, say sources, a desperation among the teenagers to succeed, to transcend their musical limitations, to always be active rather than sit back and wait for everything to fall into place. One of the first things they did was to book Keystone Studios, with the aim of putting together a high-quality demo tape that they could mail to radio stations and record labels in the UK and Ireland. Not wanting a repeat of the Hayden/CBS farce, McGuinness brought in his friend Barry Devlin, then bass guitarist and vocalist with the Horslips, to guide them through the studio session. Four tracks were committed to tape in all: "Shadows and Tall Trees," "Street Mission," "The Fool," and "The Dream is Over."

But one regrettable offshoot of U2's tigerlike hunger for the prize was their quick tendency to take chunks out of one another. As Adam later confessed in *Time* magazine: "The first couple of years, we kind of hated each other. It was very competitive, and everyone was trying to come out on top." It was during this restless and combative period that Larry was identified by the others as the runt of the litter and a potential barrier to success. In many ways, the first founding member of the group was the least committed. He had landed a steady job as a motorbike courier for the oil exploration company Seiscom Delta and expressed lingering doubts about whether or not U2 was a realistic career.

His work commitments also meant that he often couldn't make their rehearsals or first few publicity shoots, so Guggi, who bore a passing resemblance to the baby-faced teen, had to stand in for him. Eventually, the others auditioned their sometime roadie Eric Briggs to replace him permanently, although Larry's lack of commitment wasn't necessarily the main reason for them taking such drastic action. According to a source: "It wasn't that Larry was dragging his arse, he just wasn't that good of a drummer. If you were around and saw them back then, you would have to say he was the weak link, and he was the weak link for a long time. Eric Briggs was a better drummer technically, but he was also difficult to get on with. That's why Myster Men fucked him out in the middle of 1980. But his significance is that he is the living proof that U2 was not four legs of a table, undividable and united forever. They did actually figure out possible better ways of succeeding and one of them was to get rid of Larry."

The idea of dropping Larry was scrapped altogether when Maureen Mullen was tragically killed in a car accident in Dublin in late November.

3

Fortune Favors the Bold

By January 1979, U2—hard on the heels of a high-profile support slot with The Greedy Bastards, an all-star band made up of members of the Sex Pistols and Thin Lizzy, at the Stardust nightclub—were ready to headline their own Dublin club gigs, starting at the relatively upmarket McGonagles, supported by Lypton Village cohorts the Virgin Prunes, who at the time were also thought, quite wrongly, to be managed by McGuinness. The Prunes—slang for "freaks"—now also included Strongman on bass, Pod on drums, and Dave-iD on narration, and were occasionally backed by Larry, Adam, and Edge on their respective instruments. U2 and the Prunes essentially represented the two sides of Lypton Village; where U2 wanted to inspire and make a connection with the audience, the Prunes wanted to traumatize and alienate them. "Art Fuck," they called it. Gavin, the lead vocalist, would tear onto the stage tarted up like an East German hooker and invite the audience to call him a "queer." Guggi could barely sing or play an instrument. His role was mostly stage theatrics, which included holding aloft a pig's head and drowning himself in its blood for an anti-abortion number. (The pigs came from the Dublin Meatpackers in Cloghran, where Gavin worked as a purchasing and stock control clerk.) The music itself was just as challenging, alternating between playful and psychotic—usually in the same song. McGuinness loathed the Prunes. He thought them childish and self-indulgent, as well as being completely counterproductive to his real clients' objectives. Nevertheless, the U2-Prunes double act became the talk of the local scene—aided by attention-grabbing graffiti plastered on buildings and bridges proclaiming U2 CAN BE A VIRGIN PRUNE—and everybody who was anybody in Dublin wanted to experience their live shows.

At the same time, U2 was making their fair share of enemies, which was precisely what Phil Lynott had warned Adam to be careful of. Rumor had it their manager was a cold and ruthless man of considerable power and wealth, and it didn't help matters when McGuinness later sued the highly regarded Dublin fanzine *Heat* out of existence for alleging in an article entitled "McGuinness (Isn't) Good for U2" that he had used unscrupulous methods to ensure U2 secured a prestigious support slot at Trinity College Dublin at the expense of rival band Modern Heirs. U2 also attracted the attention of a small gang of youths originating from Bono's neighborhood called the Black Catholics, who prided themselves on disrupting other people's gigs. On more than one occasion, U2 was forced to defend themselves against a barrage of heckles and the odd flying bottle courtesy of the Black Catholics, who referred to them as "dirty, stuck-up Proddies." McGuinness ejected one such misguided pest by the hair from a gig at the Project Arts Centre, adding the potential for physical violence to his reputation in Dublin.

However, it should be noted that tales of the Black Catholics' so-called reign of terror have been wildly exaggerated, be it from U2 or ex-gang members hoping to gain street-tough cred. As one source explains: "The Black Catholics were completely insignificant. There were maybe half a dozen [members] and they acquired this reputation afterward as some kind of threat or sectarian threat; anytime I see a reference to them it's always wrong because it's coming from these gobshites themselves and they had such an exaggerated notion of themselves. The perception was that these people were hostile to U2 on two grounds: one, on a sectarian basis, and two, on a class basis, that the members of U2 were somehow middle-class Protestants. The irony of the Black Catholics was that they were all nice middle-class boys who had gone to nice middle-class Catholic schools and literally went on to go into jobs in the civil service, the department of foreign affairs, and banks. They all lived very respectable lives afterward."

Between gigs, the Lypton Village crowd began to experiment with street theater, reenacting scenes from *Monty Python,* taking electric drills and stepladders onto buses. The more absurd, the better. And it was here that they came across an inner-city group as eccentric and unconventional as themselves. One evening while hanging out in a McDonald's restaurant on Grafton Street, they overheard two strangers engaged in a heated argument about religion, one of whom had the Bible clutched tightly against his chest. When the war of words had ended, the inquisitive teenagers approached the God-fearing man and asked him his name. He introduced himself as Dennis Sheedy, a preacher and prominent member of Shalom, a Charismatic Christian sect devoted to surrendering their egos and material desires before the healing grace and fiery breath of the Holy Spirit. Sheedy spoke of signs and wonders and asked the teenagers if they had a relationship with the Lord. His fanaticism gave most people the willies, but Bono was reminded of the men that had so fascinated him when he attended the Plymouth Brethren church with Guggi's family. More recently, Bono and Ali; Larry and Ann; Edge and his new girlfriend, Aislinn O'Sullivan, whom he had first locked tongues with at a Buzzcocks gig; and the rest of Lypton Village had formed their own "Monday Night Prayer Group" at the Willows, the Rowen brothers' rented house in Glasnevin and Lypton Village HQ. It was an attempt to explore their faith in a DIY fashion and find a direct line to their deity away from the iron rule and hypocrisy of the Church establishment. Soon, they opened their doors to Shalom and became full-fledged members of the sect, having fallen under the spell of its main leader, Christopher Rowe, a magnetic preacher who had been raised in a missionary station in China, and unable to resist the promise of salvation and enlightenment—Adam refused to tag along on the grounds that he believed Rowe and company to be one Hail Mary away from a straight-jacket. In time, Shalom's membership number would outgrow the Willows, and the meetings moved to more suitable premises in the city center, just off Capel Street.

Dublin had its fair share of urban religious movements and cults, especially in trendy areas like Grafton Street where buskers were often outnumbered by Hare Krishna practitioners and white-robed men and women wielding clipboards, while groups such as the Church of God, the Unification Church, and Scientology lurked in the shadows, weighing up potential disciples and fine-tuning their respective recruitment pitches. Newspaper reports read like a parent's worst nightmare, with stories of fresh-faced teens turned into non-autonomous zombies through brainwashing or mind control. Such was the widespread concern that the Catholic Church—which many would argue is the biggest and most far-reaching cult of all—purportedly put in place a special unit to monitor the behavior and growth of these competing organizations.

Rumors of U2's conversion to born-again Christianity quietly began to make the rounds on the Dublin scene, producing a mixture of mild irritation and bemusement. Bill Graham, a self-described "ex-Catholic agnostic," couldn't bring himself to believe such gossip when he traveled out to the Willows to interview U2 and the Prunes for a lengthy *Hot Press* feature intended to sell the two groups to a wider audience. But then, twenty minutes into the taped conversation, Bono told him, apropos of nothing, that there was "one other thing you should know about the Village—we're all Christians." Although this did little to dampen Graham's enthusiasm for either group, the journalist chose to leave Bono's unprovoked confession out of his final draft when it hit newsagents' stands in March. He could see U2's potential and felt that such an un-rock-and-roll statement would only hinder their career, both at home and in the UK. "He wanted to protect them from the start," says a source. "But they [U2] weren't making any secret of it. They were sensible enough to know not everyone would see it the way they saw it."

That same month, McGuinness, armed with a new U2 demo tape recorded at Eamonn Andrews Studio in Dublin, flew to London in a confident mood to strike a deal with a major record label. He hit all the usual offices nestled within the two square miles of Manchester Square and Soho Square, each time mustering all his urbane charm and dapper dress sense to negotiate his way past the reception area and into the warmth and seemingly endless possibilities of the A&R department. But the only one to show even a hint of genuine interest in U2 was Chas de Whalley, a talent scout at CBS Records. Listening to the tape at his Soho office, de Whalley thought them to be loud and coarse, but the manager talked an awfully good game, whetting his appetite with news of a successful appearance on national television and a dramatic victory at a CBS Ireland–sponsored talent contest—of which the CBS man himself was completely unaware, such was the nonexistent level of dialogue between the company's London and Dublin offices. Although indifferent to U2's music, de Whalley promised McGuinness that he would make every attempt to see them play live in the near future.

Unfortunately for U2, no amount of praying or group hugs could alleviate their financial woes. Despite a succession of headline shows, they were desperately low on cash. McGuinness had set aside a money pot full of loose change in his flat-cum-office for travel expenses, while the band even played the odd university lunchtime gig, during which a roadie would go around with a bucket to collect a few bob for them. But it wasn't nearly enough. So Bono got a part-time job as a petrol pump attendant, only to quit once the cars started to queue for miles at the first sign of the petrol crisis. Adam earned his keep as a van driver transporting pottery for a small retailer based out of Malahide. He used the van at weekends to haul U2's gear around until he was fired when he misinterpreted a corner on the way to a band meeting and flipped the vehicle over. Adam recalled: "All I remember is waking up, upside down, dangling, and my glasses had come off. And I thought, 'Fuck, I've got to get to the meeting!' "

Edge was less concerned about money. Aside from music and Shalom, the only thing on his mind of late was Aislinn. She was a smart, attractive brunette, the kind that ought to come with a warning label. Suddenly money worries and the pact that he had made with his parents rarely seemed to bother him. They would just have to be dealt with further on down the road.

Larry, too, had been struck by Cupid's arrow. He and Ann had enjoyed hanging out together at school, but their relationship had since blossomed into something more serious. They were opposites in many ways. Larry was introspective, cautious of strangers or anything in general. Ann was warm, gregarious, and emotional. She had nursed him through the trauma of his mother's death, offering him a sympathetic ear when he felt ready to talk. Bono, another contrasting personality, had also been a rock for Larry during his hour of hurt, the U2 front man understanding what he was going through better than anyone. And it was both the shock of Maureen's death and the subsequent support of Bono that compelled Larry to quit his messenger job and commit his future wholeheartedly to the band. It was now all or nothing for the little drummer boy.

As for Bono, he was, on the surface, a confident, gracious young man—the support of Ali, the humor of Lypton Village, and the emotional catharsis of the Shalom meetings and performing on stage went some way to achieve this. But he was still capable of fierce mood swings and chair-hurling outbursts. Behind his infectious enthusiasm and cheeky smile, a terrible anger seethed away inside him. Life at 10 Cedarwood Road had become unbearable. He and his father were constantly butting heads, Bob growing more frustrated by the day at his son's so-called music career and still refusing to acknowledge the death of Iris or, as Bono saw it, even her existence. Bob was hurting all right. He just knew how to bottle it up, keep it private, lest he be viewed as weak. He retreated behind sarcasm and biting wit, a typical old-school Irish male response. Norman, the unlikely peacekeeper on so many occasions, had left home by now, spreading his wings for more tranquil surroundings. The writing was on the wall. The Bono and Bob Show was going to end in broken bones.

But Bono was, for once, being practical about U2's current situation.

The four teenagers had very little money, and he wasn't about to go crawling to his old man, who seemed to relish telling him this rock-and-roll thing wouldn't pan out. No, Bono went straight to what he thought was the root of the problem—he went to McGuinness. He stormed into his manager's office and accused him of dragging his backside. He demanded to know where the international deal was and questioned his so-called management philosophy. McGuinness tried to reassure him but to no avail. Bono was further frustrated when Adam, in the wrong place at the wrong time, sided with their manager, and he almost took the door off its hinges on his way out. Bono, ambitious, restless, and bull-headed, decided he was going to take matters into his own hands. He borrowed three hundred pounds from Ali, and the two of them—along with a new friend-cum-advisor called Andrew Whiteway—caught the ferryboat to England to see if they could succeed where McGuinness had not. They hit practically every record company and music magazine in the capital, dropping off copies of the recent demo tape and imploring them to come and see U2 perform live in Dublin. Dave McCullough of *Sounds* magazine was particularly impressed with the demo, and later marveled: "Here was a band that defied trends, blends, or bombast, a band that revealed direction, assurety, and downright arrogance, letting you know from the Mickey Mouse confines of a C-60 cassette that they had something vital to contribute to the rock and roll of 1979."

In June, Chas de Whalley and his CBS Records colleague Howard Thompson arrived in Dublin to check out U2 and received the full VIP treatment from the seemingly well-heeled McGuinness. De Whalley recalls: "It was 'Strawberry Time' in Dublin as they called it, which was when all the chic companies threw parties and ate strawberries and drank champagne, and Paul managed to get me and Howard invited to one of these things. So we got off the plane and ended up getting well and truly drunk at a party held in the garden of a top Dublin ad agency. Which was great."

The U2 gig took place later that evening at McGonagles, one of four Thursday-night "Jingle Bells—Christmas in June" shows in which the stage was adorned with Christmas decorations as a publicity stunt. But despite being plastered on expensive alcohol, de Whalley wasn't exactly blown away by what he heard. "As a band goes they weren't particularly special," he says, "but Bono did have a certain something which was really impressive. When I was at university I had seen Ian McKellen in the Jacobean tragedy *'Tis Pity She's a Whore* and Bono seemed to have all of McKellen's moves and had a definite charisma on stage. That's what struck me the most. I remember saying to Howard, shouting in his ear over the music, that I thought Bono was either going to be the next Alex Harvey and be a larger-than-life character who burns out after a couple of hits, or he was going to be the next David Bowie and be a major force in pop music."

Unbeknownst to de Whalley, Bono—along with key members of Lypton Village—had begun studying mime under theatrical actor and ex-con Mannix Flynn to develop his stagecraft. Flynn helped Bono create the stage character of "the Fool," whose routine consisted mainly of bumming a cigarette from a member of the audience during "Boy/Girl" and then struggling to light it. The hard thing, of course, was making it look spontaneous.

On the strength of Bono's stage presence, de Whalley pitched the head of A&R, Muff Winwood, the idea of taking U2 into a studio in Dublin and releasing the end product on the Irish division of CBS Records as a means of capitalizing on the band's growing popularity there and recuperating some of their own travel expenses. De Whalley emphasized that if it didn't work out, he would take full responsibility. Winwood gave him the nod to go ahead subject to one provision: the talent scout also produced the session. And so it was that U2 signed to CBS Ireland for five years. The deal put a bit of money in the coffers, and since it only covered Ireland they were free to negotiate with other labels overseas. McGuinness was adamant that if they had a hit single on home turf, an international deal would soon follow.

With the ink still wet on the contract paper, de Whalley returned to Dublin to see U2 perform at the community center in Howth and once more on August bank holiday weekend at the Dandelion Market, a disused indoor car park at the top of Grafton Street. Their latter gig—one of eight hosted there over the next few months—was intended to introduce the band to a younger demographic, as strict licensing laws prohibited anyone under the age of eighteen from setting foot in a pub. (Incidentally, this period marked the end of the Black Catholics' premeditated disruptions, after Bono asked a group of burly bikers to man the door at the Dandelion to stop them getting in.) De Whalley then led U2 into Windmill Lane Studios, where they worked for two days on three tracks: "Out of Control," "Stories for Boys," and "Boy/Girl." De Whalley had never produced before and was by no means a skilled musician, so his inexperience coupled with U2's own naïveté was only ever going to spell trouble.

"They were a bit ramshackle," remembers de Whalley. "When it actually came down to things going on tape they weren't very tight. Adam has a very strange sense of rhythm and also Larry was a bit of a young thrasher, he wasn't the controlled drummer he is now. We had a particularly difficult session laying down the drum track to 'Out of Control.' There's a section where the whole band breaks down to just a bass drum figure and then it all slowly builds up again. But for whatever reason, Larry's timekeeping was appalling and Adam would be out of sync with the rest of the groove, and so the whole thing would fall apart. It would work okay live when you've got all the excitement to cover the cracks, but actually on tape, under the forensic microscope, it just didn't work. So we had to go back and back to record it and things got very, very fractious. I believe I was being somewhat condescending and patronizing and I know that Larry was getting really upset. I've subsequently discovered that Bono was also getting really angry with me but biting his tongue the whole time. He kept saying, 'Larry's a great drummer, he has lessons with the best drummer in Dublin. He can't be making the mistake!' And I'm going, 'But he is!' "

As tempers flared in the studio, McGuinness sought peace and plied the makeshift producer with ready-made joints, which he gratefully accepted. "Finally we managed to patch something together that was . . . workable," says de Whalley. "But because Edge didn't have any of his echo effects in those days he was basically just chugging away like a somewhat poor man's Ruts guitarist [a.k.a. three-chord power punk Paul Fox]. So in the final mix, myself and Bill, the engineer, slammed a whole lot of flanger all over the guitar to try and give it a contemporary hit sound."

Upon arriving back in London, de Whalley knew in his heart that he and U2 had failed to deliver the goods, and he wasn't at all surprised when Winwood informed him that CBS UK wouldn't be pursuing the band any further. But the news hit the teenagers and McGuinness hard.

■

In late August 1979, U2 received a morale-boosting visit from members of the British music press. Dave McCullough of *Sounds* was smitten with the group, having met Bono earlier in the year and then having heard "Stories for Boys" on an early promo copy of *Just for Kicks*, a compilation album designed to showcase up-and-coming Dublin rock acts to UK audiences, and he convinced his editors that they warranted a blurb. With McGuinness and the magazine agreeing to share the costs, McCullough and photographer Paul Slattery boarded a plane for the Irish capital.

"They all met us at the airport," recalls Slattery. "They were a very friendly bunch of guys. They'd driven up in Adam's old Austin A40, which was literally held together with string. I don't know whether it was legal or not, but you could get away with those things in Ireland. On the way into Dublin I thought I was going to die."

Later that evening, the band treated their guests to a thrilling performance at The Baggot Inn. "It was a tiny little pub," remembers Slattery. "There must have been one hundred and fifty to two hundred people in there, and it was an amazing gig. They were supported by The Blades, who were an Irish mod band and pretty good too. U2 came on and I shot two rolls of film when I probably would have had the money for the one, but I thought they were worth it. Very theatrical. Bono was kneeling on the stage and jumping on various chairs around the bar and stuff like that. Obviously most of the crowd knew him anyway and they went crazy.

"Then we went back to McGuinness's flat, which was in a nice Georgian square, and had more Guinness after quite a few pints at The Baggot. I'm not sure about the band, though. They probably stuck to the orange juice. Bono was an earnest kind of chap and we talked about them wanting a serious record deal—one which would give them total artistic control and allow them to remain in Dublin. He asked us which gigs would be good for a short tour of London later on in the year. There was no question Bono had real charisma. He loved talking; he was always spouting off about some topic or another."

Back at CBS Ireland HQ, de Whalley's three-track tape was put into production, remixed by the Boomtown Rats' soundman Robbie McGrath and packaged as *U2–3,* complete with picture sleeve by Steve Averill. In a popular move, the band appeared on Dave Fanning's RTÉ radio show and asked the listeners to choose the A-side for them. "Out of Control" came out on top. A thousand copies were pressed in twelve-inch format and personally numbered one to one thousand by CBS Ireland's Jackie Hayden in a marketing gimmick devised to give record shops and the industry as a whole the sense that this release was something very unique and special. *Hot Press,* meanwhile, counted down the days to *U2–3* by putting together a U2 cover story, an extraordinary feat for an act without a previous release. It seemed like just about everyone in Ireland was rooting for them. So it wasn't much of a shock when all one thousand copies of the EP sold out on the first day of its release in September. A seven-inch version was then distributed to meet the demand, which was further stimulated by two televised appearances on RTÉ, the first opening for the Horslips at the Cork Opera House and the second performing "Life on a Distant Planet" on *Aspects of Rock.* All said, *U2–3* peaked at number nineteen in the Irish singles chart.

Elsewhere, Geoff Travis of the influential London-based independent record label and store Rough Trade imported a substantial number of copies of *U2–3* into the UK, and within weeks the British music press was on the case. First in line was Dave McCullough of *Sounds,* who persuaded his editors to turn the interview he had conducted with U2 in August into a full spread in light of the EP and his absolute belief in the band. On November 10 *Record Mirror* provided U2 with their first cover story outside of Ireland. Chris Westwood wrote: "The thing that makes Bono and U-2 so believable is their awareness of vulnerability; both in themselves and in other individuals. They see acceptance of this as central to the very concept of harmony, unity, and self-belief. And that's important." Bono told Westwood: "I want people in London to see and hear the band. I want to replace the bands in the charts now, because I think we're better."

These and subsequent articles raised U2's profile on the mainland and strengthened A&R interest tenfold. Consequently, Muff Winwood reconsidered his position and accompanied de Whalley to Dublin. He was now eager to snap them up for the right price. Conversing with McGuinness in a wine bar, Winwood explained CBS Records would be delighted to have such a young, talented group on board. He name-dropped The Only Ones and The Clash, and implied how lucky U2 would be to share the same label. McGuinness nodded politely, then cut to the chase. He wanted a replica of The Boomtown Rats' deal: fifty thousand pounds up front, another fifty thousand in tour support, and a house in London that they could use as a base when touring the UK. More importantly, he wanted U2 to be given complete artistic control and assurances that the label was in it for the long haul. Winwood nearly swallowed his wineglass when he heard McGuinness's demands, and a deadlock ensued.

De Whalley recalls: "Paul was still very anxious to sign to CBS Records on a worldwide basis because he took the view they were the biggest record company in the world and therefore they would do the best job. In actual fact, I'm not sure that was the wisest viewing of the way the market worked at that time, but that was the one he took. Muff was prepared to offer them a singles deal, which were fairly prevalent at that stage, which would have been a single with an option for second single and then an option for an album, but Paul was adamant that what he wanted to do was follow The Boomtown Rats' route. But this was too rich for CBS's blood. They'd have taken a punt on a single, but they weren't prepared to go all the way. So the deal didn't happen."

It was, in retrospect, a bold and highly unusual stance for McGuinness to take on behalf of his clients, what with the teenagers finding funds in short supply and Edge now studying at the College of Technology at the behest of his parents. But if U2 was going to make it internationally, the band members needed the right deal for *them*. Bono, for his part, agreed with McGuinness wholeheartedly. He told Dublin fanzine *Imprint*: "We're building ourselves up, holding out for a record deal that gives us what we want—total artistic control, allied with the marketing power of a big record company. It's a high price, but we feel justified in asking it. We want to sell records. We want to be big. Independent labels are all very well, but mostly they preach to the converted. We don't want to be a cult."

Hot on Winwood's heels was EMI's Tom Nolan, who made no secret of his admiration for the band. Nolan convinced his label to send over talent scouts Chris Briggs and Ben Edmunds to watch a gig at The Baggot Inn and meet McGuinness afterward. However, demonstrating little interest in U2 or professionalism in general, the duo returned to their hotel after the opening number to catch The Specials on *The Old Grey Whistle Test*. McGuinness was furious. He tracked them down and gave them a good old-fashioned tongue-lashing. The day Briggs and Edmunds got back, Nolan was dragged into the head office and accused of wasting the label's time. A row broke out, and four months later when the redundancies came, his name was at the top of the pile.

In what was perceived by some as the last roll of the dice, McGuinness organized around a dozen showcase gigs in London for December, two of which were supporting Talking Heads at the Electric Ballroom. When a publishing deal with Bryan Morrison Music intended to finance the tour fell through at the last minute, each member of the band had no other option but to borrow five hundred pounds from their already exasperated parents, with the exception of Adam, whose relationship with Brian and Jo had become so strained that any begging-bowl scenario was simply out of the question. Bob Hewson was the surprise package. He and Bono still had slinging matches that shook the walls of 10 Cedarwood Road, but deep down, in spite of all the arguments, Bob only wanted what was best for his son. McGuinness, meanwhile, squeezed another fifteen hundred pounds out of two former film industry colleagues, Seamus Byrne and Tiernan MacBride. And with that, U2 vowed to make a lasting impression on their English counterparts.

However, on the day before they were due to leave, Adam offered Edge a ride to rehearsals in his mother's decrepit Austin A40 and clipped the back of a truck en route. His passenger, who was not wearing a safety belt, emerged from the accident with a bloody left hand. Doctors informed Edge that he had damaged the tendons and required heavy bandaging. On the boat over, he could barely move his wrist, let alone play guitar. Yes, they were going to make an impression all right.

The U2–3 Tour got under way favorably at the Moonlight Club in West Hampstead, where they opened for the all-girl pop-punk trio Dolly Mixture, and *Sounds* man Dave McCullough was on hand to write an encouraging review. But from there, things deteriorated fast. At the grubby Nashville Rooms on Fulham Palace Road, for example, only twenty-five people showed up—the majority of whom appeared more interested in the bar's selection of beverages. The biggest blow of all, though, came at the Hope & Anchor in Islington in front of nine paying customers and an assortment of London's finest A&R scouts. Billed as "The U2's," the band played a stinker, with Edge strung out on morphine tablets to block out the pain in his hand. In a rare moment of rage, he snapped a guitar string and staggered offstage with his bandmates in hot pursuit. McGuinness, entertaining his record company guests in the wings, scurried backstage to see what the problem was. When he got there, Larry was having to physically restrain Edge from knocking Bono's head off with his beloved Gibson Explorer (a '76 limited-edition reissue model that he had picked up for around $450 while on holiday with his parents in New York the previous year). The gig was over, and the A&R scouts left as skeptical as they had arrived.

Among the attendees at the Hope & Anchor was Paul Slattery. "I wasn't there to take pictures," he recalls. "I just wanted to hook up with the band and have a few drinks; I mean, you can't go and take pictures of every gig. But it was bad, really bad. They tried to put on a good show but Edge just couldn't cope with his hand anymore. They looked like they'd blown it, to be honest. But then they did a gig at Dingwalls about a week later and that was really good. I took pictures that night and it was a great gig."

U2 was staying at an apartment in Collingham Gardens, South Kensington, which belonged to a wealthy acquaintance of McGuinness's. It was a comfortable place to rest their heads at night, but travel expenses to and from gigs in their hired van meant they had a daily food budget of just two pounds per teen, although McGuinness, who often claimed that he'd rather starve than dine on cheap food and wine, occasionally treated them to a meal at the Poons restaurant in Chinatown. Slattery arranged to meet U2 at the apartment, and shot photos of them hanging out there. He felt sorry for the young band, and the next day he drove them out to his home in Sunbury-on-Thames with assurances of a warm meal. On the way, they did another photo session along the banks of the River Thames in Chiswick. "They were absolutely penniless at this time," he says. "I just took them home and thought I better give them something to eat, feed them up a bit. So I made them a load of bacon sandwiches and soup and cups of tea. They were like waifs; they had holes in their shoes and their clothes were threadbare."

Despite the circumstances, U2's spirits remained high. "I think there was no question things hadn't gone as well as they had been expecting on this short tour, but Bono was still positive and always humorous," recalls Slattery. "I remember him saying he loved London but he wouldn't want to live here. No fucking way!"

Desperate to get things moving, McGuinness visited the office of Dave Robinson, founder of the seminal independent label Stiff Records. The U2 manager explained that he planned to sign the band to a big record label, but in the meantime he'd like Robinson to do him the favor of putting out a few of their songs as singles in the UK. Robinson would have obliged him, if not for one small problem. "The songs were crap," he says. "They were like a pseudo punk-pop band. Very Irish. Because in Ireland, blindly following the English and American pop charts, having very few gigs to play, and being able to get onto television at a very early stage, bands didn't progress very far. They didn't have that deep examination. So it wasn't like you had to be phenomenal to get to the top of the milk, you just had to be creamy."

Still, Robinson, who himself hailed from Dublin, sympathized with their predicament. "Once they'd had four or five English record companies look at them and turn them down, they were kind of stuck, because traditionally in Ireland bands would break up at that point and re-form and then try and get the record companies to look at them again. It was a real effort." Robinson advised McGuinness to instead try Chris Blackwell's Island Records out in Hammersmith, often the last port of call for departing unsigned acts, due to its proximity to the M4 motorway and Heathrow Airport.

But unbeknownst to either one of them, Island already had U2 firmly on their radar. Rob Partridge, who co-ran the indie label's press office with Neil Storey, was more than just a little taken with the Irish group, as a result of Bill Graham formally introducing him to McGuinness at a social function in 1977 and then inundating him with U2 tapes in the intervening years. Soon, Graham had turned Storey and A&R scout Annie Roseberry onto them as well. Storey recalls: "Bill—who was one of the key writers for Ireland's *Hot Press,* a kinda *NME*-like, biweekly publication—was in and out of our office the whole time. We liked Bill; we trusted his ears. He kept going on and on about this little band that he'd found who he thought were rather good and we should hear them because they weren't getting much joy in terms of record company attention."

Partridge had in fact caught U2's opening show at the Moonlight Club, and then a later London date with Storey and their significant others. "There were literally just nine people in the room," says Storey. "I can remember Edge breaking his guitar strings and then Bono sat at the edge of the stage and everyone gathered around and we all chattered. Then, when Edge had fixed his guitar, they just got back on with it and carried on again. Honestly, I didn't quite know what it was I was seeing; I just knew that there was something remarkably special. Adam couldn't play particularly well, Edge was obviously a really extraordinary guitar player, at that point in time Larry was perfunctory but solid, and the singer . . . hell, Bono was right in your face. And the songs were pretty good."

McGuinness booked an appointment to see Roseberry's new A&R boss, Nick Stewart, then referred to by his middle name of Bill or nickname "the Captain," and played him a copy of *U2–3*. Stewart was an extraordinary figure. He was a six-foot-two ex-Guards officer and rumored to have been a part of the SAS at one stage. He was absolutely obsessed with music, to the extent that he had gone along to see The Undertones and bands of that ilk perform while serving undercover in Northern Ireland. At Island, he would mastermind the reinvention of Grace Jones and earn a reputation as somebody with his finger on the pulse. Although the U2 EP failed to do anything for him, Stewart was immediately impressed with McGuinness. "He struck me as someone who—rather than being a friend of the bass player, or someone who couldn't count to twenty—knew what he was doing," says Stewart. He and McGuinness agreed to keep in touch.

Before U2 headed home, CBS Records sanctioned one more Irish single, "Another Day," which was recorded at the label's Whitfield Street studio, with de Whalley again on production duties. "Bono had lost his voice, which was a bit tricky," remembers de Whalley. "He was gargling with honey and lemon and got enough of his voice back to be able to sing and I suggested a couple of tricks, like the David Bowie trick of whispering the lead vocal as a sort of double-track to the sung one. Something to put a bit of extra texture in there. But basically speaking, they did very well.

"The second single was supposedly to see whether, in actual fact, that might ease the logjam [with regard to contract negotiations]. But it didn't and CBS in London passed on officially signing the band to the rest of the world, as a result of which the Irish company went off the boil on them and didn't work the second single at all. I've got a handwritten note on the back of a flyer from Paul when he sent me the only copy I've got of the single. He says, 'Things are so bad now that CBS Ireland are charging me for these records so only one enclosed. They are also refusing to advertise it or pay for the bag. . . . Best wishes to you, Paul & U2.' "

For de Whalley, CBS's inability to recognize U2's raw potential was the straw that broke the camel's back, and soon after, he handed in his notice. "I thought, 'What the hell am I doing here? They don't really like the kind of music I like, and even if they do they don't want to promote it.' So I left."

▪

In January 1980, U2 beat established Irish acts such as The Boomtown Rats and Thin Lizzy to win five categories in the *Hot Press* readers' poll, including the award for Best Group, which only seemed to add to the confusion on the local scene as to why they remained unsigned outside of the country. U2 milked the polls for all they were worth and set off on their most extensive Irish tour so far, culminating with an ambitious gig at the two-thousand-capacity National Stadium in Dublin.

With Nick Stewart's blessing, Annie Roseberry caught the band at Belfast's Queen's University. In harmony with popular belief, she felt that musically they were rough around the edges, but was in awe of how they worked the stage. Roseberry recalls: "The show which I attended was memorable for two reasons: there were very few people in the audience and the band played like they were playing Wembley Arena. I was captivated by Bono's electric performance more than anything else, plus the fact that they just worked together as a unit—something that you see very rarely. It was evident that other than Edge, who was always an extraordinary talent, the others were not the greatest players, but it didn't matter as there was a chemistry on stage, and when you see that it is unmistakable. Coldplay have it, too."

Roseberry hung out with U2 at their hotel afterward, after experiencing a somewhat intimidating car ride through the Belfast cityscape. "We were stopped by armed security on our way back as Adam was in the boot and there were rather too many of us in the car itself," she says. "The Europa Hotel was at the time surrounded by high security fencing and had the dubious reputation of being the most bombed hotel in the world."

In a departure from their straitlaced ways, U2 stole what they believed to be McGuinness's room key from the hotel's front desk and proceeded to overturn the furniture and fill the bathtub with shaving foam—only to later discover that they had actually trashed the wrong room, much to the annoyance of the returning occupant. Another juvenile lark almost destroyed their chances of landing a contract with Island altogether when Adam tripped while chasing a friend in the corridor with a pint of lager in his hand and spilled it all over Roseberry. "McGuinness could see the last glimmer of hope of a deal disappearing into the night by the look of horror on his face," she laughs. "It didn't worry me at all and I remember returning to London just remembering this as a great evening and that what I had seen and heard was something really special."

Island's interest moved up a gear when Stewart returned from a winter break playing cricket in East Africa in late February. McGuinness called him at his office on literally the first day he got back and invited him to attend U2's gig at the National Stadium. The venue, the first purpose-built boxing stadium in the world, was also often home to popular Irish folk groups and visiting superstars, like Eric Clapton and Genesis. That was the reason McGuinness booked it. He wanted to portray U2 as champions, and he did, filling one-third of it with enthusiastic friends and family of the band, as well as local press and freeloaders. Stewart recalls: "I landed in Dublin airport on a cold, wet January night thinking, 'God, what have I let myself in for here?' If there could have been a royal box for this gig, I was in it. The band came on and the first thing they played was '11 O'Clock Tick Tock,' which had that big powerful Edge guitar riff, and the stage was mobbed. I turned to Michael Deeny, the manager of Horslips, halfway through the gig and I said—rather unwisely, I suppose—'This bunch could be the next Led Zeppelin! They're amazing!' "

Post-gig, Stewart rushed backstage to meet U2 in "the smallest dressing room I've ever been in," and he was immediately taken aback by how young they looked. "Larry at that time would have failed the audition for *Oliver Twist*. He was painfully small," laughs Stewart. "But I said to them, 'Guys, you were fucking brilliant, and I'd like to sign you to Island Records.'" Now all he had to do was convince the label's owner, Chris Blackwell.

The son of Joseph Blackwell, an heir to the Crosse & Blackwell food family, and Blanche Lindo, a powerful landowner of Jamaican ancestry and Bond writer Ian Fleming's muse, Chris Blackwell had inherited all the right ingredients to build Island Records into one of Britain's most innovative and artist-friendly independent labels, with a roster that boasted acclaimed singer-songwriter Cat Stevens, blue-eyed soul singer Robert Palmer, and reggae artist Bob Marley, whom Blackwell had personally molded into a pop rebel white consumers could buy into. He had a reputation for treating Island as a musical family rather than a conventional company, and also encouraging the development of artistic talent, sometimes to the point of recklessness. "It's my money, I'll do with it what I want," he once told a marketing director who questioned his decision to spend a large chunk of the label's ad budget on the moderately successful Jamaican hard-core reggae group Black Uhuru.

Upon returning to Island HQ, Stewart called Blackwell at his home in Nassau and told him of his discovery. "I've found you a real live Island-type rock band," he said. However, around this time, Blackwell was trying to stake a claim in rising New Romantic act Spandau Ballet, whose look fascinated him. Stewart recalls: "I said to him, 'The Spandau Ballet guy can't really sing. It's all a bit limited. And the manager is rushing around looking for lots of money and wants his own label.' So we had this debate, and it became a bit of a thing in the company." Stewart leaned on Island's two-man press department of Rob Partridge and Neil Storey—whose opinion Blackwell valued the most, on account of them being around the longest—in terms of trying to understand how he was going to get the owner on board. Eventually, Stewart spent some time with Blackwell in Nassau, where he played him *U2-3* and got into a lengthy discussion about each member of the band. "At one point, Chris said, 'If the singer and the guitarist are so good, why don't we just sign them?' And I said, 'No, you don't quite understand. This is a real unit.'"

And with that, despite finding little to like about U2's music himself, Blackwell gave Stewart the go-ahead to snap them up, such was his employee's belief in their long-term potential. So after taking one more look at them on St. Patrick's Day at the Sense of Ireland Festival in London, Stewart signed U2 to a four-album contract four days later at an Echo & the Bunnymen gig at the Lyceum—the papers were signed in, of all places, the venue's ladies' room, as boozed-up male revelers missed the mark in the dimly lit gents' toilets next door.

For all McGuinness's careful planning, it was a relatively ordinary indie record deal at the end of the day. It weighed heavily in favor of tour support, after it was agreed that, although U2's shows were wildly inconsistent at the best of times, an intense concert itinerary would be the most effective strategy for them to build up a fan base. The band would be afforded artistic control, from the music to the packaging. And in return, Island obtained world rights for U2, excluding Ireland, where they would remain on CBS Ireland. In the United States, meanwhile, the band's music would be released through Island's distribution partner, Warner Bros. Records.

McGuinness strongly advised his four clients to split everything equally, including songwriting royalties, to maintain a sense of democracy and avoid all the clichéd money quarrels that had torn apart so many of their favorite groups. Curiously, he negotiated an equal slice of the pie for himself, thus giving birth to his adage: "U2 are a band of four; a corporation of five."

4

Boy Meets Man

U2 was overjoyed to be the latest addition to the Island family and vowed to embody moral values such as honesty, compassion, and loyalty while climbing the ladder of a distinctly venal industry. "They were keen, they were eager, they were unfailingly polite," remembers Nick Stewart. "But if they thought something had to be said, they would say it. They were on a mission. There's no doubt about that. They were on a mission."

Stewart's first order of business was to pair U2 with a producer who could figure out how to polish their sound without losing any of the energy of their live performances. At the time, he was a huge admirer of the Manchester music scene and reached out to Martin Hannett, the maverick in-house producer at Factory Records. "I thought that Martin, who at the time was working with Joy Division, would in a curious sort of way give them a push," says Stewart. "The man had something that very few producers have—Phil Spector's one, George Martin's another. He was a genius."

Annie Roseberry, then assistant to Stewart, adds: "Martin was an extraordinarily talented producer and stood out head and shoulders above most of the producers who were making records at the time. He did not follow the rule book and he was a perfectionist and I liked that. The records he had made were exciting, and U2 needed to capture that live excitement since they were not going to necessarily leap onto radio."

As Joy Division fanatics themselves, U2 welcomed the chance to work with Hannett, and joined him in Dublin's Windmill Lane Studios over the Easter weekend of 1980 to record their British debut single "11 O'Clock Tick Tock." But the marathon session didn't exactly go to plan, with the quartet's inexperience in a professional studio again painfully obvious to all; Hannett, for better or worse, living up to his mad genius reputation; and Dublin band The Atrix storming the studio and accusing U2 of plagiarizing one of their songs.

Kevin Moloney, who was then a sound engineer at Windmill Lane, recalls: "We were up with Martin for three days straight with no sleep making tape loops because the timing was not good within the band. They really didn't know how to do things in the studio, and Bono wasn't a great singer at that point. I remember that he had heard that Frank Sinatra ate cheese sandwiches before a vocal, so every time he was doing a take he'd be like, 'Time for a cheese sandwich!' They were completely out of their depth.

"It was a wild, wild session," continues Moloney. "We always suspected that Martin was doing acid in the studio. He was completely off his tree and doing crazy stuff with the electronics which we'd never heard been done before. But it sounded great. I think the band got freaked out by him because he was very much out there and not like anything they'd dealt with at the time. He had a very different attitude about him."

Hannett insisted that every sound be isolated and recorded in individual bits. The bass, for example, was recorded in three or four different parts. He sat down with Adam trying to get a certain sound on the bass amp and then got him to record a note, then another note on another track—trying to build up the bass line piece by piece, like sequencing. He obsessed about everything. He even had this thing about the time. He'd say, "The mixing will be at three o'clock in the morning. Three o'clock is the most creative time!"

As for the allegation of plagiarism hurled at U2, The Atrix felt that the guitar riff in the intro to "11 O'Clock Tick Tock" had been stolen from their song "Treasure on the Wasteland," and they marched down to Windmill Lane and demanded that it be changed. After words were exchanged, The Atrix went away and everyone was left standing around in the studio not knowing what to do about the problem until Hannett stood up and quipped, "Maybe we if put the intercom on, this 'beep beep beep?'" But no one else saw the funny side of it, especially the band, who were all very dour about the situation. Eventually, engineer Paul Thomas suggested that they put a backward cymbal on the track, which is what they did. Hannett sat in a swivel chair during the playback, and at one point he fell backward and screamed, "Jesus Christ! I've just hallucinated a gherkin!"

Despite his altered state of consciousness, Hannett recognized that he and U2 were far from compatible, with the band clearly resenting his master-and-commander production style and massive drug intake. The quartet didn't even hang around when he was mixing the song. By the end, Hannett felt rattled by the whole experience and indicated to an aide that he knew he wasn't going to be asked to come back and produce their debut album.

Review copies of "11 O'Clock Tick Tock" landed on the desks of British music journos in early May, along with U2's first official press release, which Island had commissioned Bill Graham to write. The song failed to dent the UK singles chart, but it did result in two positives: one, it was hailed by the critics as a promising appetizer, and two, Hannett's wild studio experimentalism and the sparse, monolithic soundscape it spawned, replete with deep reverb and digital effects, encouraged Edge to spurn punk retreads and think outside the box himself. The young guitarist remained a minimalist at heart; he focused on building songs around open chords, repeating arpeggios, and ringing harmonics. The key hardware component was the Electro-Harmonix Deluxe Memory Man analog delay he first introduced during the writing session for a track called "A Day Without Me," resulting in an otherworldly, echo-drenched sound much bigger than the sum of its parts—certainly too big for Dublin's parochial scene. And with that, U2's early signature sound was born. "This Memory Man had this certain sound and I really loved it," Edge later recalled in *Musician*. "I just played with it for weeks and weeks, integrating it into some of the songs we'd already written. Out of using it, a whole other set of songs started to come out. It gave me a whole other set of colors to use. It also helped to fill out the sound."

In late May, U2 bought a van with money from the Island deal and embarked on a UK tour in support of "11 O'Clock Tick Tock," visiting northern cities like Manchester, Birmingham, and Leeds for the first time. But the audiences, which ranged between ten and fifty venue regulars more attuned to gloomy post-punk acts and mod revivalists, were tough nuts to crack and rarely even feigned interest in the band. Dave McCullough, U2's most vocal cheerleader on English soil, caught one of the shows: "The esteemed U2, a murderously good and genuinely subversive young pop group, played this converted cocktail center and, yeah, it was a bummer. No communication, no interest, no fun, no vitality, U2 did their turn and went away." Meanwhile, among key figures of the self-styled übercool British music press, U2 was regarded as one of the most divisive and polarizing live acts of recent years. In the words of *NME*'s Paul Morley, himself a fan of the foursome, "Live, U2 have been appallingly erratic: nervous, overeager, musically unsure. . . . Since they've signed to Island I've been faced with almost unanimous derision from friends whose musical passions are usually the same as mine: they don't like U2. At all. . . . The problem is, U2 try too hard, go for something special, transcendent, EPIC, and nearly miss out. Too much style, not enough experience."

Fortunately for the band, their small but influential group of supporters at Island remained as devoted as ever to their cause. "At that point, don't forget there were maybe only four real fans of the band at the label; there was me, Rob, Annie, and Nick. That was it. Tony the Greek who did radio promo in the North of England came on board a bit later," recalls Neil Storey. "I probably went to more U2 shows than anybody at that period. Why? Because I loved them as human beings and because nobody else was going to. So it was not unknown to do a day's work, drive way up north, see them and the support act play, and then drive home. If you want corroboration on that, I'll give you my ex's phone number."

Storey was particularly impressed with U2's own strong work ethic and determination to put on the best show possible for punters, no matter how small in size, to advance to the next level. "You'd walk into what passed for a dressing room after the show and the first question would be, 'Did we get the set list running order right?' It was total concentration in terms of what they were doing. And a little bit later on both Bono and Edge were using us to source a lot of videos for them to watch on tour buses, of early Stones and stuff like that. They were studying the greats on stage and how they did this and that. Bono, especially, had an incredibly inquiring mind. It sounds a bit cut and dry, but it was all a part of learning how to reach an audience."

U2 also demonstrated a keen interest in the business side of things from the get-go. This was clearly a band looking at the big picture. "They were very, very bright," says Storey. "They were certainly full of questions. The first time I properly sat down with them I ended up being quizzed by Larry for what seemed like hours about the history of Island. Bono was being interviewed by the editor of *ZigZag,* a chap called Kris Needs—this was upstairs in a pub in Dublin—but Larry wasn't that interested in the interview, he wanted to know all about this record label that they'd signed to; how it started, how we worked with the artists, what happens when a single or album is released; all that kind of stuff. He was very shy, but absolutely charming. The other thing was that his flight cases were the wrong color," laughs Storey. "They were some ghastly shade of pink and he was really pissed about that. Everybody else was taking the mickey out of him, going, 'Ooh, look! They're a bit girly!'"

Joining them on the road, the Island press man developed an almost evangelical belief in U2, to the extent that during an unrelated business trip to the United States he packed a copy of "11 O'Clock Tick Tock" in his briefcase and tried to sell the band as the next sure thing in a one-on-one meeting with the head of Island New York. "Basically, I was the first person to take a U2 record to America," says Storey. "I played it to the head of the company over there at the time, Ron Goldstein, and he sat there very patiently, listened to it, and then said, 'You know what? That's not going to go anywhere. That band's not going to go anywhere.' And I said, 'No, you don't understand. They're fucking brilliant!' I just went off on one, because I was very passionate about their music. And he didn't get it. I walked out of his office thinking I'd really screwed up, because I really thought I could help them here and really push this. It was pretty awful. . . . Anyhow, I got back to London and told Rob what happened and he said, 'Oh no! That's terrible! What are we going to tell Paul?' So I said, 'The truth?' I just couldn't get it into this guy's head that this band are really special. It felt like a disaster. Obviously, in the greater scheme of things, it wasn't . . . but, at that moment in time, it felt like one."

▪

Undeterred by the mixed reception they received in the UK and the Island MD's outright snub stateside, U2 went back into Windmill Lane Studios in early July to record their second British single, "A Day Without Me," a deceptively chirpy-sounding contemplation of teenage suicide, with a young English engineer/producer by the name of Steve Lillywhite, who had previously collaborated with Siousxie and the Banshees, Peter Gabriel, and The Psychedelic Furs. Although the song would also be a chart flop, the band and Lillywhite liked one another and agreed to do a full album together there and then. The studio atmosphere Lillywhite fostered was very different from that of Martin Hannett. Both were experimental at heart, but whereas the eccentric Mancunian was more of a dictatorial leader, Lillywhite encouraged the creative input of others. Each song had an ideas sheet that he stuck up in the control room so everybody was allowed to contribute, to put up ideas about things to try. From day one, everybody felt involved in the project.

According to Kevin Moloney, there was a real DIY approach to making the record, with some of the more unconventional recording techniques involving hitting a kitchen fork off a spinning bicycle wheel for percussion, smashing milk bottles in the studio's backyard for sound effects, and moving Larry's drum kit out into the reception area after everyone else at Windmill had clocked off for the day to get a bigger sound. "The studio itself was a late '70s design, a very wooden dead kind of room, and the drum sound just wasn't working for the band," explains Moloney. "So when the rest of the building would empty out after five or six we'd record them out there late into the night. It was a spectacular sound at the time. Sometimes people like to do things by the book and then others like to tear up the rule book, and that's what happened with U2. There was a real studio atmosphere where you're trying to create something new, and Steve was absolutely instrumental in making that happen for them."

Most of the backing tracks were recorded over a two-week period, and then it was left to Lillywhite and his engineers to make sense of all the different takes, as well as tighten up the problematic rhythm section. "Steve really put it together and whipped them into shape," says Moloney. "I remember Steve recording a lot of the bass parts for Adam in order that he could learn the part he wanted him to play and then we would painfully record, many 'drop ins' later, Adam as he played the part. Larry's drumming on those early records also wasn't very good. We used to spend most of our hours late at night putting tape loops together, editing multitrack tapes to try and put a drum track together that was somehow close to the beat in time. There was a lot of tape splicing going on, a lot of razor blades. It was a highly pressurized situation, but pretty exciting too. U2 was hungry, and the sound was something fresh and new—very atmospheric and mystical, yet big and melodic."

Bono's lyrics were, for the most part, written live on the microphone—that is to say, ad-libbed. He claimed that he was hoping to emulate the emotional rawness of his idol Iggy Pop, although everyone else in the studio suspected that it was simply because he hated the idea of going off and writing by himself. It was almost as if he only felt motivated when around other people. Bono's yearning for an audience dictated the choice of recording equipment and room as well. He was frustrated for a while because he wasn't getting a performance by putting on headphones and singing into an expensive microphone. So he got into the habit of singing in the control room with a handheld mic and that made a big difference for him. It was like singing on a stage with the music turned up. He would do six takes of a vocal and Lillywhite would make composite vocals of the best bits. Bono would listen to what had been compiled and then he'd go out and do the same thing again, six more takes. That was the general way of working with him.

The predominant lyrical theme that emerged was the preservation of childhood innocence and purity in the face of encroaching adulthood, and all the complexities associated with that dramatic physical and mental change. "Out of Control," for instance, was about Bono waking up on his eighteenth birthday and realizing that birth and death were inevitable and out of his hands (although it should be noted that his birthday actually fell on a Wednesday, not two days earlier as he claimed in the song). "Stories for Boys" was about retreating into the world of comic books, music, and television to escape reality. "An Cat Dubh"/"Into the Heart," two songs combined into one, alluded to a fling that Bono had had with a girl during a breakup with Ali, as well as touching upon the human impulse toward savagery, which was at the heart of his favorite novel, *Lord of the Flies*. "Twilight" dealt with sexual orientation confusion. "I Will Follow," meanwhile, was about the unconditional love between a mother and son, as emphasized by Bono's emotional pledge to follow Iris to the other side. The album's lyrics were, according to the front man, the opposite of machismo. And for that reason, U2 decided to call it *Boy*.

As news of *Boy*'s forthcoming release spread across the Dublin scene, U2 found themselves being targeted by a gang of young skinheads. "There was an emerging skinhead subculture and one or two catcalls of 'Protestant Band' and that kind of thing," says a source. "But it wasn't sectarian. They were just assholes, people growing up in a very unpleasant way." During that period, the London music journalist Paolo Hewitt and photographer Tom Sheehan arrived in Dublin for U2's first *Melody Maker* feature and caught a glimpse of life for the group in their hometown. "We went to a café with them to get a cup of tea and on the way people were throwing stones at us," recalls Hewitt. "Bono just kind of brushed it off and said, 'Yeah, this happens a lot around here!' "

Hewitt had become a real champion of the band after seeing them play at The Clarendon Hotel in London in early July. "There weren't many people there, but it was great," he says. "At that time you had a lot of intense groups and there wasn't a lot of joy going around. It was quite a gloomy era with bands like Joy Division and the Comsat Angels, where it was more about the intellectual side of things. On the other side, you had the 2 Tone scene, but that was engulfed in a lot of right-wing skinhead stuff. So even that, which is a very joyful music, was quite political. I mean, I used to go see Madness down at the Electric Ballroom and there would be two thousand skinheads howling for your blood. And then here comes U2 and they've got passion, they've got drive, they're upbeat and the singer's actually trying to sing—people weren't singing at all back then, just kind of mumbling. That fluid guitar sound Edge had, combined with Bono's passionate voice and stage presence, just made you go, 'Wow!' It cut through everything."

U2 also quickly won over Sheehan with their hospitality, with McGuinness picking the two *Melody Maker* men up at the airport and dropping them off at the studio door. Later, they took Sheehan for a quick drink at a local pub that shared his surname and snapped a few pictures of him outside it for his family album. "Like a lot of Irish folk, they were very welcoming, very friendly, and extremely courteous," he says. "They were quite thoughtful of why you were there. There was a youthful exuberance, but with a professional one-direction edge to it. No fucking around." But in terms of having a unified visual identity, U2 was still very much a work in progress, according to Sheehan. "Bono had on tight black jeans, Cuban heels, and a deep red and black hooped T-shirt. Larry was wearing a black Harrington and looked just like a little kid. Edge was wearing a pair of trousers that were covered in paint and graffiti. And Adam was wearing what can only be described as slippers. They weren't comfortable in front of the camera. With the exception of Bono, I think they saw it as a necessary evil."

Sheehan's experience shooting the band around Dublin mirrored that of Colm Henry, their chief Irish photographer at that time and for much of the decade that followed. "They didn't feel comfortable standing together in a picture at all," says Henry. "They had no idea of what they should be doing and were very self-conscious. They did photograph very well individually though. It's a completely different story now, as I suppose they are more practiced and rehearsed—they know exactly how to stand and how to present themselves.

"They were always driven as a unit," continues Henry. "Individually and away from the others in the band they were very pleasant and modest easygoing people—but as a group, difficult. They had a different kind of outlook on things because of their religious ethos, which was far more intense than the average person in Ireland. They believed in the hard-work ethic and rationalizing stuff to get them to where they wanted to go. Other bands were into the image of being in a band and they would pose around a bit thinking that this was what it was about. U2 didn't really have an image at all—they were so unfashionable. They were totally uncool in fact, particularly to the British, who needed their bands to be completely cool to connect into them. U2 were so uncool, and uninteresting in a way. Eventually they actually made that uncoolness their main thing, [that] what they were doing was more important than fashion cool. They occasionally asked for my opinion, but I cannot remember them ever taking it on. What they did was take many opinions and then dissect them to make up their own minds. There was a lot of post-photo-session analysis with them—they threw away more stuff than any other band I ever photographed."

U2's debut LP *Boy* was released in the UK in late October, with Island shipping only eight thousand copies of it to retailers in the first week. It peaked at a lowly fifty-two on the album chart, but did garner positive reviews and a small army of loyal fans. Writing in *Melody Maker*, Lunden Barber described *Boy* as "a succession of heartfelt experiences and feelings, that balances light against shade, optimism against poignancy. I suppose it'll attract sneers, but what the hell—the music here is enough to make you cry. Welcome to the new Eighties." Paul Morley of *NME* said that he found *Boy* "touching, precocious, full of archaic flourishes and modernist conviction, genuinely strange. It won't eradicate the gray feelings people have about U2, but it reinforces the affection I have for their character and emotionally forceful music." Meanwhile, back home in Ireland, Declan Lynch of *Hot Press* wrote: "I find it almost impossible to react negatively to U-2's music. It rushes your senses, it's so sharp; every song seems like it's been lying under the tree all year, and at Christmas it's taken out of its box and shown to everybody, open-mouthed."

The Boy Tour was already under way by the time the album was available to buy, which included another support slot with the Talking Heads at the Lyceum and taking up a four-week Monday-night residency at the Marquee. However, the British audiences largely remained indifferent to U2's live charms. The Lyceum concertgoers, for example, chatted among themselves during the band's set, and a frustrated Bono slammed the microphone onto the floor as he left the stage. Also in the audience that night was *NME*'s Chris Salewicz, who dismissed U2 as "basically little more than nonsense, or perhaps the new Boomtown Rats—one of the two, and they both amount to the same thing, anyway." Salewicz scoffed at what he perceived to be Bono's attempts to imitate Rod Stewart and the inevitable Iggy Pop, and concluded that "U2 are really quite awful."

U2's future, at least in the UK, clearly rested on the ability of Island's press office to deliver positive media coverage. McGuinness worked closely with Storey and Partridge over the next few months, consulting and strategizing. "We liked him," says Storey. "He knew what he was doing. He didn't ask the impossible and allowed you to get on and do your job. He was inter-strategizing as well, looking ahead all the time. Good guy, not frivolous. It wasn't a case of, 'Let's go do all the business we need to do in the pub.' He was dead serious. But at the same time there was a nice, light side to Paul. He was a great storyteller. He was somebody who when he called you took the call, as opposed to pretending to be somewhere else. Paul rang for a reason. I'd like to think there was a lot of mutual respect there."

Also fighting the big U2 PR battle was Tony Michaelides, Island's newly appointed head of artist development and regional promotions in the UK and Ireland, whose enthusiasm for the band was both infectious and invaluable. "You just had these guys who were so full of themselves in the way that they had so much belief in their own ability and what they were going to do," recalls Michaelides. "You couldn't help but take that belief elsewhere. So I was chomping at the bit talking to people about this band. And there were some people who couldn't quite see it, but fortunately I had built up good relationships with them so I was assured they would go back and listen again."

Michaelides took U2 up and down the motorways of the UK and into virtually every radio and television station. He'd tell them, "I can get you into this station, but only you can get yourself back in." Although not everyone liked the band's music, especially live, where they were, at times, considered brash and overeager, they got by on Bono's gregarious charm. "You've got to remember Adam, bleached-blond hair and all, wasn't the greatest of bass players. But Bono was the consummate performer. Pouring with sweat, he would be climbing up the PA speakers and along the balcony trying to hit the high notes and would lose his voice and croak. When I took them in to do an interview with someone like Billy Sloane [veteran Scottish DJ] or Colin Sommerville [music controller at Radio Forth], these people would then phone me up after they'd talked with Bono and say, 'Great, Tone. Loved it. Anytime they're around, be sure to have them pop in.'"

Tony Wilson, the opinionated, populist TV presenter at Granada Television and mastermind of Factory Records, was another U2 skeptic who succumbed to Bono's charm offensive. Michaelides recalls: "Wilson said to me, 'I'm not really that into it [U2], but I can see you guys are working hard on it. Yeah, bring them in.' And he told me afterward that he liked Bono. He said from a presenter's perspective, the guy's passionate and articulate about what he's doing. See, Bono was on this mission. If you put him in front of a microphone, he was off. He was an incredible communicator. So that would make my job easier, because in those days it was very hard to get records onto daytime radio unless it was a

Bob Marley or Robert Palmer single. But luckily you also had these crucial specialist radio shows like, for instance, in Liverpool there was a rock show on five nights a week from seven to ten."

To that end, Michaelides got U2 two live sessions on BBC Radio 1; the first was on DJ Mike Read's nighttime program that championed new acts, while the second was on DJ Peter Powell's evening show and recorded at the old BBC Playhouse Theatre in Hulme. "It was right in the middle of street [race] riots," remembers Michaelides. "They wanted to go walkabout and I was trying to keep them indoors because the place was like fucking Beirut! But to get four tracks by an unknown band on national radio at seven o'clock midweek was huge; they'd never had a break like that on national radio at all [in the UK]. I remember they did a track unreleased to this day called 'Father Is an Elephant' and Bono wanted to have an echoey sound to the vocal so what he ended up doing was trailing a microphone wire up to the balcony and into the gent's urinal and he sang in the gent's toilet."

U2 also recorded their first television performance outside Ireland on the children's show *Get It Together,* which was cohosted by an owl glove puppet called Ollie Beak. "That was quite surreal," laughs Michaelides. "But Granada was the one TV station that was very innovative in what they did—they'd had the first TV appearance of The Beatles, Blondie, Elvis Costello, the Sex Pistols. They were great at supporting new music."

Still, that much-coveted exposure on daytime radio remained elusive. Storey recalls: "The radio people at Island at that time couldn't get arrested with a U2 record [during peak hours]. They relied on us, Rob and I, to deliver acres of print, and that's what we did. It's all about careful targeting and building on alliances. It was hoped that if we could build on the print coverage we were already achieving then sooner or later the people at Radio 1 and the rest of it would go, 'Err, we're ignoring this? Don't think we should.' And then of course they'd get on the bandwagon and say, 'Guess what, guys? We've just discovered this great band from Dublin!' I hate all that, but that's the way it works.

"From time to time, we'd also kinda hijack journalists. That was a small part of the strategy we evolved with Paul. 'Okay, we've got important people coming over from America and they trust our musical taste buds, therefore why don't we see if we can bring them along to the shows?' And that's how we did it. Maybe hijacking is a bit of a strong word, but when Fred Schruers arrived to do an interview with Robert Palmer, the very first thing that happened was I picked him up at Heathrow and, instead of heading off to his hotel, I took him down to Southampton University and he got to see U2 for the first time like that. That's how the very earliest pieces in America by him and James Henke ran, simply because we sort of dragged them off to see the band."

The Boy Tour also went continental, with U2 venturing into Holland, Belgium, and France for the first time. Larry, who was still a virgin despite being in a long-term relationship, found life on the road to be a daunting experience, where he was faced with the temptation of drugs and groupies at various stops along the way. As the youngest and least capable musician, he was also often the object of internal ridicule, which went beyond just playful banter. Bono, whose pathological need to be loved coexisted, paradoxically, with his need to gain ascendancy over others, was especially rude and condescending toward him. Theirs was a complex relationship. "The dynamic within the band was that Bono was Larry's emotional big brother," says a source. "Larry roomed with Bono, [while] Edge roomed with Adam. To some extent, there was a sense that Larry was also patronized and put down. I think there is quite a controlling quality in Bono's makeup. A lot was taken out on Larry; he was the kid of the operation and he wasn't a great drummer and wasn't able to keep time."

With the exception of Adam, who rarely passed an opportunity to go wild, the sight of youthful rebellion and rock-and-roll hedonism filled U2 with disgust, and they drew on their born-again Christian faith to shield themselves against it. Early in the tour, Bono had written a letter to his father back home outlining the three Shalom members' commitment to living an intense life of prayer and their intentions to bring about a purer way of approaching life and music: "You should be aware that at the moment three of the group are committed Christians. That means offering each day up to God, meeting in the morning for prayers, readings, and letting God work in our lives. This gives us our strength and a joy that does not depend on drink or drugs. This strength will, I believe, be the quality that will take us to the top of the music business. I hope our lives will be a testament to the people who follow us, and to the music business where never before have so many lost and sorrowful people gathered in one place pretending they're having a good time. It is our ambition to make more than good music."

U2 and Island's targeted PR push had given the band a small but dedicated fan base, enough to sell out the Marquee in London. However, early UK press champions such as Paul Slattery and Paolo Hewitt had started to do a U2 U-turn in light of Bono's increasingly pious and messianic behavior—whether that be claiming his voice was a gift from above, acting even more theatrical on stage, or referring to Darwin's theory of evolution as a "fairy tale." Slattery recalls: "Dave [McCullough] and I were driving back to the *Sounds* office in Covent Garden after interviewing him and Dave turned to me and said, 'Bono's just told me he's a Christian.' And I thought, 'Fucking hell. Good luck with that!' He was becoming more stagy and messiah-like so I just moved on to other music. At least you could have a drink and a smoke at an Echo & the Bunnymen gig without the guilt trip. All that savior stuff wasn't for me."

Fearing a backlash from more of their key supporters, and in accord with McGuinness's business strategy, U2 decided to take the fight to the largest and most evangelical market in the world: America.

5

A Kind of Religion

McGuinness, ever the proactive and preemptive strategist, had already been over to America in September 1980 to put in place the necessary infrastructure for U2's launch there. This included working out a deal with the legendary booking agents Frank Barsalona and Barbara Skydel at Premier Talent in New York and touching base with the powers that be at Warner Bros. out in Los Angeles. "I think I was the first person in the U.S. music business to meet Paul," says Tim Devine, then product manager at the record label. "In those days Warner's New York office was in the same building as the Premier Talent agency. I remember meeting Paul on the street with his suitcase as he was heading to his first meeting at Premier, which was ironic as I had just been assigned to handle the band and he was heading out to meet me and the Warner's staff in California next. At that point in time, Premier was the top agency for UK bands touring the U.S. Frank Barsalona and Barbara Skydel had put together a roster that included everyone from Led Zeppelin to The Who to eventually U.S. acts like Bruce Springsteen, Tom Petty, The J. Geils Band, and others. That was the kind of company U2 wanted to be in with. It was equally important to Paul to develop and maintain relationships with the right promoters in the U.S. (Bill Graham, Ron Delsener, etc.) as these were the people who booked the rooms that would be important to stage the band's development and growth in the live arena. What I gleaned from that was that Paul knew just how important the touring career would be for the band and he wanted the agency to have ownership of that even before getting to the record part of the equation. In retrospect, that turned out to be very wise thinking."

McGuinness and Premier Talent agreed that a ten-day mini tour of the East Coast would be the ideal way to introduce U2 to the States. Meanwhile, at Warner Bros. HQ, he and Devine, with the help of vice president of artist development and publicity Bob Regehr and his assistant Ellen Darst, pulled together the U.S. marketing plan for the launch and sustain of the band in their early days. Like others before him, Devine was swept away by McGuinness's enthusiasm and absolute faith in U2. "I can tell you with 100 percent certainty, McGuinness knew from day one that this band was going to be the biggest band in the world, and every action sprang from that core belief," he says. "Now, today, it's easy to look back and say, 'Oh, sure. Who wouldn't?,' but this was before they had set foot in their first U.S. gigs at places like the Mudd Club and The Ritz in New York or the Country Club in L.A., before one note of music was ever played on the radio. I certainly had to agree with him as the songs and the sheer sonic production on *Boy* showed such musical vision and strength, but this was far from a given back in those days. You have to remember that when we began working together, U2 had yet to release an album anywhere in the world. I remember telling people that U2 would be as big and as important as a band like The Who. Not everyone got it just yet, but Paul and I and a small number of believers inside the company pressed forward with this band as though our lives depended on it. That was the nature of the campaign. Creating believers and spreading it from there. To call our zeal 'religion' at that point would not be far from the truth. We wanted to get the word out but we assiduously wanted to avoid the stigma of declaring them as 'the next big thing.' That was felt to be anathema at the time; too hypey, over the top. So instead, what we did was we booked a full-page ad in *Billboard* announcing the album and the debut U.S. tour dates. But instead of telling the industry what we thought of U2, we got some of the top voices at radio, press, and retail to tell us what they thought of the band. We built a whole campaign called 'U2: The Band People Are Talking About' and we named those people and what they had to say. It was very powerful in getting the next group of people to take notice. I still have the ad framed above my desk."

So it was on December 6, 1980, that U2 played their first American show at The Ritz club in New York. Being as it was a Saturday, a night normally reserved for discos, the open dance floor was packed with around eight hundred city slickers looking to let loose to a mix of oldies and top-forty hits spun by resident DJs. Hence it began as it always did for a band up against it. U2 played, and the audience mingled at the bar. Barsalona looked on anxiously from the balcony. He'd seen this gig play out a hundred times. U2 would carry on until frustration crept in and they turned on one another, or the audience grew tired of shouting over the music and they turned on the band—and this wasn't any old audience, this was New York, tough and cynical. But U2 must have ordered a set list change. Bono was in inspired form, scaling speakers, swinging from the ceiling, breaking down walls; Edge, with his expansive, echo-laden notes, punctured the hardest of skins; and Larry and Adam just about held it all together. Slowly but surely after each number more and more people gathered around the front of the stage, leaving their conversation back at the bar. As the night drew to a close U2 had won over the entire floor. People were singing along to the choruses. Women were hoisted on the shoulders of their partners. Even the suit-and-ties in the balcony were tapping along. It was like the ending of a Hollywood musical, the entire cast singing and dancing as the credits rolled. An agent since the '60s, Barsalona had seen nothing like it, and he raced downstairs to congratulate the band after their second encore. There, meeting them face-to-face for the first time, Barsalona said, "Guys, I promise you you're gonna be big in this country." This was music to their ears.

U2 claimed another crucial victory when opening for Capitol Records' Detroit rockers Barooga Bandit at the Paradise Theater in Boston, which New England promoter Don Law had opened three years earlier as a showcase for emerging acts in the area. Boston in general was identified as a key market for U2, as it was home to a large number of Irish immigrants and college students, many of whom often flocked to the local independent record stores in Kenmore Square and Harvard Square to snap up the latest pop imports and flick through copies of the British music weeklies *NME* and *Melody Maker.* The Boston DJ Carter Alan had stumbled upon a copy of the band's single "A Day Without Me" at one such store, and proceeded to regularly play it, and later "I Will Follow," on the two radio stations he worked at, WBCN-FM and MIT campus radio station WMBR, thus earning the distinction of being the first person to spin U2 records on American radio. So there was a definite buzz and anticipation among students for the band's arrival, which would explain what actually went down at their gig at the Paradise. "What happened that night was once U2 had finished, most of the audience left," recalls Don Law. "The poor band that was supposed to be the headliner really suffered. But it was a resounding success [for U2]."

Carter Alan elaborates: "U2 came out and there was like 150 people there, which is good for one of those new music nights. They got a really nice response and did a second encore, which is unheard of. Then we went upstairs to the backstage room and met the band afterward because BCN was co-promoting the show, and we're talking and I'll never forget it—there's a window that you can look out into the main room, and Adam goes, 'I believe everyone has left!' in that soft-spoken distinguished UK accent of his. And we all went to the window and there couldn't have been more than thirty people there. They'd all left after U2, and they weren't even the headliners! The record company guy from Capitol was devastated. He just started pouring Scotches for himself and drowned his sorrows. It was that dramatic."

As far as U2 was concerned, America was theirs for the taking.

■

Boy was finally released in the United States in March 1981, where it peaked at number sixty-three on the *Billboard* 200. The original album cover, which featured Guggi's diminutive six-year-old brother Peter Rowen posing shirtless with his hands behind his head and staring directly into the camera as a symbol of innocence, was replaced by a distorted picture of the band by Warner Bros., out of fear that it could easily be misinterpreted as child pornography. However, unaltered copies made it into the States on import, and this, combined with the sexually ambiguous nature of some of the lyrics, led to U2 attracting a large gay following in New York and San Francisco. The group's popularity also received a major boost from the publication of James Henke's *Rolling Stone* feature headlined "U2: Here Comes the Next Big Thing." Bono told the writer: "I don't mean to sound arrogant, but even at this stage, I do feel that we are meant to be one of the great groups."

The Irish quartet embarked on a grueling three-month promotional campaign in America in support of *Boy,* with the likes of Frank Barsalona, Tim Devine, and Ellen Darst acting as their mentors and advocates. While most other foreign bands' ambitions stopped at receiving airplay in a major city like New York, since they were convinced that was enough to claim they had cracked America, U2 understood that U.S. radio was severely fragmented; being played on a radio station in Boston, for example, didn't mean diddly-squat in Los Angeles or Chicago—which is why they traveled up and down the country on a dilapidated tour bus, played at every available venue, and cozied up to every rock DJ, promoter, and music journalist they encountered. They were systematic and relentless in their efforts. "From the very beginning, it was clear that this band took success very seriously," says Devine. "They wanted to do everything right. I remember, it was not just Paul, but the entire band who would sit in my office asking questions about who was who and what was important as far as breaking in the States. They all took an interest in getting their message out there, particularly the singer.

"After that, it was up to Paul and me to 'work the building.' We'd go around finding supporters and tapped their budgets for what we needed. I would bird-dog people who had marketing money left and Paul would go in and politely retrieve it. We worked quite well together in those roles. We communicated a lot in those days to get every advantage we could. You have to remember, this was a band who hadn't yet sold a hundred thousand records in the United States. Clearly, we were on a mission."

Early in the tour, U2 returned to Boston's Paradise Theater to perform two shows in one day, the first of which was recorded for distribution to radio throughout both the United States and Europe, providing Warner Bros. and Island with another weapon in their armory in the battle to get U2 heard. "Here we've got this 'official bootleg' and we just slide it out to the tastemakers," says Neil Storey. "A trick like that goes back forever. In the early days of Tom Petty there was a one-sided, twelve-inch 'official bootleg' and we were just sliding out these bits of vinyl to all the right people, and then when he came into the UK supporting Nils Lofgren, what happened? Suddenly people were turning up in their masses."

The U2 campaign gained another influential voice when the Denver promoter Barry Fey endorsed the group. Fey was a towering figure who had transformed the state of Colorado into one of the strongest live concert markets in the country, as well as promoting in Missouri, Kansas, Texas, Utah, and New Mexico on a regular basis. He had established a large network of press contacts on account of his propensity to provide controversial sound bites, and he wasn't afraid to get his hands dirty to move the needle on ticket sales or protect an asset. He was clearly a man to have on your side. "The scene here was whatever I wanted it to be," Fey told the author in an interview in May 2010. "I found out what the kids wanted and I brought it. I'd hang out on the streets."

U2 made their Denver debut at the Rainbow Music Hall, and Bono's strong charisma made a huge impression on Fey. "He won me right over," the fiery impresario recalled. "They played two or three numbers and I went into the office and I called Barsalona [in New York] and I said, 'This is gonna be the biggest band in the world!' I was so impressed with them that I went into the box office, took four fifty-dollar bills out, and gave one to each of them. I said, 'Listen, you guys go have a nice meal on me.' And then a few days later Jonathan King, the Englishman with the BBC show *Entertainment USA*, called and asked if I'd seen any good bands recently, and I said to him, 'U2. They have the musical integrity of The Who.' They told me once that they were watching King somewhere and they heard what I said. So that began our great relationship, and I brought them back to the Rainbow a few months later and they sold it out."

Likewise, esteemed Chicago promoter Jerry Mickelson was quick to fly the U2 flag after putting together a five-dollar radio show for them at the seven-hundred-seat theater Park West. "They were so nice, so appreciative," he recalls. "They loved the fact that promoters like us were behind them and trying to do all we could to help them become the band they are today." Mickelson believes that much of U2's appeal, especially in the God-fearing states of the Midwest and Deep South, rested on their strong Christian faith and much-publicized clean living. "Absolutely," he says. "They were very spiritual. They made the kind of music that you could probably sit there and sing in church. Going to a U2 show was a religious experience." Many others tend to agree with him. It was U2's apparent piety and virtuousness that encouraged Carter Alan to take his Christian friends to see the band play. "I said, 'You know, because of who they are and what they believe, it affects the kind of personality that they have and it's only a good thing. They try to give an honest effort to the audience because of their beliefs.' So yeah, I would say it did help them. But there was also that aspect of the conservative Christian community that was a little bit upset because they thought they were too rock and roll to be considered Christian. I don't think a lot of those people gave them a chance."

At the beginning of the year, Bono, Edge, and Larry had attended a weekend retreat for Christians at the Gaines Christian Youth Centre in Worcester, England, where, holding a copy of the Bible, Bono had reiterated their Christian commitment. He identified Isaiah 40:3 as "the Scripture that the Lord has basically shown us with regards to the band," adding: "I see our position as Christians as to make way, make straight a path for the Lord for a second time. In that sense we have to make the rough smooth and get involved in making the rough smooth." Bono expressed his hope that members of the Contemporary Christian music scene would stop preaching solely to the converted and join U2 in the mainstream where together they could "destroy the image that has got through . . . which has [given] God almighty and Jesus Christ . . . an image of a weakling. A slightly effeminate image. A sort of Sunday image. A religious image."

Nevertheless, the singer tried to be careful about just who in the mainstream he disclosed the true extent of U2's faith to, for fear it could be sensationalized or used as a weapon against them. He'd already fallen into that trap once too often. Storey recalls: "Dave McCullough was the first journalist who broke that whole Christianity/spirituality thing [in the UK], and Bono was onto us at Island a lot at that point. 'Oh no, what have I done? I've mucked everything up. I trusted this guy and he's just kind of [exploited] it,' and stuff like that. And it was like, 'Hold on a minute. This is what you believe in. It's no big deal, it is what it is. Don't forget we have the most important Rasta on the planet signed to Island, and he has his own spiritual beliefs, so what's the big deal? It doesn't matter.' That was our attitude."

On May 30, U2 taped their first U.S. television appearance on the late-night talk show *Tomorrow Coast to Coast* with host Tom Snyder, performing "I Will Follow" and "Twilight." It was a complete success, with Bono at one stage venturing into the studio audience and getting them to stand up and dance. Snyder was visibly impressed by the band's passion, and concluded a brief chat with Bono and Edge by saying: "Judging by what people have written about these fellas in *Newsweek* magazine and some of the music publications, we will be hearing a great deal of 'The U2' in this country in the years to come."

The following night, U2 brought the American leg of the Boy Tour to an end in New Jersey, having played around sixty shows in the space of three months. Then they headed back to Europe, eager to commence work on their sophomore album and fulfill Snyder's prophecy.

■

U2 entered Windmill Lane Studios in July to record *October,* with Steve Lillywhite once again at the controls. It was an uphill battle from day one. With the exception of "Fire," which had been completed during a short break in the band's U.S. schedule at Chris Blackwell's Compass Point Studios in Nassau, the song structures derived from a three-week prerecording period of rehearsal at Mount Temple, while all of the lyrics were written in the studio in a mad panic. "They had a few ideas but no songs as such because they'd been out touring the first record," recalls Kevin Moloney. "It was definitely a struggle. I think it opened their eyes a bit with regard to the potential of what you can do in a studio and what writing a song is all about. They had more of an adolescent attitude to it, a bit of a gung-ho spirit of, 'Whatever we do, it'll be brilliant.'"

Regarding the lyrics, Bono claimed that a briefcase he owned, which went mysteriously missing after a show in Portland, Oregon, in March, had contained a blue notebook with almost two years' worth of lyrics and song ideas, although few people actually believed him. "There was a lot of myth about that," says Moloney. "He just wasn't ready. I remember him driving his car into the wall outside the studio because he'd got to the parking lot and forgot to stop because he was working on some lyrics—I ran out to the car and pulled him out of it."

Many a time the studio crew would be at a situation where, having spent ages working with the rhythm section and Edge doing overdubs, they'd be waiting for Bono to record his vocals and he'd march in and complain about everything—he'd kick arse with everybody. He wouldn't have a definite explanation as to what was wrong with something. He couldn't articulate it in a musical/scientific way, just something along the lines of, "It should have more of the Spirit in it!" A lot of the time the crew just felt he was having a mental block, trying to come up with lyrics and things like that. He once told a crew member, "Whenever everybody's going black, I'm going to say white and see where it brings me." That was also one of his strengths, in many respects. That he'd somehow make the opposite way work. But as it turned out, the crew were right to question the legitimacy of the case of the missing lyrics: when Bono was reunited with his notebook twenty-three years later after a female fan found it in the attic of her rental home, its contents amounted to nothing more than a list of potential song titles and stage introductions.

"Fire" was released as a single in the UK in late July to maintain U2's career momentum and hopefully shake Bono out of his creative stupor. It failed on both counts. "'Fire' charted at number thirty-five," recalls Neil Storey, "which, somehow or another, got them a slot on *Top of the Pops*. But for some reason the record actually dropped the next week. It was like, 'Fuck! What is happening here?' Because after *Top of the Pops* a record is guaranteed to go up. Everybody was mystified by that."

A few weeks later, U2 gave their only Irish show of the year, supporting the legendary Thin Lizzy at the annual open-air festival at Slane Castle. The huge crowd was mostly comprised of heavy-rock fans, and U2 made the questionable decision to try and win them over by performing a bunch of half-finished, barely comprehensible material from *October*. Sure enough, bottles and other missiles rained down on them in almost biblical fashion and they were lucky to escape in one piece. "They were dreadful," says an associate. "It was one of the most embarrassing things I can remember. They'd just released 'Fire' and they had fireworks go off in the background. It was one of their big Spinal Tap moments."

Compounding U2's *October* problems was the fact that behind the scenes a sharp divide had emerged between the three born-again Christian members and Adam. During the course of the Boy Tour, Bono, Edge, and Larry had gradually removed themselves from the world around them. They didn't drink, didn't smoke, and rarely socialized with anyone in the crew other than ex–Virgin Prune Pod, who had been appointed head roadie and was as devoted to Shalom as them, and their girlfriends when they occasionally joined them on the road (although always sleeping in separate rooms). They would be at the back of the tour bus reading the Bible and praying together while Adam sat at the front with McGuinness and everyone else, smoking dope and planning their next rock-and-roll escapade. Adam felt alienated and confused. He was worried that U2 was fast turning into an out-and-out Christian rock band, and made a pact with McGuinness to back each other up during any disputes with the three believers regarding their conflicting lifestyles and the direction of the band.

Now, back home in Dublin, a major point of contention was that the U2 trio's Shalom meetings were taking precedence over the recording of *October* and cutting into valuable studio time. "They used to have those Christian meetings in the studio where they'd down tools and we'd be told to shag off," recalls Moloney. "They'd have a bunch of people in and studios cost a ton of money, but that had to come first. Everything would stop. It was very out there because in the early '80s there was a lot of hedonistic attitude going on in the studio and they were very straitlaced apart from Adam—Adam was certainly the odd man out. He'd go to the pub with us or get up to the shenanigans of whatever we were doing that was not exactly appropriate. There was a sort of studio crew atmosphere; a lot of blow going on, a lot of smoke and a lot of hash, and he was very much a part of that. Then there was a sort of band attitude where they'd have tea and toast and Christian meetings and catch the last bus home."

"I actually went out with Adam and Paul [McGuinness] once or twice and did cocaine with them," says another former U2 employee. "Adam was always the exception to the Christian-right rule that existed. He seemed to be the one ready and willing to have a good time in the traditional rock-and-roll manner."

The Shalom meetings grew more intense with each passing day, with the sixty-strong flock beginning to speak in tongues, fast, and weep in ecstasy as they surrendered themselves to the Holy Spirit; the most radical members were even "slain in the Spirit" (in other words, they passed out) as evidence of deliverance and exorcism inside the evangelical furnace. At weekends, they'd all drive out to Portrane in County Dublin, where they had a number of caravans dotted along the beach, sheltered from so-called urban decadence. Bono was baptized there in the Irish Sea.

During this period, Bono's relationship with childhood friends such as Guggi and Gavin Friday also disintegrated under the weight of his fanatical allegiance to Shalom and his insufferably earnest and preachy attitude. Guggi was the first to leave the sect, with Friday and his girlfriend Rene behind him, after the elders began to exploit the considerable sway they held over the younger members. They told them what they could and couldn't wear, who they could be friends with, and who they could date. The last straw for Guggi and Gavin was when they were ordered to change the name Virgin Prunes to Deuteronomy Prunes.

One of the two leaders handpicked the prettiest female member to be his wife, after claiming God had come to him the night before and told him that she had to be with him. He was a strange man in many respects. He was forever warning the youngsters about using changing rooms and getting undressed in front of other men. Years later he would swap Shalom and his wife and children for the world of transvestism, and could often be seen parading around the bars and restaurants of Dublin in a pink frock and matching hat. Nevertheless, he was a great influence on Bono. One day, the singer marched into the control room at Windmill Lane, where Lillywhite was hard at work with the rest of the crew, and he stood in front of them all and said, "I don't know if you guys know this, but the Second Coming is going to happen and it's going to happen within the next ten years!" Then he marched right back out the door he came through. Everyone in the control room fell into a deathly silence, until Lillywhite finally turned around and said, "You know what? That idiot thinks he is the Second Coming!"

"Cults attract dreamers," muses Meiert Avis, the acclaimed Irish music video director who, along with James Morris, Russ Russell, and Brian Masterson, had founded Windmill Lane in 1978. "I think 'speaking in tongues' really freed Bono's stream of consciousness and may have helped his lyric writing and singing, let him find and trust his own spirit. [William S.] Burroughs's 'cut up' technique has much the same creative function, but reversed.

"Bono's songwriting sometimes starts as a narrative of real people and situations," adds Avis. "Then he cuts out all the specifics and is left with a universal emotional equation expressed in Edge's time-warped Welsh choir music, as played on a guitar. These two 'Irish' have a unique creative process that is the product of history, geography, religion, and genocide."

Bono's unrestrained declarations of faith would find expression in the bulk of *October*'s lyrics, from the Latin chorus of "Gloria," which translated to "Glory in you, Lord/Glory, exalt [him]" to the unapologetic "Rejoice." It was U2's most overtly religious album, with many of Bono's hastily written words in fact ripped directly from the pages of the Bible. "For all its naïveté and for all its stained-glass approach to lyric writing, if Joy Division were mining the gothic end of a very large cathedral, *October* was the folk mass/rave—'cos it was ecstatic," Bono reflected in *Mojo* in 2005.

"Gloria" was released on October 5 as the second single from the album, reaching number fifty-five in the UK and number ten in Ireland. Avis directed a low-budget promotional video for the track, depicting the band giving a free concert on a barge in Grand Canal Basin, within spitting distance of Windmill Lane. It became one of the first videos to air on the new cable channel MTV in America, and helped an import version of the single to gate-crash the U.S. chart at number eighty-one. Avis recalls: "The basic idea of putting on a raw show with fans in an unexpected place worked out, and became the model for thousands of videos, including the 'Streets' video. As for [the impact of] 'Gloria' in the USA I had no idea at the time. My focus after 'Gloria' was on trying to get work from UK record companies and bands who were prejudiced against U2 and anything Irish. I would go around the various commissioners' offices with my reel and get rejected. America seemed a million miles away."

October itself followed a week later, featuring a rather crude group shot of U2 on the cover, which the band fought tooth and nail with

Island to get green-lit, only to regret it in later years. The reviews were mixed, leaning toward the negative. Joe Breen of *The Irish Times* appreciated Edge's contribution on the album—"he saves the day with a rush of stirring notes guaranteed to move the coldest heart"—but thought the song arrangements lacked fluency and the lyrics were repetitive and thin on content. He concluded thus: "*October* is a good album though not the great set I expected of a band which has the ability to do something special. It is still all before them and the evidence is still very strong that U2 have the talent to make the big breakthrough and the album to achieve it. *October* is not the crucial set, but it is enough to make me still believe." In *Rolling Stone,* Jon Pareles said the album was incoherent, and that "the way to enjoy U2 is to consider the vocals as sound effects and concentrate, as the band does, on the sound of the guitar."

October debuted at number eleven in the UK but failed to dent the U.S. *Billboard* Top 100. In the end, it sold fewer copies than *Boy* in either market. But it was the checkered notices that stung the most, and angered Bono in particular. One adjective seemed to pop up again and again when describing the LP over the next few months: "rushed."

"The second album was not reviewed as well as the first one was," says Storey. "Everybody [in the band] kind of went, 'Oh dear. What's happening now?' And it was a case of gently saying, 'Because it's not a very good record, guys. So, okay, we've got some bad reviews, but the live show's as hot as hell. Look at the positives as opposed to the negatives.' "

Bono's frustration when something wasn't going his way usually manifested itself in two ways: he'd either lapse into stony silence or throw a full-blown temper tantrum. At times, he was impossible to live with—especially for Larry. In November, around six hundred fans at Toad's Place in New Haven, Connecticut, caught a glimpse of big bad Bono for themselves when Larry came in too late on "11 O'Clock Tick Tock" because he was adjusting his drum kit. Bono thought the diminutive sticksman was hiding from the audience members and charged at him like a grizzly bear, kicked the kit onto its side, and hurled parts of it into the stunned crowd. Then he cornered Larry and almost throttled him, if not for Edge grabbing him by his hair and planting a perfectly aimed right hook on his chin. The gig ended early in riotous confusion, with the singer and guitarist engaged in a shoving match on stage and the drummer cowering in the dressing room backstage.

▪

U2 spent the beginning of 1982 in Ireland in full crisis mode after Bono, Edge, and Larry revealed that they were seriously thinking about walking away from music altogether. The persuasive Shalom leaders had begun exerting pressure on them to quit the band and fully commit themselves to Christianity, concluding that the two were irreconcilable. For Adam, it was the moment that he realized his bandmates were more unstable than he first thought. Although he had distrusted the intentions of the Shalom sect from day one, he had no problem with the concept of spirituality and always assumed that it and music were on the same song sheet. So he was completely baffled by the news, and tried to convince them that they were about to make a huge mistake. McGuinness also weighed in, saying with sarcasm, "If God had a problem with our tour, He should have raised it at the planning meeting." As tension mounted, the exasperated manager reached a compromise with the want-away trio: they would fulfill their remaining business obligations with U2 and then take it from there.

Around that same time, unbeknownst to U2 or McGuinness, Island MD Martin Davis was leading an in-house effort to cut the band loose, amid well-founded fears the indie label was dangling precariously over the precipice of financial ruin. According to Island insiders, the amount of money U2 owed the company for legal fees, producers, and other expenses was close to £400,000 (£1 million in 2014 money), and Davis wrote a letter to Chris Blackwell warning him that, following the poor sales of *October* and lack of support from mainstream radio and television, there was little chance of recouping their development costs, therefore immediate action was required. "We're too much in debt with this band, we must drop them," he said. But Blackwell was enamored of McGuinness and his vision for the still-young group, and also retained sufficient faith in the members of staff who had signed them and continued to fight in their corner. Thus, Blackwell scribbled "No" on the letter, underlined it, and promptly mailed it back to his MD. By late March, Davis had cleared out his desk at Island HQ.

"In fairness to Martin, he was in a pretty unenviable position," says Neil Storey. "He was the head honcho at Island and the company wasn't in great financial shape at that moment in time—whatever the reasons were—and he had to make tough financial decisions on cost cutting. But Chris believed in McGuinness and U2. He could see the groundswell, and he was very aware of what Rob [Partridge] and I were creating in terms of the press. He could see this building on a global level at this point. So it was a case of saying, 'No, I'm going to back this.' You also have to understand that Blackwell in his formative days had a reputation as a bit of a poker player. So look at this in terms of poker."

Unfortunately, U2 did not receive the same level of support from Warner Bros. when the October Tour returned to America for the second time in February. The label refused to subsidize the tour any further due to *October*'s frosty reception, so McGuinness was forced to pick up the tab with his own credit card until Frank Barsalona came to the rescue and arranged a fourteen-date support slot with The J. Geils Band, who were at the height of their stardom after scoring a number-one hit with "Centerfold," and therefore ensuring U2 got to showcase their live prowess in front of large arena-sized crowds. "My memory [of opening for The J. Geils Band] is we won over their audience and people were there who clearly liked U2," Adam recalled in *San Diego Union-Tribune*. "So we started from a position of being expected to get booed off the stage, and we got encores."

U2 also agreed to take part in New York's annual St. Patrick's Day Parade, in which they were to perform on a large float to around a million people lining the curbs along a rain-swept Fifth Avenue. However, they pulled out at the last minute after learning that the official parade committee, naming deceased Irish hunger striker Bobby Sands as its honorary grand marshal, was dedicating the event to the theme "England Get Out of Ireland." It was a quietly noble move on U2's behalf. At a time when a substantial portion of Irish-Americans were captivated by the shit-stained glamor of the hunger strikes in Maze Prison, even the slightest pro-Republican sentiment would have been beneficial for an Irish band in America. It was a situation they'd faced numerous times before on the October Tour, with second- and third-generation Irish-Americans throwing money on stage and yelling pro-IRA slogans in support of Sands. U2 mostly thought them misguided, but just bit their collective tongue and pretended not to notice.

6

The Battle Cry

It was the summer of 1982. In only a few weeks, Edge would turn twenty-one. His career up until this point had been remarkable in many ways. Although the sweet taste of commercial triumph still eluded U2, he had been credited with creating a whole new "less is more" approach to guitar playing in which rhythm and lead were no longer segregated and simple notes bled with emotion—one which compelled aspiring musicians to cram the classified sections of British and American music journals with ads seeking "Guitarist—U2 style." And he had performed to thousands on both sides of the Atlantic, almost reduced to tears as the little-known Irish band and hardened audience became one. However, the contradictions between his career as a rock-and-roll musician and his life as a committed Christian and member of Shalom remained at the forefront of his mind and gnawed at his soul. Larry (who, incidentally, had added the "Jr." suffix to his name in order to prevent his namesake father from receiving his tax bills) had in effect already left the religious group, having come to realize the hypocrisy of the hierarchy's ways and grown tired of the persistent calls for U2 to cease propagating the so-called Devil's music and devote their lives entirely to the sect. "I got out before anybody else," Larry later told *Q*. "I'd just had enough, it was bullshit. It was like joining the Moonies." Bono, too, had begun slowly backing away from the evangelical furnace, having reached the conclusion that "it would be a very unusual, maybe even perverse, God that would ask you to deny your gift." Edge respected their decision and had in fact expressed similar concerns but ultimately tolerated Shalom's increasingly fanatical and manipulative behavior because of the overwhelming sense of joy and peace he felt during the prayer meetings, and he attributed the dialogue established between himself and God to the group. Therefore, according to insiders, he told his bandmates that he needed time to reflect on what it meant to be a born-again Christian and how he could "best serve God"—and whether or not rock and roll had a part to play in this wholly spiritual existence.

Edge found himself standing at a crossroads with an indefinable ache and two lives pulling him in opposite directions. Eventually, after two weeks of intense soul-searching, he also left Shalom, having determined that Christianity and rock and roll did not have to be mutually exclusive and that it was absurd to suggest otherwise. He could, he felt, use music to share his beliefs, to offer something positive to the world without turning it into an evangelical tool. And while Shalom had been a great source of spiritual strength and balance to him, he also firmly believed that we are all on a spiritual path, one way or another, and that it is ours to walk alone, free of religious bigotry and prohibition. "I think the sort of spirituality that I believe in transcends religion, leaving it looking stupid," Edge told *Jamming!* in 1984. "Religion for me is like politics in a sense—something to belong to. It's a set of values that people accept a lot of the time without thinking about it."

In the ensuing years U2 would maintain that their Shalom experience had helped shape their spirituality, honing their knowledge of the Scriptures and ultimately strengthening their opposition to organized religion. But many intimates believe that the secretive, authoritarian nature of the evangelical sect also became an indelible part of U2's psyche. "The most important thing about Shalom for U2 was that they absorbed a cultlike mentality," says a former member of the sect. "They became more ruthless and very, very good at protecting themselves as a direct result. The whole U2 organization has cultlike qualities."

■

On August 8—Edge's birthday—U2 entered Windmill Lane Studios with a renewed focus on their mission to conquer the music industry on their own terms, aided once again by Steve Lillywhite and house engineers Kevin Moloney and Paul Thomas, after unsuccessful trial runs with Blue Öyster Cult producer/manager Sandy Pearlman and Blondie's Jimmy Destri. And with the stakes so perilously high—and the war chest empty—the studio dwellers got straight down to business, working eighteen-hour days from the get-go. "There really was an air of desperation and absolute hunger about those sessions," recalls Moloney. "They were very lucky to have made it past *October*. They were certainly lucky to still be signed [to Island Records]. I remember they were having so many difficulties financially, and it was around two grand a day to hire the studio, which was a hell of a lot of money for a band that had nothing. It was real backs-against-the-wall stuff."

Originally, the project was intended as a reaction to what was happening in the UK music charts at that time; the antithesis of the synth-pop sound most commonly associated with the New Romantic fashion movement. Or, as Bono would say, "a slap in the glossy, made-up-to-be-pretty face which is the music of most of our contemporaries." To achieve this, Bono felt that U2 needed to capture the raw power and energy of their live shows and pushed Edge to be more aggressive in his playing—"Don't be like the Edge. Be like Mick Jones from The Clash!" he would often urge his ethereal songwriting partner. Bono was also concerned that Edge's echo-laden guitar sound had become too predictable and encouraged him to jettison his beloved Electro-Harmonix Deluxe Memory Man, to which the guitarist responded by experimenting with an amplified Washburn Acoustic Festival and a Second World War–era Epiphone lap steel, positioning the strings in couples an octave apart to produce his own idiosyncratic sound. "There were people regurgitating

'A Day Without Me' for an entire LP . . . like flocks and flocks of stealers," Bono later told *Creem* magazine. "Lots of people are playing just like the Edge, to the extent that he was being asked if he was being influenced by them! He was in danger of parodying himself. So we sat down for this album and said, 'Look, we must strip the sound bare.' "

With two albums under his belt, Edge now felt more at home in a studio environment, and his mind fixated incessantly on developing basic ideas he had come up with on the road and pushing his slight frame and suppressed aggression to the very extremities of their capabilities. Bono, at once motivator and profiteer driven to seize upon the creative moment—which he referred to as "the moment when God walks through the room"—as swiftly as possible and to then share this vision with a planet spinning at a mere fraction of his natural speed, would often "Bongolese"—that is to say, speak in tongues—over Edge's raw outpourings until a structure or, at the very least, a dominant feeling was agreed upon. The much-criticized rhythm section also played their own small but significant role in the creative process, providing Edge for perhaps the first time a solid foundation on which to develop his ideas, which was attributed to Larry being asked to use a click-track to improve his timing. It was a hi-hat on a tape loop, a hard-sounding thing. Larry didn't particularly like it, but he got into the spirit of it eventually. He had to. Bono and Lillywhite would push him. Bono would push everyone.

"He [Larry] was very anti-click-track," says Moloney. "He'd heard from some other drummer in the business that click-tracks were killing records. I think it was just insecurity on his behalf. But he certainly needed one, and then when sequencers came along he was able to use them live and that really helped him a lot. But he was very reluctant to begin with."

Two weeks into the sessions Bono and Ali tied the knot at All Saints' Church in Raheny. It was a typically unconventional affair, falling somewhere between a traditional Protestant wedding and a radical Charismatic Christian ritual. Jack Heaslip, Bono's guidance counselor at Mount Temple, presided over the ceremony, having since been ordained as an

Anglican priest. The sermon was given by Shalom leader Chris Rowe, with whom Bono remained on good terms despite having officially left the sect. For many of the guests who crammed into the small church, it was their first glimpse into the secretive world of Shalom and they were visibly perplexed as other fellowship members formed a circle around the altar and began to chant ecstatically. Bob Hewson, who was said to have been quietly proud of his son's commitment to Ali, appeared uncomfortable. For Larry, Sr., it was confirmation that he had been right to encourage his son to distance himself from the religious group. The wedding reception was held at Sutton House Hotel, during which Bono was hoisted onto the shoulders of his brother Norman and carried through the main rooms like a triumphant prizefighter. According to guest Shay Healy, "It was like he was fated to be a leader." Later, with the party in full swing, U2 and Irish singer-songwriter Paul Brady grabbed the wedding band's instruments, climbed onto a table, and burst into a spirited rendition of Little Richard's "Tutti Frutti" which blew out the electricity in the building, leaving Bono and Ali to spend their first night together as husband and wife in pitch-blackness.

For U2, the ceremony represented not just the union of two lovers—the zealous, charismatic fireball and the serene, apple-cheeked girl next door—but a major step toward reconciliation between Bono and Adam. Of all the relationships in the band, theirs was the biggest casualty of the spiritual conflict. During the recent recording sessions, Bono had even accused the estranged bassist of becoming a rock-and-roll caricature and told him to wise up. Yet at a time when, in the words of one insider, "Adam may very well have believed he was about to be kicked out of the band," Bono asked him to be his best man. And Adam grasped this olive branch with both hands.

Bono and Ali honeymooned in Jamaica, enjoying free board at Chris Blackwell's Goldeneye estate, which had once belonged to Ian Fleming. Adam and McGuinness, meanwhile, took full advantage of U2's first break in years by jetting off to Tuscany, Italy, with Lillywhite and Moloney in tow, determined to have a good time. "We rented a house for a week off a friend of McGuinness's in the advertising business," recalls

Moloney. "It was the wildest time I've ever had. I remember one night he [Adam] desperately wanted to drive the rented car into the swimming pool in the house. I swear to God, and it nearly bloody happened too. We all awoke late the next day to find the car only feet away from the pool. Luckily it didn't make it, but we were very close."

Edge opted to stay at home and focus on the album, much to the horror of Aislinn, who had trouble accepting the fact that she and her man were to spend the last days of summer in dreary Dublin. Following a heated exchange with his apoplectic girlfriend, Edge secluded himself in U2's newly rented beachfront bungalow on the north side of a peninsula known as Howth Head—which the band used as a rehearsal space and Bono and Ali would squeeze into on their return—and put all his "fear and frustration" as a songwriter and boyfriend into a musical composition *Rolling Stone* magazine would come to describe as "the bone-crushing arena-rock riff of the decade." Then, as the waves crashed onto the shore outside the rear window of the bungalow and the sheer force of the guitar riff reverberated through his skull like a tower bell sounding the alarm of an approaching storm, came the lyric that would dictate the direction of the song and much of the album that followed: "Don't talk to me about the rights of the IRA, UDA." It was a real breakthrough moment, shaped by U2's firsthand experience of Irish-American Republican sentiment while on tour in the United States. But to the others working on the album, it suggested that while Edge was prepared to take off his armor and convey his inner turmoil through his guitar playing, he was hesitant to do the same when putting pen to paper.

Bono, by his own admission, was also reluctant to examine the self, to confront the bitterness, hypocrisy, and spiritual unrest that had almost torn U2 apart and supply the public with a raw, uncompromising autobiography. Consequently, he suffered terribly from writer's block, with his only tangible contribution at that stage being a love song he wrote for Ali on their honeymoon, called "Two Hearts Beat as One," which he envisaged Barbra Streisand or Aretha Franklin one day belting out. Therefore he took Edge's external, politically charged concept and ran with it, pausing only to temper the opening IRA/UDA dig to avoid the risk of reprisal and contrast the Bloody Sunday incident in Derry in 1972, in which British paratroopers shot and killed thirteen unarmed Catholic civil rights protesters, with the death and subsequent resurrection of Jesus Christ on Easter Sunday to emphasize the futility of The Troubles in Northern Ireland and promote the principles of nonviolence. A militaristic drum pattern that recalled Larry's youth learning under Joe Bonnie and a choppy, frenetic electric violin from nomadic musician Steve Wickham, whom Edge met purely by chance at a Dublin bus stop, were then added in the studio, completing U2's aggressive-pacifist anthem "Sunday Bloody Sunday."

"We all had a hand in that song," Edge later explained to *NME*, "because it's probably the heaviest thing we've ever done, lyrically. It's hard for us to justify a title like 'Sunday Bloody Sunday,' and we are aware of that. We realize the potential for division in a song like that, so all we can say is that we're trying to confront the subject rather than sweep it under the carpet. We thought a lot about the song before we played it in Belfast, and Bono told the audience that if they didn't like it then we'd never play it again. Out of the three thousand people in the hall about three walked out. I think that says a lot about the audience's trust in us."

Other political and social issues U2 addressed on the album they came to call *War* included the Polish Solidarity movement ("New Year's Day"), the effects of war on family life ("The Refugee"), and the threat of nuclear proliferation ("Seconds")—the latter track, which boasted Edge's first lead vocal performance and incorporated a sample from the 1982 television documentary *Soldier Girls*, was considered so sparse in its final form that a visiting journalist once commented to the band, "That's going to be great when it's finished." The album cover, a new shot of *Boy*'s child subject Peter Rowen posing against a weathered sheet of corrugated iron, his face at once angry and afraid and sporting a cut lip, symbolized what the world can do to a child, the loss of innocence. Moreover, it reflected Bono's own lack of faith in human nature. "The century that we are living in is the most barbaric ever," he told *NME*. "In the past, men committed atrocities without being fully aware of what they were doing. Now man has been educated, but the atrocities are still going on. But I still have my beliefs, not so much in people, but in what lies behind people. That comes across in the music."

Elsewhere, the up-tempo "Like a Song" was written as a response to British music journalists and rock contemporaries who accused the band of being far too earnest and safe—the Cliff Richard and the Shadows of the waning post-punk movement. Bono argued in *Rolling Stone* that he believed U2 to be "totally rebellious, because of our stance against what people accept as rebellion. The whole thing about rock stars driving cars into swimming pools—that's not rebellion. . . . Revolution starts at home, in your heart, in your refusal to compromise your beliefs and your values."

"Drowning Man" was an acoustic ballad Edge considered "one of the most successful pieces of recording that we've ever done." Originally conceived as the score for Bono's shelved "Sam Beckett–style play" of the same name, the finished article was notable for its 6/8 rhythm and Steve Wickham's Celtic-inflected violin. The mostly improvised lyrics drew upon Isaiah 40:29–31, and Bono claimed it was the voice of God speaking through him—"You know, 'Take my hand, I'll be here if you can—I don't want these famines to take place, these car accidents, this world of chance, this is not how I intended'"—although U2 intimates believe the song subconsciously alluded to Bono's intolerance of Adam's lifestyle and his wish for the bassist to seek the truth of God as he himself had done.

"Red Light" and "Surrender" both retained the cinematic feel of *Boy* and *October* while introducing elements of contemporary R&B and funk. They were also tied together thematically, inspired by the hellish reds and steamy sidewalks of '70s New York as depicted in Martin Scorsese's *Taxi Driver*. Adriana Kaegi, Cheryl Poirier, and Taryn Hagey of the globe-trotting tropical funk group Kid Creole and the Coconuts provided the background vocals on both tracks after McGuinness, a friend of Kid Creole's ZE Records boss, Michael Zilkah, called Kaegi and invited the trio and their trumpeter Ken Fradley down to Windmill Lane. "Not what we had in mind," recalls Kaegi, "but we agreed anyway, only to find a bunch of very young innocent lads at the studio who turned bright red when Cheryl told them she sings better in the nude and started taking off her pullover. She was just having fun. . . ." Poirier adds: "They were young, shy, and polite—uncommonly polite for early '80s rockers. Bono was energetic and enthusiastic and very 'hands on' in the studio, working alongside Steve Lillywhite. The drums, bass, and guitar tracks had already been recorded, so Adam, Larry, and Edge were mostly bystanders during our sessions. Adam was engaging and funny. Edge was pensive, with his guitar in hand, and Larry was really, really shy! When we recorded 'Red Light,' Bono kept telling us to sing softer and softer, until the words sounded like whispers. So, after a bunch of takes and retakes I figured out what he wanted and blurted out 'Oh, you want it to sound sexier, sort of orgasmic, right?' Then there was a hush in the control room . . . not a word from the guys . . . oops . . . I was unaware of their strong religious beliefs and had stepped out of bounds rather bluntly!"

As October turned into November, U2's *War* album was behind schedule and over budget, an all-too-familiar occurrence that concerned the powers that be at Island. The final song to be recorded was in fact the album's closing track, "40," a hymnlike ballad based on Psalm 40 that belied the manner in which it was created. The band and crew had been working through the last night of recording, tired and mentally exhausted, when one of them pointed out that they were still one song short of a full-length LP. So Lillywhite sprang into action and said, "Right, take this outtake and slow down the drums. I think we can make something out of it," and Edge switched back and forth between guitar and bass, because Adam had already gone home, and Bono sat in the corner with a copy of the Bible, frantically writing down lyrics. It came together in about fifteen minutes, but that's all the time they had because ephemeral synth-pop romantics Minor Detail had booked the studio and they were waiting outside to come in—for the last few weeks of recording, U2 had to fit around the schedule of other artists at Windmill, working exclusively at night and then also preparing the equipment for the next act scheduled to arrive at half past eight in the morning. It was strenuous stuff. "That was part of the deal," recalls a crew member. "It was a bit of a nightmare, but it was done."

Remarkably, U2 was soon plotting their next career move. Upon returning from London to perform *War*'s first single "New Year's Day" on *Top of the Pops* in January 1983, the band immediately caught a taxi back to their bungalow to work on new material. "They've always been like that—very driven in the pursuit of their goals," says a source. "They're not like anybody else, that's for sure. I think a lot of people don't understand the amount of work they put in."

U2's doggedness was rewarded when "New Year's Day" cracked the UK Top 10 singles chart, while in America it was FM radio's most added track the week it was released, thanks in part to the tireless campaigning of Island's new VP of promotion, Michael Abramson. Abramson also persuaded MTV executives to put the dramatic "New Year's Day" music video directed by Meiert Avis on heavy rotation, as a result placing U2 on the radar of young, hip Americans almost overnight—although a lack of support from CHR (contemporary hit radio) programmers ensured the single stalled at number fifty-three on the *Billboard* Hot 100. Bono viewed the success of the song as a victory not only for U2 but for rock music in general. "It just appears that people are getting disillusioned with the usual sort of 'snap, crackle, and pop' and they want something different," he said, adding that American radio in particular "is run by commercial enterprise, therefore by its nature it will be bland. I feel that our music can cut through that. I feel it's like a knife to that whole surface of MOR [middle of the road] music." For Edge, it was the speed at which the band's fortunes had changed on the previously impenetrable U.S. radio that was most satisfying. "I talked to many program directors [when promoting *Boy* and *October*] and the line was always the same: 'I listen to you when I go home, I think your album's great, but I'll never play it on my station, because if it means one kid pushes that button, it's a mistake.' One guy said something which I felt was very important to remember being a foreign band coming into America: 'If my station is the last station to add this album in the whole country, we'll be okay. But if we're the first and it dives, then we suffer.' So for the change to have happened so quickly... it's amazing, it really is phenomenal."

War followed in late February, topping the UK album chart in its first week of release and entering the United States at number ninety-one before eventually peaking at twelve—a slow but steady climb considered equally impressive given the general apathy toward new imported music at that time. Reviews from critics both at home and abroad were largely favorable. Writing for *Hot Press,* Liam Mackey acknowledged *War* as "a record which bears witness to its time and context with a mixture of fear, courage, and hope." J. D. Considine of *Rolling Stone* wrote in a four-star review that "U2 may not be great intellectuals, and *War* may sound more profound than it really is. But the songs here stand up against anything on The Clash's *London Calling* in terms of sheer impact, and the fact that U2 can sweep the listener up in the same sort of enthusiastic romanticism that fuels the band's grand gestures is an impressive feat." And Philip Smith of *The New Zealand Herald* hailed it as an instant classic, saying "U2 have set out to make a big statement on a subject close to the Irishmen's hearts—and they have succeeded."

But that wasn't enough for Bono. He wanted to be accepted by everyone, including the influential trinity of British music weeklies—*NME, Melody Maker,* and *Sounds*—who had all but washed their hands of the band at the height of the post-*Boy* religious fervor. So when a *Sounds* critic deemed *War* "too straightforward, too literal" and claimed the lyrics to "Sunday Bloody Sunday" had failed to move him whatsoever, Bono became so frustrated, so fixated, that he brought up the review during a show in Portsmouth on the UK leg of the War Tour and called the journalist "deaf, dumb, as well as blind." And he was practically inconsolable when Gavin Martin of *NME* stated that the album "cranks out blank liberal awareness" and "is another example of rock music's impotence and decay."

Nick Stewart notes that Bono was by far the most thin-skinned of the band. "I remember having quite an emotional conversation with him in the Portobello Hotel after they played at the Hammersmith Odeon. He said, 'Captain, *NME* don't like us!' And I said, 'Well, this may come as a bit of a surprise to you, Bono, but you've gone past *NME* now and you want to be worrying a bit more about whether *The Times* and *The Guardian* like you.' Which they did. I said, 'Don't worry about some snotty little student journalist who wants to make a name for himself. It's not important.' But he wanted to be liked by everybody. And it's not easy seeing yourself being traduced or criticized in print by someone you don't even know, saying that you're pompous and overblown when you know in your heart that that's not what it is at all."

▪

U2 continued to prove themselves a viable business investment when the War Tour—marketed as "The War on Boring Music"—landed on American soil in late April. Playing against a backdrop of three large white flags and Ian Finlay's photograph of Peter Rowen from the cover of *War,* their distinctive brand of militant pacifism and anti-nationalism was received enthusiastically by audience members and critics traditionally not averse to big emotional statements and theatricality. Indeed, while the inherently cynical British media and public had scoffed at the very notion of Bono, clad in black peasant freedom fighter garb, marching around the stage and scaling theater balconies while waving a white flag and imploring them to shout, "No more! No war!" to a martial beat, their burgeoning American audience lapped it up with abandon. Journalist Rick Miller attended the opening night in North Carolina and wrote: "Here is this happy maniac, playing human lightning rod with a white flag of peace on the first day of the tour, just to break through to us. There are no words for the warmth of the thrill that U2 gave the crowd. I surrendered and I know I'm not alone."

Carter Alan, who remained an invaluable ally to U2 in the New England region, joined the band and their traveling crew of eight on the road for a couple of weeks, starting with two sold-out nights at Boston's Orpheum Theatre—the second of which was taped and broadcast on the nationally syndicated radio concert series "King Biscuit Flower Hour." It was immediately apparent to Alan that U2 had honed their craft since their last visit. "On previous tours they were a raw and undisciplined entity on stage," he says. "But on the War Tour—at least initially—they had a more focused energy. There was a greater sense of balance between Bono's stage act of going into the audience and what the other guys were doing musically, especially Edge, who was conjuring up these rich and aggressive guitar textures. And the fans were going nuts." The high ticket demand, coupled with the band's commercial breakthrough with "New Year's Day," convinced Don Law that they were ready to graduate from small colleges and theaters to sports arenas. The New England promoter booked their first U.S. arena date to be held a month later at the eleven-thousand-capacity Worcester Centrum on the outskirts of Boston. "It was the right time," says Law. "They had steadily built up a live following through relentless touring and positive word-of-mouth and then when the hit single came along, the numbers multiplied overnight. So we stepped up ahead of everyone else and then Barbara Skydel filled in other dates. That was the big step up." Naturally, U2 welcomed the move, having made no secret of their ambition to follow in the footsteps of Bruce Springsteen and perform on the biggest stage possible as soon as humanly possible. They even inquired about playing at New York's twenty-thousand-seat Madison Square Garden, but it wasn't available on the date specified. "If we stay in small clubs, we'll develop small minds, and then we'll start making small music," Bono told *Trouser Press*.

However, U2 soon discovered that playing the big game came at an equally big price. They had always prided themselves on the close relationship they had with their fans. It was intimate and passionate, yet respectful and unobtrusive, a genuine bond that had developed over time and was largely absent of the mindless adulation and star fucking rock-and-roll careers are typically built upon. But as the War Tour clocked up more miles and the shows got bigger, the opportunity to meet and interact with each other became more scarce and enviable. Meanwhile, the popularity of "New Year's Day" attracted a different breed of audience member to their shows altogether: one who appeared to have little interest in the meaning of the lyrics and was only there to hear the hit single or because, in the words of a visibly frustrated Bono, it was now "fashionable to be into U2." This disparate audience—the territorial superfan suddenly starved of intimacy, the hit-hungry pop fashionista whom U2 felt an obligation to educate—produced an intense and at times unpleasant atmosphere which was at odds with the uplifting spiritual effect the band were normally associated with. The quartet looked on helplessly as fans trampled over one another to get nearer to the stage and heavy-handed concert stewards fought them back. Bono, who at that time was considered the unlikeliest of sex symbols, also found himself being mobbed on stage by groups of shrieking women, one of whom tried to handcuff herself to his leg, in scenes reminiscent of a Duran Duran concert. The singer often tried pleading with everyone to calm down, but to little avail.

The excitement U2 aroused for better or worse at each stop on the road suggested they were on the brink of something colossal. On May 14, Carter Alan witnessed an incident outside the Tower Theater in Philadelphia that he defines as "the beginning of U2 hysteria." He paints a scene that falls somewhere between The Beatles' *A Hard Day's Night* and George A. Romero's *Dawn of the Dead*. "We were all sitting on the tour bus—minus Bono and Ali who had hitched a ride with Bruce Springsteen, as you do—getting ready to head off to a party McGuinness was throwing back at the hotel, when suddenly a large group of fans and autograph hunters swarmed around the bus," recalls Alan. "We were parked there for what seemed like an eternity when Larry, who was sitting up front with the driver, slid open a side window to chat to the folks outside. Well, a riot immediately broke out as people fought to get within earshot of him. It was crazy. They were screaming and holding on to whatever parts of the bus they could as we tried to pull away from the curb. Eventually, Larry convinced Dennis Sheehan [U2's tour manager] to open the door so he could ask everyone to back away. Bad idea! Within seconds he was being pulled from the moving bus, and Dennis and I had to dive across the aisle to grab the one arm still inside before he was dragged outside. It became this huge tug-of-war. Then the driver slammed on the emergency brake and helped us pull him back inside to safety. Larry was visibly shaken by the whole thing and couldn't really wrap his head around what had just happened because it was all so foreign to him. I think there was definitely something in the air that night, something prophetic. You could feel it."

The group's new level of success in the United States created all kinds of difficulties, especially for Bono, caught as he was between being "the next big thing" and devoted husband to Ali. On and off stage, it seemed like just about everyone wanted a piece of the front man: Hollywood players, groupie flies, rock-and-roll scribes, even college professors and students preparing papers on the band's music. "I'm the singer in the group U2 and people expect things from me that I can't quite honestly give them—which is to be the life and soul of the party," he told *Hot Press*. "There are nights when I'll stand up on the table and I'll take my clothes off and there'll be another night when I'm afraid to even sit down." It was, he said, "something for Ali to understand."

Bono could often be seen putting a protective arm around his wife, literally and figuratively, as if to safeguard her purity as together they navigated the big-city party scene that goes hand-in-hand with a modicum of fame and success. The rock journalist Ethlie Ann Vare joined them one night at the Hollywood hotspot Club Lingerie and noted that Ali looked "as out of place as a dairymaid in a brothel." Bono's marriage, according to one friend, kept him on the straight and narrow and made life bearable for everyone who was part of his inner circle during that period: "[Because] here is this horny, emotional guy who also needs to live as a Christian."

Bono, rather than taking comfort in U2's rise in popularity, fretted about them being perceived as "just another fashion band passing through" and sought extreme ways to connect with the audience and make a lasting impression. Thus, he became even more animated and theatrical on stage, with his roadies heightening the sense of danger by frantically scurrying around after him. Guitar technician Stephen Rainford describes the nightly routine as "organized chaos," with everyone in the band and road crew having a well-rehearsed role to play. "Steve Iredale, who was the production manager at the time, was always staging little ad hoc events for the evening where Bono would venture into, and occasionally over, the crowd," he recalls. "Some of it was quite dangerous. I mean, how Bono could walk along the balcony with a microphone in his hand without falling I have no idea. But Steve, Dennis Sheehan, or one of the other guys was always right there, pulling him in the right direction. And it always got a reaction, which was the intention."

Bono took his stage act to new heights when asked to perform to an audience of 125,000 people at the second US Festival, held on Memorial Day weekend in Southern California. Organized by Apple cofounder Steve Wozniak, the festivals (featuring everyone from The Clash to Oingo Boingo) would forever serve as a cautionary tale to rock promoters, hands bloodied by over 180 arrests and two reported deaths, not to mention $20 million in lost revenue. Still, Bono—having already sweet-talked promoter Barry Fey into moving U2 from their original fifty-minute slot on day one (otherwise known as "New Wave Day") to day three ("Rock Day") because, according to Fey, "they didn't want to be viewed as a punk band"—grabbed a fair amount of newspaper headlines himself when, during "Electric Co.," he took a white flag and climbed the lighting truss all the way to the roof of the 120-foot canvas stage, where he proceeded to serenade the cheering mass of festival-goers below.

"That was two years' wages," Bono panted backstage at the customary post-gig debriefing, before slumping into a chair. "And I'm not talking about money." (Incidentally, the US Festival marked the demise of the iconic lineup of The Clash, following the expulsion of founding member Mick Jones from the group. Not that U2 was exactly cut up about it. Adam, for one, already believed they had surpassed their one-time heroes. "I think that we're actually better than The Clash," he said. "I think we're in a different league to them.")

Although three studio albums in, U2 was considered first and foremost a powerful live act, and McGuinness was adamant that they exploit this by putting together a live concert video and mini LP. He identified the band's June 5 gig at the nine-thousand-capacity Red Rocks Amphitheatre in Colorado as the ideal setting. More importantly, McGuinness remained on good terms with local promoters Barry Fey and Chuck

Morris—who had first introduced U2 to the grandeur of Red Rocks in '81—and negotiated a three-way partnership between U2, Island Records, and Feyline Productions to finance the ambitious project, in addition to sponsorship deals with Coca-Cola, Denver superstation KWGN-TV, and local rock radio station KAZY. The production team of Channel 4's flagship music program *The Tube,* led by Malcolm Gerrie, were flown in from the UK to film the show with the understanding that they had the first option to broadcast it, free of charge. Randy Ezratty, the owner and founder of the world's first portable multitrack recording system, Effanel Music, was hired to record the audio. Steve Lillywhite was called upon to mix it. Everything, it seemed, was in place for a smooth production.

Then came the wind, sleet, and snow, turning the venue and steep climb leading up to it into a treacherous mud bath. A natural amphitheater nestled between towering sandstone cliffs in the Rocky Mountains, Red Rocks was accustomed to witnessing Mother Nature at her most temperamental, and often the city of Denver gave promoters until 1 P.M. to move their event to a more suitable location nearby should the need arise. But U2 had other ideas. Having sunk around thirty thousand dollars of their own money into the preproduction, and with royalties from *War* still going toward paying off their label debt, they argued that canceling or relocating the show would be tantamount to financial suicide.

"I wanted to move it," recalled Fey, who was known for his volcanic temper, which on one occasion led him to punch out the lead singer of Sha Na Na. "I was coming back from the 'Country Day' at the US Festival and I could see snow through the plane window. When we landed at the airport, I ran straight to the phone and I called my production people and I said, 'Where has it been moved?' So then they started stammering, and I said, 'What the hell's a matter with you?' They said, 'Someone wants to talk to you' and Paul got on the phone. See, they'd wanted to call me all day but he wouldn't let them. Paul says, 'We can't move this, Barry.' Then Bono gets on the phone. He says, 'Barry, I must tell you I've just gone on all the radio stations, personally, and told people that I don't care if they come out tonight. We'll play tomorrow for free in

Boulder at the Events Center. But the show will go on.' He said several years later that we had a discussion about why I tried to move the show. According to him, I said, 'You don't understand. You're raining on my audience!' But I don't remember that."

Contrary to popular belief, Fey was not alone in questioning the decision to go ahead outdoors. Almost everyone in the stage crew, particularly the local hired guns, expressed major concern. "We were all looking at each other going, 'Is it going to happen?'" recalls Stephen Rainford. "Everything was on again, off again because of the weather. I don't know why it went on. There was so much about it potentially off-putting, including electrical problems. But what do you do? I was surprised even during the show they had a helicopter with a spotlight camera that was flying in the fog with poor visibility."

A mutiny was brewing. "The guys from the American sound company were not at all enamored with being out with this band," says Randy Ezratty, whose own assistant was shocked on one of the lighting trusses while setting up. "I can remember them saying, 'Oh, we could be out with Asia right now!' So they decided to pull the plug on it. They said, 'It's a matter of safety. We're going to pull the system down and we're not going to do it.' And in a moment that I will remember for the rest of my life, Paul called everybody down into the bowels of Red Rocks where they fed everybody. It was cold and raining and everybody was shivering, and Paul made a speech, saying in no uncertain terms that we were going to proceed as one, that the band's entire livelihood was riding on this, and that this was one of the most pivotal moments in their career. He said that if it were deemed that this show was in any way possible to happen, it was going to happen, and it was not going to be tolerated that anybody would do anything but add their effort to a successful and positive outcome. I just stood there and went, 'This is so cool. This is like a general rallying the troops.' That's what makes Paul a great manager."

Eventually, the downpour receded to a penetrable veil of mist and drizzle, and Fey introduced U2 to the four-thousand-strong faithful who had braved the elements to take their place at the foot of the stage, lit by three flaming torches placed atop the craggy rock face. As it turned out, the inclement conditions actually had a positive effect on the concert production once the cameras started rolling, with the band engaged in a dramatic "man-versus-nature" battle on a medieval-looking film set no amount of money could buy. G. Brown of *The Denver Post* later wrote: "It's doubtful that any other band could have turned the adversity at Red Rocks into its favor so convincingly. . . . The event ceased being a concert after the second song—it was more akin to a church service, a tangable [sic] exchange between a band fulfilling its promise as a premier musical outfit and its soaked yet ecstatic devotees." In 2004, *Rolling Stone* featured the concert on its list of "50 Moments that Changed the History of Rock and Roll."

"If it had been a nice June day it would have been just another concert," Fey said later. "But the fire, the mist, and the fog . . . I had another show that night with Neil Diamond downtown, and I was supposed to go to that. But I could not leave the stage. I was mesmerized. If you ask one hundred thousand people today, they were there. But the attendance was only, like, forty-two hundred people."

Another factor in the production's success was the subsequent marketing campaign. Over a six-month period, McGuinness and Malcolm Gerrie managed to get various edited versions of the concert shown on *The Tube,* MTV, and its sister network Showtime, as well as significant radio time on NBC's *The Source,* thus preselling the aptly titled *Under a Blood Red Sky* project to a wide audience on both sides of the Atlantic. The impact was enormous. *Rolling Stone* concluded that "the sight of Bono singing the antiviolence anthem 'Sunday Bloody Sunday' while waving a white flag through crimson mist . . . became the defining image of U2's warrior-rock spirit and—shown in heavy rotation on MTV—broke the band nationwide."

Yet perhaps the most inspired promotional move of all came from none other than Stiff Records founder Dave Robinson, who was installed as the new president of Island Records after going into business with Blackwell. "We marketed that album and [U2's] back catalog on TV at a cheap price," recalls Robinson, who loaned Blackwell £1 million to fund the 50 percent share purchase in Stiff and keep Island afloat. "It was that TV marketing that actually cracked them from being an interesting cult band into a major player. Island up until that point had only pretended to market people. Blackwell had an attitude not to spend too much money on marketing; he thought a group on the road was as much marketing as you needed. It was a slightly old-fashioned attitude. They had a poster that they used to send to people saying, 'If you don't promote, something happens' and then at the bottom 'nothing.' And when I got there that's pretty much what they were doing for their acts."

Consequently, the low-cost mini LP *Under a Blood Red Sky,* which ultimately featured only two tracks from Red Rocks, with the other six taken from what U2 adjudged to be superior performances in Boston and West Germany, was released in November, reaching number twenty-eight in the United States and number two in the UK, where it outsold *War* to become the best-selling live album in British chart history up until that point. The concert film, released on home video the following year, was an international bestseller and was nominated for Best Long Form Music Video of the Year at *Billboard*'s annual Video Music Conference.

But before that, there was the small matter of U2 completing the War Tour in one piece—an increasingly unlikely scenario given Bono's nightly high-wire routine amid the screaming hordes battling it out for close proximity. It all came to a head at the Los Angeles Sports Arena on June 17 when the singer found himself trading blows with a fan in front of a crowd of twelve thousand. "It was disgraceful," he recalled in *Hot Press*. "I went into the audience with the white flag and it was a manic audience that ripped me and the flag apart. I ended up attacking this guy, flooring this guy in the audience. I was about twenty feet from the stage, right up in the balcony, and I was in a fracas with a member of my own audience. I mean it's a white flag and I'm going . . . phootf . . . completely with the adrenaline." Cornered, Bono dived from the balcony into the sea of outstretched arms below, hotly pursued by his new sparring partner and half a dozen copycats. The scuffle resumed until Dennis Sheehan pulled Bono back onto the main stage. *Los Angeles Times* critic Robert Hilburn called it one of the most thrilling incidents he had ever witnessed at a rock concert, and one of the stupidest.

Post-gig, Bono sat in a corner of the dressing room, his clothes torn to shreds and scratch marks on his chest. He cut a dejected figure. The band told him that he had gone too far, that he had put himself and the audience at risk, that he had "undermined the dignity and nobility of the music." They would have to find new ways to connect with the crowd. Bono agreed. "We don't need to use a battering ram," he said. "It has to be down to the music."

Following appearances at a series of European festivals, including a headlining spot at Dublin's Phoenix Park Racecourse where they received a hero's welcome from twenty thousand fans, U2 concluded the War Tour with six sold-out shows in Japan. Grossing around $2 million, the tour marked the first time the band had turned a profit on the road. "They were kind of frugal living and then suddenly they seemed to have a few bob between them at the end of it," recalls a source. Nevertheless, they remained motivated not by money but recognition and the chance to effect positive change. And they realized that the battle for ascendancy and their souls had just begun. "We're not naïve enough to think we're there yet," Edge said. "But I think what we have is a passion and belief in the thing we're trying to do and where we're actually going and that determination that we're not going to fall by the wayside . . . to this business which can easily chew up all the best intentions, all the best principles and just spit them out. There's a lot of bands that would speak about the music business like some sort of piranha fish. We're not scared. We're not worried about it. We're just determined that our ideals and principles will not go under, will not be compromised for convenience sake."

7

The Professor and His Students

U2 had more reason to celebrate at the beginning of 1984 with the arrival of the annual music awards: they were victorious in almost every category they were eligible for in the *Hot Press* readers' poll, including Best Polling Act, Group, Live Band, Irish-based Act, Album (*War*), Male Vocalist (Bono), and Instrumentalist (Edge); readers of *NME* defied the magazine's anti-U2 stance to award Edge Best Guitarist; and in the *Rip it Up* poll in New Zealand they walked away with Best Group of '83, Best Album (*War*), and Best Vocalist (Bono) despite having yet to tour there. *Under a Blood Red Sky* was also certified platinum in the UK, with sales for the mini LP already eclipsing three hundred thousand, and gold in the United States. Nevertheless, U2 maintained a low profile in and around Dublin. "All that period you would not see U2," says a source. "You might have seen Larry in a burger place on the north of the city, but other than that they kept to themselves. They didn't go to gigs much. They kept their heads down the whole time, and they kept things very tight."

With one glaring exception: Adam was arrested for dangerous driving and driving with excess alcohol in the early hours of March 3. The

Dublin District Court was later told that he had failed to stop at a Garda checkpoint at Harold's Cross Road in Dublin, after which he was pursued on motorcycle by Garda Gerald Walsh and forced to pull over at Brighton Avenue. Adam told Walsh that he was an Irish celebrity and to "stop messing." After warning the officer that he would cause himself a great deal of harm because he (Adam) was well known high up, Adam turned on the car engine and refused to switch it off. When Garda Walsh leaned in the driver's window and attempted to do so himself, Adam drove off, dragging the officer along the road for approximately forty-five feet.

Upon regaining his footing and composure, Garda Walsh continued his pursuit of the vehicle, which came to a stop close to Adam's home. Garda Walsh approached the car for a second time. "You will be sorry for this," Adam said, before adding that he was the bass guitarist in U2 and he wanted to go to bed. Garda Walsh eventually called for backup and hauled Adam off to Rathmine's Garda Station where he was found to be twice over the legal limit. He was disqualified from driving for three years. However, District Justice Sean Delap later reduced the term to two years because he was satisfied that Adam had apologized after the incident.

"Once you're done for drink-driving that's usually a sign that there's more stupidness to come," Adam chuckled in *Q* years later. "There's a bit more mileage there for a while!"

But, notwithstanding Adam's collision with the law, U2 members found Dublin to be a place where they could remain off the radar, and it allowed them the opportunity to hold on to a sense of normality they believed was crucial to their artistry. Thus, ignoring the seductive siren calls of big-city music centers like London and New York, Edge and Aislinn, who had tied the knot in a low-key ceremony in July '83, bought their first home together in Monkstown, south Dublin. Adam resided in the leafy southern Dublin suburb of Rathgar with his new girlfriend Sheila Roche, who would later work under Paul McGuinness. And Bono and Ali moved into a small Martello tower—similar to the one James

Joyce had stayed at in Sandycove in 1904 and used as the setting for the opening chapter of his novel *Ulysses*—overlooking the seafront promenade in Bray, County Wicklow. Only Larry opted to remain at his parental home on the north side of Dublin, acutely aware of the ephemeral nature of success in the music business.

Bono's Martello tower, which was built by the British in the early nineteenth century to withstand an invasion by the French, was as unlikely a writing and rehearsal space for a rock band as it was a home for a young married couple. But over a four-week period, U2 sketched out around fifteen pieces of music there that they felt represented a significant break with the past. It was a departure they felt was necessary for the longevity of the band. The *War* era had been conceived as a counterattack to the New Romantics then storming the charts. But they could never have foreseen that the album and tour would in fact make them trendsetters, leading a whole movement of stripped-down guitar and political optimism the U.S. music press referred to as the New English Invasion. Now they were in danger of becoming caricatures of themselves and needed to change course.

The idea to write new material at the Martello tower was, in hindsight, no surprise. Edge told Tony Fletcher of *Jamming!* that the band had grown tired of working in "a dead, acoustic atmosphere, which is the usual studio sound, and then trying to revitalize the recorded work using effects and reverberation and all the standard music trappings." In late 1983 they had charged Dennis Sheehan with the task of finding an alternative recording space for their next album, and Sheehan suggested Ireland's Slane Castle, an eighteenth-century gothic structure overlooking the River Boyne and just a few kilometers from the site of the Battle of the Boyne, the most famous of Irish battles. Facilities included guest rooms and a restaurant, and it was only a forty-minute drive from Dublin. More importantly, Slane Castle was home to a cavernous ballroom built for George IV's state visit in 1821. McGuinness promptly booked it for four weeks, beginning May 1984.

It was assumed that the L.A.-based hit-maker Jimmy Iovine, whose production credits included Stevie Nicks's solo debut *Bella Donna* and U2's own *Under a Blood Red Sky*, would produce the album, having inundated Nick Stewart with phone calls, practically begging him for the job. Iovine and his trusted engineer Shelly Yakus had even gone as far as to meet up with Randy Ezratty, whose mobile studio U2 would be renting once again, to discuss the logistics of recording at Slane Castle, and the trio hit it off immediately. But then the band had a last-minute change of heart. "We were all getting it together to go," recalls Ezratty, "and then I get word from Paul [McGuinness] that Brian Eno's going to do the record and he insists on bringing his own engineer, this guy called Daniel Lanois."

Brian Eno had burst into public consciousness as a member of the British art rock group Roxy Music in the early '70s, playing the libidinous, gender-bending keyboardist and studio experimentalist to Bryan Ferry's debonair front man and pop careerist to both critical and commercial acclaim. As Ferry later recalled, "I did all the work. Brian did all the girls." The descendent of several generations of postmen and a student of a then newfangled policy of art school education that stressed the importance of randomness and gave expression to his innate iconoclastic style, Eno had remained with Roxy Music for just two albums, until his low tolerance for boredom necessitated that he fly solo. This consisted primarily of inventing what he called "ambient music," which, according to Eno, was about "creating an ambience, a sense of place that complements and alters your environment," as well as producing such acts as Robert Calvert, David Bowie, and Talking Heads. He had, in the words of *The Irish Times*, assembled "possibly the most influential and uncategorizable body of work in the history of recorded sound."

The members of U2 were big fans of Eno's ambient records in particular (with the exception of Adam, who thought they weren't nearly rock and roll enough) and felt that he ticked all the right boxes for the European-sounding album they had in mind. But at the time, Eno was entertaining the possibility of retiring from music production altogether and had doubts about whether a collaboration with the band would work. He explained in an hour-long telephone conversation with Bono, who he found to be articulate, smart, and sympathetic, that he wasn't a U2 fan and that he feared he would drastically alter the sound that had defined their career thus far. "I'm not interested in records as a document of a rock band playing on stage," Eno told him. "I'm more interested in painting pictures." To which Bono replied: "That's exactly what we want to do!"

And so Eno agreed to join the project, his first with a rock band since Talking Heads' *Remain in Light* four years earlier. But as an insurance policy he insisted that he bring along the relatively unknown Canadian producer Daniel Lanois, who he had collaborated with on his ambient records and believed had a talent for getting the best out of musicians. "I knew that even if it didn't work out with me, the record would be in a safe pair of hands," he later told *The Mix*. "Working with Dan, I was allowed to be as far out as I wanted, but they wouldn't be left there thinking, 'God, what's going to happen to our record?!' "

As it turned out, Eno wasn't the only one to have initial concerns about the collaboration. Chris Blackwell and the vast majority of others at Island argued that it was tantamount to commercial suicide. "There was a feeling that Eno was this sort of twiddly-diddly bloke, and what the hell were U2 going to be doing with a twiddly-diddly bloke?" remembers Neil Storey, who, along with Rob Partridge, was one of the few in favor of the move. "Everybody was saying, 'Come on, let's bring Steve Lillywhite back!' "

Consequently, Nick Stewart was put under enormous pressure by Blackwell to talk U2 out of it. Stewart recalls: "He said, 'You better sort your band out because they're going in a very odd direction.' So I spoke to Bono and promptly got another call back from McGuinness saying, 'You shouldn't be speaking to him!' And I realized then that they had made their mind up and Bono wasn't for turning. I said to Chris, 'I can do no more about it. They're going to do it and that's the end of it.' " But Blackwell was having none of it and hopped on a plane to Dublin—where he too succumbed to Bono's powers of persuasion. "He actually sat down and had a summit with them," says Storey, "which is probably the worst thing possible to do, because Bono sat there and outtalked him and suddenly it was like, 'Hey, this is a good idea!' "

Two weeks later, Eno and Lanois drove out to Slane Castle where U2's crew were readying the makeshift studio ahead of the band's arrival on May 7. Neither the crew members nor the staff at Slane gave Lanois the kind of welcoming he had hoped for. "Nobody knew him," laughs Ezratty. "I was setting up the equipment and Henry Mountcharles, the guy who owns the castle, saw Danny, and because Danny has that sort of Latin complexion, he sent him to the kitchen thinking that he was a waiter there to work at a banquet. Danny kept his cool and explained that no, he was there to work with U2.

"Nobody really cared to have Danny there," admits Ezratty. "He was a bit of an interloper in everybody's mind. The band wanted Brian, so there was a little bit of tension there and Danny bore the brunt of it for at least the first few weeks, until everybody realized how brilliant he was."

Like U2, Eno and Lanois relished the idea of leaving the traditional studio behind and making full use of the gothic ballroom, but within a day or so they realized that the sound in there was too wild, with too much reverberation. "Okay for chamber music, but no good for rock and roll," says Stephen Rainford. "So there was lots of draping and sound absorption added around the walls, and then other rooms like the library, which had a punchier sound, and the drawing room, which was converted into the control room, were used as well. Edge's amplifier was often at the bottom of the staircase and there would be a microphone there and another at the top, so it wasn't even in the same room as the band. There were lots of different experiments we tried out."

Rainford remembers the work hours being long and arduous from the outset. "I was there for weeks on end and a day could be 10 A.M. to 1 A.M. I mean, Eno wouldn't be around for that kind of schedule; he had more of an 'executive schedule.' But it was nose to the grindstone for the rest of us." But as they were all living together at the castle, there was a certain camaraderie that developed between the men, which made life easier. Lunch was always a big part of the day. U2 and crew would gather around the dining table and Eno would wheel in a blackboard and monitor their progress: which instruments were completed for which song, what was set in stone, what wasn't. It was evident to all at the castle that Eno was the one driving the buggy. "U2 were still young and the great 'small' man was very self-contained and intimidating," recalls Colm Henry, who the band brought in to photograph the sessions. "I got the impression that he was possibly playing around with a young band to see where it went for him as much as them."

"They [U2] were starstruck," nods Ezratty. "Brian was really being Brian; he needed to impart that kind of wisdom and Zen-Eno thing. He knew the band gravitated to him and he played the part very well. He had a sort of aura that for them at that young age was really sweet to watch. You could see that Bono was just enamored with the guy. Although Larry was a little bit annoyed," he laughs. "They weren't allowed to have any of the British fan magazines in the control room because Eno thought they were 'too pedestrian.' You could just see the eye rolls on Larry's part. It was a very interesting atmosphere."

Eno loved the fact that U2 had only drawn up rough sketches before entering Slane, and rather than sculpt these into shape, he insisted that they explore more ideas in a series of group improvisations. Eno often set the tone, creating rhythmic and atmospheric backdrops on his synthesizer for U2 and Lanois to play along to on their respective instruments. He posed the question, "What wouldn't you do?" and encouraged them to follow their first instinct, to embrace spontaneity, to recognize the opportunities afforded by errors. The experiment resulted in an additional fifteen pieces of music that immediately changed the identity of the LP the band had envisaged. Eno, engaged with the experimental ideas of John Cage and Cornelius Cardew, shunned conventional techniques and found clarity in the chaos. "Brian Eno loves things that are broken," says Rainford. "He likes mathematical chaos. I remember helping him to lay an old Yamaha synthesizer on its side with instructions to leave it like that over the weekend. 'Let's record it on Monday morning. See what it sounds like then.' There was a willingness to try things a different way."

Edge particularly flourished under the tutelage of Eno. Looking to reinvent his sound, Eno ran much of Edge's guitar through an AMS harmonizer, a Lexicon Prime Time, and a reverb chamber, to the point that even Lanois confused the parts for keyboard overdubs when listening to the playback. He also encouraged Edge himself to use the studio as an instrument and broaden his range of guitar tones. Thus, Edge experimented further with alternative guitar tunings on a Fender Telecaster, played slide with an echo, got to grips with an E-Bow, and developed the "zero sustain" method in which he would dampen the vibration of the strings with masking tape near the bridge. Edge had no idea what the outcome of any of it would be, but like Eno he was aroused by the sense of discovery.

Eno's and Lanois's roles overlapped in some parts, but mostly served different functions. "I was concerned with the broad picture," Eno said later, "while he was more concerned with the day-to-day conditions of working in a studio, which he understands very well, and he is extremely diligent." Lanois, himself an accomplished songwriter and multi-instrumentalist, also brought a certain kind of musicality, and because of his firm grasp of music manuscripts and notation, he was able to simplify the process of musical composition for the band (none of whom could read music themselves) in a way they felt Lillywhite couldn't. Lanois had a particular interest in rhythm and taught Larry how to properly utilize brushes, percussion, and tom-toms on drum parts he mapped out for him, as well as encouraging him to add a few different snares and timbales to his kit. For Larry, who had felt neglected and unappreciated on previous recordings, the experience of working with Lanois was especially gratifying.

Recording at Slane wasn't without its issues, however. The castle was water powered, and when the River Boyne was at low tide, the U2 team was forced to use an old diesel generator, which had a tendency to break down or catch fire, as their main power source. "When that stupid river started to run low, the voltage would go down and it would beat the crap out of my equipment," says Ezratty. "You could see the lights dimming on the gear and the power supplies fighting to stay alive, and I'd be going, 'Oh no!' And of course Danny would have nothing of that. You had to be ready to go at all times regardless of what the river or the generator was providing."

On June 6, U2 relocated to the more reliable Windmill Lane Studios, at which point a certain amount of tension loomed over the sessions, like a pregnant rain cloud threatening to burst. The original plan was to record the basic tracks at Slane and then mix at Windmill, but during an internal discussion certain band members expressed concern that much of the Slane material remained in skeletal form and that it was far too soon to even contemplate entering the final production stage. Adam worried that they were essentially making a Brian Eno record and disagreed with some of his production ideas. Bono politely bemoaned his own lack of mic time and Eno's insistence that they do as few takes as possible.

Eno, who at that time appeared more interested in the songwriting process than the actual result, explained that the skeletons were the songs and stressed the importance of preserving a genuine moment in time. "The reality is that a writing session is a bunch of demo-ing and jamming and it develops in unusual ways," says Rainford. "So if Eno thought he had the take, well he's the producer. I can understand why they weren't comfortable with the results out of Slane, but that was the experiment they were running." Eventually, a compromise was reached: U2 would reassess and in some instances rerecord entire song parts, but without undermining the original impressionistic vision.

■

During the recording of the album, McGuinness and his two financial advisors, the New York lawyer and self-described "dealmaker" Owen Epstein and the ambitious Dublin accountant Ossie Kilkenny, to whom he entrusted his most personal affairs, set out to renegotiate U2's contract with Island Records to reflect what they believed to be the group's true value to the label. According to Island sources, it was a testimony to McGuinness's business integrity and vision that he had managed to keep the original deal alive for almost four years before the money started rolling in, especially when taking into account the label was on the brink of financial collapse for much of that period.

But 1984 was shaping up to be a phenomenal business year for Island under Dave Robinson, the pub-rock-manager-turned-entrepreneur. Robinson's solution to Island's money problems had been to cancel the label's entire release schedule because, he says, "there were no hits in it. We didn't have the money to really put it out and the bands had all got fairly fat. Blackwell hadn't been paying attention for a long time; he'd been living in Nassau and had a real yen to be in the film business." Robinson masterminded the Bob Marley & the Wailers greatest hits collection, *Legend,* which went on to become the best-selling reggae album of all time, with current worldwide sales estimated in excess of 35 million copies, and promoted Frankie Goes to Hollywood, whose debut LP featured the number one singles "Relax," "Two Tribes," and "The Power of Love." What's more, Robinson sold an additional 1.5 million copies of U2's back catalog through television advertising—a feat that also told Robinson that the group were "about to become colossal."

McGuinness, Epstein, and Kilkenny had picked an opportune moment to talk numbers. Under the terms of a new four-album deal thrashed out at Island HQ, U2 would receive an advance payment of $2 million per album as well as an increased royalty rate. Island would produce three music videos (each with a budget of $75,000) per album and grant U2 the power to appoint their own record producer(s). And in what is still considered as one of the shrewdest moves of all time in the music business, McGuinness and company saw to it that U2 got back the publishing rights to all their music and recordings—something not even The Beatles accomplished. Like most managers and accountants before them, the trio were well aware that the music industry strongly stacked deals in favor of the record label and publishing company, but unlike their predecessors they had successfully tipped the balance of power back to their clients. U2 now had complete control over their affairs and, along with their manager, were set up for life. McGuinness, Epstein, and Kilkenny popped open a celebratory bottle of champagne as they returned home on the Concorde.

Upon learning the good news, U2 immediately held a meeting at Windmill Lane where they vowed never to yield to the corruptive power of money. "That is the biggest single threat to this group: money," Edge later explained to *Jamming!* "I've struggled with that, I've thought I'll give it all away, I'll just put it somewhere and forget about it, but it's something you can't run away from, it's something you've just got to respect. You've just got to be aware of the dangers of losing what you've got due to this thing called money."

It was during this period that McGuinness also established his own management company, Principle Management. He appointed ex–Warner Bros. mover Ellen Darst as head of operations in New York. Anne-Louise Kelly, who had served as his personal assistant since the previous summer, working out of his spare bedroom, was put in charge of the Dublin office above Windmill Lane, with a staff of five working under her. Consequently, the entire U2 organization was, as a visiting journalist once remarked, "run with a military precision that I, for one, have never seen matched."

Most sources agree that a substantial amount of U2's success should be attributed to McGuinness. "I cannot underestimate the importance of Paul in the success of the band, the way he has guided them," says Nick Stewart. "He is the fifth member. And very few bands have that strength of manager. There have been some great and powerful managers—one thinks of Tony Smith who did a wonderful job for Genesis and Led Zeppelin's Peter Grant—but none better than Paul McGuinness."

"He's their [U2's] guiding light," nods legendary concert promoter Harvey Goldsmith. "He comes over as Mr. Nice Guy, but behind that façade he's a very tough guy. As much as the band in their own right were strong enough and different enough to make their mark, it's his guidance that really made it work."

But Dave Robinson begs to differ; he suggests McGuinness merely carried out the orders of U2's master strategist, Bono. "Paul did a good job for them, but he's never broken any other band. He's never managed anybody else really well. Bono was the real brains in my book and he towed the rest along. McGuinness handled the money well, but Bono handled the marketing angles, the promotion, the positioning of the band. He was the best salesman around in a group, certainly nowadays. The band's survival was down to Bono's thinking."

■

U2's contract celebrations were put on hold when, just twelve days before the album's August deadline, Bono, true to form, revealed that he didn't think he was going to be able to finish the lyrics in time. No one could quite believe what they were hearing. Adam, also still at loggerheads with Eno over some of the mixes, accused Bono of not pulling his weight. Eventually, McGuinness had to step in and calmly remind everyone that U2 was contracted to play their first Australian/New Zealand dates in less than a month, and neither Eno nor the studio would be available upon their return. Now was not the time for a crisis of confidence or pointing fingers. Now was the time for hard graft. According to U2 sound engineer Kevin Killen, in the last week they worked on the LP "twenty-four hours a day. Brian taking this first half of the day with me, Danny the second half. There was not a lot of sleep but we managed to finish it at 7 A.M. on the last day." Then Lanois jumped on a plane to London and mastered the record in the basement of Blackwell's office.

The level of intensity at which U2 had worked was something none of them was eager to repeat. "The album was very tough," Adam said. "It's a lot of hard work and obviously musical rows occur. And we've just said at the end of it, 'Okay. It's a great record, but we know each other well enough and respect each other well enough that we never actually want to make a record again and strain the relationships to that extent.' It should never be that important that that friendship gets pushed to the background. That is the most important thing. U2's humanity is the most important thing."

With the album in the can, U2 turned to Dutch photographer Anton Corbijn to shoot the album artwork and publicity stills, most of which was captured at Moydrum Castle, outside Athlone. "The burned-out castle is the end of a period," Edge told *NME*. "The golden hour is over, the thing that interests us is the faded glory and the creepers, the fact that there is new life getting on in there." But not everyone at Island was happy about their choice of photographer or the shot of the castle they stuck on the LP cover. "There was a lot of debate about the album cover," says Neil Storey. "I remember Robbo [Dave Robinson] throwing it around the office, going, 'I hate this fuckin' thing! I fuckin' hate it!' He wanted them to use somebody other than Anton, but they'd met Anton through Rob [Partridge], really—he'd done the *NME* pictures in New Orleans and Rob had taken him over so that's how they met. So, I suppose that's a bit our fault. And, of course, Anton got into a spot of trouble because he plagiarized the sleeve. . . ." Indeed, it soon emerged that Corbijn's photo was practically identical to the picture on the front cover of Simon Marsden's 1980 book *In Ruins: The Once Great Houses of Ireland*. U2 agreed to pay compensation for Corbijn's error of judgment. (This was the second time in less than a year that U2 had incurred the wrath of copyright lawyers; the original version of "Electric Co." on *Under a Blood Red Sky* included an unauthorized snippet of Bono singing Stephen Sondheim's "Send in the Clowns," for which they were ordered to pay fifty thousand dollars and ordered to remove it from future pressings.)

U2 named the album *The Unforgettable Fire,* after an exhibition of the same name featuring paintings by survivors of the atomic bombing of Hiroshima and Nagasaki in 1945. The band had first seen the paintings in late 1983 at the Chicago Peace Museum, to which they had donated the stage backdrop from the War Tour as part of an exhibit on rock music entitled "Give Peace a Chance," and they had a profound emotional impact on them. Bono realized that this image of "the unforgettable fire" was applicable not only to nuclear holocaust but also an all-consuming force like heroin, or, in Pentecostal theology, the Baptism of the Holy Spirit. It was something he could apply in a much broader sense.

U2 took in another exhibit at the Peace Museum dedicated to civil rights leader Martin Luther King, Jr. During the making of *War,* Bono had read Stephen B. Oates's book *Let the Trumpet Sound: A Life of Martin Luther King, Jr.* and noted the parallels that could be drawn between the civil rights movement and The Troubles—and the great distance between how each struggle was handled. "[When] the arms struggle, as it was called, was taken up to defend the Catholics, who were definitely being brutalized, we despaired for the lack of vision of the kind Dr. King offered people in the South," Bono said later. Consequently, the unforgettable fire that had burned within Dr. King and fueled his aggressive pacifism had a huge bearing on the lyrics to U2's new single, "Pride (In the Name of Love)." Originally, the song was about Ronald Reagan and his misguided pride in building nuclear weapons. But something about that didn't sit right with Bono. "I was giving Reagan too much importance; then I thought Martin Luther King, there's a man," he told *NME*. "We build the positive rather than fighting with the finger."

"Pride" was one of only three songs on *The Unforgettable Fire* to predate the Slane sessions in any form. The basic rhythm parts and melody were conceived at a War Tour sound check in Hawaii, then Edge and Bono worked on the arrangement at the front man's Martello tower. From the very beginning "Pride" was regarded as a traditional U2 song, yet when it came to recording it at Slane and later at Windmill it proved nothing but troublesome. "The original structure was a lot more complex," Edge explained to Tony Michaelides on Piccadilly Radio, "and it was Eno's influence that led us to cut it down, to strip it down to the bare essentials of that piece, and in so doing I think we produced probably one of our only true single releases. It wasn't envisaged originally as a forty-five, but it just became obvious when we mixed it that it was actually a song that could get very far in the charts."

Released in September, "Pride" charted at number three in the UK and number thirty-three in the United States. U2 and McGuinness expressed disappointment that it didn't break into the American top ten, and laid the blame on Island's short marketing reach stateside. Not that all of U2 coveted hit singles exactly—according to Island sources, neither Adam nor Larry wanted to even release a forty-five from *The Unforgettable Fire,* citing the throwaway nature of the single format and the importance of the LP being viewed as a whole. But Bono and Edge saw the guitar-dominated "Pride" as a transitional song, a stepping-stone from the past to the future, and a way in which to ease U2 fans into their radical new direction. Edge acknowledged that some fans would ultimately be disappointed with the new U2, but subscribed to the belief that artists should make music for themselves first and foremost. "I think when you start catering for others first you lose a certain hook to what you're doing, a certain vision for it and an understanding for what you're doing," he said. "You've got to really work for yourself first, for that vision that you have. When you're pleased with what you're doing for yourself, that's when you really are doing your audience the best service. If you start trying to analyze what they want, trying to cater for other people, I think you're in a very dangerous area. I know a lot of bands who do that and I think it can really backfire."

The album's opening track, "A Sort of Homecoming"—which Eno called "a cinematic piece"—was intended to state U2's purpose clearly and set the tone of *The Unforgettable Fire*. Liam Mackey of *Hot Press* noted that the "primary colors of yore are here absorbed into a much broader canvas, the totality almost symphonic in its orchestration of sounds (as distinctly opposed to instruments) but without any unnecessary grandiosity that description might imply. There's a subtle but effective Irish undercurrent in both the melody and lyrics. . . ." During the many months U2 had spent on the road promoting *War*, Bono had gained an insatiable appetite for the written word; he spent less time at the back of the tour bus rereading the Bible and more time exploring books on philosophy and poetry. He had become a great admirer of Seamus Heaney, whom he was first exposed to while studying at Mount Temple, and described the lyrics to "A Sort of Homecoming" as trying to play around with Heaney's style. He also devoured the collected poems of the Holocaust survivor and nonpracticing Jew Paul Celan, whose faith Michael Hamburger, Celan's first major English translator, described as a negative theology and countered Bono's own positive convictions about the nature of God—as usual, he was interested in hearing both sides of the argument. The title and theme of the song were inspired by Celan's acceptance speech when receiving the George Buchner Prize in 1960, in which he said poems were "the paths on which language becomes voice. They are encounters, paths from a voice to a listening you, natural paths, outlines for existence perhaps, for projecting ourselves into the search for ourselves . . . A kind of Homecoming."

"Wire" was, according to Bono, "the hypodermic needle" of *The Unforgettable Fire,* an attempt to express the hopelessness of the heroin epidemic in a Dublin City already marked by poverty, multigenerational unemployment, and high population density. It was against this backdrop that U2 also recorded "Bad," in which they aimed to provide a glimpse into the mind of a heroin addict without taking a moral stance. "Bad" was Bono's first attempt at writing in the first person from someone else's point of view, although the addict's true identity would remain a mystery for the simple reason that the front man often revised it in the ensuing years to suit the situation; for example, in 1987 Bono claimed he wrote "Bad" about a close friend called Gareth Spaulding who, for his twenty-first birthday, was given enough heroin to kill him, and then in 2011 he said it was about Andy Rowen, Guggi's brother who was still very much alive. Bono's compulsion to embroider the truth whenever he told a story was something Edge had learned to put up with over the years. "I've just realized that the facts aren't that important, it's whether it's a good story or not that's important, and as long as there's some relation to the original, it's fine," he told *NME* in 1985.

Musically, "Bad" was just one example of Eno championing the value of spontaneity and instinct. The basic arrangement—the repetitive pattern of which was inspired by The Velvet Underground—was completed in just three live takes. Then Eno added a keyboard arpeggio and a few overdubs. Similarly, the ghostly instrumental track "4th of July"—named to mark the date of birth of Edge and Aislinn's baby daughter, Hollie—took form when, unbeknownst to Edge and Adam, Eno overheard them playing around with a little bass figure and bottleneck guitar in the next room and recorded it through a series of treatments that he had set up for the vocals for "Bad."

Meanwhile, the largely unintelligible "Elvis Presley and America" saw Daniel Lanois acting as a conduit for randomness to occur. He was mixing "A Sort of Homecoming" at real speed and repeatedly hitting a wall when he decided to slow down the tape from thirty inches per second to twenty-two. At that precise moment Bono walked into the room and failed to recognize the song. He asked for a mic and started ad-libbing about the genius of Elvis Presley in response to Albert Goldman's infamous 1981 biography that portrayed the rock-and-roll idol as, in the words of *The New York Times*, "an illiterate bumpkin who, propelled to fame by an unscrupulous manager, spent the bulk of his life indulging in drugs and sexual fetishes." Bono later told *Star Hits*: "Elvis was a genius; he didn't have to say it, he expressed it in his hips and in the way he held a microphone. I despise Goldman, this book, and anyone who thinks that Elvis was an idiot."

U2 had gained another instrument on *The Unforgettable Fire* with Bono's voice, which had deepened dramatically through age and years of touring. On "Promenade"—in which he offered a romanticized view of the seaside resort of Bray, as seen through the glass roof of the Martello tower he shared with Ali—Lanois captured it for the first time, presenting the singer with an old valve microphone similar to the model Elvis had used to produce a warm, live sound. "We managed to capture a bottom end and depth to Bono's voice that surprised even him," Lanois said.

The symphonic title track evolved from a short piano piece Edge had written during a demo session with Blondie's Jimmy Destri in 1983. Edge revisited it at Martello, where he applied a simple backbeat and treatments using a DX-7 synthesizer. Then Bono, singing from lyrics he had sketched in a hotel room on the Japanese leg of the War Tour, experimented with a number of melodies, and within an hour they had nailed the basic chord structure. Edge and Eno later embellished it with harmonics and a string arrangement by Noel Kelehan of the RTÉ Concert Orchestra.

The Native American mantra "Indian Summer" was regarded as one of the most "Eno-esque" tracks on the album, with its choppy, African-inflected funk and tribal chants calling to mind the producer's work with Talking Heads, while Bono's soaring vocals about spiritual renewal in urban America were seen to possess the same liberating spirit that defined gospel music, Eno's favorite genre despite him being an atheist. It was what attracted him to U2's music: the sense of abandonment.

Not unlike *War*, *The Unforgettable Fire* closed with a prayer: "MLK," an ambient lullaby dedicated to Martin Luther King, Jr. and a companion piece to "Pride (In the Name of Love)." Despite the difficult and potentially depressing subject matter throughout the album, U2's positive vision once again shone through; they focused on the power of the individual to overcome adversity and change the world around them.

Although over time *The Unforgettable Fire* would be widely accepted as a classic U2 album, it was originally met with mixed reviews when released in October 1984. Most critics complained that it was maddeningly vague, both sonically and thematically. Kurt Loder of *Rolling Stone* wrote: "U2 flickers and nearly fades, its fire banked by a misconceived production strategy and occasional interludes of soggy, songless self-indulgence. This is not a 'bad' album, but neither is it the irrefutable beauty the band's fans anticipated." Likewise, *People* stated that "[t]he sound, and the group's yearning, melancholy melodic style, cast an incantatory spell. But like a fog, it can make you soggy if you stay out in it too long," and that the words "add up to little more than allusions."

NME's Gavin Martin, an early champion of the band until "the dull litanies of *October* and the routine agitpop of *War*," wrote that *The Unforgettable Fire* "in a cautious way bespeaks a rebirth for U2," and praised Eno and Lanois for helping the band tap into "the spirit and celestial wonder at the core of their music once more." Nevertheless, Martin expressed "a suspicion that it amounts to little more than an experimental diversion, that the big, bold rock sound will soon surge forth again." It was perhaps Tony Fletcher of *Jamming!* who best explained the LP's enduring legacy when he acknowledged that "this is not an album full of hits. What it is, however, is a forceful collection of atmospheric ideas and themes, forgettable at first but strangely haunting and soon firmly implanted."

Naturally, U2 was hurt by the criticism, but found great comfort in the fact that the album debuted at number one in the UK and Australia, and eventually climbed to number twelve in America, emulating the chart success of *War*.

8

The Rising Flame

Last-minute rehearsals for the Unforgettable Fire Tour got under way at Dublin's Oscar Theatre in mid-October 1984. It was a frantic time for U2. They had found it impossible to replicate the multi-textured sound of the new album as a three-piece band and vocalist, and had been forced to reschedule or cancel altogether the first few dates of the tour to afford themselves more prep time. The nineteen-date Under Australian Skies Tour, which spanned from August 29 to September 24, had failed to present a solution; lacking time, know-how, or even the appropriate sound equipment, U2 had stuck closely to the set list from the War Tour, with the addition of only "Pride (In the Name of Love)" and "The Unforgettable Fire," for which Edge alternated between guitar and piano. "We weren't ready to do a full-blown version of the album," recalls Stephen Rainford, "because there was nothing for the live production [to work with]: no keyboards, synthesizers, drum machines. Stuff we needed."

Adam was vehemently opposed to the idea of adding an extra musician on stage because he believed it would upset the group's chemistry.

Edge suggested simplifying the song arrangements, but that didn't go down too well with the others. In the end it was decided that they would add programmed sequencers to their live mix, despite some concern that it would dehumanize their sound. The job of loading the programs and fading the keyboards in and out during each show was given to Rainford, who remained hidden away under the stage floor to maintain the illusion of four musicians playing on stage. "The keyboards and synthesizers were fairly rigid in what they needed to do," he says, "[but] we didn't necessarily want to make it so rigid that they stuck to a particular song format, although it was necessary for certain parts. So there was a lot of manual interaction like, for example, I would turn sequencers on and off during the performance to accommodate Bono if he wanted to take off on a tangent for ten minutes."

U2's live sound wasn't the only thing to undergo a radical makeover. Bono realized the importance of looking good on stage and during the recording of *The Unforgettable Fire* he had asked Adam to convince his friend Marion Smyth, a London-born fashion stylist, to come up with a few ideas as to what the band should wear for the Under Australian Skies Tour. Smyth enjoyed the assignment so much that she agreed to become U2's stylist on a permanent basis, sourcing clothes from various fashion shows and shops in London and Paris in preparation for the Unforgettable Fire Tour. Her only directive was to avoid what Bono disparagingly referred to as "pop colors." As a result, Larry sported a spiked crew cut, earrings, and a black leather jacket reminiscent of James Dean. Edge wore no-frills white shirts. Adam's bushy blond hair had already been cut into a shorter, more urbane style, and a selection of muted checked shirts completed his new look. Bono slipped on black knee-high military boots and leather trousers, and sported a jet-black mullet haircut which *VRS* magazine likened to a "porcupine's quills." It was a hairstyle Bono would live to regret. "I had one of the worst haircuts in the 1980s," he said later. "I know that it launched a million second-division soccer players. But the truth of it, if I'm really honest, is that I thought I looked like David Bowie."

The Unforgettable Fire Tour opened to a crowd of seventeen thousand at the Espace Tony Garnier in Lyon, France. It was, however, plagued by teething problems. The band spoke at length about wanting to challenge their live audience and gently nudge them out of their comfort zone, but struggled to strike the right balance between the direct and theatrical U2 of old and the more restrained and esoteric U2 of new. "[The audience] may have to sit for half the show and actually listen to what's going on," Adam said at the time. "I don't think that's too much to ask." Bono reflected the tone of the new material by acting more reserved on stage, rarely venturing out from behind his mic stand to work the crowd. His past propensity for wild and excessive gesticulation was, Edge explained to *Musician*, "a gesture that made sense to the front row. It was Bono saying, 'I can get to you, I can be with you.' But the cynics at the back of the auditorium said, 'That's a bit cornball.' Now we're turning our eyes to the cynics, to the world-weary music fans, non-music fans, and critics as well. We're approaching them in a more subtle way. We'll be communicating directly through our work." But at first U2's understated approach only succeeded in confusing and infuriating much of their French audience, and the new songs were often drowned out by cries for the full emotional and physical release of the *War* and *Under a Blood Red Sky* era. It was a period of adjustment for all concerned.

The tour also didn't fare well in the English capital in November where U2 endured two hostile nights at the Brixton Academy. Some members of the audience were so restless that several fights broke out and a noticeably rattled Bono was reduced to rambling incoherently between numbers. David Quantick wrote in *NME*: "The most boring band in the world. There may be groups equally as dull, but I fail to see how any of them can be worse."

U2 found *NME*'s criticism especially hard to take because the *Unforgettable Fire* project was created in part as a response to the earlier charges of bombast and blatant rockism brought against them by the British music press. They had now adopted a more subtle, genre-shifting approach, and yet still the usual suspects greeted them with blows. They felt that they were being treated rather harshly. And they hit back. "I think it stinks," Adam said of *NME* and company's brand of music journalism in *BAM*. "I wish somebody reviewed those papers every week. . . . You get sick of all that negative reaction to bands and stuff and just think 'Why bother?' Unfortunately, you're an asshole if you're still into music, according to those papers."

As much as they longed for critical acceptance in the London press, U2 was gradually becoming more distrustful of the media in general, and sanctioned fewer interviews. In fact, Larry refused to take part in press engagements altogether. Nevertheless, they discovered an unlikely ally deep in UK territory, in Dave Dickson of the heavy metal magazine *Kerrang!* Dickson attended U2's second gig at Glasgow's Barrowland and hailed them as "the single most important new rock band to emerge since, probably, The Clash, and in terms of actual musical influence, since Led Zeppelin." He acknowledged the dilemma that U2 faced in maintaining "street-level" intimacy while applying their trade in larger venues populated by rock's goliaths, but concluded that "if they succeed—and I believe they will—there's hope for everyone because it will mean that strength and compassion still have a place."

U2 was followed around Europe by Marc Marot, the newly appointed managing director of Chris Blackwell's publishing company, Blue Mountain Music. The twenty-four-year-old Marot had been encouraged by Blackwell to develop a close relationship with the band, and one of the first things he did was to suggest putting together a sheet music book for U2; it was, he explained, a way in which to exploit their catalog in terms of showing other professional and amateur musicians how to cover their songs. In order to get the process started, Marot worked out the guitar chords and wrote out the lyrics while listening on headphones. He then suffered the humiliation of having Edge and Bono perform his incorrect versions in fits of laughter at the back of the band's tour bus. Originally, U2's print publisher refused to produce the book, as they thought there was no market for it, so Marot arranged for the book, entitled *U2 Portfolio,* to be printed in Korea and then shipped to the UK. "I think we only produced something like a really modest run of five thousand books at first and they sold out immediately," he recalls. "Then we printed another load—twenty thousand—and they sold out immediately. And, eventually, it went on to sell over a hundred thousand books and was very, very successful not only for Blue Mountain Music but U2 as well in terms of the royalties and everything else. That was partly how I created my relationship with the band, because I said I was going to do something, I did it, and it worked. There was a reason for them to trust me."

McGuinness, on the other hand, took a little longer to warm to Marot, perhaps afraid that there was suddenly another rooster in the hen house. "I think he was quite rightly suspicious of me at first, because I was just another industry guy coming into their world," says Marot, who freely admits to being scared of the U2 manager at the start. "He's a very smart man and he doesn't suffer fools. And so I found it was best not to bullshit; be straight, do the job, be discreet, keep your head down. And that's what I did." Consequently, *U2 Portfolio* marked the beginning of what would become one of the most fruitful long-term business relationships in the music industry.

■

In late November, Bono and Adam agreed to participate in the Band Aid charity single "Do They Know It's Christmas?," organized by Bob Geldof and Ultravox front man Midge Ure to raise money for the Ethiopian famine of 1983–85—despite McGuinness's advice that the U2 duo should distance themselves from such a potentially uncool project. Geldof was an unpopular figure at the time, known primarily for his foul temper, scruffy appearance, and being married to the flirtatious British television presenter Paula Yates (hence the sardonic moniker "Mr. Paula Yates" which only served to anger him further). He cowrote the song with Ure after watching news footage of starving Ethiopian children while sitting at home with his more famous wife in apparent despair over the demise of his pop career. The news reporter Michael Buerk described the scenes of human suffering as a "biblical famine existing in the twentieth century." Aid workers called it "the closest thing to hell on earth."

The song was recorded within a twenty-four-hour period at Trevor

Horn's SARM West Studios in Notting Hill, London, with Geldof recruiting more than thirty leading British and Irish performers, including George Michael of Wham!, Simon Le Bon of Duran Duran, and Phil Collins, to ensure maximum media attention and sales. Rock veterans Status Quo also received an invite, and they were at the center of the drug mayhem—coke, dope, whatever they could get their hands on. "Everybody was just totally out of it and Rick [Parfitt] and I were the drug center," Quo's Francis Rossi later told *The Observer.* "People were saying 'let's go and see Dr. Rossi and Dr. Parfitt, shall we?' "

At first, Bono was reluctant to sing the lyric Geldof set aside for him. "This is not about what you want, okay?" Geldof snarled. "This is about what these people need." It was the song's most provocative line: "Well, tonight thank God it's them instead of you." Geldof reminded Bono that the song was about people "dying of hunger a few miles away from the richest continent in the world that's paying taxes to burn their surplus food." He added: "Imagine if it was you." Bono did. He sang the line. The pair also got into the first of what would become many heated exchanges about religion. "Well, Bob, you've written your first hymn then, haven't ya?" Bono teased. To which Geldof, an avowed atheist, simply replied: "Fuck off!"

Band Aid's "Do They Know It's Christmas?" was released on November 29, 1984. It sat atop the UK charts for five straight weeks, shifting over 3 million copies and becoming the biggest-selling single of all time there, until 1997, when it was finally outdone by Elton John's Diana, Princess of Wales, tribute single "Candle in the Wind 1997"; even so, not everyone was enamored with it, including Geldof himself. "I am responsible for two of the worst songs in history. [One is] 'Do They Know It's Christmas?' The other one is 'We Are the World,' " Geldof told Australia's *Daily Telegraph* in 2010. "Any day soon, I will go to the supermarket, head to the meat counter and it will be playing. Every fucking Christmas." Outspoken singer Morrissey was even less generous in his assessment of the Band Aid project altogether in a 1985 *Time Out* interview: "I'm not afraid to say that I think Band Aid was diabolical. Or to say that I think Bob Geldof is a nauseating character. Many people find that very unsettling, but I'll say it as loud as anyone wants me to. In the first instance the record itself was absolutely tuneless. One can have great concern for the people of Ethiopia, but it's another thing to inflict daily torture on the people of Great Britain. It was an awful record considering the mass of talent involved. And it wasn't done shyly; it was the most self-righteous platform ever in the history of popular music."

■

U2 undertook their first all-arena tour in America and Canada in February 1985, performing forty shows in twenty-nine cities, with multiple nights in several key markets. Willie Williams, U2's stage designer, also convinced them to utilize every available seat in the house by playing in the round. Williams explained that the sight of two thousand screaming fans would provide an impressive backdrop and lend the shows a more intimate feel, not to mention the obvious financial benefits. McGuinness agreed with the latter point. U.S. critics validated the preceding two. The band somehow seemed looser and more at home in larger venues, the critics noted. And while crowd trouble still erupted at certain stops, the power of U2's music often transcended it.

Russell Smith's review in *The Dallas Morning News* reflected the general consensus among American critics: "The Irish foursome—merely great on record—very nearly defies praise live. . . . Maybe it's Bono. The lead singer's presence is dynamic, to say the least. It's a spiritual magnetism—as opposed to animal—and the result was absolutely mesmerizing. At one point, he brought a young woman—stunned to the point of tears—onto the stage, and gave her a long embrace that, in another show, would have seemed sexual. But Bono's embrace called up another sort of image—more like a faith healer administering to a cripple. . . . It's the only band that's ever moved me to question the Rolling Stones' seemingly definitive statement, 'It's only rock 'n' roll.' "

As the tour progressed, Bono handled most crowd problems one of two ways: either by hurling a white flag into the cauldron of faces and then rebuking them for scrapping over a symbol of peace, or by inviting a fan on stage to play guitar with the group on Bob Dylan's "Knockin' on Heaven's Door" in an attempt to demystify the "rock idol." "The most memorable moment I've witnessed at a rock concert occurred during U2's Unforgettable Fire Tour in San Francisco," recalls Jas Obrecht, former editor of *Guitar Player*. "Midway through the concert, Bono stepped up to the microphone and said, 'You don't need expensive equipment or a big PA to make music. You just need an acoustic guitar and a few simple chords. Does anyone here play guitar?' Thousands of hands shot into the air. Bono reached into the crowd and pulled a skinny teenager onstage. He handed him an amplified acoustic guitar and quickly showed him the chords to Dylan's 'Knockin' on Heaven's Door.' The band launched into the song, and then one by one the other instruments dropped out, until the young man stood alone in the spotlight, strumming the chords as ten thousand people sang along. Point made, Hewson."

U2 found the fanaticism that they encountered offstage somewhat harder to deal with. The band members flippantly referred to it as "Beatle-mania," which was arriving in towns to find hundreds of young fans camped outside the airport and hotel, often trying to dodge past security guards in the hope of catching more than a quick glimpse. U2 felt it was an invasion of their privacy and, eventually, beefed up their security team with the addition of Ron McGilvray, Kiss's security expert. "If people want to treat me with respect they should treat me as a person," Bono sighed. But U2 insiders insist that the group's then-new mode of transport and accommodation more than compensated for any loss of privacy. Gone were the endless hours spent on a cramped tour bus and flying on commercial airlines. U2 now had their own private plane, an old four-engine Vickers Viscount, and saw the world at street level from the back of a chauffeur-driven limousine. And the hotels were of the luxurious variety, including the Parker Meridien Hotel in Midtown Manhattan, the Hershey Hotel in Philadelphia, and Stouffer's Inn on the Square in downtown Cleveland. It was a high-priced existence at odds with their reputation as the people's band, and they readily embraced it.

All except Edge. The guitarist found life on the five-star road problematic with a baby and wife on board, despite the help of a full-time nanny. It was, he later confessed, mostly trivial things that troubled him, like having to constantly remind U2 staff that he and Aislinn required a hotel room with an adjoining nanny's quarters. Edge also suspected that the other band members saw his family as a burden, the weight of which was too great for them to carry on their ascent up the rock-and-roll ladder. But such concerns faded away over time, and Edge credited his daughter Hollie with keeping him grounded and sane amid the intense fan worship.

In March, *Rolling Stone* magazine put U2 on the cover under the headline: "Our Choice: Band of the '80s," stating that "for a growing number of rock-and-roll fans, U2 have become the band that matters most, maybe even the only band that matters." It was the highest accolade U2 had received in America, but it also emphasized the unrealistic expectations and pressure placed upon them. Their fans had elevated them to a lofty position: that of social crusaders capable of diagnosing and curing all the world's ills. "Their music means a lot to world peace," a male fan in Chicago was quoted as saying at the time. "I think it really can help change the world." In an interview with *The New York Times,* Bono balked at "the condescending thing of being a singer-prophet leading the mass." He said: "How can you be the spokesman for a generation if you've got nothing to say other than 'Help!'" Edge, so often the foil to Bono's idealism, was apt to play down the band's influence over youth culture. "Honestly, the whole U2 phenomenon is probably going to amount to little real change," he told *NME.* "I suppose you could put in the liner notes: 'Please do not mistake Bono for God.' Perhaps you have to accept it as an inherent flaw."

U2's core audience tended to lean to the far left of the Reagan Revolution, which the majority of American youth swore its allegiance to, so the band doubted that this era of revived conservatism would have much of an impact on the size of their fan base. "I think they [U2 fans] are, by and large, a more thinking core of American society," Adam told *The Dallas Morning News.* "So I suppose, unless we move to the right in terms of our music, we perhaps won't get to those people, anyway."

Nevertheless, U2 was keen to stress that they were only a political band in a humanistic sense. In an interview with *The Christian Science Monitor,* Adam spoke of their music as a type of communication and healing force, saying that ultimately he would like to write music that "doesn't go to the brain. It goes straight into the ear and to the heart. And you plug straight into the emotional plane of a generation of people." The message, he explained, was simple: "I don't think it would be how to fiddle your taxes.... Love is almost too clichéd, but certainly a security and a sense of well-being."

The highlight of U2's hugely successful U.S. tour came on April 1 when they played their first-ever concert at New York's Madison Square Garden, which sold out in just over an hour. Aware of the significance Irish people attached to one of their own performing at such an iconic American venue, the band spared no expense in flying their family and friends over from Dublin, as well as a number of handpicked journalists from Ireland and the UK. *Hot Press* editor and longtime U2 champion Niall Stokes was one of the chosen few, and noted that it was "a long way from Limerick Civic Week to Madison Square Garden but U2 have made that transition—and in such magnificent style.... In Madison Square Garden twenty thousand hearts beat as one. On stage the unforgettable fire and conviction of U2's music had won them over, and won them totally."

The following morning, U2 capitalized on their Big Apple triumph by holding a press conference to announce their first headlining stadium concert, which was to take place in June before a crowd of fifty-seven thousand people at Dublin's Croke Park. Bono and Edge then fielded questions from their guest-reporters "like champions the night after a title fight," as one attendee put it. "Last night's show was in a way a peak for what we've been doing in this country for the last three or four years," Edge said. "We all know what it took to get to this stage. It will take a few weeks before it sinks in."

U2's rise in the fiercely competitive North American market had drained the physical and mental reserves of the four band members and their twenty-strong road crew, but the financial rewards were extraordinary. Four of U2's five albums were in the *Billboard* Top 200—three of which had sold over a million copies—and the all-arena leg of the Unforgettable Fire Tour had played to around 578,000 U.S. punters by May 4, when it wrapped up at the Hollywood Sportatorium in Florida. U2's reputation was that of the biggest cult band in the States, akin to Bruce Springsteen before *Born in the U.S.A.* propelled him to superstardom.

According to Neil Storey, U2's success was a testament not only to their own efforts, but also to the support and commitment provided by a number of very committed men and women working behind the scenes: "At that time, certainly from signing [to Island Records] until Madison Square Garden, there are a few people who played quite a big role in things: Rob [Partridge], Annie [Roseberry], Nick [Stewart], Dave Robinson, Tony the Greek [Michaelides], and obviously CB [Blackwell] within Island alongside the guys at Wasted Talent [UK booking agency] and the main people in the crew like Dennis [Sheehan], Joe O'Herlihy [U2's long-serving live sound engineer] and Willie [Williams], and Anne-Louise [Kelly] in the office; the guys at *Hot Press* and the English journos who got it. There was a massive loyalty aspect in those early days. Why? I suppose it was a belief in this something that the band had. Whatever this something was, was there the first time I saw them play and it was pretty bloody special witnessing close-up that . . . something . . . emerge at a variety of landmark moments. There was a long road traveled from the early days and I'll happily admit to a moistening of the eye when the band walked out onto the stage at The Garden. Without—in any sense—knowing it way back when, it was like a confirmation of that belief: Yes! This is where this something is meant to be."

Tony Michaelides agrees that it would be foolish to ignore the many people—particularly those on the Island payroll—who played an integral part in the development and success of U2. "What happened in the early stages was always about a team of people," he says. "Don't ever underestimate Island and the people that were around U2 that benefited them. I doubt that would have happened back then with a company like CBS (Sony)."

U2's story was just beginning, however. In April, Bono had received another phone call from Bob Geldof. On a recent whistle-stop tour of Ethiopia to show the British public that the money raised from Band Aid was being well spent, Geldof and the various television crews documenting his visit had discovered that the emergency food aid was being held up at the docks of Port Sudan by a trucking cartel charging extortionate prices to move it. BBC News reported back home that "an acute shortage of transport is still hampering the distribution of food aid and while the supplies lie in the port they are at the mercy of the weather." Geldof explained to Bono that the only way to break the cartel and deliver the aid was to raise enough funds to buy a fleet of trucks, and that he, along with Midge Ure and promoter Harvey Goldsmith, were organizing a charity concert in July to do just that. It was to be called Live Aid.

9

The Two Americas

Live Aid was a dual-venue benefit extravaganza held on July 13, 1985, at London's Wembley Stadium and Philadelphia's JFK Stadium to raise money for famine victims in Ethiopia. The self-proclaimed "Greatest Show on Earth" was broadcast live to an estimated 1.9 billion viewers in 150 countries and reportedly raised $250 million. U2 played a starring role at Wembley, one that brought them to the brink of superstardom, and yet their performance almost didn't happen—just hours before the band was due to arrive at the venue with promoter Barry Fey, they telephoned Bob Geldof and threatened to pull out of the charity event altogether because they weren't allowed to have a sound check. But by showtime, U2 had relented, having managed to secure a much-sought-after early evening slot on the bill, which meant they were the first Wembley act to perform via the transatlantic video linkup. "They made some incredible decisions as a unit at the right time," says Tony Michaelides. "When you've got something like Live Aid that's got a massive amount of publicity, everybody's going to tune in to see the start of it and then they might go and do some other stuff and pick it up later on, because you're not going to sit in front of the TV for ten hours. So when America tuned in U2 was the first band that they saw—they basically opened the Wembley show for the American TV audience. And to pull something like that off is extraordinary."

U2 took to the stage at 5:20 P.M. London time, following an introduction by Jack Nicholson from Philadelphia. They launched into their twenty-minute set with "Sunday Bloody Sunday," the receptive audience, dotted with U2 peace flags, swaying and punching the air in time with the martial rhythm. Then came a twelve-minute version of "Bad," during which Bono signaled stewards to pluck three girls out of the seventy-two-thousand-strong crowd, one of whom he slow danced with in the security pit after leaping from the lower part of the stage. It was one of Live Aid's—and U2's—defining moments. "Bono picked that up from Bruce Springsteen," says Dave Robinson. "Springsteen had this routine where he would dance with a girl from the audience and Bono nicked it. He used to do that in every show, but at Live Aid everyone thought it was a brand-new thing. But it was just like him climbing the PA stack—it was the same thing. It was marvelous and the whole world saw him do it and they all thought 'What a geezer. This guy is Live Aid!' "

However, because of Bono's stunt, U2 didn't have enough time to perform "Pride (In the Name of Love)" as originally planned, much to the disappointment of his manager and bandmates. "McGuinness was going nuts at the side of the stage," recalls Stephen Rainford. "It was going on too long and he told me to get out there and drag Bono off by the scruff of his neck. Which you can't exactly do!"

Says Michaelides: "After that gig there was no conversation backstage; the band was so pissed off with Bono. He went back home and was literally a recluse. Like the others, he thought he'd blown it, and he was just saying to people, 'I don't know what I've done.' Because the only song that anybody knew was 'Pride.' It was an opportunity for a global audience to hear their hit single and Bono, who was just wrapped up in the moment, goes AWOL."

Bono later claimed that he considered quitting U2 after Live Aid. "I was really bummed out," he told BBC Radio 1. "I thought I'd just shot the band in the head in front of a billion people." Dejected, he fled to the medieval port town of New Ross in County Wexford, where he encountered a local sculptor working on a nude bronze statue. The man, in his late fifties, knew relatively little about popular music but he had watched Live Aid on television. He explained that the statue was called *The Leap,* inspired by Bono's own "leap of faith" from the stage to dance with the girl. It dawned on Bono that rather than committing career suicide, he had captured the spirit of Live Aid, of a global community pulling together, and in the process established the band as a prominent act on the international stage, nowhere more so than in America. U2's album sales (including the newly released EP *Wide Awake in America,* none of which was actually recorded in the States) tripled over the next few months as a direct result of their participation at the charity event.

Music historian Paul Gambaccini, who was part of the BBC broadcasting team at Wembley, notes: "It was very interesting how in Britain over 50 percent of the viewers on the BBC panel said that Queen had stolen the show, which had been the sense of the performers backstage at Wembley, but to Americans who were concentrating on the Philadelphia part of it, it was U2 and Bono taking the risk with that young woman. It was a real game changer from a commercial point of view."

Of course, U2 wasn't the only act on the bill to profit so handsomely, intentionally or otherwise. The aforementioned Queen's twenty-minute jukebox set was so well received that, the following year, the original lineup embarked on their first and only moneymaking tour of their entire career—a remarkable turnaround of fortunes for a band that had walked into Live Aid as public enemy number one after playing nine gigs at the infamous Sun City gambling resort in South Africa, which was a direct violation of the United Nations cultural boycott and led to accusations of them supporting apartheid. (Later that year, Bono featured on the "Sun City" single and album of the same name by the Artists United Against Apartheid, an all-star protest group created by Steven Van Zandt to speak out against South Africa's apartheid policy.) Bob Geldof, meanwhile, received an honorary knighthood for his work on famine relief in 1986. Geldof—henceforth referred to as "Sir Bob" by the UK press, even though he was not a citizen of a Commonwealth realm—also launched a solo pop career and published his best-selling memoir *Is That It?* that same year.

However, Live Aid—which became the template for all future celebrity charity concerts—had less of a positive impact on Sub-Saharan Africa, according to aid experts. "Live Aid did harm as well as good," says David Rieff, a senior fellow at the World Policy Institute and author of *A Bed for the Night: Humanitarianism in Crisis*. "I have little doubt that they [the organizers and performers] had the best of intentions, but there is no connection between raising money for a good cause and that money being well spent."

Rieff—whose views on the causes of the Ethiopian famine and Live Aid's legacy are largely supported by other leading authorities on Africa and Western aid—argues that both Live Aid and the media blitz surrounding it failed to acknowledge Ethiopia's problems were largely man-made, the product of civil war and immoral policies practiced by a Soviet-backed Marxist-Leninist military junta, led by Mengistu Haile Mariam, who had overthrown (and later quite possibly executed) Haile Selassie in 1974, and thereby created a necessary risk-free charity operation that allowed an international television audience to donate their money with confidence and, in the process, feel good about themselves. Indeed, as the BBC's Michael Buerk later confessed, the foreign press deliberately tiptoed around the complex political causes of the famine amid fears that reports of "yet another stupid African war" would draw little sympathy or cash from the public back home: "[A]t the back of your mind, is: if I overemphasize a negative angle to this, I am going to be responsible for . . . inhibiting people from coughing up their money."

Rieff accepts that money raised from the telethon was distributed to a number of humanitarian relief agencies. But the "no-strings-attached" manner in which it was distributed through the non-governmental organizations (NGOs) and private charities enabled Ethiopia's communist junta, then at war with rebels in the northern provinces of Eritrea and Tigray, to carry out Stalin-styled forced programs of resettlement and agricultural collectivization which exacerbated the famine and, quoting famine scholar Dr. Alexander de Waal, "prolonged the war, and with it, human suffering."

Dutch author Linda Polman relates in her book *War Games: The Story of Aid and War in Modern Times* that the thousands of aid workers and journalists who flew into Ethiopia "were forced to change their dollars for local currency at rates favorable to the regime, and this alone helped to keep the Ethiopian war machine running. Food aid was used as bait to lure starving villagers into camps. They were held there awaiting deportation to the state farms in the south. A life of forced labor lay ahead. The government army that guarded the camps took a share of the food aid and even requisitioned trucks from aid organizations to move people out."

The French charity Médecins Sans Frontières (MSF) refused to assist the Mengistu regime and were kicked out of the country altogether after claiming that six thousand children had died in one camp even though there was a sufficient amount of food to go around. The UN specialized agencies and other NGOs, many funded by Live Aid, mostly kept quiet and, when the U.S. government asked the aid community to oppose the resettlement program, the head of UN development in Ethiopia complained about America's "politicization" of resettlement—just one example, say critics, of the moral complexities of the multibillion-dollar humanitarian business.

MSF estimates that between 150,000 and 200,000 Ethiopians were killed during the forced resettlement that was facilitated by the relief effort. They claim that it killed more than famine and war during 1985. MSF president Claude Malhuret said in late 1985 that humanitarian "aid to victims was unwittingly transformed into support to their executioners." Nevertheless, Bob Geldof publicly defended the NGOs. In an interview with *The Irish Times* in November 1985, he said: "The organizations that are participating in the resettlement program should not be criticized. . . . In my opinion, we've got to give aid without worrying about population transfers." When the reporter put it to him that an estimated hundred thousand people had at that point died in the transfers, Geldof replied that "in the context [of the famine], these numbers don't shock me."

■

Two months after Live Aid, Bono and Ali spent five unpublicized weeks in Ethiopia as volunteers for the Christian charity organization World Vision. Upon arriving at the Addis Ababa airport, the married couple were greeted by World Vision communications officer Steve Reynolds, who was assigned to be their guide throughout their stay. "[Bono] was scared out of his mind," Reynolds later told *The Seattle Times*. "Like a first-termer at boarding school." Reynolds had seen his fair share of celebrities passing through the main office in the wake of Live Aid, most of whom wanted "just to be seen in the context of the famine," and he was suspicious of the U2 singer's intentions at first. But any doubts he had about Bono were put to rest when he and Ali went to work at an orphanage of three hundred children in a feeding camp in Adjibar, in southern Wollo Province, where they helped staff to teach the children about health and hygiene through a series of songs and drama programs. The children affectionately nicknamed Bono "The Girl with the Beard," which was a reference to his mullet hairdo, earrings, and feral facial hair.

For Bono, working at the orphanage was a hugely rewarding experience. But he was left haunted by an incident in which a middle-aged man approached him, dropped to his knees, and begged him to adopt his young boy because he couldn't afford to feed him. "You take him with you," the man pleaded through a translator. "If he stays here, he will surely die!" Soon after, Bono was escorted around the various camps and compounds in Addis Ababa. "Something in him had changed," Reynolds noted in *World Vision Magazine*. "As we walked through row after row of makeshift huts and shelters where people waited for the next food handout, Bono showed tireless compassion. It seemed he wanted to hold every child and comfort every mother."

Bono later claimed that he experienced a "culture shock" when he and Ali flew back home to Dublin. "I saw this big, fat, spoiled child of the West," he said in 1987. "And I started to see our cities as deserts and wastelands." Bono became fascinated with desert symbolism, the idea of an unforgiving environment that stands between man and his dreams as well as being a source of divine presence in Judeo-Christian tradition, and he tapped into this when penning the lyrics for U2's next studio album, *The Joshua Tree*.

Early writing sessions for *The Joshua Tree* took place in Larry's new home in north Dublin throughout November. U2 crammed into the drummer's spare bedroom and sketched five musical pieces, two of which would later evolve into "Red Hill Mining Town" and "With or Without You." Then, in January 1986, the band set up camp in Danesmoate House, a neglected twenty-roomed Georgian mansion in Rathfarnham in the foothills of the Wicklow Mountains, six miles outside of the capital. Yet again, it was an attempt to avoid the sterile environment of a traditional recording studio. The dining room was turned into a control room, while the adjoining drawing room, with its high ceiling and wooden floor, became the live band room, which was where most of the jamming and recording was done. Adam liked the two-hundred-year-old protected heritage building so much that he later bought it for $487,000 and made it his home after extensive renovations. That it also happened to be near St. Columba's College, the private boarding school from which he was expelled, had little bearing on his property investment, he claimed.

U2 was joined in their new studio by Brian Eno and, eventually, Daniel Lanois, as well as two new faces altogether: chief engineer Flood (a.k.a. Mark Ellis) and assistant engineer Dave Meegan, both of whom were recommended to the band by Gavin Friday following their work with the Virgin Prunes. "I stayed with them for about a month and a half, just recording everything they did while they jammed and worked on song ideas," recalls Meegan. "Lanois wasn't there at that point, but Eno was. Usually he was in first every morning and he'd start some dodgy sequence on his DX-7—it would be just like a cello line with no intentions of ever staying forever, just something to inspire people when they walked into the room. So that would be chugging away on some eternal loop and then usually Edge would be in next and he'd start playing along with it. Then all the others would join in eventually, and that would develop into something else or crash-dive pretty quickly. But it would start the day off on a very creative level."

Eno, although once again assuming the role of chief sonic catalyst, was keen to keep the sessions as uniformly creative as possible. "Eno would light the fire, but also allow everyone the space to be creative at that particular point," says Meegan. "It didn't start breaking down into individual bits until later in the process. But at that early stage it was all for one and one for all, really. And what was nice to see was that both Adam and Larry pulled the ideas off on a tangent. They have a unique way of doing things that are unpredictable. If Edge started a riff, you'd kind of picture in your head what someone might do normally behind that as a rhythm section and they never did that. So it was like rolling the dice when those two joined in because it could pull the whole idea anywhere. Sometimes with drummers and bass players when they join in at that stage they're quite reluctant to stretch the idea, because they're afraid of upsetting the idea, whereas Adam and Larry wouldn't give a toss. They'd do whatever they felt was right emotionally in that piece of music. Very rarely did Bono or whoever else go, 'Oh, shut up for a minute!' They all followed that flow, which was nice to see. It was quite democratic and I think that's why those early ideas worked really well. There were absolutely no rules set on any of them because they had no idea what the album was going to be like. They wanted it to be very different from *The Unforgettable Fire*, but they didn't know how they were going to do that."

That is, all but Bono. Bono pictured a U2 album steeped in American and Irish roots music and would often jam some blues with Stephen Rainford or another crew member at hand in the hope of convincing his three bandmates that this was a direction worth pursuing. He argued that U2's long-established rejection of music genres predating the phlegm-encrusted punk movement of '76, otherwise known as the "Year Zero" concept, was founded on musical ignorance and no longer something to boast about. What's more, by snubbing it, they were denying their own musical heritage and hindering their development.

It was, in fact, Bob Dylan who first turned the perpetually restless and forward-looking Bono on to the notion of checking his rearview mirror for the first time. When interviewing the American singer-songwriter in 1984 on behalf of Ireland's *Hot Press* (just moments before accepting an invitation to join him on stage at a huge open-air concert at Slane Castle, where, to the horror of Dylan purists, he ad-libbed his way through "Leopard-Skin Pill-Box Hat" and "Blowin' in the Wind"), Bono, conscious of U2's decision to reject the past, told him: "The music of U2 is in space somewhere. There is no particular musical roots or heritage for us. In Ireland, there is a tradition, but we've never plugged into it." Dylan, who was no stranger to exploring and nurturing American and Irish folk tradition, replied: "Well, you have to reach back into the music. You have to reach back." His words troubled Bono for quite some time, never more so than when, in 1985, he was invited along to a Rolling Stones recording session with The J. Geils Band's Peter Wolf while in New York to take part in the *Sun City* project. Keith Richards, Mick Jagger, and Wolf fell into a blues jam and encouraged Bono to join in. But he couldn't. He didn't know any of the blues standards they were playing. Returning to his hotel room, Bono promised himself that he wouldn't let that happen again. He picked up a guitar and wrote the sparse antiapartheid blues song "Silver and Gold," which he recorded in the studio the following morning with Richards and Ronnie Wood and donated to the *Sun City* album.

As an avid reader, Bono's next logical step was to immerse himself in the literature of the American South: Walker Percy, Zora Neale Hurston, and Flannery O'Connor, whose 1952 novel *Wise Blood* was recommended to him by Bruce Springsteen. He was also drawn to the New Journalism movement of the '60s and '70s, as well as the Dirty Realism movement pioneered by writers like Charles Bukowski, Raymond Carver, and Tobias Wolff. "The new American writers, particularly the Southern ones, tend to write in a very direct way," Bono told *NME* in 1987. "They also use a lot of biblical imagery and, as someone who has read the Bible, I can see a lot of power in that elemental imagery. Everyone can relate to those simple, powerful images. They are helpful when you want to convey just what a wasteland last year was politically, especially in America."

Bono even went so far as to plan how U2 would look and present themselves to the public during this proposed exploration of all things Americana, beginning to gather ideas and inspiration as far back as late 1984. "I got a phone call late one night from Bono's personal assistant, a guy called Greg Carroll," remembers Tony Michaelides. "He introduced himself and said, 'Bono wants to know if you could possibly send him copies of all your Spaghetti Westerns on VHS, he's got this idea in his head for an album.' So I made him copies of all my Clint Eastwood movies, including *The Good, the Bad and the Ugly,* which he'd seen lying around my house. So even then, Bono was putting together a presentation that was very appealing, both thematically and visually."

Larry responded the most positively to Bono's proposal. The no-nonsense drummer was instinctively attracted to simple song structures, and had appreciated the directness of the blues and country music he'd caught on radio stations and truck-stop jukeboxes when the band's battered old tour bus sputtered and limped its way through the American South in the pre–*Unforgettable Fire* days. Soon enough, Larry was digging through Dublin thrift shops and specialist country record outlets, and he fell in love with the music of Hank Williams, Patsy Cline, and Dolly Parton, among others. Edge, on the other hand, wasn't entirely convinced. His interest was in European-sounding groups like Can and Brian Eno's solo work, not blues, country, or folk music, and certainly not the derivative white blues-rock of the mid '70s, which he rebelled against as a teenager. Edge had just completed the soundtrack album for the low-budget British crime thriller *Captive,* in which he and his Canadian collaborator Michael Brook, inventor of the Infinite Guitar, expanded upon the lulling and drifting dreamscape of *The Unforgettable Fire,* and he had expressed a desire to continue in this Eurocentric vein. It wasn't until he had heard Robert Johnson and other early blues that he eventually warmed to the idea.

Bono wanted the new album to be more focused and disciplined in its songwriting than *The Unforgettable Fire.* He spoke of writing songs that adhered to traditional song structures and could be played on mainstream radio around the world; "songs," he said, "that would also appeal to an ordinary working man and woman . . . capture a people's imagination." The idea took root in his mind following a conversation with Barry Fey in 1985. Fey later recalled: "We were in Paris and it was late, about two or three o'clock in the morning, and I was kind of bugging him. I said, 'You might be the biggest rock band in the world, but you still don't have your "Hey Jude."'" Luckily for Bono, everyone in the band, including Edge, was happy to move in a more song-focused direction on this particular project. Even Eno, the eccentric avant-garde artist, was up for the challenge.

In typical U2 fashion, the Danesmoate sessions were long and challenging, but also fun. It wasn't all work and no play, according to Rainford. "I was there pretty much twenty-four hours a day. Sometimes late at night Bono would come back with a bunch of people after the pub and sing overdubs on something. Guggi and Gavin Friday would be around quite a bit. Charlie Whisker and Catherine Owens, too. That would be like 'Wednesday Night Painting' where they'd all be doing a little art project on the second floor. People were invited around for inspiration."

Undoubtedly what Bono appreciated most about this long period of creativity was that it afforded him the chance to clear the air and reconnect with his old childhood friends Guggi and Friday. And scaling the dizzying heights of fame, he needed them more than ever—particularly Friday's candor. "Gavin's job as a friend to Bono was to tell him he was an idiot," laughs Meegan. "Because no matter who you are, if the world tells you you're God it's very hard not to believe it. But Gavin would just go 'Oh, fuck off!' and he would drag him straight back down to where he should be. They were kind of like brothers, to be honest. Even visually I could have problems telling the difference between the two of them when they walked in the room."

But there was one former Virgin Prune and U2 roadie conspicuously absent from the reunion: Pod. "He fell out with U2 after *The Unforgettable Fire* and wasn't around for *The Joshua Tree*," explains a source, referring to the split caused by differing religious views. "It was quite a bitter falling-out, but Pod was a megalomaniac. His ego just got the better of him. So certainly U2 are ruthless individuals and they cut people loose, but in many cases you couldn't really blame them."

■

In May, U2 headlined Self Aid, a televised benefit concert held at the RDS stadium in Dublin that urged people to pledge money and jobs to alleviate the unemployment crisis in Ireland. Other guests included Christy Moore, Van Morrison, and Elvis Costello. It wasn't the first time U2 had tried to give something back to the community that had supported them: in 1983, Bono had served on Irish prime minister Garret FitzGerald's Select Government Action Committee on Unemployment, albeit briefly; in 1984, U2 had launched their own record label, Mother Records, to help discover and develop new Irish music talent; and in 1985, they had donated proceeds from their Croke Park show toward the building of a music rehearsal center for young musicians (although this was perhaps of little consolation to the two hundred people injured, including six police officers, or the local stores that were looted as concertgoers embarked on a violent rampage after the gig). But nothing could have prepared U2 for the barrage of criticism that greeted their involvement in Self Aid. The event, like Live Aid before it, was attacked by many for conforming to the new economic policies championed by Margaret Thatcher and Ronald Reagan, which shifted the responsibility of social welfare from the state to the individual. U2 was accused of liberal hypocrisy, and the magazine *In Dublin* ran a hard-hitting cover story titled "The Great Self-Aid Farce—Rock Against the People" with a photograph of Bono. The criticism cut deep. U2's performance on the day included a blistering indictment of Thatcher's government in the shape of Bob Dylan's "Maggie's Farm," and an incensed Bono ranted about "cheap Dublin magazines" during "Bad." Niall Stokes of *Hot Press* later called it "the blackest and most ferocious set of their entire career."

John Waters, author of *Race of Angels: The Genesis of U2* and the *In Dublin* article in question, suggests that U2 felt embarrassed for allowing themselves to be talked into such an ill-conceived and reactionary scheme. "At the time, I thought they were just plain crazy with rage on account of being criticized by us," he says. "I think they certainly felt they were unfairly singled out, which is probably reasonable. But then again they were U2, and the headline act. In fact, I subsequently apologized to them for the over-the-top elements in my own article, which really stung them. My sense is that there was this phony attempt by certain people in Dublin to jump on the Geldof bandwagon, and they got caught up in it, because they didn't think it through. I suspect that U2 understood at the time that most of what we said was true and right, but were caught up in the anger. I think if they were honest today, they would say it was an embarrassment, but nobody is really pressing the issue."

In June, U2 again interrupted the recording of *The Joshua Tree* to join the likes of Sting, Lou Reed, and Peter Gabriel on Amnesty International's whirlwind twenty-fifth anniversary U.S. tour, A Conspiracy of Hope, to raise awareness of the human rights organization and its campaign for the release of prisoners of conscience. U2 also saw their support of Amnesty as "a major opportunity to redefine the band in America," according to Adam. "We had broken through with *The Unforgettable Fire* and felt the time was ripe to show as many sides of the band as possible. . . ."

U2 was in fact the first act to sign up to the six-date tour and played an integral part in convincing other artists to follow suit. "Every time Bono came off the phone from talking to one of them he would run back into the room and then they would mimic them," recalls Dave Meegan. "He was on cloud nine. And all the people they talked to reminded them of the music that they were into—they were just open to everything at that point. Their musical heroes were bleeding into the music and they weren't embarrassed by it, which gave them a lot of space to work in."

The final concert at New Jersey's Giants Stadium was a sold-out, eleven-hour affair shown in its entirety on MTV. It was also notable for featuring the last public performance by The Police until they re-formed two decades later. In the middle of their 1981 hit "Invisible Sun," Sting was joined by Bono on vocals, and after its conclusion each member of the English rock band handed over their instrument to their U2 counterpart in a symbolic passing of the torch. "Every band has its day," Sting said later. "[W]e were the biggest band in the world, and I figured it was U2's turn next. And I was right." Amnesty's A Conspiracy of Hope

Tour was hailed as a resounding success, attracting around thirty-four thousand new members and netting a cool $2.1 million in box office receipts for the organization. And it did U2's post–Live Aid reputation no harm, either. "To tell you the truth, I remember the travel between shows more than I remember the shows themselves," says Stephen Rainford. "We got to share this big jet and it had no partitions from front to back and everybody was on board, all the bands and crew, and it was quite the thing to see hurtling through the sky. Quite the party machine!"

■

U2 came crashing back down to earth on July 3 when Greg Carroll, Bono's twenty-six-year-old personal assistant and roadie, smashed the singer's Harley-Davidson motorbike into a car on Dublin's Morehampton Road. He died instantly. "That was a tough thing," says Rainford. "Everyone was obviously devastated. And that was such a beautiful experience we were having with Greg Carroll, all of us. We met him in New Zealand [on the Under Australian Skies Tour]. He showed up on the first day as stage crew working for the promoter and by the end of those few days down there, he was working with us. He left New Zealand with only a plastic bag for his clothes and stuck with us all around the world. I thought he was an exceptional individual, really. Lovely guy. He didn't deserve to die so young."

A visibly shaken Bono, Ali, Larry, Ann, and Katy McGuinness (Carroll's girlfriend and sister of Paul), as well as other members of the U2 entourage, brought his body back to New Zealand for his tangi (a traditional Māori funeral rite that lasts three days) at Kai-iwi Marae, near his hometown of Wanganui. During the main service, Bono, who was ringed by two plainclothes detectives and eight Māori wardens for much of his stay, read a poem to the two hundred mourners, and said that Carroll "believed in New Zealand, believed in his Māori background . . . we all believed in him." At the "last supper," which is treated as a time of celebration, he sang "Let It Be" and "Knockin' on Heaven's Door" with The Ponsonby DC's Gavin Buxton accompanying him on violin. The whole experience inspired Bono to write the poignant "One Tree Hill," named after a 182-meter volcanic peak and memorial spot for the Māori people that Carroll took Bono to on his first night in Auckland in late 1984. U2 would also dedicate the *Joshua Tree* album to Carroll.

Following the burial, Bono and Ali flew straight from New Zealand to Nicaragua to meet up with David Batstone, founder of Central American Mission Partners (CAMP), which was an organization that sent U.S. citizens to live with Salvadorans targeted by the right-wing security forces—otherwise known as the death squads—financed and trained by the U.S. military in accordance with the "Reagan Doctrine" that pushed to extend covert assistance to numerous anticommunist guerrillas and resistance movements in Central America and other territories. Bono had first learned of CAMP's work while in San Francisco for the Amnesty tour—which itself had exposed him to the dark side of U.S. foreign policy. U2's set designer Willie Williams was an old friend of Batstone's and he arranged for him to give Bono a guided tour of a street in the Mission District called Balmy Alley, home to a collection of politically motivated murals by refugees fleeing the violence in Central America. Bono arrived with Edge and Lou Reed the following morning, and within an hour he had invited himself to join Batstone on his next trip south.

"So here we go six weeks later," recalls Batstone. "I picked him up at the Managua airport and Ali was with him—he didn't tell me Ali was coming. We go get a coffee and he says, 'What do you want from me?'—Bono's just full of candor and frankness. And I said, 'To be honest, you're the one who called me and told me you want to go. I have no agenda with you. If you want to get involved and do something, fine. But my goal in life isn't to get a rock-and-roll band involved in my human rights work. If that's something that you want to pursue, then let me know how you want to pursue it.' So that comforted him."

But that warm feeling deserted Bono once the small party arrived in El Salvador. Says Batstone: "We had an agricultural camp in the countryside working with people who were marginalized economically and politically. It was in a conflictive area and a couple of things happened on that journey as we were heading toward the village. First, we see a dead body on the side of the road where we'd just parked, and as we are walking by it there's a note on it from a death squad warning anyone who tries to participate in the economic projects we were doing, or tries to help the poor with reading and education, this is what happens to them. It was a common thing that I saw. But imagine coming straight out of Dublin and this is what you're seeing." Then, as the group continued up the steep trail to the camp, they heard the ominous sound of gunshots being fired close by. "I think they were just trying to scare us, to be honest. But there's a certain amount of irrationality when it comes to violence and dictators. I wouldn't say it was not without its fear. I remember Bono saying some colorful piece of language about what was happening, what we do next. And I said, 'You just keep walking forward, and hope that they don't have better aim.' "

The group was within two miles of a neighboring village when they spotted the first Salvadoran military F-16 fighter jet circling the sky above it. Others appeared like roaring birds of prey. Military helicopters, too. What happened next was like a scene from Francis Ford Coppola's *Apocalypse Now.* "We're on a knoll and we're looking down," remembers Batstone, "and we see the bombs dropping on this civilian village they suspected were providing food and maybe even recruits to the opposing rebels. I still remember the shock on [Bono and Ali's] faces that this could happen, the callous treatment of people. I think all of that really jarred them. So when Bono left El Salvador, as we finished our trip, he said, 'This will find its way out some way. I can't make any promises, but just know that this has shaped the way that I see the world.' "

Consequently, Bono wrote the lyrics to "Bullet the Blue Sky" based on his experience in Central America when U2 resumed work on *The Joshua Tree* in the autumn of '86, alternating between Windmill Lane and Melbeach House, Edge's newly renovated property overlooking Dublin Bay. Bono wanted the music to depict the horror of war and told Edge to "put El Salvador through your amplifier." But it was the returning Dave Meegan, hunched over the mixing console at Melbeach, who realized its thunderous potential. "I thought it should sound a bit like Led Zeppelin so I adjusted a monitor mix of it and made it really heavy sounding," recalls Meegan. "Lanois walked into the room and he was blown away by it, because they'd been treating it quite soft. So he got the band in and they went straight off to Windmill and put all the drums through the live room and made them sound like John Bonham. And that was quite a buzz because I felt I'd been an influence." The result was U2's heaviest rock song to date, built around a dive-bomb slide guitar, Bono's aggressive, confrontational vocals, and a powerful drum-based riff that owed much to Zeppelin's "When the Levee Breaks," itself an adaptation of the 1929 Delta blues original of the same name by Kansas Joe McCoy and Memphis Minnie. This was not the romanticized America of the Old West, but Reagan's America with a "k." "I love America and I hate it," Bono told *NME*. "I'm torn between the two. . . . I'd gone to America and embraced America and America had embraced U2. But now I had to rethink and a song like 'Bullet the Blue Sky' is a result of that. I have two conflicting visions of America. One is a kind of dream landscape and the other is a kind of black comedy." Hence the album's working title: *The Two Americas*.

"Mothers of the Disappeared"—described by *NME* as "a simple, plaintive lament of stunning beauty and sadness"—was dedicated to the CoMadres, a group of women who had lost their families to the Reagan-backed death squads and who themselves risked being kidnapped, raped, and severely tortured by their government for asking too many questions. Bono spent an afternoon with the mothers at their office in San Salvador and sat in silence as they shared with him their stories of human suffering and perseverance. "I still remember he and Ali being brought to tears by these mothers whose kids had disappeared and were never seen again and the work that they were doing in El Salvador to keep the profile of their sons and daughters alive," says Batstone. "That was a very moving experience for them."

"Mothers of the Disappeared" would not only close the album, but serve as the last piece of what Edge called the "suite of death," which also included "One Tree Hill" and "Exit," a dark and sinister tale about a religious man who, Bono explained, "became a very dangerous man when he misunderstood the hands of love." Inspired by *The Executioner's*

Song, Norman Mailer's Pulitzer Prize–winning novel on convicted killer Gary Gilmore, who was executed in 1977, "Exit" would see U2 being pulled unwittingly into a Los Angeles murder trial in 1991 when the defendant John Robert Bardo told forensic psychiatrist Dr. Park Elliott Dietz that the line "pistol weighing heavy" had given him the idea to kill the television actress Rebecca Schaeffer two years earlier. According to the Associated Press, "Bardo, who had sat motionless through the trial, sprang to life when the song was played in court. He grinned, bobbed to the music, pounded his knee like a drum and mouthed the lyrics." It emerged that Bardo had stalked Schaeffer for three years before shooting her at point-blank range on the doorstop of her apartment building. He was convicted of first-degree murder.

U2 was in such prolific songwriting form that by October there was enough material for a double album. Bono proposed the idea to the others, but he was ultimately persuaded to pare it down to eleven tracks. "There would have been two records, depending on which songs we decided to finish," Edge explained in *Musician*. "There was this one album, the 'blues' album that Bono was talking about, and another, much more 'European,' which is kind of the way I was led. . . . We hustled to try to finish it, and to get our own views across, but it is a democratic band, and neither my nor Bono's feelings came through completely." In the end, U2 opted to sacrifice sonic cohesiveness "to present what we felt was the strongest material." Nevertheless, an important characteristic of the music during the selection process was that it gave the listener the sense of an actual location. "We used to call it cinematic music," Edge told VH1's *Classic Albums*. "Music that actually brought you somewhere physical as opposed to an emotional place."

More often than not that place was the American Southwest. Bono wrote the lyrics to "Where the Streets Have No Name" because the idea of going "somewhere where the values of the city and the values of our society don't hold you down" appealed to him, he told *Propaganda*. He cited Ethiopia as a major influence, but also German director Wim Wenders's 1984 road movie *Paris, Texas,* which used the image of a man wandering insane with grief in the desert as a metaphor for an American culture that had, to quote a character in another Wenders picture, *Kings of the Road*, "colonized our subconscious"; and therefore *Paris, Texas* and "Streets" were both inspired by the inconsistencies of the mythic American Dream, as seen through European eyes. Another song, "In God's Country," depicted the Statue of Liberty as a temptress whose dress was "torn in ribbons and in bows." "[Has] this woman come to rescue you from drowning or whatever," Bono pondered, "or is she the siren that's actually drawing you onto the rocks?" The lure of America was, and remains, particularly strong for the Irish. "The Irish fascination with America goes back to the famine, when large numbers fled to the new world on a mission of hope," Adam explained. "There's something about the great expanse of America that resonates in the soul of the Irish, whose grandiose ambitions are held in check by the physical limitations of their country."

Musically, "Streets" came from a demo Edge recorded on a Tascam four-track tape at Melbeach. It was a rather complex piece, with the celestial guitar-keyboard intro composed in a different time signature to the rest of the propulsive rock anthem, and when Edge presented it to the others, there was an audible collective groan. It was a painstaking process to get the band's performance just right, and required Lanois to write the arrangement on a giant blackboard and walk them through the time signature jumps and recurring chord changes. Eno estimated that around 40 percent of the time it took to make *The Joshua Tree* was spent on "Streets," and according to U2 legend, at one point he became so frustrated at the lack of progress that he had to be physically restrained by tape operator Pat McCarthy from wiping the master tape altogether. The truth is somewhat less dramatic. "That song was recorded, so there was a version of it on tape," Eno told *Classic Albums*. "It was a nightmare of screwdriver work and my feeling was that it would be much better to start again—I was sure we would get there quicker if we started again. So my idea was to stage an accident to erase the tape so we'd just have to start again. But I never did." "Streets" was one of several tracks mixed by Steve Lillywhite and Mark Wallis at Windmill Lane while U2 continued to record and re-record live off the floor the designated album cuts at Melbeach right up until deadline day.

The elegiac piano-driven "Running to Stand Still" was about a junkie couple in Dublin that Bono had read about in a newspaper. "Such was their addiction that they had no money, no rent," Bono told *Musician*. "The guy risked it all on a run. All of it. He went and smuggled into Dublin a serious quantity of heroin strapped to his body so that there was on one hand life imprisonment, and on the other hand riches." Incidentally, the line "I see seven towers but I only see one way out" was a reference to the Ballymun tower block estate that had become synonymous with Dublin's heroin crisis.

Under the working title of "The Weather Girls," "I Still Haven't Found What I'm Looking For" was considered the bastard child of Patti Smith's "Redondo Beach" until a spot of studio surgery by Eno and Lanois steered it in the direction of contemporary gospel, providing an uplifting counterpoint to Bono's lyrics about spiritual doubt. Eno explained to *Classic Albums* that he lobbied for songs that were "self-consciously spiritual to the point of being uncool. And I thought uncool was a very important idea then, because people were being very, very cool. And coolness is a certain kind of detachment from yourself, a certain defensiveness actually, and not exposing something because it's too easy to be shot down.... And of course everybody was in the process of shooting U2 down. Critically they were not favored... they were thought to be rather 'heart on their sleeves.'"

"Red Hill Mining Town" was the embodiment of the earnest emotion and bleeding-heart leftism that had made U2 such a polarizing band. Inspired by the Tony Parker book *Red Hill: A Mining Community*, the sweeping rock anthem focused on the breakdown of a marriage set against the backdrop of the doomed British miners' strike of 1984–85. Ian MacGregor, the Thatcher-approved head of the National Coal Board and scourge of miners, was also alluded to in the song.

Around this time, Bono confessed that his own marriage was under immense strain because of U2's work commitments. He and Ali—who was studying social and political sciences at Dublin's University College—had a stormy relationship, and Bono half-joked that he occasionally found himself being thrown out on the street. "Ali will not be worn like a brooch, she is very much her own woman," he said. "My life is a mess. I haven't been able to handle juggling my marriage with recording and touring." Meanwhile in the background, the tabloids linked the singer to a number of women, including Lone Justice chanteuse Maria McKee and Clannad's Máire Brennan. Bono had collaborated with both women, and facetiously referred to McKee—whose American roots rock band had opened for U2 on many occasions—as his "second wife."

Interestingly, Bono addressed sexual temptation on "Trip Through Your Wires," a drunken, blues harp–filled romp that evoked the rough-and-tumble spirit of Bob Dylan's *The Basement Tapes*. Production-wise, it was the epitome of the organic, band-in-a-room sound U2 was striving for. Bono had an aversion for anything that sounded "posh," and drummed it into everyone that the LP should never sound bigger than the people listening to it. Mark Wallis recalls: "The key word at the time was 'humble.' I think all we used during the mixing of that album was a couple of spring reverbs and tape delay, and I can remember at the time all of us had a sort of inner feeling of 'Do you think the public are going to like this?' We were trying to sound simple and honest rather than spending hours making everything sound huge, like atomic bombs going off, which is what was happening with records at the time. Just put some nice colorization on and paint a nice picture with the basic ingredients. I think *The Joshua Tree* started a chain of events where people were starting to un-produce their records a little bit."

Bono also wrote about the "violence of love" on the Scott Walker–inspired ballad "With or Without You." "I see it in myself and in other people around me that love is a two-edged sword," he said. "I didn't want to write about romance because that doesn't interest me as much as the other side." The song was a slow burner, with Bono's restrained vocals and Edge's eerie guitar wails, produced by a prototype Infinite Guitar given to him by Michael Brook, eventually building to a cathartic climax. Bono said it "whispers its way into the world," and much of that must also be attributed to the studio wizardry of Eno. Wallis reveals: "Steve [Lillywhite] and I were mixing it and Brian just came in and went, 'I want to change the intro.' And it was kind of awe-inspiring because he said, 'Right, send this guitar through those ten effects over there and send that guitar through those ten effects over there and then feed them back into each other.' So what started as a traditional bit of rhythm guitar, bass, and drums suddenly became something quite otherworldly and spiritual, and the sound of the music you were hearing started to give you a feeling of where the song was going to go prior to the lyric. I thought that was really visionary."

"With or Without You" was considered to be Bono at his lyrical peak, effectively mixing the sexual and spiritual in the context of a masochistic relationship. But to reach that level required an intervention from his bandmates. "He had a whole set of lyrics for most of the album but the band weren't happy with them," recalls Meegan. "They were really critical of Bono at the time and they sent him off to rewrite them all, and what he came back with was just absolutely stunning. That was a critical moment that never gets mentioned. It's what forced lyrics like 'With or Without You' to happen. I don't think that is a pressure he has nowadays; lyrically he gets away with murder. But it knocked him back to being a schoolboy again and made him insecure, and that place of insecurity is why he came up with some great things. And that was the atmosphere that was around on *The Joshua Tree*. They were all capable of telling each other when something was shit and not letting each other get away with it no matter what confrontation that would cause. They were all very tough, especially at the latter stages."

No one more so than Larry. "Larry was black and white," continues Meegan. "He said it as it was. But he was also very chilled as well on some levels. He'd walk into a room and go, 'Nah, that's crap.' He'd refer to some other band of the moment that was awful and say, 'That sounds like them,' and that was it and then walk out. And straightaway that idea would be put on the back burner. Because if Larry wasn't into something, that would take the life out of it and people would definitely lose interest in it. I think everyone thought it was hell; but whether they liked it or not, what he said they held in high regard. That's one of the main reasons why they survive. They accept that band democracy."

"With or Without You" seemed like an obvious choice for the album's first single to U2's studio crew. But the band always had their doubts about its quality, let alone single potential. Meegan recalls: "Bono brought it back from the mix at Windmill and said, 'You've got to listen to this. I don't know if it's good enough.' And he played it to me and it absolutely blew me away. I just said, 'That is going to be number one everywhere in the world. You're mad!' They were so close to the material that they couldn't tell when they had moments of greatness. To me, it was staring them in the face. I think that's why they also got bogged down with things like 'Streets.' They just couldn't see it anymore, it had gone on that long." Eventually, Gavin Friday stepped in and convinced them to release it. And the decision paid off. "With or Without You" became U2's biggest hit, topping the U.S. charts for three weeks in May 1987.

It was the photographer Anton Corbijn who was ultimately responsible for *The Joshua Tree* as an album title. In December 1986, U2 and Corbijn embarked on a three-day bus journey through the ghost towns of the Mojave Desert in California shooting the artwork. Corbijn told the band about the Joshua tree, a strange yucca palm that grows in the deserts of the American Southwest and which most likely got its name from the early Mormon settlers heading farther west, who believed that the tree, like the prophet Joshua from the Old Testament, was waving them on toward the Promised Land. On the second day, Corbijn spotted a lone tree in Death Valley, two hundred miles north of the hippie mecca of Joshua Tree, and took pictures of the band standing in front of it. Corbijn's stark monochromatic imagery of U2 would become just as iconic as the music it adorned and, for better or for worse, cemented the public's perception of the group as earnest, po-faced men. Larry later told Neil Perry of *Sounds*: "If you look at the cover of *The Joshua Tree* there you see four very unhappy men. Now, you may ask, why? A lot of people will say they're feeling guilty, they've got the weight of the world on their shoulders. They've been involved in the Save the Whale campaign and they're very unhappy about it. What nobody realizes is that it was twenty below out there! We were freezing. Put any bastard out there and see if he's happy."

The Joshua Tree was completed in January 1987, just hours before the deadline enforced by Island. On the last night U2 held a competition in Edge's bedroom at Melbeach to see who could come up with the best running order for the album. Kirsty MacColl, the wife of Lillywhite at the time, came out on top. Meanwhile downstairs, Edge, ever the perfectionist, was finding it difficult to let go of the project and suggested the unthinkable. Meegan recalls: "The mastering was booked for 9 A.M. in London, it was now 2 A.M. and Edge still wants to do a backing vocal on 'Streets!' And no one would say no to him, not Eno, not Lanois, no one. The only person that would stand up to him was Lillywhite, and it was just brilliant to watch him do it in a very diplomatic but absolutely black and white way that you couldn't argue with, because he was so right. He said, 'The album's finished, that's it. That version of "Streets" is going on the album. If you want to do the backing vocal then we'll take the multitrack to my [Meegan's] SARM studio in London and I'll get it all sounding the same, Edge can do his backing vocal on it in Dublin, and then we can remix the new version in London and that can be the single.' So there's a backing vocal on the single, but not on the album. And that was because of Lillywhite's compromise at the end.

"Then I had to jump on the first plane out of Dublin and personally take the album to Island in Hammersmith, hand it over officially before it went to mastering, and then meet the tapes at the mastering room," continues Meegan. "Lillywhite just got there on time as well. And the rest, as they say, is history."

10

The Ground Beneath Their Feet

U2's *The Joshua Tree* landed on Island's desk at a crucial point in the company's history. Once again, it was fighting for its survival, after a series of bad investments in the film industry by Blackwell had undone all the progress made by Dave Robinson during his hugely successful 1984–85 tenure as Island president. Blackwell, via his film production subsidiary Island Alive, had funneled the label's profits into the production and distribution of three critically acclaimed pictures, Spike Lee's feature-length debut *She's Gotta Have It* and the Academy Award–recognized *The Trip to Bountiful* and *Kiss of the Spider Woman,* but also, regrettably, into numerous others that failed to materialize. Needless to say, Robinson took umbrage at Blackwell for "pissing away" money that he felt would have been better spent on signing and developing new music talent, and their relationship soured to the point where Robinson was pushed out of the company altogether. "Robinson just thought it was self-indulgent and he would say so," recalls an Island source. "He would turn around and say, 'What the fuck are you doing?' I mean, how could you get rid of a guy who turned a deficit into a profit? Why would you get rid of him unless it was personal?"

Says Robinson: "The film business is not something in which you can make a quick decision and hope for luck in. You need to be more technical and know what you're doing, and there are so many sharks in the water that even if you're a big barracuda they will eat you up. And he [Blackwell] fell for it. It was a great shame because quite honestly it messed up my life insofar as the money that I made for the record company that would have then gone on to push Stiff Records and Island was used in a couple of really bad movies which never saw the light of day. Blackwell put about £6 million into them which was our profit for that year. So we were back to owing money and not having a lot of hits. So a great year in '84 was wasted because of Blackwell and his movies. And Stiff suffered a great deal because Island weren't paying their bills—when Blackwell supposedly bought the shares in Stiff we got rid of our accounts department to save money because Island's accounts would be able to handle it, but they didn't. They paid Island's bills, but not Stiff's. It took me a while to find that out. I'm not wishing to be bitter in the story, they're just facts. You know they call Blackwell 'The Babyface Killer?' I should have paid attention.

"Island made more money that year when I was running it than they'd ever made in their lives," continues Robinson, "and yet Blackwell didn't pay me for my shares in Stiff. I did get some small part back eventually [after taking legal action], but it was a lot of effort, and in that long time getting it back, it put financial pressure on Stiff which up until then had been doing much better than Island. I mean, Island was a great label but it hadn't had a lot of tender love and care for a while. Blackwell was the head of it, but he wasn't running it. I spent too much time worrying about his label and not enough about my own." As a result, Stiff Records folded in 1986 with reported debts of around £3 million. Its assets were later bought for £300,000 by ZTT Records.

It is often said in the business world that one man's misfortune is another man's gain, and Paul McGuinness, ever the opportunist, was able to use Island's turmoil to U2's own advantage. McGuinness was still sore about the group's 1984 single "Pride (In the Name of Love)" underperforming in the U.S. charts and made it his personal mission to ensure that the Island head honcho overseeing the release of *The Joshua Tree* would have an intimate knowledge of the inner workings of the American music industry. He identified Lou Maglia, the former executive vice president of Elektra Records, as the ideal candidate. Maglia, who also happened to be a good friend of Ellen Darst, had resigned from Elektra in 1985, after he was forced to terminate two hundred employees and relocate the label from California to New York in the wake of the deep financial crisis of its parent company, Warner Communications, which was mainly brought about by its troubled Atari computer division. McGuinness called Maglia at his home in the Big Apple in mid-1986 and arranged for him to meet with Blackwell in a restaurant in London's Soho to discuss the Island opening. There, Maglia explained to Blackwell, who had just flown in from Jamaica and was wearing flip-flops in the middle of a freak snowstorm, that in order for the appointment to work, he needed to be the final decision maker on all issues relating to the record company. Blackwell agreed, and that was the premise their relationship was based on.

Nevertheless, Maglia was in for a shock when he met with Island's CFO and learned the full extent of the company's financial situation. Maglia recalls: "I went over and I said, 'Chris wants me to come in and run the company,' and he said, 'Did he say how we were going to pay you?' He took me on a little tour around the place and he brought me to this room and said, 'This is where the copying machine was before it was repossessed. . . .' Then I talked to the promotion guys and they said, 'We haven't gotten expense checks in six months. We had to borrow money to pay our American Express bill,' and all this business.

"But I researched the company and I saw things like catalog that hadn't even been released on cassette [in the U.S.], let alone on CDs, which were just coming into vogue. It was pretty much a British company and that was their primary interest. So I laid it out in a very diplomatic way that it had to be marketed from the United States. We had to release things based on what the needs were there. It was a transition, but I think people like Marc [Marot] realized what it would take to get it done and they were always very supportive."

U2's *The Joshua Tree* was to be an integral part of Maglia's game plan. In late '86, after hearing the rough mix tape and playing it constantly to anybody he knew who was influential, Maglia drew up a hundred-thousand-dollar marketing budget and then went before a WEA distribution committee and requested that the album be directed at the U.S. CD market from the get-go. "A lot of people thought I was crazy," laughs Maglia. "U2 was on Atlantic (WEA) at the time [in America] and it was pretty much if that record didn't sell, if that band didn't take off on that album, then they would have been looking someplace else. So it was a key situation for everyone. And what I did was I actually went to WEA and promised the guy that was in charge of manufacturing that if he manufactured me a million CDs on the day of release that I'd give him a week of gold. So I shipped more CDs than any CD in the history of WEA up until that point. And that's what got that record to jump onto the charts and debut high in the United States." Indeed, in March 1987, *The Joshua Tree* entered the *Billboard* album chart at number seven, the highest album debut in the States in over seven years, before rising to number one its fourth week, where it remained for nine successive weeks. Meanwhile, in Britain it became the fastest-selling album in UK chart history when it went platinum within the first forty-eight hours of its release. Overall, *The Joshua Tree* topped the charts in over twenty countries, and made U2 a household name.

It was also reviewed favorably on both sides of the Atlantic. Bill Graham of *Hot Press* wrote that "*The Joshua Tree* rescues rock from its decay, bravely and unashamedly basing itself in the mainstream before very cleverly lifting off into several higher dimensions." Writing in the *Los Angeles Times,* Robert Hilburn said that "[i]n a time when the rock 'n' roll world feasts on the banality of such acts as Bon Jovi, *The Joshua Tree* is asking more of mainstream audiences than any pop-rock album since Bruce Springsteen's *Nebraska*." He added: "*The Joshua Tree* finally confirms on record what this band has been slowly asserting for three years now on stage: U2 is what the Rolling Stones ceased being years ago—the greatest rock 'n' roll band in the world."

Says pop historian Paul Gambaccini: "*The Joshua Tree* is the pinnacle of U2's career, and happily it's also the commercial pinnacle of their career. It's one of those rare cases where art and commerce meet. It's also the one that comes in highest in all of the various voting competitions for the best albums of all time, and indeed in one VH1 poll it actually was number one. There was such a quality to the songwriting and Bono just sounds like the voice of rock music at that time. Of course, Eno had such a wonderful contribution. One is always hesitant to credit a producer too much, but on the other hand in some arrangements you cannot discuss the album without discussing the producer—I refer of course to George Martin and The Beatles, and Gus Dudgeon and the early Elton John period from 1970–76. And the combination of Eno's soundscapes, as Paul Simon called them, and U2's material was perfect. The fading in of 'With or Without You' and 'I Still Haven't Found What I'm Looking For' is a marvelous idea. And just that first little pining note on 'With or Without You' has so much soul. He really was the perfect foil or counterweight to their style.

"I don't think people were expecting *The Joshua Tree* to be that great because U2 had only been occasionally great," continues Gambaccini. "I seem to recall that it crept up on the industry. And then when it happened of course everyone thought, 'Oh, fantastic!' But it was only number one in its fourth week in the American charts, so it was building. It was a grower and it just kept going. A lot of those early U2 records were on the chart in America forever: *War*: 179 weeks, *Under a Blood Red Sky*: 180 weeks, *The Unforgettable Fire*: 132 weeks, and even *The Joshua Tree*: 103 weeks. People didn't buy them straightaway; they were word-of-mouth successes. It was only with *The Joshua Tree* that U2 became the number-one rock group."

■

Two weeks after the release of their landmark album, U2 headed to America for the first leg of the Joshua Tree Tour, which would see them playing multiple nights in arenas. But for all its box office triumph, the tour was cursed from the moment their flight left London en route to

Los Angeles. Some six miles above the Atlantic, their commercial plane was hit by lightning, temporarily knocking out the radar and lights. "Don't worry, it's only God taking your photograph," Bono reassured his neighboring passenger, Sophia Loren. Unbeknownst to him, the Italian screen siren and self-described "Neapolitan witch" had once claimed that her powers of ESP prevented her from boarding a Rome-bound plane that crashed and killed everyone aboard in 1955. Luckily for U2 and Loren, her psychic abilities hadn't abandoned her, and their plane landed safely on U.S. soil.

The tour began, to a certain extent, on March 27, when U2 filmed the music video for "Where the Streets Have No Name" on the rooftop of the Republic Liquor Store at the corner of Seventh and Main Street in Los Angeles—a clear homage to The Beatles' final gig on London's Apple Building in 1969. The video shoot, which was directed by Meiert Avis, saw the band play four additional songs to the crowd of people that gathered below, and in effect brought downtown L.A. traffic to a standstill. "This was more art project than cynical marketing operation," says Avis. "We were there to have some iconoclastic fun, identify with fans, and stick our tongues out at the world and get noticed. It was a flash mob, agitprop. That's why it begins with the commissioned graffiti 'Art Saves Lives.' "

But despite popular belief, the so-called impromptu performance was actually the product of weeks of careful planning, which involved putting in place the necessary safety measures for fans and leaking the location of the shoot to numerous radio stations and newspapers. Avis recalls: "It was very meticulously planned from a safety point of view. We spent a week reinforcing the roof of the building so that if the fans got up there it wouldn't collapse. The local residents had no issues with what we were doing. We had city permits, it was all legal. We even had our own assigned LAPD for traffic control. You can see them open it up and let the fire brigade through at one point. The fans were always considered and everyone was safe."

However, Avis was forced to abandon his original plan to film U2 during magic hour when one of the radio stations, looking to get the jump on their competitors, broke the story too soon and eager early birds flocked to the liquor store before the band had even got there. "LAPD management started arriving and had natural concerns," says Avis. "It looked like we might get shut down before we had enough fans to make the video. The fans were the wild card, and miraculously they started showing up, first one or two, then hundreds. So I started shooting while the producers negotiated with the LAPD, who really were trying to balance the different needs of the situation as best they could." In fact, the LAPD were so accommodating that U2, anxious to appear rebellious on camera, tried to provoke them into pulling the plug. Eventually, the LAPD took the bait, and the film crew captured the police officers confronting producer Michael Hamlyn and ordering the band to come down off the roof to a chorus of boos from the crowd.

"We had a spare generator on the roof so that when they shut down the main generator we could still run the PA," recalls Avis. "So when they pulled the fuse on the main genny, we fired up the backup generator and then someone pulled the fuse on the scissor lift so they couldn't get up on the roof and we kept shooting. Rock-and-roll rebels. The second genny was cut eventually and Bono ended up with just the megaphone to talk to the crowd. The edit compresses time obviously, but it's a documentary record of the event. And things were more heated if anything. Ultimately someone suggested that we might go to jail and get AIDS if we didn't stop. By then I knew I had the video so I wrapped it up and we went back to the hotel and watched it all on the news. Instant gratification. You can only imagine the feeling."

Indeed. Avis's video won Best Performance Video at the Thirty-First Grammy Awards in 1989 and went on to become one of the most celebrated, and imitated, rock promos of all time. "It's been ripped off hundreds of times," says Avis. "Someone tried to rip it for a Heineken commercial. They even had the gall to call us up to try and find the exact location downtown. [But] the excitement comes from the rebellion; the taste of freedom lights up the fans and the band. I hate it when they rip you off badly. Michael Moore's RATM video on Wall Street got it right."

In April, U2 walked straight into another storm when arriving at the State University Activity Center in Tempe, Arizona, for the official launch of the tour. Only this time the storm was entirely man-made. Unbeknownst to the band, ultraconservative Arizona governor Evan Mecham had recently rescinded the state holiday honoring the birthday of Martin Luther King, Jr., saying its creation had been illegal and King "didn't deserve" it. Other artists, most notably Stevie Wonder and The Doobie Brothers, canceled their shows in Arizona in protest, and U2 was criticized by a statewide campaign for not following suit. The negative press was particularly embarrassing for U2 as they had been such vocal supporters of King in the past, even going so far as to dedicate two songs to him.

The band saved face by announcing that they would be making a "sizable financial contribution" (five thousand dollars) to the Mecham Watchdog Committee, a grassroots campaign to remove the governor from office. Still red-faced, they also prepared a statement describing Mecham's actions as "an insult to a great spiritual leader" and begged Barry Fey to read it out to the audience ahead of their first show. "They called me into the dressing room," Fey said later, "and they asked me to make the statement. I said, 'What do you want me to make it for? You should do it.' 'No, no, Barry. You do it!' And that got me into a running battle with Mecham. What an asshole! I started getting on *Entertainment Tonight* all the time and the last thing I told them was, 'You don't have to live in Arizona to be ignorant.' "

U2's stay in the Grand Canyon State went from bad to worse. Adding injury to insult, during the final rehearsal on April Fools' Day, Bono fell backward off the stage and cut his chin on the handheld spotlight he wielded for dramatic effect in "Bullet the Blue Sky." He was taken to a local hospital, where the wound was stitched up, leaving behind a small but permanent scar. Bono was accompanied there by Ali, who had showed up unannounced in Arizona following a heated transatlantic telephone conversation between the married couple just forty-eight hours earlier. Ali had blasted him for asking her parents to keep an eye on her in his absence, before slamming the phone down on him. She returned home to Dublin five days later.

The extensive tour rehearsals, coupled with the dry desert air, also wreaked havoc with Bono's vocal cords. On the opening night, he found himself unable to sing and relied on the kindness and enthusiasm of the audience to belt out the songs for him. Nevertheless, the critical response was generally positive. *The Phoenix Gazette* wrote: "Flying in the face of defeat is precisely what this band is about, and Bono and company showed a determination and spirit that would have convinced any unbeliever." Even so, U2 delayed the second Arizona show by twenty-four hours to allow Bono's voice time to recover.

On another day of rest, U2 hit Las Vegas and saw Sugar Ray Leonard beat Marvin Hagler in a controversial split decision at Caesars Palace. Later, they got Barry Fey to score them free VIP tickets (normally going at twenty-five thousand dollars a table) to Frank Sinatra's midnight charity engagement at the Golden Nugget casino-hotel, during which the warm-up comedian Don Rickles brought them to the attention of Ol' Blue Eyes himself. "Hey, Frank. Before you start, there are some people in the audience you really should meet," Rickles said. "It's a band called U2. They're going to be very, very big!" Rickles shone the spotlight on the Irish quartet as they stood up and waved. Sinatra took one look at them, turned to Rickles and said, "They may be getting big, but they haven't spent a dime on clothes."

Bono recalled on BBC Radio 1: "We got to meet Frank afterward and an ongoing relationship started with him. He and Larry hit it off because Larry was talking to him about Buddy Rich and oddly, I don't think many people talked to Sinatra about music. I remember after the meeting, because there was a whole host of celebs he wouldn't go out and meet because he was talking to us, we got out of the room and there was a lot people going, 'Hey, U2! Wanna race horse named after ya? Ya wanna go down to the track in New Jersey?' We were very hip that week in the neighborhoods that would be portrayed in *The Sopranos*."

U2 returned to Vegas on business on April 12, when they performed at the Thomas and Mack Arena. After the show, they took to the neon jungle of Fremont Street pretending to be buskers for the Barry Devlin–directed video for "I Still Haven't Found What I'm Looking For." Pulled together on a shoestring budget, the promo clip was later nominated for five MTV Video Music Awards.

Initially, U2 was opposed to releasing "I Still Haven't Found . . ." as the follow-up single to "With or Without You." They much preferred "Red Hill Mining Town," and even shot a bizarre music video for it with the Irish filmmaker Neil Jordan in which they were featured as sweaty, sexed-up coal miners. The fact that plan A was scrapped altogether and U2 was saved from certain embarrassment was down to Island president Lou Maglia. Maglia had recognized the chart potential of "I Still Haven't Found . . ." right away and mailed copies of the song to radio stations throughout the United States. The response from DJs and listeners was extremely positive, and it consequently received heavy airplay across the country. And yet, U2 remained unconvinced. Maglia recalls: "I had 'I Still Haven't Found What I'm Looking For' at number one at album radio—which is a very important format in the United States—while 'With or Without You' was number one at Top 40. Then I got a phone call from Chris [Blackwell] and he said that the band's decided that they don't want to go with 'I Still Haven't Found . . .' and I said, 'What?!' He said McGuinness was in agreement so I screamed at my secretary, 'Where's U2?' And he said, 'Houston.' So I got right on a plane and went into their dressing room after the show. They're like, 'Lou, what are you doing here?' I said, 'Well, if I didn't come here and talk to you guys it would be a disservice to you.' So I talked to them and Edge said, 'What if we come back with the song in September?' and I said, 'No way. We'd be looked at like buffoons if we changed the single right now. The record is set up to be a number-one record, as well as "With or Without You." It's very important that you keep it going the way that it is. Ultimately, it's your decision. But this would be a very awkward situation."'

U2 dragged their feet for another five days before finally giving Maglia the go-ahead to release it as a commercial single. And Maglia's judgment was vindicated when the song climbed to the top of the *Billboard* Hot 100, giving the band their second (and last) number-one single in the States. "I had those experiences a lot in my career," says Maglia. "But I think that was a pivotal point in their career as far as launching them into that megastar status."

U2 was undoubtedly the toast of America. And though they publicly cursed the burdens of superstardom, the prying of the press, the unrealistic expectations of fans, they also reveled in their privileges. In Los Angeles, they once again rubbed shoulders with music royalty when Bob Dylan joined them on stage to duet on "Knockin' on Heaven's Door" and "I Shall Be Released." After the gig, Bono returned to his rented villa at the Sunset Marquis with Edge, Dylan, and the revered musician/producer T-Bone Burnett, where they jammed together until the break of dawn. Bono and Dylan's relationship quickly progressed from casual acquaintances to genuine friends, and Dylan later wrote in his 2004 memoir, *Chronicles, Volume One*: "Spending time with Bono was like eating dinner on a train—feels like you're moving, going somewhere. Bono's got the soul of an ancient poet and you have to be careful around him. He can roar 'til the earth shakes." U2 also became known for their star-studded aftershow parties, attended by the likes of Jack Nicholson, Faye Dunaway, Harry Dean Stanton, and the warring couple Sean Penn and Madonna. Before long, Bono became infatuated with the Material Girl and confided to an aide that she had a starring role in many of his erotic dreams.

Their faces already splashed across the cover of every major music publication, U2 then rose above the strata of pop stardom to some even more revered atmosphere by becoming only the fourth band ever to appear on the cover of *Time* magazine, after The Beatles, The Band, and The Who. Full of admiration, critic Jay Cocks described the group as "citizens of some alternative time frame spliced from the idealism of the '60s and the musical free-for-all of the late '70s. Their songs have the phantom soul of The Band, the Celtic wonderment of their compatriot Van Morrison, and some of the assertiveness of punk, refined into lyrical morality plays." He added: "They are about spiritual search, and conscience and commitment, and it follows that some of the band's most memorable performances—and, not incidentally, the ones that have helped U2 break through to an even wider audience—have been in the service of a good cause, at Live Aid or during last summer's tour for Amnesty International. This is not, then, just a band for partying down." Perhaps the most revealing comment in the *Time* profile came from Edge, who implied that the intensity of the U2 phenomenon was having a detrimental effect on his mental well-being. "My life revolves around the music, the keyboard," he said. "My family should make a difference, but I am not able to spend enough time with them."

Under the glare of the spotlight, Bono was becoming increasingly paranoid about the band's image—that they appeared bland, disjointed, and uncool. He turned to Lola Cashman, a highly sought-after London fashion stylist, to help him perfect a look and style for them that embodied the sexy, rugged frontiersmen of Western fiction (something he had been working on solo, with mixed results, for the last couple of years). "Bono knew in America, more so than anywhere else at that time, you also had to look good," says Cashman. "People want to be tantalized, they want all their senses to be indulged. So it would matter visually, aesthetically, what you looked like. And when you're creating someone's image, it's not necessarily just the clothes you put on them, it's teaching someone a certain attitude. He was really intrigued by it all." Up until that point, Cashman had shown little interest in leaving her beloved fashion industry behind to join the rock-and-roll circus, but Bono piqued her curiosity. "Bono won me over, basically. He arranged to meet me in Dublin and we had an instant rapport. He was so charming and persuasive that I thought, 'Hey, maybe this could be fun after all!' I knew I could make them look so fucking hot and I loved hard work and the fact that I was going to get my teeth into such a big project."

Bono's enthusiasm was such that he personally negotiated the terms of Cashman's contract (including a large salary and no outside interference) without consulting the other members of the band or McGuinness and Principle Management, which put her in a very awkward position. Says Cashman: "Ellen Darst, who was in charge of hiring and firing [at Principle and U2's holding company, Not Us Ltd.], resented the fact that I was brought in without her consent, and we had a huge row during our first meeting where she basically tried to assert her authority over me and told me in a quite offensive manner that I would have to take a pay cut if I wanted to keep my job. I told her where she could shove it, reminding her that I was happy to return to the fashion industry. She was obviously under a lot of pressure to keep U2 happy because she quickly apologized and started to backtrack. Of course, that didn't last long. As far as she and Principle were concerned, I was an 'outsider.' I had no idea about corporate politics, and boy did it come back to bite me in the arse."

During the image-making process, Bono confided to Cashman that he was "absolutely petrified" about what people would think of the band if they knew they were making lots of money, and encouraged her to perpetuate the myth that U2 was the people's band. Even the clothes she bought for the band, which were mostly expensive, well-made designer labels, she would then configure to give the impression U2 was just like their fans.

Naturally, given their day-to-day proximity to one another, Bono and Cashman grew close, to the point where U2 management expressed concern about the nature of their relationship. "Bono was very much in the zone before going on stage," recalls Cashman. "He never talked to anyone and the only person around him was me. It was almost like, 'C'mon, put your foot in this, put your foot in that.' I mean, he does zone out. I think one of the reasons we got on so well was because I could read his moods, read where he was at, and I knew when to talk and when not to. I knew how to meet his needs, basically. But that's all part of my job. My job was like you had gone into service; you worked morning, noon, and night. He later admitted he became codependent on me. That wasn't my doing, it was all him. But it created me to be a bigger threat and caused all the jealousy and backstabbing."

The tension bubbled up in New England, where Darst and McGuinness accused Cashman of being infatuated with Bono after he was discovered asleep in her hotel room in Boston following a night of heavy drinking on his part. Cashman denied the charge, which she calls "ludicrous." "All I was interested in was doing a brilliant job," she says. "Ellen was clearly worried that the proximity of my job and creative input were undermining her own authority. 'Do you really think you can take us all on?' she asked me in a rather chilling tone with McGuinness at her side. The whole thing deeply upset me and when I informed Bono of the treatment I received from Ellen and Principle on a regular basis, he kind of shrugged his shoulders and said he wasn't the least bit surprised. I just had to get on with it. [But] I do know he later told his management that he respected my honesty and the fact that I was the first person in a very long time who wasn't afraid of the band professionally."

Cashman viewed Bono as a compelling contradiction; he was often very humorous, but also incredibly intense, and he obsessed about every detail, no matter how small or trivial it appeared on the surface, in his relentless pursuit of perfection. "I will say this about Bono: you do feel like you're in the presence of someone very gifted. He definitely has that aura about him. I kind of had him down as a poet warrior and I wanted to dress him in a way to portray that. The clothes were just an enhancement of who he is, which is a very powerful individual with these words and this magnetism." But there was also, in Cashman's view, an unhealthy amount of anxiety and self-loathing attached to Bono's obsessive behavior. As the U.S. tour progressed, he became more and more depressed about his appearance, especially his fluctuating weight, which was caused by his heavy drinking. He was so desperate he eventually asked Cashman to inquire about a fitness instructor and liposuction on his behalf. "He had to be constantly reassured," says Cashman, who chronicled her experience in *Inside the Zoo with U2*. "He was very childlike in that way."

Bono was desperate for the others to take an active interest in how they looked, particularly Adam, whose bookish appearance really concerned him. He urged Cashman to forge a relationship with them without being too obvious until they felt comfortable consulting her. "You catch more flies with honey," he told the stylist. But it took a lot of work. At one point Larry, the most masculine and resistant of the four, accused her of trying to make him look like "a fucking nancy boy" when she bought him a pair of black leather chaps after learning he was a motorbike enthusiast. "This was around the time Boy George had come out and said he had a huge crush on him," laughs Cashman, "so he was obviously feeling vulnerable. I can remember Adam teasing him about it and Larry storming out of the room, slamming the door behind him, in a fit of temper."

As Cashman's relationship with the rest of the band developed over time, certain members saw it as an opportunity to get things off their chest and ask for advice about U2 and life in general, in the midst of their empire of secrets and whispers. "I became a bit like a part-time counselor," says Cashman. "But because the whole U2 setup was so hush-hush, with the band members keeping so many secrets from each other, I was then sworn to secrecy. It almost got to the point where I was afraid to speak lest I let slip some secret." However, recognizing America is a predominantly Christian country, U2 made it quite clear to Cashman and each other that it was in their best interest to preserve, and even augment, their image as altogether virtuous, God-fearing men despite indulging in hedonistic lifestyles, with backstage Bible-reading now being a thing of the past. "They wanted to give an image that they were Jesus lovers. We thought that'd be good. That was all part of an image, creating an image. Everything was absolutely contrived: their looks, their image. I mean, the job that I do obviously is what is said on the package. I'm not saying they weren't religious, but not like it was made out to be. They were more relaxed, shall we say, by the time I went to work with them."

None more so than Adam, who indulged the most. "He was really out there," remembers Cashman. "He and Paul McGuinness were absolute bosom buddies. They partied hard and did more wild stuff than everyone else, and the rest of the band used to get very worried about their antics, that it would be exposed. In many ways, Adam was the odd one out. When he wasn't around Paul he cut a very lonely figure. He didn't have much in common with the other band members and spent very little time with them offstage. He would carry around in his jacket pockets a pair of nasty threadbare socks from his childhood as a kind of security blanket. He wouldn't go anywhere without them. It was so bizarre.

"I never felt completely at ease around Adam," she adds. "He had no real personality. He was a mystery, and I don't think he himself even knew who he was."

From day one U2 had been quite transparent about the fact that they wanted to be the biggest band in the world, adored by fans and critics alike. It was as if Bono in particular had spent his whole life preparing for it. And yet, fame and success appeared to knock them against the ropes like a surprise left hook and none of them knew how to handle it. Between May and August, the Joshua Tree Tour roared through Europe, where it graduated to huge football stadiums, during which time the backstage area was one of fear and insecurity. It took Bono hours to come back down after a performance, after which he would invariably fall into long periods of depression. He'd sit alone with his notepad of lyrics and concepts, practically daring anyone to approach him. Bono and Larry were not seeing eye to eye at all during this period, and the singer was apt to take out his frustrations on nearby doors, almost ripping them off their hinges. In August, he was included in *Playboy* magazine's list of the "10 Sexiest Men in America," but that did little to alleviate his concerns regarding his physical appearance. At one point, he told Cashman that he was "totally freaked out and uncomfortable" about his ballooning weight. Desperate, he began to starve himself in a bid to shed the pounds. "I was genuinely concerned about Bono's health," says Cashman. "I would catch him vomiting before going on stage and when I'd gently confront him about it he'd brush it off saying it was only a hangover. But I knew he'd been fasting. He was really sensitive about it."

Edge, too, was a sensitive soul. He believed that the pressures of fame and his marital problems were the cause of his hair loss, which he hid under a variety of hats and bandanas. "He was so down [about his baldness] he felt it hard work to walk on stage and pretend to be having such a great time," recalls Cashman. Edge eventually asked the stylist to make an appointment for him with a hair specialist in London, which she did, but he backed out at the last minute because he was worried the press would find out.

These were strange days for U2 all right. They appeared as tight a unit as ever on stage, yet in truth they scarcely exchanged a "hello" between shows, and when they did they'd only start bickering over the most trivial of things, such as Bono accusing Larry of attempting to steal his identity by wearing the same brand of aftershave as him. Nevertheless, the band somehow always managed to put their differences aside long enough to get the job done, thanks in part to their pre-gig ritual. Each night, two minutes before showtime, they would huddle together and exchange words of encouragement. It was almost robotic in manner, but it worked, putting them in the right frame of mind to go out and deliver the kind of high-energy intensity that left their fans breathless. "I'm not one for hero worship," says Cashman, "but there were times when I stood by the side of the stage with tears rolling down my eyes, because to hear that much adulation given to someone was electrifying. You didn't know where the tears came from. It was overwhelming."

▪

Looking to capitalize on the interest surrounding U2, McGuinness put pressure on them to not only return to the States for a huge arena/ stadium tour in September, but also to document it on film, with a full worldwide cinema release in mind. The mood got extremely desperate. "You have to understand, they were physically and mentally exhausted and the public scrutiny they were under was so intense," explains Cashman. "They'd simply had enough and wanted to go home. But McGuinness and his accountants convinced them it was the right thing to do financially, and the boys never could resist the lure of more money." According to another source, U2 began to use and structure their operations around The Rolling Stones' profit-maximizing business model.

"Bono didn't lick it off a stone; he licked it off Mick Jagger," says the source. "Jagger was the exemplar."

U2 was a fast-expanding conglomerate, employing accountants, lawyers, bankers, publicists, and around sixty tour personnel. Their financial performance was shrouded in utmost secrecy, although often the topic of discussion between crew members as they saw sound checks take a backseat to never-ending business meetings (mockingly referred to as "money checks"). But unlike The Stones, U2 cared deeply about what the outside world thought of them, which was what prevented them from accepting tour sponsorship, having concluded that such a close and visible association with a particular product always introduced the risk of negative publicity or controversy. They knew exactly what the market wanted from them, and how to exploit it without tainting their image. "You try and brand the artist in the way that U2 are branded—the most brilliant corporate branding I have ever seen, without anyone ever thinking that they were being corporately got," Keith Negus writes in *Producing Pop: Culture and Conflict in the Popular Music Industry*. "You never saw a picture of U2 if it wasn't in front of the Joshua tree. Bono was out there. . . . He was an okay kind of guy because he was saying the right things. . . . Brilliant piece of marketing."

Around that same time, U2 and McGuinness were presented with another remarkable business opportunity, the likes of which perhaps not even Jagger and his band would have exploited, when Chris Blackwell notified them that Island Records were unable to cough up the £10 million owed to them in back royalties, after he had continued to squander the company's profits in the film industry. "It was a situation where he [Blackwell] was working on five films at one time and they were all cross-collateralized," explains Lou Maglia. "If one went bust, they all went bust."

Marc Marot elaborates: "In Island's first year as a film distributor and film production company we won three awards at the 1985 Oscars, but the trouble is, is that gave a false confidence to everybody. Everybody forgot that the films were what were termed 'negative pickups,' where they were almost completely finished and just needed a bit of deficit financing to get them on the road—Island hadn't actually commissioned them, made them, and then had them become successes. So on the back of two things: one, the first year of fantastic trading and three Oscars, and secondly, the massive foreign income that was coming in from U2's *Joshua Tree,* Island started making its own pictures and in effect we used U2's royalties to fund them. And that's what got Island into trouble—when it came to being able to pay the royalties, we weren't able to do it because the money had been spent elsewhere."

U2 and McGuinness were initially shell-shocked by Blackwell's announcement. McGuinness went to Frank Barsalona in rag order and confessed, "I don't know what to do. We're fucked!" As in past years, Barsalona provided him with more than just a shoulder to cry on. Applying his business acumen, the booking agent/mentor suggested to McGuinness that U2 enter into a new agreement with Blackwell whereby they forgo their royalties for *The Joshua Tree,* which at that stage had shifted 7 million copies worldwide, in exchange for a 10 percent equity stake in Island, including all the subdivisions, with the understanding that Blackwell would sell the company. "That was Barsalona's idea," reveals a source. "It wouldn't have happened otherwise if Frank hadn't educated Paul." And it proved a masterstroke. In 1989, Blackwell sold Island to the Dutch-owned music giant PolyGram Records, for which U2 received an estimated £25 million—a sum significantly greater than the value of the unpaid royalties.

■

The final North American leg of the Joshua Tree Tour coincided with the publication of Irish sportswriter and McGuinness chum Eamon Dunphy's authorized U2 biography *Unforgettable Fire—The Story of U2.* The book received quite favorable reviews, but critics close to the group pounced on a number of embarrassing inaccuracies, such as Dunphy's claim that British pop punks The Buzzcocks were a local Dublin band. And despite its hagiographical tone, the ultra-secretive U2 didn't appreciate Dunphy's prying into their family album and religious beliefs. In fact, while researching his subjects, Dunphy had numerous run-ins with Bono, whom he came to view as a control freak and cold-blooded careerist infatuated with the world of celebrity. In the press, Dunphy called the front man a "pompous git" and a "bigot" whose only redeeming quality was Ali, and referred to the U2 setup as a "very hierarchical world which reeks of the old 'lord of the manor' thing." Bono, meanwhile, called Dunphy "rat poison." It was a vicious falling-out, and yet, oddly enough, Dunphy and McGuinness remained good friends throughout.

When it came to choosing a director for their self-financed $5 million rockumentary *Rattle and Hum*, U2 opted to play it relatively safe and hired Phil Joanou, a graduate of the prestigious University of Southern California film school whose directing credits included two episodes of Steven Spielberg's *Amazing Stories* and the $6 million high school comedy *Three O'Clock High*. The twenty-six-year-old Joanou also happened to be a massive U2 fan and wanted nothing more than to portray them in a positive, almost mythological light. During filming, "E.T.," as he was affectionately nicknamed by the band, captured his four idols paying their respects to Elvis Presley at his grave at Graceland; recording the euphoric Billie Holiday tribute "Angel of Harlem" at Sun Studios in Memphis with The Memphis Horns, considered the soul of the unmistakable Stax sound of the '60s and '70s, while "Cowboy" Jack Clement looked on approvingly; performing "I Still Haven't Found What I'm Looking For" with The New Voices of Freedom gospel choir at their Harlem church; and rehearsing the redemptive jukebox stomper "When Love Comes to Town" in Fort Worth, Texas, with blues legend B.B. King, who was seen commending Bono for writing lyrics beyond his years.

Joanou's cameras were also rolling for U2's highly charged performance of "Sunday Bloody Sunday" in Denver on the day eleven people were killed by an IRA bomb at a Remembrance Day parade in Enniskillen, Northern Ireland. Pacing the stage like a man possessed, Bono raged: "I've had enough of Irish Americans who haven't been back to their country in twenty or thirty years who come up to me and talk about the resistance, the revolution back home; and the glory of the revolution, and the glory of dying for the revolution. Fuck the revolution!"

Joanou's decision to shoot much of *Rattle and Hum* in grainy black and white was intended to highlight the importance and weight of U2's message-rock music. He also avoided the cut-and-paste editing techniques employed in contemporary music videos and relied instead on Bono's flair for drama in an attempt to create a greater sense of authenticity and an organic flow. It wasn't all plain sailing for the director, though. Given the camera-shy dispositions of Larry and Edge throughout the '80s, Joanou found making the movie was occasionally, he told the *Los Angeles Times,* "a bit like a big game hunt."

Truth be told, U2 was afraid of what Joanou would find. They worried constantly about him having access to their world, even though McGuinness assured them that they and Principle Management had the final say on what went into the film. And just as well. Bono later described the tour as one of the worst times of their musical life. He was drinking a lot and was on painkillers after falling into the lighting pit in a rain-soaked Washington, D.C., and dislocating his left shoulder, which only exacerbated his mood swings and made him even more unpredictable. Bono's obsession about his physical appearance also reached new heights. Upon learning from management that Bruce Springsteen was in attendance at their show at Philadelphia's JFK Stadium and had also agreed to join them on stage for a rendition of "Stand by Me," five-foot-seven Bono became agitated and pleaded with Cashman to make him look taller than the American rocker. "I thought, 'Fucking hell, I'm not a magician!' So I made some crack like, 'Well, look, you can wear my high heels,' and he thought it was a brilliant idea," recalls the stylist. "So there he was, hanging out with Springsteen at the aftershow party wearing my red high heels and a long pair of trousers to hide the fact. He would do this a few more times with certain famous people until I commissioned John Moore [a London shoe designer] to make all his footwear with raised insoles and wedges. You know, truth's stranger than fiction. If only people really knew."

U2's clandestine world had an element of real darkness. Crew members could often be heard boasting about receiving sexual favors from female fans in return for promising them entry to the backstage area. Bono, meanwhile, alluded to U2's own hedonistic lifestyle in a 1988 *Hot Press* interview: "Members can get a bit out of control on a tour and forget where they've come from and who they've left behind. You can live out any side to your character, and there are many sides to all of our characters. . . ." Speaking to *Rolling Stone* in October 1987, he said, "If you could see into the dressing rooms and the offices of a lot of bands in our position, you would see the real abuse of power. Like making a promoter crawl because you are paying his wages; like making the road crew wait for four hours because you are late for a sound check; like the sexual abuse of people who are turned on by your music. I don't know whether I am guilty of all of those. Maybe I am. But that is the type of power I worry about in rock and roll." Furthermore, Adam told *Hot Press*: "It's great if people get comfort from what we do. Great. What more could you ask from a pair of shoes? But that's what we do. It's not what we are. I mean we're pretty crazy. The Bono I know is a lot crazier than the Bono people see on stage or whatever. We all have our own demons and his ones are bigger than everyone else's."

Following the arrival of Joanou and his film crew, the U2 members felt compelled to call a cease-fire and close ranks. During this period, the others consulted Bono at almost every opportunity, even Larry. But that is not to say the singer and drummer were suddenly the best of friends, or that all childish behavior was a thing of the past. In Memphis, for example, Bono and Larry came to blows post-gig after the latter saw Bono slipping on a pair of gray underpants identical to his own after taking a shower. Larry, who was drying himself off with a towel, was apoplectic and demanded Cashman explain to him why Bono was wearing the same style of underwear as him. Bono chuckled and replied that the underpants were "not exclusive" to Larry, a line the drummer himself often used during their routine quarrels over fashion items, such as the aforementioned aftershave. Larry paused, as if to fully digest Bono's gibe, and then charged at him like a bull at a rodeo, knocking him to the stone floor of the dressing room. Bono immediately sprang to his feet and gave as good as he got before Edge and Adam, also naked, burst out of the shower room and pulled them apart. "All hell broke loose," says Cashman. "I couldn't believe it. There I was watching two naked grown men fistfight over a pair of knickers."

The Dublin and New York branches of Principle Management, meanwhile, squabbled among themselves for access to the band and creative and corporate influence, splitting into groups of self-interest. Often depicted as a large family rather than a business, the U2 empire was in fact engaged in a toxic power struggle. "I'd come from a fashion background and that's quite bitchy, but nothing could have prepared me for life on the road with U2," says Cashman. "It was like *I, Claudius* and the courts of the Caesars where they're all trying to overthrow each other. It was so juvenile, the behavior. I'd never experienced anything like it."

Yet still, the U2 machine rolled on. On November 11, just weeks after the stock market crash of 1987, the band threw a free outdoor concert at the Embarcadero Center in the heart of San Francisco's financial district and jokingly dedicated it to the endangered power-suit-wearing stock traders—many of whom, according to Lou Maglia, had sent their secretaries down to the nearest Tower Records store when *The Joshua Tree* was first released and snapped up around a dozen copies of it each. Wall Street loved U2, and U2 loved them right back. "Seeing that the business sector has been having such big problems, we decided to do a 'Save the Yuppie' concert," Bono quipped. "That's why I'm wearing this hat. We'll be passing it around later. We've already got one man who donated a three-piece suit and a briefcase."

During "Pride," Bono climbed into the interior of the much-maligned Vaillancourt Fountain, which the renowned architecture critic Allan Temko once described as something "deposited by a concrete dog with square intestines," and spray-painted the words, "Stop the Traffic, Rock and Roll," before twenty thousand cheering fans. The following morning, San Francisco Mayor Dianne Feinstein, in the midst of a major crackdown on graffitists wreaking havoc across the city, released a statement condemning the act. "I am very disappointed that a rock star who is supposed to be a role model for young people chose to vandalize the work of another artist," she told reporters. Bono faced a misdemeanor charge for defacing public property. Meanwhile, back home, Bob Hewson was furious, and told the Irish papers that his youngest son "deserves anything he gets convicted of."

Bono escaped punishment after he wrote an apology to local city officials and U2's promoter Bill Graham promised to pay for the cleanup. But the singer's admission of guilt was perhaps not entirely genuine. Three nights later, when U2 performed the first of two gigs in Oakland, Bono invited the fountain's designer, Armand Vaillancourt, on stage to graffiti their stage backdrop as a public show of support. Vaillancourt obliged him, and wrote: "Stop the Madness!" During the second night, Bono told fans that Mayor Feinstein should know the difference between "an act of vandalism and graffiti art."

In December, U2 returned to Tempe, Arizona, to shoot concert footage in color for *Rattle and Hum*. Tickets for the two shows at the sixty-thousand-seat Sun Devil Stadium were priced at five dollars to ensure a good turnout, as well as to compensate for Joanou's ten cameras and eighty crew members blocking fans' view of the action on stage. The first night of filming was dubbed an "utter fucking disaster" by the director, with Bono focusing all of his attention on the tepid audience rather than the cameras. For weeks, the front man had been working methodically on adapting his stage presence to a stadium crowd. It was, he said, about projecting a sense of power and danger, as well as approachability that captivated everyone in attendance and pulled them in. Brought intimacy to stadium rock. To that end, he had a video monitor installed for Cashman so that she could help him art direct the show. "We'd look at it in the morning and everything would get analyzed: his movement on stage, how the clothes looked in a particular lighting, etc.," recalls Cashman. "There's nothing spontaneous about Bono or U2. Even with his outburst [about the Enniskillen bombing] he had a mind to think, 'Look, I'm going to say something that might be a bit on the edge and that'll get a big reaction.' Then it'll sell records, then it'll make money. He's the master of spin."

To Joanou's relief, Bono agreed to limit his stage movement on the second night, and the last show of the Joshua Tree Tour was captured on celluloid for posterity. "I am so hyped and so pumped," the director said amidst the sound of laughter and clinking glasses at the end of tour party, "because it was a great show and we nailed it visually."

"We had problems with this movie, but tonight I think we did it right," Bono added.

Little did either of them know that *Rattle and Hum* would almost be their undoing.

11

Standing on the Shoulders of Giants

U2 and Phil Joanou spent the first couple of months of 1988 to-ing and fro-ing between Dublin and Los Angeles, working on the final stages of *Rattle and Hum*. They had compiled over 160 hours' worth of raw footage, and now came the unenviable task of editing it down to a ninety-five-minute film suitable for theatrical release. Just to keep things interesting, the band also began writing new songs for a mooted part-live, part-studio double-album soundtrack at Dublin's STS Studios and L.A.'s A&M Studios with superproducer Jimmy Iovine, who oversaw the postproduction of their live mini LP *Under a Blood Red Sky* in 1983. They delved even further into American roots and '60s pop, and vowed to put a modern spin on the music and culture they had become so enamored with over the past couple of years.

In February, U2 was afforded the opportunity to revel in the full backslapping tradition of awards season when they picked up the gong for Best International Group at the Brit Awards. Three weeks later, they stole the show at the Thirtieth Annual Grammy Awards, taking home two gongs: Best Rock Performance by a Duo or Group with Vocal for

"I Still Haven't Found What I'm Looking For" and Album of the Year for *The Joshua Tree,* beating awards heavyweights Michael Jackson, Prince, and the trio of Emmylou Harris, Dolly Parton, and Linda Ronstadt. "It really is hard carrying the weight of the world on your shoulders," Bono quipped on stage during his acceptance speech, before mentioning his political concerns over South Africa; backstage, he insisted: "We don't see this as a peak for U2. It's just a beginning." Edge, for his part, pulled out a list as he accepted the first award, and thanked such diverse personal heroes as Martin Luther King, Jr., Amnesty International, Frank Barsalona, Batman and Robin (a.k.a. Brian Eno and Daniel Lanois), and Pee-wee Herman.

In May, U2 moved their music gear into Dublin's Point Depot—which was then a neglected train yard, before being renovated into a concert hall later that year—to shoot additional footage for *Rattle and Hum.* Also on hand was the band's photographer Colm Henry, who noted that they seemed far more guarded in their interactions with non-full-time U2 employees than in previous years. "There were a lot of people around them at this stage, a lot of minders," recalls Henry. "Each of the guys had a roadie and a runner, and the presence of these guys kept people at a distance from 'their' guy—a bit like bodyguards. So they were no longer approachable. They still liked to hang out and give the impression that they were, but this was not the case. I remember at that time Bono still had a kind of gentleness to him which he doesn't seem to have anymore. He has now become such a good actor at playing Bono that the regular guy Bono is hardly detectable."

Creatively, U2 was in fine form, and Joanou filmed the foursome running through two freshly baked tracks. The first, "Desire," which Bono would later concede was about his own "lust for success," mimicked the beat of The Stooges' "1969," itself a facsimile of the Bo Diddley beat. The second, "Van Diemen's Land," was a sparse folk ballad written and performed by Edge and dedicated to the nineteenth-century Irish-born poet and journalist John Boyle O'Reilly, who was deported to the penal colony of Western Australia for his role in Fenian resistance to the British rule of his homeland, before boldly making his escape on an

American whaler and becoming a pillar of the Boston Irish-American community.

"That was a good experience working at the Point," recalls engineer Dave Meegan, who recorded the film's audio in a truck parked on the ground floor, directly below the fake tape machine seen on screen. "Going over I thought, 'Oh no, because they're the biggest band in the world they're going to be all relaxed and they won't be taking it all so seriously.' But it was quite the opposite. I think that's what makes them great; no matter how big they are, they don't get complacent. They still treat it like their first album and they still have that insecurity which is what forces them to do good things."

U2 returned to Los Angeles to wrap up recording and postproduction work on *Rattle and Hum*. Edge and Aislinn rented a property in the millionaires' playground of Beverly Hills, and the others shared a gated compound in the equally affluent Bel Air. With the exception of the lead guitarist, who devoted pretty much every waking hour to the project as a way to escape the reality of his crumbling marriage, the band also used it as an opportunity to let their hair down after the grand madness of the Joshua Tree Tour. Larry rode the streets of L.A. on his motorcycle, while Adam and Bono explored the seedier side of the City of Angels and drank with abandon. Adam gained entry to Hugh Hefner's Playboy Mansion via Jimmy Iovine's wife Vicky, where he rubbed shoulders with Hollywood legend Tony Curtis and Motown Records founder Berry Gordy. Bono often frequented LSD guru Timothy Leary's favorite paparazzi-free hangout The Flaming Colossus, which at the time was described by the *Los Angeles Times* as "a noisy clubhouse for black-clad fashion models" and appeared to base its concept around "packaging Third World culture for European consumption." He enjoyed the club's nightly entertainment, including belly dancers, fire-eaters, and young black men, naked but for billowing pantaloons, banging on African instruments, although given the wealthy, all-white context the latter act was said to carry the whiff of a minstrel show. Amid the L.A. debauchery, Bono, in the words of the late *Rattle and Hum* sound engineer Bob Vogt, "played Mr. Greenpeace, but proved he would do your girlfriend behind your back in a heartbeat, if he got the chance." U2's world was no longer black and white, but shades of gray.

Work on the soundtrack dragged on until August, partly as a result of Bono's preoccupation with L.A.'s nightlife. Three other studio tracks were finished during this period: the curiously lustful, gospel-tinged rocker "Hawkmoon 269," featuring Bob Dylan on Hammond organ, and the title of which alluded to both the 1985 book *Hawk Moon* by Sam Shepard and the number of times the song was mixed by engineers; the industrial-edged, Albert Goldman-hating "God Part II," a loose sequel of sorts to John Lennon's "God" and U2's own "Elvis Presley and America," as well as being a complete anomaly on an otherwise roots-focused project; and the plaintive country ballad "Love Rescue Me," which Bono had cowritten with Dylan during the dizzying highs and gut-wrenching lows of the Joshua Tree Tour. The U2 front man had got so drunk one night that he had crawled into the spare bed in Edge's L.A. quarters and passed out. There, a song came to him in his dreams, about a drifter/false prophet who was worshipped by lost souls despite crying out for some salvation himself, and Dylan was the voice of this damaged protagonist. The next morning Bono, nursing the hangover from hell, drove out to Dylan's Shangri-La Ranch in Malibu to ask him if the song belonged to him. Dylan said it didn't, but they could work on it together, and the two of them sat down and brought Bono's whiskey-fueled dream to life. Dylan actually recorded a lead vocal track, but later requested that it be removed because of his involvement at the time with the supergroup Traveling Wilburys.

U2 also approached the eccentric songwriter/arranger/producer Van Dyke Parks to frame "All I Want Is You," written at the Point Depot between film takes, with a string section in order to heighten the emotional resonance of the song. Parks agreed, and returned two days later with a haunting string arrangement, complete with a climax remarkably similar to Larry Fallon's string coda on Van Morrison's "Astral Weeks."

The *Rattle and Hum* soundtrack was completed in the early hours of August 31, after which the studio crew threw a playback party and raided Bono's secret stash of Cabernet. "Life wasn't to [sic] grand if Jimmy [Iovine] didn't get that applesauce," said Vogt.

Three weeks later, U2 released "Desire" as the lead single from *Rattle and Hum,* earning them their first number-one hit in the UK, while in the United States it peaked at number three. The much-anticipated double album—marketed as a tribute to the American artists that had influenced U2—followed on October 10, and the band, sans one blond-haired drummer, delighted their die-hard Irish fans by making an unannounced appearance at its midnight launch at Dublin's HMV store.

But impressing the international music press proved a much more difficult task. The *Rattle and Hum* soundtrack was met with derision by most critics, who interpreted it as an arrogant attempt by the band to, in the words of Jon Pareles of *The New York Times,* "grab every mantle in the Rock-and-Roll Hall of Fame." In a scathing review entitled "When Self-importance Interferes With the Music," Pareles concluded that "Each attempt is embarrassing in a different way.... What comes across in song after song is sincere egomania." *Rolling Stone* thought it was "calculated in its supposed spontaneity," and noted that it "ably demonstrates U2's force but devotes too little attention to the band's vision." And in the *Village Voice,* Tom Carson said: "By almost any rock-and-roll fan's standards, U2's *Rattle and Hum* is an awful record. But the chasm between what it thinks it is and the half-baked, overweening reality doesn't sound attributable to pretension so much as to monumental know-nothingism." Carson, never one to hold back, also referred to the band as "the priggish, thin-skinned egoist and the three dullards."

There was of course the odd notable exception. U2's two most reliable cheerleaders, Robert Hilburn of the *Los Angeles Times* and Bill Graham of *Hot Press,* both waxed lyrical about *Rattle and Hum*'s worth. Hilburn called it a "frequently remarkable album—a work that not only lives up to the standards of the Grammy-winning *The Joshua Tree,* but also places U2 more convincingly than ever among rock's all-time greatest groups." Graham, for his part, said it was "the most ambitious record U2 have yet released." *NME*'s Stuart Baillie also participated in their mini love-in by giving the album a rating of eight out of ten, although it later emerged that his glowing review was in fact an eleventh-hour replacement for Mark Sinker's original critique of four out of ten—in which Sinker dubbed *Rattle and Hum* "the worst album by a major band in years"—after market research carried out by the magazine concluded that a U2 cover story increased circulation by thirty thousand copies. Sinker quit the magazine in protest.

But in the end, the negative reviews appeared to have little, if any, impact on the commercial performance of *Rattle and Hum*. For the time being at least, U2 remained critic-proof, and the double album went to number one in most territories, shifting almost 3 million copies in the first month alone. Within time, *Rattle and Hum* sold 14 million copies worldwide.

In late October, U2 hit the promotional trail for the film in style, having cut a multimillion-dollar distribution deal with the Hollywood studio Paramount Pictures. As part of an aggressive marketing strategy, they threw red carpet benefit premieres in Dublin, London, Madrid, New York, and Los Angeles, where they posed for cameras and signed autographs for adoring fans. With the exception of the UK premiere, they also performed a short acoustic set outside each venue. "We did four countries in as many days," recalls Lou Maglia, "and to be in Dublin especially and go through the streets in limos and see the crowds of people on both sides and the flashbulbs—that was probably the most exciting night of my life."

But neither Paramount's money nor U2's dedicated followers could prevent *Rattle and Hum* from being an expensive box office flop. The rockumentary's theatrical run in North America was cut short after it made just $8.4 million in three weeks, despite a big advertising push and opening in over fourteen hundred cinemas. Critically, too, it suffered the same fate as the soundtrack. Only now the gloves were well and truly off. Iain Johnstone of *The Sunday Times* called it "possibly the worst rock documentary ever made," adding: "U2 emerge as the most bland, uninspiring, and uninteresting quartet of musicians assembled since somebody shook the Monkees out of their plaster casts." Hal Hinson of *The Washington Post* wrote it off as "an exercise in rock 'n' roll hagiography," and seemingly gained pleasure from ridiculing Bono's outward display of vanity. "Has there ever been an entertainment figure more in love with his upper arms than Bono?" Hinson pondered.

Many of the charges leveled against the band related to their live cover version of The Beatles' "Helter Skelter." Bono introduced the opening track by saying, "This is a song Charles Manson stole from The Beatles. We're stealing it back," which critics immediately read as U2 depicting themselves as the true heirs to the Fab Four. And Bono's comments in a *Rolling Stone* interview did little to dispel this notion. "Let's get down to The Beatles here," he said, clearly agitated. "We're not saying we're a better band than The Beatles. But we are more of a band than The Beatles. We are. There's four of us—a street gang, essentially, who drew no lines. Not Lennon and McCartney songwriting and Ringo's the drummer. When we walk onstage, it is the band that is the real work of art, the four of us."

But perhaps the most valid common criticism concerning the film was that it wasn't revealing enough, as there was very little focus on any of the band members or what it was like to be a part of the world's biggest rock-and-roll group. For many, the U2-approved final cut of *Rattle and Hum* only posed more questions. "We never get close to U2 at all, never find out anything about them," wrote Andy Gill in *The Independent*. "[I]n their urge to avoid looking daft, they have re-edited their reality to the point of solemnity."

The accompanying onslaught of official *Rattle and Hum* merchandise, including books, T-shirts, mugs, and keyrings, as well as the omnipresent black-and-white billboards featuring U2 at their most po-faced and airbrushed, also proved too much to bear for their growing number of detractors. The band were seen as humorless, narcissistic opportunists hell-bent on elevating themselves to the pantheon of rock gods. Jokes of egomania running amok began to make the rounds in offices, college dorms, and bars. One particular favorite: "This guy dies and goes to Heaven, and St. Peter takes him to see a band made up of dead rock stars. The guy is shocked when he sees Bono running around the stage waving a white flag. "I didn't know Bono was dead!" he says, scratching his head. "He's not," St. Peter replies. "That's God. He just thinks he's Bono!"

It was a humiliating experience for yesterday's heroes.

As further salt rubbed into U2's wounds, Bono's heavily scripted anti-IRA outburst featured in the film was thought to have earned him a brief spot on the organization's hit list, driving him into a state of absolute fear and paranoia, according to an aide. Of course, this was not the first nor the last time Bono feared for his own life. He later claimed that a gun-toting racist offended by U2's public support of the Mecham Watchdog Committee at the beginning of the Joshua Tree Tour had threatened to shoot him if the band refused to drop "Pride" from their set list when they returned to Arizona in December 1987. "Some people want to kill the singer," he recalled at the Rock and Roll Hall of Fame in 2005. "Some people are taken very seriously by the FBI, and they tell the singer he shouldn't play the gig, because tonight his life is at risk, and he must not go on stage. The singer laughs. You know, of course we're playing the gig, of course we go on stage. And I'm standing there, singing 'Pride (In the Name of Love),' and I've got to the third verse, and I close my eyes, and I know I'm excited about meeting my maker, but maybe not tonight—I don't really want to meet my maker tonight. I close my eyes, and when I look up, I see Adam Clayton standing in front of me, holding his bass like only Adam Clayton can hold his bass.... Adam Clayton would've taken a bullet for me—and I guess that's what it's like to be in a truly great rock-and-roll band." However, according to a piece in *The Arizona Republic* in 2010, "[n]either Tempe police nor Arizona State University police could find a report about the incident. The Phoenix office of the FBI also came up empty. Special Agent Manual Johnson, the FBI's spokesman, said he was at those shows as a fan but could not locate any report of a threat." Barry Fey, U2's promoter in Arizona at that time, also didn't receive any requests for security to be beefed up. "[Bono] never talked to me about that," Fey later told the author. "I know he got hurt when he fell through the pit, but I don't remember him getting threats."

But two years after that disputed incident, Bono received a very real, and very chilling, death threat from a disturbed Irish-American called Pat Harrison, who claimed that he had furnished the singer with over one hundred U2 songs—including everything on *The Joshua Tree*—and demanded songwriting credits and royalties. Harrison told *News of the World* in 1989 that "most of them I provided in two long letters in 1986. But the last eleven I handed to him personally in a plastic carrier bag when he was appearing at Tempe, Arizona, a year later." Harrison was believed to have set a date for revenge, adding: "If I took a gun and shot him, that would get everyone's attention."

▪

U2 spent much of what remained of the decade defending themselves against criticism, and not all of it was related to *Rattle and Hum*. The mercurial Irish singer-songwriter Sinead O'Connor emerged as perhaps their most vocal detractor during this period, accusing the band of being a mafia-like organization that secretly ran the Irish music scene. She took particular umbrage at revelations that McGuinness had a financial stake in *Hot Press*, having bailed out the magazine in return for shares, and viewed this as U2's attempt to dictate media content, all the while keeping up the façade of promoting equal opportunity through their label Mother Records, established ostensibly to nurture young talent and ensure a level playing field. U2 refused to take the comments lying down, and became embroiled in a public feud with O'Connor. "The people who listen to our records—they're not fooled by it," Adam seethed in *Hot Press*, pointing out that Bono had "pioneered" O'Connor, and Edge had used her on the soundtrack for *Captive*. "I don't know why she's doing it—but I don't think people believe it. It's stupid. It's immature. She'll learn."

Much of O'Connor's antagonism toward U2 could be traced to the fact that the group had dismissed her mentor, Fachtna O'Ceallaigh, from his position as general manager at Mother Records the previous year, after he had described their role as "precious and meddling" in a *Hot Press* interview. O'Ceallaigh was always a curious appointment, given that he despised U2 before he even got the job, based on what he says was Bono's eagerness to "enhance his own position in the perception of the public" by attaching himself to the likes of Live Aid and Nelson Mandela and at the same time know that, in the case of the latter, "the ANC went out and decapitated people, planted bombs, etc." He adds: "Bono could big up Mandela and end apartheid—and rightly so—but he couldn't say anything about what was going on a hundred miles up the road in his own country except to denigrate and call people—who were doing exactly the same thing—psychopaths. So I could never allow myself to offer any kind of respect to Bono in particular."

O'Ceallaigh accepted the offer to manage Mother Records in 1986 because he respected McGuinness and he bought into the altruistic concept of the label as originally presented to him. "The idea seemed to be that—and it seemed to happen in some cases, at least the legend about the Hot House Flowers—somebody within the four members of the group would come across something that intrigued them and eventually a decision would be taken that yes, this is the right thing to release through Mother," he says. "It was to be a one-off single which Mother would pay for the recording of. If the group wanted to record in a certain studio, that's where the recording would be done. Every effort would be made to put them together with their producer of choice as well. The record would then be released on Mother which was going through Island Records—so sales distribution, promotion, publicity, every aspect of it would be handled as a major label release would be handled. And then if EMI came along and wanted to sign the band, well then everybody would shake hands and say, 'That's great. Thanks for the lift up, Bono.' And Bono would say, 'Good luck, lads. Be on your way. You have our blessings,' and that would be it. So it was basically to give a leg up to new talent without any of the normal strings being attached to it, like, 'I paid for your demos therefore I own them and you can't use them unless I get a slice of the future earnings.' "

O'Ceallaigh was informed that Mother's record sleeves were to be "generic" with a label-specific design. But even though each sleeve basically looked the same—except for the name of the artist and occasionally the color—they still had to be approved by U2, whose decision-making process O'Ceallaigh likens to "walking through glue."

"You would present ideas to them for possible releases and chase the artwork and then there'd be torturous weeks of thinking and speculating and so forth, none of which I was involved in," he recalls. "I was an employee so I should have understood that, I suppose. But everything had to be, as it seems in all of their activities from day one, mulled over and examined from every possible angle to ensure that none of it was contrary to whatever they think they represent and would not in any way detract from what U2 is. It all seemed very nervous, very enclosed, and very controlled. So all of these things took forever and in the meantime you had this young group in Ireland somewhere going, 'What's happening with our record? What's the delay about?'

"And then eventually I came across this group from Glasgow called The Painted Word and got the material over to Dublin so that U2 could hear it and urged that they consider releasing it. I got the go-ahead and booked whatever studio it was in Scotland that the group wanted to record in and notified the U2 office in Dublin that this was happening, these were the costs. And then I got a phone call from Paul McGuinness asking me what was going on with The Painted Word thing and had any arrangement been made about acquiring the publishing of the material on the proposed record. He suggested that the record could not be done without the publishing rights being assigned to Mother, otherwise there would be no opportunity to recoup the recording costs. And I said, 'But I thought that was the whole point? That you have Mother Records to give relatively new young groups the chance to be seen and heard in the way they want to be, and allow them to be signed onward and upward and with you cheering from the sidelines? Now it seems that there are strings attached.' So there was a discussion, if you like, and I said, 'Okay, Paul. I'll tell you what. I'll give you the phone number of the group, right? You can ring them and tell them you want their publishing and explain to them how that reflects the altruism of this concept in the first place. Go ahead. Do it. Because I'm not fucking doing it.'"

McGuinness never called, and The Painted Word record came out on Mother. But as far as O'Ceallaigh was concerned, that was the turning point. "In my naïveté, I accepted what I was told from the word go, that there would be no strings attached to these releases. That was the attractive thing about it, besides the fact that they were going to pay me. But the parallel attraction was that something can happen for some young whippersnapper and they won't be screwed, that the music business is clean. So when I discovered that actually it wasn't clean or as clean as it had been presented, I didn't feel that I could honestly go to a group or hear something and jump up and down about it and go, 'This is perfect for Mother Records!' It kind of removed the purpose as far as I was concerned."

O'Ceallaigh had lost whatever enthusiasm he had working for Mother and in a move tantamount to job suicide, he went public with his abject hatred for U2 in *Hot Press*. Needless to say, his employers were not amused, and demonstrated as much when they ran into him at a taping of the BBC2 late-night music show *The Old Grey Whistle Test* in Belfast in March 1987. U2 was the headline act, while O'Ceallaigh was there with Sinead O'Connor, whom he represented in an advisory capacity. O'Ceallaigh recalls: "We went up to Belfast from London and Sinead did her sound check and everything seemed to be hunky-dory, and then there was a flurry of activity and everyone was going, 'U2 are here! U2 are here!' So U2 wandered in and I got perfunctory nods from Bono and Edge, and then Larry walked in the door and looked at me and said, 'What the fuck are you doing here?'—in other words, 'Get out of my space.' And I just ignored him and thought, 'Well, fuck you as well,' and went about my business with Sinead which subsequently developed into my managing her."

That was to be the last time O'Ceallaigh encountered U2 before the inevitable ax fell. He recalls: "I got a letter in June of that year from Anne-Louise Kelly saying, 'Paul and the boys have decided to end your employment. We really appreciate the work you've done.' I was fired, in other words. But I didn't give a shite anyway. I was excited about working with Sinead, excited about her energy. I was pissed off that I wasn't going to get paid in a practical way, but that was the sum total of my reaction."

In the months that followed, others joined O'Ceallaigh in voicing their frustration over U2's handling of Mother Records. Paul Byrne, a former member of In Tua Nua, for example, described the label and Bono as "wacky," and expressed his disappointment that the group's first single "Coming Thru" "sat there for three months when they [U2] realized there was no 'record label' to take it any further." Charlie Rafferty, then singer/bassist with the Real Wild West, was more blunt in his criticism of dealing with Bono in particular. "He promised the sun, the moon, and the stars," Rafferty fumed. "He made me feel spiritually enriched. He kept saying, 'I'll see if I can get this done and that done.' And I stopped him and said, 'Hang on a minute, you own the fucking company.'"

In an interview, again with *Hot Press,* Bono accused those criticizing U2 and Mother of seeking to "put us in the clichéd role of being Led Zeppelin and therefore casting themselves as The Clash and the Sex Pistols, without having a thimbleful of the talent that those two groups have." Eventually, he got tired of the responsibility of running the label, and handed over the reins of power to Adam.

■

Throughout this period, Bono remained almost bipolar in nature, according to observers. One day he was the extremely charismatic, passionate, and gregarious band leader, then the next he was the painfully depressed and agitated rock martyr reduced to grunts and curses under the seemingly unbearable weight of U2's own godhead myth. He remained a man of extremes and contradictions. "It's very . . . difficult at the moment," he said of being Bono in an interview with *Spin* magazine in January 1989. "I don't know. If I talk too long now I'll say something I'll regret. It's important that I keep things together, but it's not easy sometimes. Everything I say becomes some sort of statement, something of vast importance. I could go on stage, unzip my pants, and hang my dick out and people would think it was some statement about something."

But the troubled singer had cause for a double celebration on his twenty-ninth birthday when Ali gave birth to their daughter, Jordan (an Old Testament name, and the name Bono originally wanted to call their new Killiney mansion by the sea), at Dublin's exclusive Mount Carmel Hospital. Having previously joked that he had probably fathered a hundred children already, Bono described the arrival of his and Ali's first child together as the greatest experience of his life. "She's a truly beautiful baby, just like her beautiful mother," he told reporters camped outside the hospital. He also admitted that his was a "very selfish kind of lifestyle," and that he would need time to adjust to fatherhood. "The idea of looking after somebody else, this little girl, I haven't quite got used to it. It's a whole new thing for me. I think it'll turn my life upside down, but I think that's a good thing."

U2's "All I Want Is You" was released as a single in June, and Bono dedicated it to Ali. The romantic ballad failed to melt the hearts of an American market that had overdosed on U2 content in the past two years. But in the UK, it was a top-five hit, boosted by Meiert Avis's cinematic music video, which transformed the song into a poignant meditation on the anguish of unrequited love, as told from the perspective of a doomed circus dwarf besotted with a female trapeze artist. "Barry Devlin wrote the scenario," recalls Avis. "Pure genius, using the little man to personify the emotion. It's a strange video to watch now. It feels like it exists in its own space." The video—in which U2 made only a cameo appearance—was shot on Ostia Beach outside Rome using the very first Technocrane. It was a difficult production. "There were tears and fights and sleepless nights behind the scenes, everyone on the team had a very hard time of it," says Avis. "For me it was the most ambitious thing I had ever directed, and I was very scared. The stakes were high and there were a lot of power players circling the honeypot. Meanwhile, I have been set up with the task of making a black-and-white video with a dwarf and no band performance whatsoever. It was absolutely the right thing to do with this song, but it was a very difficult experience.

"After the shoot I blacked out in a bathroom screaming in a weird epileptic fit and woke up on the tile floor naked and shivering with no idea where I was. When I got back to Dublin and put the film up on the telecine I found there was major camera fault and more than half of the material was totally fucked up. The edit was heartbreaking, looking at all these magical shots and performances that I couldn't use because most of the film was fogged, scratched, and jumping around in the gate. No one except me will ever know what a great video this could have been. Fortunately what we were able to salvage from the wreckage just about works."

As for who or what dies at the end of the video, the director says: "People are still working it out on YouTube, twenty years later. Perhaps the little man only fantasizes that he climbs the ladder. For me it's a psychological allegory, not meant to be literal at all. That's what makes it universal. Hope and love die, and are reborn, a little wiser."

In August, Adam, still a bachelor at large, put another dent in U2's straitlaced image when he was arrested by two undercover policemen in a car park outside the Blue Light pub in Glencullen for possession of nineteen grams of marijuana and with intent to supply. But more importantly, it threw the band's live future into doubt. The twenty-nine-year-old was immediately released on $710 bail, and ordered to stand trial at Dundrum courthouse on September 1. The main event attracted widespread attention, and Adam arrived in a black chauffeur-driven Mercedes with Larry and McGuinness by his side. The U2 trio were ushered through the media scrum and into the courthouse without making any comment. There, standing in the middle of the courtroom, his hands clenched tightly in front of him like a naughty schoolboy, Adam listened closely as it was revealed that the supply charge was being dismissed, and he pleaded guilty to the lesser charge of possession. His solicitor, Garret Sheehan, referred to him as "a talented and successful musician," and said that he had "brought honor to the country and not inconsiderable employment." Sheehan asked for clemency, and stressed that a drug conviction would cause his client—who had gained Irish citizenship earlier that year—serious problems when applying for visas in Australia, Japan, and the United States.

The somewhat eccentric Judge Windle displayed little interest in rock-and-roll music, however, and reprimanded Adam for the "dreadful example" he was setting for the small children who looked up to him. Judge Windle was also "distressed" to learn that Adam had a previous conviction under the Road Traffic Act, but acknowledged that the drug offense was "on a very low scale of importance." He concluded that, under the Probation of Offenders Act, he was willing to drop the charge without conviction if Adam agreed to donate twenty-five thousand pounds to the Women's Aid Refuge Centre. Sheehan turned to McGuinness—who sat expressionless beside Larry throughout the trial—awaiting instruction. McGuinness paused for a moment, then nodded. Disaster averted, yet again. U2 could go on tour when they saw fit. "Nothing to say," McGuinness told the reporters as the trio emerged from the courthouse and jumped back into the Mercedes.

U2 saw out the '80s with the Lovetown Tour, which took in Australia, New Zealand, and Japan, but steered clear of the United States and much of Europe. The tour was an opportunity for them to make up for canceled dates on the Joshua Tree Tour, and also to invite B.B. King and his band to be their opening act. But the forty-seven-date trek proved to be one step too far for the Irish quartet. Bono endured various vocal problems as the result of bad technique and a throat virus he picked up in Australia, forcing more last-minute cancellations and rearrangements; Larry was just plain sick of being a "human jukebox," playing the same hits night after night, and complained that being in U2 was no longer fun; Adam was still trying to keep a low profile after the trial; and Edge was going through a huge identity crisis, which was reflected in his choice of raggle-taggle clothes (fans would later call this "the Pirate Years").

U2 also came under fire from Irish youth leaders and clergymen for setting ticket prices too high for their four end-of-year homecoming shows at the Point Depot. The National Youth Council of Ireland called the twenty- and twenty-five-pound prices "excessive" and argued that they would be out of the reach of many Dublin youngsters and the unemployed. The band eventually caved in to public pressure and dropped the prices to sixteen pounds standing and eighteen pounds seated, but not before McGuinness told the press that he hoped "this peculiar coalition of priests and other commentators will be bringing their enormous influence to bear on the other more essential pricing issues of the day. Petrol? The cost of travel? Should the agricultural sector be subsidized? What about interest rates? Coal and butter . . . ?" Tom Curran, director of the NYCI, said that he resented the U2 manager's "disparaging" remarks, and that they smacked of "sour grapes." Curran added: "We don't tell U2 how to play their music and Mr. McGuinness should not be telling us how to run our affairs. U2 are a group who claim to be responsible to Irish youth and also claim a social message. It would be totally contradictory to their image to charge the prices they were asking for."

In the past two years, U2 had been bloodied by the *Rattle and Hum* fallout and crushed by their own myth. Something was about to give. "This is just the end of something for U2," Bono told fans during the December 30 show at the Point. "It's no big deal. We have to go away and just dream it all up again."

12

Achtung, Berlin!

The mood in the U2 camp was somber; the tail end of the 1980s had truly knocked the stuffing out of everyone. They needed time to reflect on the past and contemplate the road ahead. Maybe even rediscover the art of smiling in public. Maybe. "We went back to Dublin in a fairly crazy state," Adam recalled in the *Los Angeles Times*. "We had all been on the move for the last ten years and this was our first chance to sit back for a few months and try to put everything into perspective."

The breather also gave band members the opportunity to branch out and pursue other projects. In January 1990, Bono and Edge co-wrote the abrasive industrial score for the British Royal Shakespeare Company's theatrical production of *A Clockwork Orange*, which received a lukewarm response from the novel's author, Anthony Burgess. "I'm a bit scared of it because my original intention was to use the music of Beethoven," Burgess told *The Times*. "It was appropriate because that was the music the hero Alex likes. He rather despises the other stuff." Meanwhile, Larry coproduced the Republic of Ireland's official 1990

FIFA World Cup anthem "Put 'Em Under Pressure," which reached number one in the Irish charts.

In June, U2 got together in Edge's basement and recorded a sinister electronic reworking of "Night and Day" for the Cole Porter–themed AIDS benefit project *Red Hot + Blue,* and along with *A Clockwork Orange* it was a harbinger of their future sound. "Night and Day" was released later in the year as a twelve-inch limited edition supplied to club DJs only. The promo consisted of two remixes by Youth, who originally found recognition as a founding member of the industrial rock band Killing Joke. "The band wanted a heavy mix, a left field, undergroundish mix and then a kind of radio dance mix as well," Youth told *NME.* "They're interested in the basic good vibes that are coming out of a lot of dance music at the moment. They were intrigued by working methods and how this kind of music is put together."

U2 invited the German art-house filmmaker Wim Wenders to direct the "Night and Day" music video specially shot for an ABC television special on World AIDS Day, and it marked the beginning of a long, fruitful alliance between the rock band and cinema innovator. The promo clip cast U2 in seedy surroundings (even if it was actually in the comfort of Wenders's Berlin apartment) with abstract references to needle-related drug use—one of the major causes of the spread of the HIV virus. Although Bono had addressed heroin abuse in songs like "Running to Stand Still," "Bad," and "Wire," his refusal to discuss his own possible dabbling with drugs frustrated many fans and critics. They wondered why a man with a reputation for being commemorated and ridiculed in the same breath for his outspokenness continually dodged the big question: "Have you or haven't you?" Cornered by a tenacious Adam Block of *Mother Jones,* Bono spelled out why: "I've written so many songs using heroin as an image, it might be interesting for me to tell you that, say, 'I've had experiences with the drug heroin.' It might be interesting for me to do it, and to own up to it. If it were misconstrued, somebody who, for whatever reason, respects me, that might lead them to get into it. If I become addicted to heroin, I can afford the trappings. I can afford the Betty Ford clinic. I can afford to have my blood changed. . . . But there is some guy who lives in a room in Dublin who can't."

The first of its kind, *Red Hot+Blue* encouraged addicts to use clean syringes and promoted safe sex through thought-provoking songs. Other artists who lent their names to the project included Neneh Cherry, Debbie Harry, and Iggy Pop.

■

Since the turn of the decade, Germany had been going through a huge transition. The Berlin Wall had been torn down and the dream of East meets West had become reality. With plans to record a new studio album, U2 was in need of inspiration and there it was: freedom and chaos. They arrived on the very last flight into the old divided city on October 3, 1990, the day of formal reunification, and immediately joined one of the many street parades. "It was really, really dour-looking German people holding up big signs, looking very unhappy," Bono recalled in *Rolling Stone*. "We're walking around, going, 'Wow, these Germans really don't know how to throw a party.' Then we discovered we were in the wrong parade. We were in a demonstration for people who wanted to put back up the wall, all these Stalinists and hard-core Communists. We could just see the headlines the next day: U2 ARRIVE TO PROTEST THE DESTRUCTION OF THE WALL."

Following a long night of barhopping, U2 checked into an old guesthouse in the former East Berlin, which had once played host to a certain Leonid Brezhnev. At around 7 A.M. a bare-arsed Bono went downstairs to pour himself a glass of water and encountered a German family standing in the hallway. With nowhere to run or hide, the singer clutched his manhood and stood his ground. The oldest man demanded to know what Bono was doing in their house, to which he replied, "Look, buddy, this happens to be my house." The man gave him a startled look and asked him, "Are you the caretaker or something?" It soon emerged that this was the man's parental home, where he had been born and raised until the Communist authorities seized it, and now he had returned to reclaim his birthright.

And so U2 swiftly flew the family's rightful nest and landed in the nearby Palasthotel, which was filled to the brim with sleazy Western businessmen. "Men in striped suits with a hooker on each knee, or at the bar drooling over a girl of fifteen," Bono later said in *NME*. "In the middle of the night I was woken by this bloodcurdling screech. I thought someone was being murdered. It was a woman in the room above mine. I was about to reach for the phone, when all of a sudden I heard her giggling. Turned out to be some kind of S&M act."

U2 began recording *Achtung Baby* with Daniel Lanois in the cavernous Studio 2 at Hansa Tonstudio, shadowed by the Berlin Wall, which was being rapidly chipped away by military guards and souvenir hunters. Once a Nazi ballroom, Hansa had been the setting for a number of seminal recordings, including much of David Bowie's so-called Berlin Trilogy with Brian Eno in 1977, and it was hoped that the ghosts of music past would inspire the band to great things.

However, *Achtung Baby* proved to be one tough baby to conceive. For starters, Hansa had fallen into a state of disrepair since the last high-profile recording there, Nick Cave's 1987 heroin-fueled opus *Your Funeral . . . My Trial*, which meant U2 had to install their own equipment at great expense. Then there were the arguments, those of the brutal kind. Before leaving for Berlin, Bono and Edge had assured the others that they would have the dozen or so demos the band cut in Dublin during the summer polished and ready to go. But all they brought was the same material plus half-baked ideas for a new sound and direction—none of which Larry or Adam were keen on. Edge had been listening to a lot of noise rock, electronica, krautrock, and industrial music: Sonic Youth, My Bloody Valentine, Nine Inch Nails, KMFDM, Tangerine Dream, and The Young Gods. Bono had been sniffing around closer to home, soaking up the Madchester scene in England, where bands like The Stone Roses and Happy Mondays were causing a stir with their colorful brand of neo-psychedelia and dirty rhythms. Bono and Edge spoke at length about how they would have to incorporate elements of these genres into their own music if they were to remain relevant. Focus on the rhythm, the sex of the music. Give it some Euro rawness. Inject some goddamn oomph!

Paul Hewson, age fifteen to sixteen, at Dublin's Mount Temple Comprehensive School, 1976.

(Alan Godden)

U2 taking in the weather on Galway Bay on the west coast of Ireland, 1980. *(Colm Henry)*

Adam working up a sweat as U2 open for The J. Geils Band at Nassau Veterans Memorial Coliseum in New York, March 25, 1982. *(Dion Simte Photography)*

U2 in America: Bono dancing with a female audience member at the Bijou Club in Dallas, Texas, April 1981—a routine he learned from watching Bruce Springsteen. *(Vern Evans)*

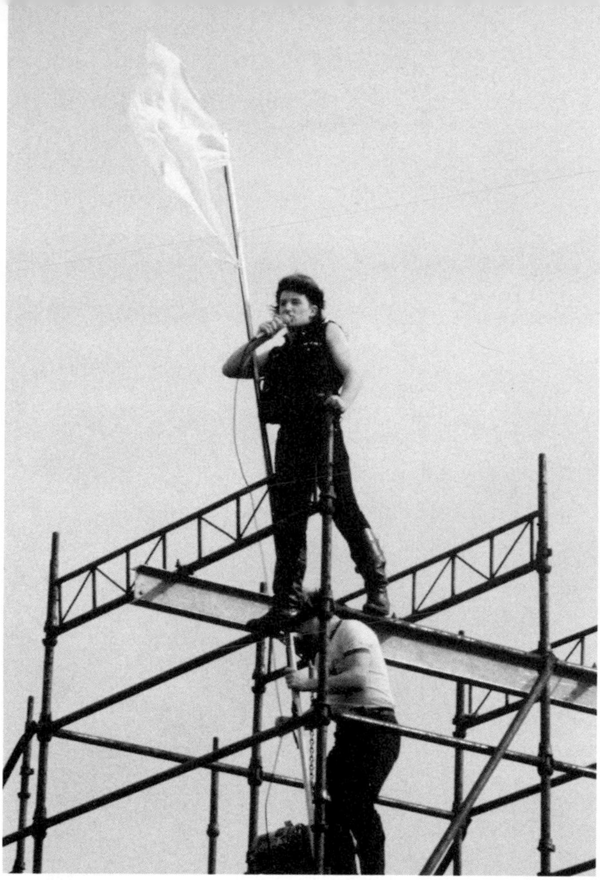

Bono plays daredevil during the annual MayFest festival at the State University of New York, May 1983. *(Neil Morganstein)*

Sonic innovator Brian Eno takes the "starstruck" band under his wing during the recording of *The Unforgettable Fire* at Ireland's Slane Castle in the summer of 1984. *(Colm Henry)*

Money matters: Edge and Bono with U2 manager Paul McGuinness, 1987. *(Colm Henry)*

U2 take a break while filming *Rattle and Hum* at the Point Depot in Dublin, May 1988. *(Colm Henry)*

Bono as "The Fly" lets loose in Cleveland, Ohio, March 1992. *(Steve Kalinsky)*

Edge down under in Australia on the last leg of the game-changing Zoo TV Tour. *(Glenn Shambrook/Feedback 1993)*

U2 out-glitz George Clinton and Parliament-Funkadelic as they emerge from a giant lemon-shaped disco mirror ball on the Toronto stop of the PopMart Tour, October 1997. *(Otto Kitsinger)*

The band in full flight on the PopMart B-stage, 1998. *(Otto Kitsinger)*

(*Above*) U2 on the 2001 Elevation Tour: "reapplying for the best band in the world job." *(Otto Kitsinger)* (*Above right*) Edge in concert on the Vertigo Tour, October 2005. *(Phil Romans)* (*Right*) A tribute to the victims and heroes of 9/11: U2 invite FDNY workers on stage at New York's Madison Square Garden, October 27, 2001. *(Otto Kitsinger)*

The U2 family: Bono and wife Ali Hewson, Adam, Edge and wife Morleigh Steinberg, and Larry and longtime partner Ann Acheson at the Seventy-Fifth Annual Academy Awards held at the Kodak Theater in Hollywood, March 23, 2003. *(Kevin Winter/Getty Images)*

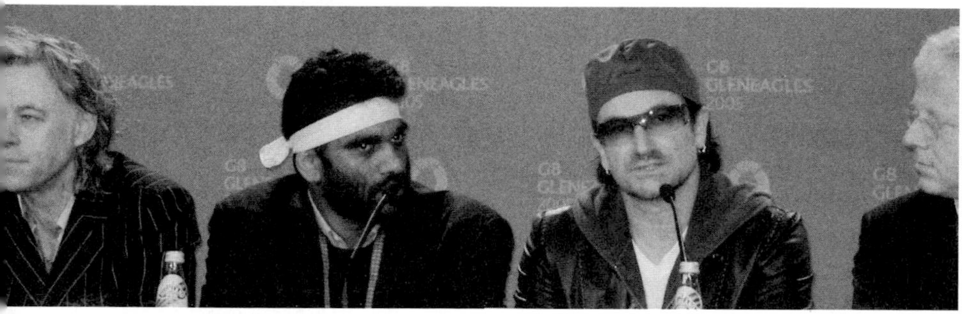

Bob Geldof, Dr. Kumi Naidoo, and Bono lock horns at a press conference during the G8 summit at the Gleneagles Hotel in Scotland, July 6, 2005. *(Christopher Collins)*

Friends in high places: Bono and U.S. president George W. Bush share a joke before a meeting at the 2007 G8 summit in Heiligendamm on the Mecklenburg Baltic coast in Germany. *(MANDEL NGAN/AFP/Getty Images)*

Adam at the book signing for *U2 by U2* at Barnes & Noble's flagship store in Manhattan's Union Square, September 2006. *(Phil Romans)*

The mothership has landed: the U2 360° Tour "Claw" at Dublin's Croke Park, July 2009. *(Peter McAviney)*

Bono and Ali with their eldest daughter, Jordan, at the Edun fashion show during Mercedes-Benz Fashion Week Spring 2014 at Skylight Modern in New York, September 8, 2013. *(Brian Ach/Getty Images)*

Larry and French costar Juliette Binoche attend the Norway premiere of their new film, *A Thousand Times Good Night*, at the Colosseum Kino in Oslo, October 16, 2013. *(Ragnar Singsaas/Getty Images)*

Larry and Adam weren't buying into it. Larry in particular had good reason not to. Often he found himself cooped up in his hotel room while the rest of U2 was in Hansa, with nothing to do but stare up at the ceiling and cancel out any thoughts of drum loops and other studio machinery reducing his role in the band. He felt like an outsider. He felt betrayed. When it got too much, he tried phoning the studio to give his bandmates a piece of his mind, but the line was busy.

Adam, the musical conscience, the one who believed in U2 before anyone else, was also uncertain—bewildered even. He felt that experimenting with youth culture was a sign that the *Rattle and Hum* critics had been right all along: they really had lost the plot. Worse still, producer Daniel Lanois felt the same way. Bono recalled in *Details*: "There was a Greek chorus of people around the record all saying 'You can't do this.' Or, 'Why don't you write a song like that?' Or, 'What has rhythm got to do with U2 anyway?' It wasn't a big deal, but it was there. From people producing the record, from people in the band at times. I mean, there was no map and we were running with the new idea."

As the mood darkened, it also became apparent that much of the tension stemmed from conflicting views over their equity structure. From day one, U2 and McGuinness had split all income equally to avoid dissension within the organization, but Bono and Edge, the principal songwriters, now resented the fact that they made the same amount of money as their three partners despite contributing more. McGuinness, accused of neglecting the band to pursue business interests in Hollywood and television, protected his position and generous slice of the pie by undermining Adam's level of input. It was a fascinating development, and one that represented a shift in relations, values, and power.

On one occasion, amid a flurry of finger-pointing and fault-finding, Adam grabbed his bass guitar and thrust it into the chest of Bono, snarling, "If you're such an expert, you fucking play it then!" The winter climate didn't help. It was always raining and it was cold, bitterly so. It seemed like the reunification party was winding down and entering its hangover phase. The city streets were a hustler's paradise, with cheap transport top of the agenda; the hotels were fully booked with the weirdest clientele Europe had to offer; and the bars were jam-packed with heartbroken communists staring into empty beer glasses. Taking a breather from Hansa, Lanois jumped into his car and headed for the railway tracks to make field recordings of passing trains. Hot on his tail was a carload of neo-Nazi skinheads chomping at the bit to take out some of their frustration on a foreigner. Lanois ran a red light and left them eating dust.

With very little sign of things improving inside the studio, U2 was left with only one option: Brian Eno. The self-described "sonic landscaper" had been kept up to date with the band's progress via tapes sent to him in London, and it was felt that if anyone could steer them in the right direction, it was him. Although he'd turned down the opportunity to work on the project from the outset because of other commitments, Eno agreed to visit Hansa on a fortnightly basis, usually staying on for a week at a time, to suggest and incorporate a few ideas of his own. "Buzzwords on the record were trashy, throwaway, dark, sexy, and industrial (all good) and earnest, polite, sweet, religious, rockist, and linear (all bad)," Eno recalled in his *Rolling Stone* journal, "Bringing Up the Baby." "It was good if a song took you on a journey or made you think your hi-fi was broken, bad if it reminded you of recording studios or U2."

The creative breakthrough came when Edge was messing around on the piano with two potential bridges for a track called "Sick Puppy." He presented the sections to Bono and Lanois, who suggested that he try combining them on guitar. Then as the band started jamming the resulting piece, Bono walked up to the microphone and began scatting lyrics over the melody. Within half an hour they had stumbled upon the basic arrangement for "One," an emotive rock ballad about a relationship on the brink of collapse that in time would be regarded as one of their finest songwriting accomplishments. The bass line from "Sick Puppy," meanwhile, evolved into the funk-laden "Mysterious Ways," in which Bono traced the link between sexuality and spirituality. Edge's stylish wah-wah riff lit the way on what would be the one truly untroubled spot on the album, thematically speaking.

Shortly after "One" and "Mysterious Ways" were bagged it was agreed that after the Nazis and then U2, there were enough bad vibes in Hansa to run a hoodoo factory. Therefore the band returned home over the Christmas period, where they held a series of clear-the-air talks in a bid to salvage what little friendship they had left, beyond Bono and Edge's close bond. Consistent with their cultlike mentality, all animosity within the group relating to money matters was kept in house for the good of the brand image. Instead, they would play up the heated but ultimately innocuous musical-differences angle, using it as a selling point to add a sense of headline-grabbing drama when promoting the album later that year.

For Edge and Aislinn—who had just given birth to their third daughter, Blue Angel, in June 1989—this was also the period that they came to a very painful understanding: their seven-year marriage was over. Edge moved out of their family home in Dublin and briefly stayed with Adam before purchasing a cottage of his own nearby. An emotional wreck, the guitarist immersed himself in the new album to occupy his mind.

The rest of U2 recommenced work on *Achtung Baby* in February 1991, renting the ten-thousand-pound-a-month Victorian manor Elsinore on the Dalkey coastline, which they nicknamed "Dog Town" because of a few adjacent dog kennels. They, and everyone else involved, maintained a code of silence throughout the making of the record, a move supported by Island's new president Marc Marot following the misguided *Rattle and Hum* campaign. "It had all got a little too big and overblown for me with the film and everything else," explains Marot. "And then *Achtung Baby* was such a change in direction in many respects that to have spent months talking about a change could have lent to disappointment and not managing expectations very well. So it was a conscious decision just to keep our own counsel, keep schtum, and just get to the point where we were confident that we had the right music and the right imagery, which is very important."

News in April that bootlegs of the work in progress had surfaced on the black market threw a monkey wrench in the works to a certain extent. Fashioned in a German pressing plant, the two identified double albums, each entitled *The New U2: Rehearsels* [sic] *& Full Versions,* featured over three hours of raw material in total, evidently stolen from Hansa, and were fetching up to forty pounds each. Island took out an ad in the British trade magazine *Music Week* threatening legal action against anyone found guilty of copyright infringement. Later investigations involved the FBI, UK police, customs, and the BPI's antipiracy unit, leading to many traders refusing to stock the albums. Bono tried to minimize the significance of the leak by referring to the tapes as "gobbledygook," although Edge later conceded that the experience was "like being violated."

Says Marot: "We never caught the people responsible [for leaking the music]. We didn't know whether it was hotel room theft by a cleaner or a tape op in Hansa who just helped themselves to it. But that was damaging. No band wants their noodling out there. And now, with the Internet, it would be terribly damaging. But at least then it relied on physical distribution and we successfully closed the pressing plant down and prosecuted."

Then came August and yet more PR problems for U2 and Island when U.S. audio hackers Negativland released an EP called "U2," containing an unauthorized sample of "I Still Haven't Found What I'm Looking For" and a profanity-filled outtake of DJ Casey Kasem introducing the song on his *American Top 40* show. The jacket also gave the impression that the EP was in fact a U2 product. Island recognized the artwork as consumer fraud and filed a 180-page lawsuit against Negativland and their label, SST Records, for illegal use of the U2 trademark. In return, Negativland and SST knocked up a well-publicized anti-U2 campaign which overnight cast the Irish quartet as the villains of the story. However, Marot is quick to dismiss the impact the Negativland storm had on the band. "In U2 world Negativland was an utter nonevent," he says. "These guys made a career out of trying to turn it into something that it wasn't. Nobody gave a shit. It was like, 'What is all this fuss about? Next!' It had nothing to do with the band." (Note: In June 1992, two members of Negativland interviewed Edge over the phone while posing as journalists, only to reveal their true identities and ask him for a twenty-thousand-dollar loan to help pay off their legal bills and establish a record label—with the guitarist getting a 10 percent cut. A tad stunned and amused, Edge said that he would think about it, but they never heard from him again. Three years later, Negativland released a book, *Fair Use: The Story of the Letter U and the Numeral 2,* which documented the copyright affair in its entirety.)

▪

Grunge music exploded out of its native Seattle and onto the global stage in September 1991, turning rock and roll on its head. At the forefront of this phenomenon was a young trio called Nirvana, fronted by the enigmatic Kurt Cobain. The quintessence of the slacker culture, their brand of stripped-down heavy rock and darkly cryptic lyrics formed the soundtrack to millions of angst-ridden youths alienated from the so-called glamor of the American dream that had colonized the subconscious of the West via Hollywood and MTV. Generation X had found its voice. Consequently, many '80s stars—INXS, Simple Minds, and, to the relief of many, hair metal bands such as Poison and Winger—would find the '90s to be a cold decade, one of artistic irrelevancy and monumental sales slumps. Even for the mighty U2, the odds were stacked against them. With the humiliation of *Rattle and Hum* still relatively fresh, many questioned whether they would be able to bounce back and ultimately have something worthwhile to say. They needn't have worried.

On October 12, U2 broke their self-imposed silence with the release of "The Fly" as the first single from *Achtung Baby.* It was an explosive fusion of distorted blues and angelic gospel, with a metallic beat-driven edge. Hard. Chaotic. Sexy. It marked a dramatic departure from the American roots exploration of *The Joshua Tree* and *Rattle and Hum.* Visually, too, U2 had undergone a sensational transformation, as evidenced in the accompanying performance music video; gone were the cowboy boots and Stetson hats, replaced in the case of Bono by a shiny black leather suit, slicked-back jet-black-dyed hair, and a pair of wraparound blaxploitation sunglasses. Stephen Dalton of *Uncut* later noted that "The

Fly" was the first step in "a bold trash-funk rebirth, with Bono's Kafka-esque metamorphosis explicitly mocking his pious public image" and that it symbolized "both a confession and a celebration of fame's Faustian pact with sin and excess." Bono, for his part, described the single as "the sound of four men chopping down *The Joshua Tree*."

However, the experimental nature of the "The Fly" presented Marc Marot at Island with a few dilemmas with regard to getting it to that crucial number-one spot in the UK singles chart. "The first U2 single for which I had worldwide marketing responsibility is probably the only one nobody can sing the chorus of," laughs Marot. "It possibly had one of the lowest airplay rotations on BBC Radio 1 that year. I was desperate that my first single would go in at number one; however, the airplay was so poor that we had to come up with a plan to help it along its way. We decided to release 'The Fly' as an unlimited one-week-only single where if people wanted to order ten thousand copies or a million copies of it in the first week, they could, but we were not going to manufacture any more after that week. And that's what really pushed that track to number one, because people didn't want to play it on radio because it didn't have the big chorus."

U2's *Achtung Baby* was released worldwide in November to both commercial and critical acclaim. The album debuted at number one in the United States and in most other major territories; and though it stumbled at number two in the UK, it spent a total of eighty-seven weeks on the chart there. Writing in *Rolling Stone*, Elysa Gardner said that, as with *Rattle and Hum*, "U2 is once again trying to broaden its musical palette, but this time its ambitions are realized. Working with producers who have lent discipline and nuance to the group's previous albums U2 sets out to experiment rather than pay homage." Gardner concluded that the album consisted of "many moments" when "we're reminded why, before these guys were the butt of cynical jokes, they were rock & roll heroes—as they still are." Jay Cocks of *Time* magazine enthused: "U2 does something unique here. The band not only reasserts itself but reinvents itself too. After *Rattle and Hum*, there was some thought that it had overreached itself, gone a little too mainstream, got a little too big even for its own grand ambitions. *Achtung Baby* restores U2 to scale, and gives the band back its edge. It's a monster."

The intriguing album title derived from U2's live sound engineer Joe O'Herlihy, who had plucked the phrase from Mel Brooks's satirical masterpiece *The Producers* and adopted it as his own in Berlin. "It's a con," Bono told *Rolling Stone*. "We call it *Achtung Baby* grinning up our sleeves in all the photography. But it's probably the heaviest record we've ever made. There is a lot of blood and guts on that record. It tells you a lot about packaging, because the press would have killed us if we'd called it anything else." At one stage, U2 had flirted with the idea of calling the album *Adam* because of a certain naked bass player brandishing a lot more than a smile on the vibrant sleeve collage (which also included photos of the band in drag), leading a number of countries in the conservative parts of the world to place a sticker over his genitals. Adam revealed all: "I had to be talked into it, I have to say. I was very nervous and apprehensive about revealing myself in such a way. But I got into the spirit of wickedness, I suppose. . . . I only wish I had an erection at the time."

Considering everything that they had been through, it came as no surprise that *Achtung Baby* was U2's most personal record since *October*. But while their sophomore release documented the lives of three born-again Christian rockers on a mission to save the world from eternal damnation, Bono, influenced by the disintegration of Edge's marriage and the fractured relationship between band members, now focused his attention on the ugly side of love, where faithfulness and betrayal collided—headfirst. His lyrics were full of disturbing sexual imagery and metaphors, mostly relating to sadomasochism and oral sex. Bono later hinted that he may also have been writing about his own marriage to Ali with regard to the album's adulterous overtones. "I've had my problems in my relationship," he told American pop journalist Bill Flanagan. "It's tough for everybody. I think fidelity is just against human nature."

Open-heart surgery, Bono called it. When the artist makes the choice to reveal rather than conceal. But at what price? Letting the world inside your head can be a dangerous game, leaving you vulnerable to attack. Since a child Bono had been fascinated by David Bowie's flamboyant alter ego Ziggy Stardust. How he enabled Bowie the freedom to spill his guts, to show his true colors and not deal with the consequences. Even Mick Jagger and Keith Richards, through their own sex, drugs, and rock 'n' roll personas, could afford the luxury of writing the odd emotionally raw tune and not be taken as overearnest. This really got under Bono's skin. It was time for him to erect a façade of his own, and it came in plastic, compliments of U2's worldly wardrobe man Fintan Fitzgerald.

In the winter of 1990, Fintan had acquired the aforementioned 1970s bug-eyed sunglasses on one of his customary scouting trips to London's Portobello Road. Aware of Bono's dilemma, he thought they might do the trick. It was a long shot, but it worked. To a degree neither he nor Bono could have possibly imagined. Bono would slide them on during the writing of "The Fly" and, in a somewhat immature way, his whole attitude would change. He became the deranged character in the song. He became the Fly. "It was written like a phone call from hell, but the guy liked it there," Bono said in *Rolling Stone*. "It was this guy running away—'Hi, honey, it's hot, but I like it here.' The character is just on the edge of lunacy. It's megalomania and paranoia." Back in Dog Town, Bono found that behind this ironic mask nothing was sacred. Matters of the heart (and bedroom) were no longer forbidden and no longer avoidable. Why would they be? It was all coming from the Fly now, a guy straight out of *One Flew Over the Cuckoo's Nest*. And, rather selfishly, *Achtung Baby* reaped the rewards.

The album launched with the industrial bellow of "Zoo Station," a downward spiral into insanity. Zoo Station, or Bahnhof Zoo, was the main transportation hub in western central Berlin. At night, it would often be frequented by pickpockets, prostitutes, and junkies, many of whom had boarded one of the station's trains coming from the East after reunification with hopes and dreams of a better life, only to be rejected by the social order. U2 used the station as a metaphor, staging their own voyage into the unknown through the eyes of an East German passenger, with heavy distorted riffs and a rhythm that suggested total confusion, while the vocals—treated through a Yamaha SPX1000—were barely recognizable. Robert Hilburn wrote in the *Los Angeles Times*: "You can't tell for a few seconds whether U2 has joined the heavy-metal camp or if it has been commissioned to write the soundtrack for a horror film. When Bono begins singing, special effects make him sound as if he is speaking to us while emerging from a deep, troubled sleep and preparing for nightmares of the real world."

Critics noted that the image of two people tearing each other apart ran right through the album. It was there in the spectral pop of "Ultraviolet (Light My Way)," a desperate plea for guidance and reassurance in a decaying relationship. It was there in the sci-fi glam rock of "Even Better Than the Real Thing," where a promiscuous lover attempted to crawl back into the arms of his companion with grand assurances he shows no sign of fulfilling. And it was there in album closer "Love Is Blindness," in all its ugly glory. Drenched in complete pathos, the final track was a moody, atmospheric piece, with guitar feedback hanging in the air like a thick fog before exploding into some kind of sonic death chant. For once there was little chance of understanding and, as the ending would have it, little of survival. This was U2 at the end of the world. "[T]he best thing about the record is Edge's guitar playing," Bono said in the *Los Angeles Times*. "To me, it's like a prayer."

And not even Jesus and Judas were let off the hook. "Until the End of the World"—originally written at the behest of Wim Wenders, who needed "a song that could represent their music ten years from then" for his futuristic epic of the same name—paraphrased the conversation between the two religious figures in the Garden of Gethsemane, told from the perspective of Judas, and the aftermath when he was consumed by guilt. On this, and indeed most of *Achtung Baby,* Bono, in keeping with the spirit of U2's new musical direction, as well as being under strict orders from a voice specialist, resisted his big, open-throated vocal delivery of old, and instead adopted a more restrained,

Sinatra-esque conversational style (occasionally complemented by a delicate falsetto) to convey intimacy; it was, he explained, the realization that a whisper can be more powerful than a scream.

Other tracks on U2's radical new album included the hip-hop-inflected torch song "So Cruel," the windswept pop anthem "Who's Gonna Ride Your Wild Horses," the woozy "Tryin' to Throw Your Arms Around the World," and the brooding snarl "Acrobat"—the latter of which Bono cited as his favorite song on the album; it was, he said, both a response to his critics and an acknowledgment of the paradoxes one faces as a performer, family man, and Christian. "I have learned to embrace the contradictions in life and that's one of the messages of the album," he told the *Los Angeles Times*. "There was a time when they were tearing me apart because I am not able to live up to a lot of the things I believe in. It's hard to talk about that and the reasons behind the songs on the album without sounding like a guest on one of those confessional TV shows, but there were definitely times when the fire you are playing with starts to play with you and it can destroy you before you even know it's there."

Lou Reed was thanked in the liner notes for his input on "Acrobat." "He has a great ear," Bono noted in *Music Express*. "He gives constructive criticism. I once asked him if there was something about U2 he didn't like. He said, 'The rhyme.' "

13

Under an Atomic Sky

On February 28, 1992, U2 embarked on their groundbreaking multimedia Zoo TV Tour at the Lakeland Civic Center in Florida, in support of an album that had already shifted 7 million copies worldwide. Five years had passed since their last show on American soil so anticipation was high. When tickets for all thirty-two hit-and-run arena dates went on sale, Pacific Bell, a telephone company in L.A., recorded 54 million attempts for calls in fewer than four hours as rabid fans kept hitting redial. In Boston, the demand crashed phone lines, while other cities sold out in less than five minutes. Outside venues, scalpers were making anything from eight hundred to eighteen hundred dollars—twice the going rate for Michael Jackson and Madonna tickets.

Zoo TV was partly devised as a complex performance-art commentary on fame and the desensitizing effect of mass media. Essentially acting as their own state-of-the-art mobile television station, U2 intercepted satellite transmissions from around the world and relayed them to the audience on four Vidiwalls and thirty-six TV monitors. Live CNN reports of the horrors of the Gulf War, terrorism, rape, and politics competed for airtime with game shows, *T.J. Hooker* reruns, pornography, and shopping channels plugging their products. Registered charity foundations asked for donations, while televangelists appealed to the faithful for generous contributions to meet their corporate objectives. And there, at the center of contradiction, was Bono, zapping his way through the satellite feeds with a remote control, highlights of which included Senator Paul Tsongas declaring his withdrawal from the race for the Democratic presidential nomination in a live news broadcast, a live satellite linkup to the MTV Video Music Awards in which the host Garth from *Wayne's World* joined the band on drums for "Even Better Than the Real Thing," and a bizarre moment in Florida when Russian astronaut Sergei Krikalev, who was "stranded" in space aboard the Mir space station following the collapse of the Soviet Union and Russian coup of 1991, agreed to talk live via satellite but fell asleep and missed his cue. "At least he wasn't at the show," Bono quipped.

There was more. Riffing off the work of word artist Jenny Holzer, the audience was bombarded with random aphorisms at brain-melting speed: "THE FUTURE IS FANTASY/IGNORANCE IS BLISS/BELIEVE EVERYTHING/DO YOU BELIEVE ME?/DEBT/PUSSY/WEAR A CONDOM/NIGGER/CONTRADICTION IS BALANCE/TOMORROW BELONGS TO ME/DEATH IS INEVITABLE/YOU ARE A VICTIM OF YOUR TV/WATCH MORE TV." Advertising slogans that populate everyday life were also thrown into the mix: "CHARGE IT/WEAR IT/HYPE/HOPE/I WANT IT NOW." (Incidentally, Holzer believed U2 failed to grasp the distinction between inspiration and plagiarism and considered taking legal action against the group.)

And then, as if all the above wasn't enough, six customized East German Trabants dangled from the ceiling like stars watching over an apocalyptic information highway. The people's car was something of a running joke with U2 as every day they made their way to Hansa they would see another one burned out by the side of the road, jettisoned by a family heading West. The Trabbies were hollowed out, fitted with stage lights, and then painted in pop culture motifs by artist Catherine Owens, giving the show another visual element and paying silent tribute to the fall of the Iron Curtain.

"Zoo TV is kind of information overload: music, visuals, and text. It's the point where it all converges and gets spurted out," Edge explained on MTV, just one of the many networks they were lifting footage from. "It's not an original idea but I don't think it's ever been done in the context of a concert before. It's good fun. We discovered that irony isn't necessarily the enemy of soul and you can do things that are very ironic yet at the same time be saying something that's actually very personal and very true, and that the two aren't necessarily in conflict."

Blame it on Bono. Zoo TV was his concept. Sitting at home watching the Gulf War unfold live on CNN, it dawned on him how desensitized he had become to it all. The advent of satellite television had changed the media landscape to the point where every couch potato from Dublin to Tokyo was on the front line. Bored? Flick over to the movie channel and watch the Duke gun down a few bad guys, then back to CNN and watch the U.S. Air Force destroy an air-raid shelter with two laser-guided smart bombs. There was no division between fiction and reality anymore. And he wasn't alone in the way he felt. "I remember this incident in Manhattan," Edge said in *Melody Maker.* "A friend of mine was sitting in the lobby of a hotel and the only TV set was at the check-in desk, and all the guests were down there watching *Starsky and Hutch* or something. Suddenly, this guy walked in off the street with blood all down his front and people averted their gaze from the TV until they'd seen everything they needed to. Then they went back to the TV. It was all a blur."

In what could be interpreted as a statement of intent or a commitment to their new vision, the Zoo TV set list was front-loaded with between six to eight songs from *Achtung Baby,* during which Bono assumed the role of the Fly, endowing him with the characteristics and mannerisms of a narcissistic rock star. Clad in his black leather suit and sunglasses, he stumbled around the dark, disorienting environment like an intoxicated Jim Morrison, goose-stepping to the contradictions and posing for the press photographers in the pit at the front of the main stage as PHOTO OPPORTUNITY flashed on the video screens. Sometimes he planted wet kisses on the Zoo TV video cameras before rubbing them up and down against his crotch. The Fly was the ultimate big shot, even gracing the cover of the British edition of *Vogue* alongside Christy Turlington, one of a troupe of statuesque supermodels to regularly party with U2 backstage on Zoo TV.

Just one alter ego wouldn't do, however. Thus, Bono returned for the encore as a southern-televangelist-cum-snake-oil-salesman named the Mirrorball Man, kissing his own reflection in a full-length mirror in mock lust and tossing fake dollar bills into the audience in a shameless attempt to buy their trust. Adam suggested he use a telephone to administer prank calls from onstage and the Mirrorball Man was only too happy to oblige. In Detroit he phoned a local pizza parlor advertised on one of the screens and ordered ten thousand pizzas—one hundred of which were actually delivered to the arena and promptly handed out to the front row. In another city he rang a live sex line and begged for his "baby." And in Oakland he made the first of many calls to the president of the United States at the White House, but George H. W. Bush wasn't available. Later, when members of U2 were guests on *Rockline*, New York's nationally syndicated radio phone-in, Democratic presidential candidate Bill Clinton called for an "unscheduled" natter after hearing they had trouble reaching him. Although the conversation got off to an awkward start—Bono: "Should I call you Governor or Bill?" Clinton: "No, call me Bill." Bono: "All right, and you can call me Betty."—the Irish rock band and future president got on like a house on fire, discussing censorship laws and America's role in world issues. The stunt brought no end of free publicity for both parties, so much so that an anxious Bush felt the need to address it on his own campaign: "So Governor Clinton doesn't think foreign policy is important, but anyway he is trying to catch up. You may have seen this in the news, he was in Hollywood seeking foreign policy advice from the rock grop, uh, rock group U2! Now, understand, I have nothing against U2. You may not know this but they try and call me at the White House every night during the concerts. But the next time we face a foreign policy crisis I will work with John Major and Boris Yeltsin, and Bill Clinton can consult Boy George. I'll stay with the experts!"

And just when fans and critics feared that U2's music would get lost amidst the machinery and theater, U2 had one more surprise: a B-stage attached to the end of a catwalk that stretched deep into the heart of the audience. Inspired by Elvis Presley's informal *'68 Comeback Special,* they played a short, gimmick-free acoustic set on it every night as if they were buskers looking for a dime.

Critics were unanimous in their praise for Zoo TV. Wayne Robbins of *Newsday* wrote: "It was a grand success. Though the show was elaborately conceived, it was often a high-spirited, self-deprecating funfest. They seem to have learned that rock and roll can deal with issues without being ponderous; that it can be pleasurable without being mindless. It seems to have taken the singer, in particular, a while to lighten up and stop taking rock stardom so seriously." Reporting in Virginia for *Melody Maker,* a converted Jon Wiederhorn beamed: "I arrived this evening fully prepared to trash U2 for predictable rock posing, uninspired musicianship, pulpit preaching, living in the past, and poor taste in clothing. But, alas, I cannot be negative about U2 tonight. Their Zoo TV show is visually stunning, musically unparalleled, downright moving and, dammit, truly entertaining. . . . I have to concede that U2 are the best band in popular rock 'n' roll."

Draped in smirking irony and knowing decadence, both Zoo TV and *Achtung Baby* were viewed as a calculated attempt by U2 to break away from their grim, holier-than-thou public image. The media had made caricatures of them, and U2 had responded by creating an even bigger postmodern cool cartoon, seemingly based on rock-and-roll stereotypes. But the real irony, insiders say, was that their new persona was a truer reflection of who they were behind the scenes. They had, through the power of irony and self-deprecation, learned how to hide in plain sight.

As in the past, U2 remained fiercely protective of their inner world. Bill Flanagan, a friend of Ellen Darst and a vocal supporter of the band in the early years, was invited to join them on the road for the duration of Zoo TV, which he documented in his book *U2 at the End of the World*. Flanagan provided a fascinating glimpse into the group's creative process, but the book is noticeably free of brand-damaging material. "The uncut version of the book was seven hundred pages long," says a source. "He was ostracized by them [U2] afterward. Flanagan really damaged himself with that book, by writing the truth. So that's the kind of people you're dealing with."

■

Zoo TV reached European shores in May, and it was there where U2's social conscience resurfaced once again when they assisted Greenpeace in an antinuclear demonstration against the proposed expansion of the Sellafield reprocessing plant on the West Coast of Cumbria in England. The owners, British Nuclear Fuels Ltd. (BNFL), had been informed of their plans days earlier and, fearing crowds of fifteen-thousand-plus would show up, went to the High Court and obtained an injunction against the protest, which stated that anyone found entering the grounds of the plant without permission would be arrested. But U2 and Greenpeace had other means of attack. Arriving at dawn in inflatable dinghies from the Greenpeace ship *Solo*, clothed in white radiation suits, masks, and designer sunglasses, they carried ashore oil drums full of contaminated mud taken from the Irish Sea as a "return-to-sender" gesture. And since they were below the high-water mark, the limit of BNFL's land, no law was broken.

Although the band had made a point to avoid such direct activism on Zoo TV, it was agreed that Sellafield was one tumor they weren't prepared to stand back and watch as it grew. "It's absurd that a rock band has to dress up in ridiculous costumes to draw attention to this problem, to bring the facts out," Bono told a flock of journalists on the beach.

"Sellafield is our back again," Edge added. "There's a particular school in Dundalk where a lot of girls have left and had Down's syndrome babies. The idea that this new plant would open up and increase emissions by 1,000 percent is completely outrageous." The band also held a

"Stop Sellafield" concert with Kraftwerk, Public Enemy, and Big Audio Dynamite, with all proceeds from this and the eventual video release going directly to Greenpeace.

U2 wrapped up the first chapter of Zoo TV in November, after expanding the show to football stadiums in North America. Dubbed the "Outside Broadcast" leg, the Willie Williams/Mark Fisher futuristic stage design was compared favorably to the hi-tech, low-tech neon sprawl of Shinjuku in Tokyo and Ridley Scott's *Blade Runner,* with steel radio towers that appeared to touch the sky. To operate it, U2 invested in a $3.5 million television studio control room—which included four broadcast-quality cameras, four surveillance cameras, two Handycams, four tape machines, eleven laser disc players, and a satellite dish to pick up pictures from outer space—and employed over 180 traveling crew members, including 12 directors. With production expenses at $125,000 a day, show or no show, McGuinness would later claim that the tour relied on merchandise sales to break even. "I think I made more money on the date than they did," promoter Barry Fey said later. "It was so mechanized, with the radio towers and this and that. But it was a great tour. We did over fifty-seven thousand people [in Denver]."

If U2 was worried, it didn't show. "All that shit about being the biggest, the best, the loudest is all meaningless," Bono said. "The biggest turn-on about having shitloads of money is the ability to do what you like; you can afford independence, a lot of so-called independent bands can't. It's a question of making the leap and not believing in the hype that rock 'n' roll has become. It would be such a total cliché to roll over at this time. After the first ten years, the rock cliché is to break up or repeat yourself ad nauseam. We've managed to avoid that, and we're nowhere near used up. In fact, we're only getting into it."

■

In January 1993, Bill Clinton, U2's new Washington pal, was inaugurated as the forty-second president of the United States, and Larry and Adam hooked up with REM's Michael Stipe and Mike Mills under the supergroup guise of Automatic Baby to perform at the MTV Rock 'n'

Roll Inaugural Ball in honor of the new president. Meanwhile, Bono and Edge were in Hamburg, Germany, for the two-day "Festival Against Racism." Bono was invited to speak at the press conference, and he told journalists: "Rock 'n' roll is for some of us an alarm clock. It wakes us up to dream. It has stopped me from becoming cynical in cynical times. Surely it is the inherited cynicism of our political and economic thinking that contributes so much to the despair of the 1990s. . . . We started the century with so many competing ideas as to how we should live together. We ended with so few." The singer then teamed up with Edge and Indian violinist Jo Shankar to perform the ever-evolving "One" to a standing ovation.

If nothing else, the band members' activities were nothing more than distractions—albeit worthy distractions—to fill the four-month gap between the end of the 1992 tour and the next European leg scheduled to begin in May. Coming down from the high that is tour life and picking up the pieces of domestic life can be tough. Ali Hewson can shudder at the thought of the number of times she's had to summon Bono down from a household table, singing and motioning to an invisible audience, as the lines between rock star and husband remain distorted for some time. But at least Bono had a home to return to. All Edge had waiting for him were echoing walls and unpaid bills. Faced with this realization, he locked himself in The Factory studio in Dublin's Docklands and started cutting demos with thoughts of recording a four-track EP to coincide with the forthcoming tour. Soon enough the others joined him, adamant they weren't ready to resume life on planet Earth just yet. Eno and engineer/producer Flood weren't far behind them, eager to see what the band could create while still in the channel-hopping mind-set of Zoo TV.

During this period, news of an unlikely romance between Adam and British supermodel Naomi Campbell began to circulate in the press. For a man who prided himself in keeping his private life just that (barring, of course, two arrests), Campbell was an intriguing choice for a girlfriend. At only twenty-two, this notoriously difficult customer had already managed to set the modeling world ablaze, domineering catwalks and fashion magazines with her sultry style and killer looks, which made her a media star and international celebrity. But it was arguably her topsy-turvy love life that had garnered the most attention, with turbulent romances with the likes of Hollywood legend Robert De Niro and heavyweight boxer Mike Tyson every tabloid and gossip columnist's dream scenario. And now here she was again, dating a rock star. The articles almost wrote themselves.

The two lovebirds had met in August 1992 after Campbell accepted an invitation from the bass guitarist to attend a U2 show at Giants Stadium in New Jersey—this following Adam's confession in the official tour program that the thing he would like most in the world was to meet the supermodel. Much small talk ensued post-gig but the pair failed to hit it off right away, with Adam uncharacteristically shy in her presence. Then, in February 1993, they were sharing room space again at Ellen Darst's leaving party in New York after Bono had brought Campbell along as his guest. Three months later, Campbell had announced her engagement to Adam on Irish television. "If I'm working late, or he is, there's an understanding," she said, wearing an antique engagement ring worth forty thousand pounds. "There's a lot of trust." According to observers, their relationship was almost childlike, spent constantly reassuring one another.

Back at The Factory, U2's EP had evolved into a full-length studio album, entitled *Zooropa,* which saw them advance farther into the world of moody experimental electronica. Sonically, it was the morning after to the late-night debauchery of *Achtung Baby.* Thematically, it was the offspring of Zoo TV, commenting on voyeurism and media manipulation. Trouble was, the tour deadline had arrived and it wasn't quite finished. They would have to steal a few days by flying back to Dublin after each show until it was everything but gift-wrapped.

The Zooropa leg of Zoo TV got under way in spectacular fashion on May 9 at the Feyenoord Stadium in Rotterdam, Holland. Breaking away from the decidedly Americanized razzmatazz of the "Outside Broadcast," U2 turned the focus on the dark shadow cast over Europe. The fall of the Iron Curtain and communism had been seen as a giant step in unifying the continent by reducing barriers but, ironically, it had divided it more than ever. The European Community was dangerously fragmented, as nations disintegrated into smaller nations and citizens and politicians struggled to hold on to their cultural/religious identity amid the influx of refugees escaping politically unstable homelands in the East, giving rise to extreme right-wing parties throughout Western Europe. In former Yugoslavia a bloody war had erupted between several factions in what came to be known as the Bosnian War—the first on European soil since 1945. These were uncertain times where no one knew who they were, never mind what they wanted to be.

U2 took this turmoil and ran with it. The Zoo TV screens flickered into action with overlapping snippets of "Fanfare" from the album *Lenin's Favourite Songs* and Beethoven's "Ode to Joy" echoing around the stadium, occasionally drowned out by droning voices asking "What do you want?" in different European languages. Looped footage of a German boy playing drums at the 1936 Olympics in Berlin from Leni Riefenstahl's Nazi-propaganda film *Triumph of the Will* flashed on-screen in a satirical nod to the parallels between rock concerts and the Nuremberg rallies, while during "Bullet the Blue Sky" Ku Klux Klan–like flaming crosses morphed into swastikas in what was interpreted as a chilling warning of the similarities between Europe's present state and that of the '30s. The twelve-star flag of Europe was also displayed, only for the whole thing to come tumbling down under the strain when one of the stars fell off.

Within this new world disorder, Bono's third and final alter ego was born, Mr. MacPhisto, a devilish creation based on Mephistopheles of German folklore and the flamboyant English-born Irish dramatist Mac Liammóir, who pranced around Dublin in full makeup twenty-four/seven. MacPhisto was certainly an eccentric fellow, dressed up like Halloween in a gold suit and matching platform boots, white face paint, red lipstick, and horns. He sang and spoke in a posh English accent on par with the king of camp John Inman of *Are You Being Served?* fame. Bono later referred to him as "the Fly when he's old, fat, and playing Vegas."

Like the corrupt preacher man before him, MacPhisto used the telephone as a weapon to pester whoever took his fancy. In Holland it was his travel agent. In Germany it was Chancellor Helmut Kohl (Kohl was otherwise engaged, but the old devil left a message with his assistant nonetheless: "Thank the chancellor for letting me back into the country! I'm baaack! I'm baaack!"). "Dressing up as the devil was great," Bono said later. "The amazing thing was a woman called Eunice Shriver who set up the Special Olympics—she's one of the Kennedys and an American Irish, I suppose—she came down to see us. She's incredibly erudite and she's up on everything, a pretty sharp lady. And she said after the show, 'I used to go and see U2 shows and I just saw these kind of angels.' And she said, 'Tonight I saw these devils as well as angels on stage, and I think I liked it better. It's a fairer fight.'"

The Zooropa shows invariably ended with MacPhisto's ghostly, childlike falsetto rendition of Elvis Presley's "Can't Help Falling in Love." "Elvis is still in the building," he would then whisper softly as he disappeared into the night, handing over the reins to the king's own version coming over the PA system. Many journalists cited it as the most poignant moment of each show.

U2's Grammy-winning cyberpunk album *Zooropa* was released in June. Pop critics described it as "both a reflection of and a reaction to Zoo TV . . . the surrealist, fast-forward distortion of the digitalized global village" [*Time*], "the sound of verities shattering, the moment when exhilaration and fear are indistinguishable" [*Rolling Stone*], and "a harried, spontaneous sounding, and ultimately exhilarating album" [*Entertainment Weekly*]. But to U2 it was primarily a bargaining chip for a lucrative new record deal with Island. "It was not a particularly successful record in terms of longevity," says Marc Marot. "It was a quick and dirty record. It wasn't supposed to have any singles and we ended up releasing only 'Stay' [the most traditional U2 song on the album] and 'Numb' [an experimental piece of electronic noise sung/spoken in catatonic repetitions by Edge] as singles and 'Lemon' [a falsetto-driven funk song which recalled Eno's work with Talking Heads and became an unlikely club remix hit] as a video-only single, and that was because frankly U2 wanted it to be a low-key release. We often wondered if it was delivered to Island as a contractual filler to get them to the point where the big negotiation could take place because they were coming to the end of their contract."

And it worked. McGuinness, flanked by U2's celebrity lawyer Allen Grubman and flamboyant accountant Ossie Kilkenny, negotiated a six-album contract extension with Island's chairman Tom Hayes worth an incredible $60 million-plus to the band, placing them above The Rolling Stones as the highest-paid rock act in music history. The deal guaranteed U2 $10 million per album and a blue-chip 28 percent royalty rate on every record sold, as well as including Internet and other multimedia provisions. "I am thrilled that U2 are renewing their deal with Island Records," McGuinness said in the official press release. "When we started out we thought all record companies must be like Island. Now that we know that's not true, we definitely want to stay with Chris Blackwell and all our new friends at PolyGram."

In July the European tour rolled into Bologna, Italy, where, in a controversial move, U2 incorporated into the show a nightly live satellite linkup to the besieged city of Sarajevo, changing both the mood and worth of Zoo TV. Their connection, Bill Carter, a twenty-seven-year-old American filmmaker and relief worker in the Bosnian capital, gave a rundown of the day's events from an abandoned television studio, depicting horrific scenes of women and children tortured and raped, bodies and limbs scattered in streets like dead leaves from shells and land mines, and poor to nonexistent food and water supplies under the constant Serb bombardment. Carter would also comb the city by day in search of residents of any ethnic background to give their own personal account of the war during the broadcast. At one stage, Bono was hell-bent on sneaking into the city and playing a free gig there, until word got back snipers would pick off members of the audience coming and going. At Carter's suggestion, U2 sent a satellite dish into Sarajevo instead and joined the European Broadcast Union so they could legally transmit (they were later sent a bill from the EBU for one hundred thousand pounds, though McGuinness refused to cough up on the grounds it was offensive to those struggling to be heard). "We were offering a true human reality," Carter recalled in *Rolling Stone*. "No one in seventeen months had allowed Bosnians—besides the politicians—to speak live to the world."

After the nightly broadcast U2 found at times it was almost impossible to continue the concert, such was the aftereffect. The most obvious example of this occurred at the first of four nights at London's Wembley Stadium when they went live to Carter and three young women—a Muslim, a Serb, and a half Croat, half Serb—and one of the girls asked them, "What do you really do for us?" And before Bono could offer a reply, she continued, her voice filled with rage, "Excuse me, I think nothing." Bono was left speechless; he had no words of comfort. And for the remainder of the show the audience stood in almost silence. Rock and roll had never felt so powerless.

The next morning British newspapers debated exhaustively the morals of assimilating rock-and-roll theater with real-life catastrophes. Some sneered that for all their postmodern irony, U2 had climbed right back up onto their soapbox at the first opportunity. Most simply found it to be in bad taste. *NME* wrote: "It was insulting. Faced with the horrific description of the situation in Sarajevo, Bono was reduced to a stumbling incoherence that was probably the result of genuine concern, but came across as bog-standard celeb banality. What does the band who have virtually everything buy with their millions? The one thing they've never had—credibility. Shame it's not for sale."

U2 dropped the satellite linkup from Zoo TV altogether after their second Wembley date. But during that same show, they had one more thing for the media to chew over. The controversial writer Salman Rushdie, who'd been in exile since the late Ayatollah Khomeini issued a fatwa on him in January 1989 for alleged blasphemies against Islam in his novel *The Satanic Verses*, joined MacPhisto on stage in front of seventy-two thousand screaming fans. "I'm not afraid of you; real devils don't wear horns," Rushdie told MacPhisto as his face was projected onto the gigantic video screens; this a man who was living his life in ghosts and shadows through fear of being killed. It was seen as a moving display of camaraderie on U2's behalf for a strident advocate of free speech, and the following morning newspapers around the globe ran front-page photos of the novelist's figurative one-finger salute to a leader and his minions.

The UK tabloid press later reported that it was also during U2's four-night residency at Wembley that Adam splashed fifteen hundred pounds on a "three-day sex and drink binge" at the Regent Hotel with a bevy of prostitutes, demanding that the ladies be "young, beautiful, and black." The reckless bassist allegedly ordered the prostitutes, at least one of whom claimed that she also shared drugs with him, on his credit card, only for the madam who ran the brothel to then pass on his details to a journalist who came in at the end of every month to go through her records. Not for the first time, Adam had a lot of explaining to do to loved ones. Campbell publicly dismissed the story as "complete crap" and stood by her man—for the time being, anyway.

▪

In September, on a month's leave from Zoo life, Bono joined Gavin Friday and Maurice Seezer in STS Studios in Dublin to write and record three original songs for the Jim Sheridan movie, *In the Name of the Father,* a searing indictment of the British criminal justice system. It was Bono and Friday's first collaboration together since the U2-Virgin Prunes ditty "Sad," performed in the early days and as yet unrecorded.

The next month, Bono and the rest of U2 helped Friday celebrate his wedding day by holding the reception at The Clarence Hotel in Dublin, which they had bought in 1992 and had since spent three hundred thousand pounds renovating. The party was held downstairs in the basement-cum-nightclub, The Kitchen, which wouldn't officially open until early 1994. A high-spirited affair, U2 performed "The Boys Are Back in Town" and later Edge and Naomi Campbell butchered their way through a number of karaoke songs, including The Monkees' "Daydream Believer."

Bono was also able to use the gap in touring to fulfill a lifelong dream of his by singing with Frank Sinatra on the crooner's new *Duets* album, his first LP in almost ten years and one that marked a return to

Capitol Records. Joining an eclectic cast of "contemporary artists," including Aretha Franklin, Barbra Streisand, and Tony Bennett, Bono traded vocals with Sinatra on the Cole Porter standard "I've Got You Under My Skin," even having the grapefruits to call him an "old fool." "I've Got You Under My Skin" was the album's first single, and a music video was shot for it in a bar in Palm Springs in November. The shoot was not without its problems and ended on an abrupt note. "It was an amazing moment, actually," Bono recalled on BBC Radio 1. "It was in a friend of his, Dominic's Place. We were waiting for Frank to turn up, and in he walks, he's kissing Dominic on the cheek, you know, the whole thing. We start the video. He's a little nervous. I think he probably had a little bit of Alzheimer's so he didn't like to be on his own too much, and one of the scenes he had to be completely on his own. He got quite agitated after it, and he started to forget where he was, who he was, and who I was, and he wanted to leave. So they [the film crew] said, 'We gotta do the thing with Bono, Frank.' And he said, 'Sonny? Sonny's here?' And they're saying, 'No. Bono!' And he's going, 'Who?'" Sinatra got up and left and that was that.

That same evening, Bono received a phone call from Sinatra's wife, Barbara, asking if he'd like to have dinner at their place by way of apology. When he got there Sinatra was in great form, knocking back tequilas with old friends. Bono handed Barbara his coat and ordered a ginger ale, much to the bemusement of Sinatra and his crew, who considered it a "girl's drink." Bono nervously brushed his hair over his gold earrings. Over Mexican dinner they drank tequila served from a glass bowl as big as the two singers' egos. Bono then treated everyone to an a cappella version of "Two Shots of Happy, One Shot of Sad," a saloon swinger that he wrote in the hope that Sinatra would one day record it.

A little later they settled down in the screening room to watch an old black-and-white movie. Unable to hold his alcohol, Bono fell asleep and woke up to discover his trousers were soaking wet around his crotch. He thought for sure he'd wet himself and watched the remainder of the film in silence. He hadn't, of course. He'd spilled his drink. Nevertheless, it was time to call it a night. In the little time he'd been there he had managed to not only be out-drunk by men twice his age, but also to stain Barbara's precious white sofa. Better to leave the scene of the crime than stick around for the sentencing.

Sinatra asked Bono to return the following day and he considered it, but he had a plane to catch to Australia where his bandmates were preparing for the final Zoo TV leg, "Zoomerang/New Zooland." Arriving in Melbourne, Bono found a band desperately clinging on to its sanity after being on the road for the best part of two years, hitting city after city, night after night, reestablishing their position as the biggest rock-and-roll band in the world. Somehow they'd even managed to fit in another studio album, a fascinating vision of a not-so-distant future. But the wear and tear of the past few years had begun to take its toll. None of them felt this more so than Adam. The bassist's drinking had spiraled out of control, and as the tour crawled into Sydney a few days later, his fractured state reached its inevitable conclusion when he failed to show up for a sound check in the hours leading up to U2's gig at the city's Football Stadium. Sprawled out on his hotel bed, lost in a fever of cheap booze and god knows what else, Adam could barely open his eyes, let alone stand on stage. He had spent the previous night trawling the bars in town and then raiding the drinks cabinet in his room, presumably hoping to wash away the rumors circulating in the press that his fiancée had been spotted in London holding hands with her ex-lover Robert De Niro.

Backstage, tempers were already fraught as the show was being treated as a dress rehearsal for the live worldwide broadcast of Zoo TV from the same venue the following night. As the gig fast approached, the three punctual members of U2 kept glancing at their watches. Adam had been late before. In fact time and Adam were never on what you'd call a first-name basis—his motto being "Give time, time." But he knew the stakes. His bandmates were anxious to know his whereabouts, even worried about him. They made a phone call. They didn't like what they heard.

U2 made the decision to go on stage without Adam, relying on his bass technician, Stuart Morgan, to stand in for him. Post-gig, they handed the self-destructive bassist an ultimatum that rattled him to the core: cut down on your lifestyle or we will cut you loose. Sure enough, Adam understood where they were coming from, and promised them one way or another he was going to clean up his act. He then rejoined them for the live Zoo TV broadcast, pale but sober, as well as the other remaining dates in Australia, New Zealand, and Japan.

Adding to the cloud of tension that had once again descended over the U2 empire was the alarming discovery that they had run into serious financial difficulties after spending exorbitant sums on Zoo TV and losing money on other nonmusic business interests. McGuinness and Ossie Kilkenny had proven to be poor money managers, plowing the group's earnings into markets they had little knowledge of. Their most high-profile mishap came in the form of LeisureCorp, in which they invested £22 million on four prime sites around Dublin and a further £8 million on six sites abroad in Germany with the intention of building leisure centers for ten-pin bowling and Quasar, a laser-gun game. But plans collapsed in Ireland when the Irish government changed the rules for the Business Expansion Scheme, while in Germany it turned out that all war games featuring replica guns were banned there. It was an embarrassing and costly error for all involved and by late 1993 U2 had bailed out, while LeisureCorp later sold off its properties at a net loss. However, according to a source, this was a "small-beer kind of mistake" compared to the money they lost during the UK property market crash between 1990 and 1992.

At one point during their latest crisis, U2 considered severing ties with McGuinness and aligning themselves with the persuasive Kilkenny, who had expansionist designs and coveted the managerial position in an official capacity. Consequently, McGuinness, desperate to remain in power, promised to beef up the business side of the organization and also agreed to take a smaller equity stake. However, this would be just the first round in an almost decade-long battle for survival and power between the two allies-turned-rivals.

In Tokyo, Zoo TV's final stop, it was left to Bono to be the wild child of the moon, as Adam opted for a relatively early night with a good book. As told in Bill Flanagan's *U2 at the End of the World*, the singer (along with Fintan Fitzgerald) lost his minders in a blur of bustling crowds and neon lights and plunged headfirst into a world of techno-slavery and after-hours hostess joints. He later surfaced on an apartment floor, his brain like a television tuned to a dead channel, and his aching body surrounded by a group of semi-naked hookers shaking off a night's worth of smack. On seeing he had momentarily come round, one of the girls kindly offered him a shot of heroin. Bono groggily shook his head, words failing him. The girl struggled to comprehend the rock star's snub, before finally offering to have sex with him. Bono waved her away, then curled up and fell asleep again. But not for long—the sexual temptress wasn't the only one who wanted to get into his leather trousers. Awakened by a strange hissing sound and a not entirely unpleasant tingling sensation working its way up his leg, he glanced down to find a pet python making goo-goo eyes at him. Bono could already see the headlines. "Rock Star in Heroin Sex Orgy." "St. Bono Loses Halo in Drug Den." "Irish Rocker Found Half-Conscious in Kinky Tokyo Snake Pit." This was not good. Fitzgerald, hearing alarm bells piercing through his own altered state, helped Bono to his feet, then guided him out through the apartment door and into the blinding morning light.

Back at the hotel, Bono wondered aloud how things had gotten so out of hand. U2 had become rock-and-roll clichés for real, victims of their own success and curiosity. This had to end. Now. "It's funny the things that happen to you on tour," Bono recalled at a Swansea literature convention in 1995. "You see people when you travel the world and some of them keep pythons. But that was a sign and that sign said 'Go home.' So I did."

So that was that. After around 5.3 million people had tuned into 157 shows, the Zoo TV screens were switched off for the last time. U2 had set out to revolutionize the live concert experience and many believed they had succeeded—not least the band themselves. "I don't think there is any better description of the '90s from the satellite point of view—looking down," Bono told *Rolling Stone*. "Not every record you make, concert you play should carry the weight, be that kind of zeitgeist. Because when it happens, it's an amazing thing."

14

Staring into the Flash

On the sun-kissed French Riviera, nestled between Nice and Monaco, is the seaside village of Èze-sur-Mer. It's a small piece of paradise, as Bono discovered when he visited for a fortnight in 1985 and was inspired enough to start writing the lyrics to "With or Without You." He loved the location so much in fact that he later cajoled Edge into going halves on two sheltered villas overlooking the Mediterranean. They renovated the largest villa with the intent of using it as a holiday home. And it was here they escaped with family and friends in 1994 following the Zoo TV juggernaut. They relaxed on the terraces, listened to music, drank a lot of red wine, and entertained acquaintances passing through, including Michael Stipe and Dave Stewart. Bono was in his element. He grew a beard, put on a few pounds (later referred to as "the fat Elvis period"), and got out the paintbrush. INXS front man Michael Hutchence and his supermodel girlfriend Helena Christensen (who was a regular VIP at U2 shows) lived a stone's throw away and they would swing by for dinner. Bono and Hutchence struck up a close friendship, often heading down to the beach to engage in drunken debates about love, life, death, music, all kinds of things, until sunrise. (Frances Cahill, daughter of the Irish crime boss Martin "The General" Cahill, would later claim in her memoir, *Martin Cahill, My Father,* that it was during this period that five criminals staked out Bono's home in Dublin with the aim of kidnapping and holding his daughter, Jordan, for a £4 million ransom, until the plan was ultimately dropped on the orders of Ms. Cahill's father. However, Paul Williams, a qualified criminologist and author of *The General,* has doubts about the credibility of the kidnapping plot. "I never heard that allegation until Ms. Cahill made it," he says. "I never encountered any information about such a plot during my research over the past fifteen years. I have interviewed several of Cahill's associates in the criminal underworld and never has this matter even been mentioned. I have also spoken extensively to a wide variety of police contacts who dealt directly with Cahill and his gang and there has never been any intelligence suggesting that Bono's family was ever targeted either. My suspicion is that it was done [by Ms. Cahill] to make mischief.")

Edge was joined in the south of France by Morleigh Steinberg, a dark-haired Californian of wealthy parentage. The couple had first met in 1987 when Steinberg, a professional dancer, appeared in U2's video for "With or Without You" and hosted a celebrity bash during the Joshua Tree Tour. She was later hired as Bono's movement coach on Zoo TV and also interacted with the singer on stage during "Mysterious Ways" as a belly dancer. By the end of the tour, Edge and Steinberg were officially an item (after she had given her then-boyfriend back home the boot). As far as the guitarist was concerned, this was the happiest he'd been in a long time.

Larry and Adam, meanwhile, bought pads in New York and began taking professional music lessons, eager to gain new knowledge and tighten up certain areas of their playing on their respective instruments. For Larry the lessons couldn't have come any sooner. "After being on the road, it's time now to advance a bit musically," he told *Rolling Stone.* "I really want to learn how to explain myself in musical terms, the basics of music theory."

Adam also joined an art class and even flirted with the occasional singing lesson from leading vocal coach Katie Agresta. It was in fact Agresta who introduced Adam to his bass teacher, Patrick Pfeiffer, who helped him to better understand mode/chord relationships, groove structure, and syncopation. "He was already using most of these techniques," recalls Pfeiffer, "but he wanted to know what it was he was hearing so he'd be in control." To his delight, Pfeiffer found Adam to be a model student in terms of work ethic and discipline. "He'd never miss a lesson. He'd always be prepared. One week he was walking in Central Park every day, tapping out syncopations. He'd come back for his next lesson and absolutely nail the stuff . . . and that particular exercise is anything but easy. He wouldn't let anything get between him and his lessons either, walking through virtual monsoons and arriving completely soaked. He was an absolute joy to be around. Easily one of the most dedicated and self-disciplined individuals I've ever met."

Although many critics have described Adam's bass playing as overly simplistic and repetitive, Pfeiffer, who is also the author of *Bass Guitar for Dummies,* maintains there is more to him than first meets the ear. "Adam's style is not simplistic, it is complex in a subtle way. Many people would miss that point by listening for the flashiness of lots of notes, but there's a deeper level of complexity. In Adam's case, he uses a technique called 'harmonic syncopation,' which is when the bass plays a consistent rhythm, usually attacking every eighth note in a measure, but anticipates the harmony by shifting the tonality before the actual chord does. This technique gives the song a forward motion, a thrust, because the bass keeps arriving early for the harmony, anticipating it. It's a technique often heard in McCartney's and Sting's playing as well. Adam also uses some interesting and challenging riffs. He's just subtle about it, but I can tell you, the cat can play."

Around this same time, Adam and Naomi announced that they had called off their planned Valentine's Day wedding and gone their separate ways—although vowing to remain good friends. Adam also faced up to his own personal demon and attended Alcoholics Anonymous meetings in a bid to get sober and avoid a repeat of the Sydney incident. "Namely that for whatever reasons—and I still don't know what those reasons are—I am one of those characters that has an addictive personality," he later told *Hot Press*. "And it's an emotional problem as much as it is a physical problem and I had to start dealing with that. And that's the hard road, figuring out the psychology of it."

▪

In November 1994, U2 regrouped for two weeks at London's Westside Studios where—under the pseudonym Passengers—they collaborated with Brian Eno on a soundtrack album of improvised avant-garde pieces for a series of imaginary films, a natural progression, if you like, from *Zooropa* and Eno's 1979 ambient opus *Music for Films*. Later joined by Scottish DJ Howie B, the collective spent a further five weeks in U2's recently purchased Hanover Quay studio in Dublin in the spring and summer of 1995. "For us, this is an opportunity to get all this stuff out that there isn't really room for on a U2 record," Adam told *NUJ*, "and the fact that we haven't been together for a year means that there's a lot of energy to make music and do something with it. The last thing we wanted was to get bogged down on a two-year song album and lose that energy."

U2 also turned their focus to a number of other projects. Bono and Edge cowrote the eponymous theme tune for James Bond's seventeenth screen outing, *Goldeneye*, which was performed by pop diva Tina Turner, as well as the Irish peace process prayer "North and South of the River" with folk legend Christy Moore. Larry, meanwhile, played drums on Emmylou Harris's *Wrecking Ball* album, which was recorded at Daniel Lanois's Kingsway Studios in New Orleans.

In June, U2 released their only single of the year, the T-Rex-esque glam-rock romp of "Hold Me, Thrill Me, Kiss Me, Kill Me," taken from the soundtrack to the third live-action Batman installment, *Batman Forever*. Originally recorded during the *Zooropa* sessions but left off "because it had guitar on it," the song explored the power and expectations of stardom and Bono's—and Bruce Wayne's, for that matter—struggle with duality. It reached number two in the UK and number sixteen in the United States, outdone in both markets by its sentimental soundtrack-mate, Seal's "Kissed by a Rose."

At one stage Bono had hoped to persuade *Batman Forever* director Joel Schumacher to give MacPhisto a role as a bad guy in the film, but alas, it wasn't to be. Schumacher told *ShowBiz Ireland*: "He wanted to play a villain in The Riddler's world. But we had Jim Carrey and Tommy Lee Jones and I didn't have a part for him. He understood my reasoning and then he wrote that fabulous song for us which was wonderful."

In September, Bono, Edge, and Eno attended the annual "Pavarotti and Friends" benefit concert in aid of War Child in Modena, Italy, where they performed "One" and "Miss Sarajevo," a Passengers track featuring an operatic solo by Pavarotti, accompanied by a full classical orchestra. The majestic "Miss Sarajevo" was written about a beauty pageant held in the Bosnian capital during the war as a surreal act of defiance. Yet without Pavarotti's perseverance, the song would never have seen the light of day. As U2 discovered, the big man simply couldn't take no for an answer. Bono explained on BBC Radio 1: "He rang to ask if we would write him a song, and I said I didn't think that would be possible because we were working on the Passengers project, and he just would not stop calling, which is pretty amazing. It would be every single day and if he wasn't called back immediately he'd shout at our housekeeper and say, 'Get God to give me a call!' He would say things like, 'I will call you, and I will call you every day and every hour. I will be in your dreams, when you wake up. I will speak into the ears of your children. Your father is a tenor, and I will tell him you won't write a song for me.' So I thought, 'Oh God, we'll really have to do this.'"

On November 6, with virtually no promotion, the Passengers' *Original Soundtracks 1* album was released worldwide to modest opening-week sales before quietly dropping off the charts. Critically, it fared better. Bill Graham of *Hot Press* wrote: "Let's not argue whether or not this is U2's best album but instead agree that it is certainly their most relaxed, and their most playful. It's to be applauded that they've set themselves a task that disassociates them from the more predictable patterns of superstardom. But better still is the fact that they have effectively created a world of nighttime atmospherics that is both very far from anything U2 have done before and yet curiously recognizable as their work." Tom Moon, meanwhile, concluded in his review for Knight Ridder News Service that "*Soundtracks* turns the rules of ambient music upside down. Anybody with a synthesizer can generate drone music. On *Original Soundtracks 1*, U2 argues that it takes skill, and heart, to make such austerity meaningful."

High praise indeed, though like many critics, Graham and Moon mistook the soundtrack for an out-and-out U2 work, which it was not, as reflected in the band's moniker and the low-key marketing. "It was a Brian Eno/U2 project," stresses Marc Marot. "I, in particular, have an aversion for side projects. I think they can be very confusing for a fan base. And I was very strongly against marketing it as a U2 record, but I don't remember having to persuade people very hard. The arguments were never with U2; the arguments were internally with PolyGram because it was the run up to Christmas and they felt they could sell some serious volume with it. But my view was that if it were a U2 record, it was a very substandard U2 record; and if you marketed a substandard U2 record, you would damage U2 as a brand, particularly on the back of *Zooropa*. So I was very keen to distance them from it and also very keen not to have conventional singles released from it—to not draw too much attention to it, just allow it to do what it did."

Incidentally, Larry, the no-nonsense drummer, was against its release altogether. Too much art for art's sake, he grumbled. "It was a good record to make. But when it was finished it was just this meandering, self-indulgent . . . It's not the sort of album I'd go out and buy myself." However, Larry was more than happy to collaborate with Adam on an updated electronic version of Lalo Schifrin's "Theme from *Mission: Impossible*" for the Tom Cruise movie based on the cult '60s spy series. The initial studio request was for the whole band to contribute under the U2 banner, but as Bono and Edge were up to their eyeballs in demos with Massive Attack producer Nellee Hooper in London and Dublin in preparation for a new album, the rhythm section volunteered to accept the mission on the group's behalf. It represented an opportunity for the duo to put their newfound musical knowledge to the test, replacing Schifrin's 5/4 time signature with a 4/4 groove to make it something people could dance to. Released in May 1996, the track was a top-ten hit around the world, shifting over five hundred thousand copies in its first month in the United States. Larry and Adam also got to attend the Los Angeles movie premiere, sharing the red carpet with Cruise and his French costars Jean Reno and femme fatale Emmanuelle Béart.

■

With U2 still losing sleep over their financial affairs, McGuinness, in full self-preservation mode, instigated a controversial bidding war between booking agents and promoters for the exclusive worldwide rights to the band's next stadium tour—which caused a great deal of resentment among those who had stood by them in the early years and expected a similar kind of loyalty at a time when the tour industry was experiencing a massive downturn. Among those invited to Dublin in March 1996 to make an offer was a consortium comprising Frank Barsalona, U2's long-serving American agent and mentor, as well as European promoters Harvey Goldsmith and Marek Lieberberg. "Frank was representing U2 and they were being wooed away [from Premier Talent]," recalls Goldsmith. "At that point he was very upset about the whole thing, and we went to see him and said, 'Look, we'll prop you up, we'll back a bid. You be the agent and we'll promote the whole tour.' Because Frank was a really good friend of mine and a business colleague and I felt that they were wrong in leaving him." According to a friend of the late agent, during the Dublin meeting U2 promised him the rights to the tour as a token of the band's appreciation for all he had done for them. However, by the time Barsalona's plane landed back home in New York, U2 had agreed to sell the tour to his archrival Michael Cohl in a deal worth up to $115 million. Feeling betrayed and deceived by those closest to him, Barsalona became a shell of the man he once was. "Frank virtually had a nervous breakdown," reveals the friend. "When it came to dollars or loyalty, dollars was [U2's] choice."

Cohl, a cofounder of the Toronto-based concert promotion firm TNA and a former co-owner of Canada's first all-nude strip club, Pandora's Box, had in fact pioneered the full-service touring system U2 and

McGuinness now favored, guaranteeing his clients an amount equal to around 85 percent of potential ticket sales and shouldering the production costs (which also included buying out local promoters or forcing them to partner for shows for a modest flat fee) in return for the global rights. He had made his reputation in 1989 when he wangled the rights to The Rolling Stones' Steel Wheels Tour from San Francisco–based impresario Bill Graham, who later likened losing the veteran rockers to "watching my favorite lover become a whore." However, Cohl was thought to have been out of the running altogether after a 1995 *Toronto Star* investigation accused him of cheating bands by charging them an extra fee for a nonexistent tax, thus also driving up the ticket price for fans. But according to sources, U2 conducted their own investigation into the allegations and found little evidence to suggest that Cohl was responsible. The U2-Cohl agreement was based on one hundred stadium shows with an average ticket price of forty-five dollars, which was double that of the typical U.S. ticket price that year. Peter Conlon, an Atlanta promoter, called it "a lightning rod for everything that's wrong with this business and they're reaping the seeds of greed."

Disillusioned at the level of nostalgia that existed in white rock and roll—and, more importantly, enthused by the critical praise bestowed upon *Achtung Baby, Zooropa,* and *Original Soundtracks 1*—U2 continued to push forward during the recording of their ninth studio album, *Pop,* integrating the sonic innovations of dance, techno, and trip-hop into sounds culled from various phases of their career. But the sessions found the quartet at their most fractured. Adam in particular was in a bad place. He was struggling to adapt to his new lifestyle and was in constant disagreement with Nellee Hooper over various creative aspects. By the autumn of 1995, U2 put out a call for additional studio personnel to aid them. Brian Eno was the odds-on favorite to come to their rescue once again, but he informed them that he was going to sit this one out to focus on his own projects. Northern Irish DJ David Holmes was straight-up busy. Bristolian trip-hop guru Tricky went as far as hanging out with Bono in Jamaica, taking magic mushrooms with him and listening to the Hooper-produced tracks. "That's the best thing you've done in years," he told Bono. "Don't mess with it." In the end, U2 settled for Flood (principal producer) and Howie B (coproducer, engineer, and mixer). Hooper, meanwhile, would later be replaced by Steve Osborne, one half of the acclaimed remix/production duo Perfecto, who had reimagined "Even Better Than the Real Thing" and "Lemon" into dance-floor hits at the request of Island's Marc Marot and Nick Angel.

Compounding U2's problems was the fact that Larry had aggravated an old back injury in late 1995, which necessitated surgery and sidelined him for the better part of three months. Therefore, the job of supplying the beats fell to "vibes man" Howie B. His elaborate record decks were set up alongside U2's own instruments in Hanover Quay so that he could contribute loops and samples at a whim. When things got flat he'd upset the flow of things by hitting a foot pedal to generate a dose of creative tension, or spin some obscure vinyl and encourage the band to improvise over it. His job was as much about turning them on as it was straightforward production. And while the jam was in progress, Flood, meticulous by nature, would be in the control room making sure everything was going onto a tape. He would then seek out the best parts and transfer them to another tape, which he'd give to each band member at the end of the week. Next day they'd come in and debate the pros and cons and ultimately what they were going to pursue further. In many ways, Howie B and Flood's creative input was not entirely dissimilar to Eno and Lanois's in the past, and U2 dubbed the dynamic duo "Batman and Robin Version 2.0."

Edge had made a conscious decision to play more guitar on *Pop* after largely experimenting with keyboards on *Zooropa* and *Original Soundtracks 1*. He had grown frustrated with all the retro-minded guitar players out there and felt that there was a real opportunity to make new ground. And it was in his approach to guitar where he connected with the trip-hop dance culture the most, focusing on creating unforgettable sounds and textures rather than traditional melodies. "I'm still fascinated by melodies, and I'm certainly not leaving that behind, but I think that for some of these songs it was a good twist to not do a conventional guitar hook kind of melody but to try to find some extraordinary sound that could create the same effect," Edge told *Guitar Player*.

The apex of his guitar experimentation was the "747" sound so prominent on both the darkly spiritual "Gone" and the Led Zeppelin–meets-Prodigy techno rock rumble "MOFO." Flood revealed in *Guitar World*: "We nicknamed it the '747' guitar 'cause originally it just sounded like this ridiculous jet plane taking off and going absolutely mad. It's him using his Korg SDD delay heavily fed back and then going into a couple of different fuzz pedals and a (Digitech) Whammy pedal. One of the fuzz pedals was a Fuzz Face. I can't remember what the other one was, to be quite honest. But the way he's got it set up, the guitar starts feeding back in a controllable way that sounds very uncontrollable."

Adam, too, was determined to take his weapon of choice to new heights, nudge it to the forefront, continue his growth as a musician. And he couldn't have picked a better time to do it. Flood was a bass man. He liked nothing better than a throbbing bottom end. On average Adam used an SVT Mark One with an 8x cabinet which Flood mic'ed with a Neumann U47 FET minus pads, filters, and other enhancements. He also had a few effects, compressors, distortion units, and boom boxes at his disposal. He'd play them into an amp, then he and Flood would choose the most suitable effect for each song. The only rule was that it couldn't be murky, it had to have definition.

By late April, U2 had accumulated thirty-eight musical pieces, yet they only had five real songs to show for it—three of which were mapped out during the *Zooropa* sessions. The band's most celebrated work was said to give listeners the sense of a specific physical location, but this was all over the place, schizophrenic and stateless. Searching for clues, they decided a spot of creative tourism in Miami would be worthwhile. Edge told *MAX*: "Miami is like candy floss. You know what I'm saying? The culture of Miami. We were determined to kind of explore that and see that up close and kind of inject a little bit of fun into that recording. We'd been in the studio for quite a while and we thought that it would be good to get away from Dublin and do some recording elsewhere and Miami seemed like a good place to blow away some cobwebs and just open ourselves up to something else." And they had a great time out there. Just U2, Flood, and family (Howie and the other crew members stayed behind in Dublin). One night, the group ended up in a late-night poker joint straight out of a Scorsese movie, with shag-pile carpet and slick mob types dealing more than just cards. Larry, who was still in no condition to sit behind a drum kit for long stretches of time, took on Howie's role in the shade of South Beach Studios, contributing loops and samples during jams. "I'm using all this shit to my advantage," he said, "otherwise I'll be out of a job."

But U2's stay in Miami was cut short after just a couple of weeks when news reached them that their early Irish mentor Bill Graham had died of a sudden heart attack. He was forty-five years old. The band returned to Dublin for his funeral, where Bono sang Leonard Cohen's "Tower of Song" and served as a pallbearer along with Edge. "He was like a brother to his colleagues and a cousin to us," Bono said later in a special edition of *Hot Press* celebrating the music critic's life.

When work on *Pop* resumed in July the impact Graham's death had had on U2 was there for all to see and hear. What was originally intended to be an exuberant, upbeat album that celebrated the moment and didn't take itself too seriously soon treaded darker terrain, with a bleak awareness of one's own mortality. Fighting it at first, Bono called in Irish artist David Donahue to brighten up Hanover with an "environment of words." He told Donahue that he wanted to explore the opposite of human nature (that is, joy) and revealed his loathing for the term "gothic." "Dark is easy," he said. "Writing a happy song, now that's hard." But Donahue wasn't convinced. He felt that Bono, like many of their fellow countrymen, had a true gift for melancholy, and he was determined to tap into this to prevent the lyricist from becoming a "prophet of sunshine." Donahue covered the studio walls with poems and passages plucked from classic literature, including William Butler Yeats's sonnet "Before the World Was Made," Albert Camus's *The Outsider,* and Samuel Beckett's *Malone Dies,* with its opening line: "I shall soon be quite dead at last in spite of all." He also printed random words such as "Dark Eyes," "Made Flesh," "Greying Sky," "Dying," "Alone," and those taken from the Bible's Sermon on the Mount on either side of small pieces of transparent plastic and dropped them into a gigantic jar of honey. Observing the words, burning vividly in their dark realism, Bono got the message loud and clear.

By late July, U2 had around twenty bona fide tracks vying for a place on the album. However, it wasn't long before they realized they'd made a few wrong turns along the way. Namely by employing loops in Larry's absence they had lost some of what was special about the band. Edge recalled in *Q*: "[It] was like the heart and soul was missing. I remember turning round to Flood and saying, 'Why is this sounding so flat and lifeless? What are we missing?' And he said, 'The band!' And it was suddenly, like, Ah, right . . . okay." And so U2 frantically went about stripping down the more mechanical elements to bring the tunes back to their essence. The member with the most on his plate was Larry, who dusted off his kit and began to replace the loops with real drums. And in the event loops were in fact required, one of his preferences was to record his drumming onto a handheld Walkman and then send it through a sampler, so even then somewhere in the mechanical-sounding beat was a human heart.

U2's radical last-minute rethink forced a delay in the album's release until 1997, resulting in all kinds of complications for both them and their label. "I loved *Pop*, but what a problematic birth," says Marc Marot. "It was supposed to be delivered to me for autumn '96 but they were having terrible problems with it in the studio. The worst thing was that they had signed a deal to go on tour in '97, which they were about to try and sell with no album out. But they couldn't finish it, couldn't finish it, and then eventually half delivered it to me in December. I remember sitting with Bono and Edge at Alain Levy's [worldwide president and CEO of PolyGram] fiftieth birthday party in New York a few days later and Edge owned up to me that the record wasn't finished, but that they had to get it out because they had the tour booked. So we were aware of that, and there was an element of making the best of a bad job."

That job was made a whole lot harder by the fact that a Hungarian fan had come into possession of a U2 promo featuring two thirty-second audio clips of music from *Pop* and uploaded it onto his Web page in late October. Within twenty-four hours radio stations around the world had begun spinning the clips on air as a preview of the "New U2."

Marot recalls: "The band gave us a VHS tape to play at a retail conference—Our Price, HMV, all the retailers would have been there—and there was a little clip of them doing 'Discothèque' and 'Wake Up Dead Man,' just a piece of raw footage. And then one of the international distributors took away that VHS, gave it to a mate who then extracted the audio off it, and this awful unmixed substandard piece of music ended up being picked up by a radio station in Hungary and then playlisted by KROQ in North America—and the band hadn't even delivered the album to us! And it's like an infection. If a station like KROQ gets it, everybody's got to have it. So we had to bring forward our release date for 'Discothèque' and get everything done in unbelievable time. The whole of the beginning of *Pop* was messy."

The swirling, groove-based "Discothèque" received its first official airing on Ireland's RTÉ 2fm on January 7, 1997, after Paul McGuinness personally hand-delivered it to DJ Dave Fanning. In the United States, the single was added to 343 radio station playlists, and was the most-played record on the *Billboard* Modern Rock chart by the end of the first week. However, while it was a favorite among U.S. radio programmers, the public response was mixed. The song seemed too trashy, too throwaway for it to be U2. This view only intensified with the much-hyped world premiere of the ultra-camp "Discothèque" music video on MTV, in which the band appeared dressed as members of the Village People inside a giant mirror ball. The single debuted at number one in the UK and number ten in the States, but quickly fell.

Pop, meanwhile, topped the charts in over thirty countries when it was released in March. But like the lead single, it had a remarkably brief shelf life; in America, for example, it dropped out of the top ten altogether after just three weeks, with the perception there being that it was an out-and-out dance album on account of "Discothèque" and its title, which was intended to reflect its eclectic scope. "We have songs that we've processed, where we've fucked up the sound and messed with new technology," Bono said of *Pop* on MTV. "But there's other songs that are very simple and are the sound of a band playing in a room. What's important for U2 is that we can do anything we want—that's important.

Soon as someone tells us we can't do it, we'll do it. Soon as someone says, 'You're a rock band, don't you try and get on the dance floor,' we just think, 'Fuck you!' You must not allow yourself to be put in a box."

The band hastily put out "Staring at the Sun," the most traditional U2 track on the album, as the second single in an attempt to salvage the situation in the United States. However, the song tripped at number twenty-six on the *Billboard* Hot 100 before performing its own disappearing act. McGuinness, who remained embroiled in a bitter power struggle with Kilkenny over the U2 empire, placed the blame for the single's failure squarely at the door of Island's marketing team. "The public knew it was there, radio knew it was there," counters Marot. "It's rarely down to marketing people for a band the size of U2. I think 'Discothèque' had undermined people's confidence in the band at that stage." Indeed, despite a sustained promotional blitz, all three subsequent singles from the album failed to find a large American audience: the Brit-pop-inspired "Last Night on Earth" missed out on the Top 40 at number fifty-seven, while "Please," a moody, intricate piece about religious divide, and "If God Will Send His Angels," which Bono described as "science fiction gospel," didn't even make the Top 100.

U2, for their part, held McGuinness accountable for the poor commercial performance of *Pop* in America. They took him to task for convincing them to go ahead and book the tour before the album was anywhere near finished. Larry, who was mostly considered an irritant by the others, was so incensed by McGuinness's schoolboy error that he even tried to block *Pop*'s release altogether (although this didn't prevent him from claiming the album was "right up there with *Achtung Baby* and *Zooropa*" when doing the promotional rounds). All in all, *Pop* sold 6 million copies worldwide, a low figure by U2 standards.

On the plus side, *Pop* initially received favorable reviews from music critics, who praised its ambition and adventurous spirit. "Super group play a blinder. . . . Different, daring, and dark," proclaimed the *Belfast Telegraph*. *Rolling Stone* believed that U2 had "defied the odds and made some of the greatest music of their lives." *Q* magazine gushed that the album was "[b]ig enough to fill the U2-shaped hole left in modern rock since Zoo TV. Excellent." Perhaps self-confessed U2 hater Phillip Smith of *The Sunday Telegraph* summed up the love best when he conceded that *Pop* was "much less unsettling and much more interesting than could have been hoped for. . . . It is time to give U2 their due."

The album was considered to be the band's most spiritually challenging work to date, juggling life's struggles with faith, doubt, and temptation amid late-twentieth-century decadence and trash—all of which U2 themselves continued to wrestle with in private. But the lyrics did draw criticism from the Christian community, who felt that the band—Bono in particular—had abandoned God. Christian journalist Steven Isaac of *Plugged In* magazine lamented: "These four Irishmen, once considered by some fans to be a 'Christian' band, dance to a darker score than they did during their *Joshua Tree* days . . . they persist in placing more and more obstacles between themselves and Truth—sex, drugs, and ego among them. Their quest has mutated into self-pity and pointless anguish. . . . Teens fascinated with the band's soul-searching should be directed to 1 Timothy 6:3–5 and Ephesians 4:10–16. Imitating U2 will only lead to confusion, temptation, and compromise."

But such Christian-based condemnation was just a drop in the ocean, and U2 basked in the positive reviews to both hide their own dissatisfaction with the record and divert attention away from the poor sales. "We're getting the best reviews of our whole life, and from the most miserable of quarters," Bono told *Hot Press*. "And generally, big groups just don't get those reviews because people don't want to give you the cream on the cake. They're wrong to think like that because they should forget about your stature and context and think about the quality of the work. But in this instance, I think we're coming out on top, because the reviews are unbelievable."

Enter PopMart. The death of stadium-rock spectacle.

■

U2 had unveiled the PopMart Tour on February 12, 1997, at a world press conference held in the lingerie section of a Kmart store in downtown New York. The supermarket-themed stage design comprised of a gigantic McDonald's-style yellow arch that towered over the main stage and supported a thirty-ton PA system, the world's largest drive-in LED screen, a twelve-foot-wide illuminated stuffed olive perched atop a hundred-foot cocktail stick, and a forty-foot hydraulic mirror-ball lemon from which the band would emerge during the first encore to perform "Discothèque" on a large Plexiglas B-stage-cum-dance-floor—all powered by three on-site generators that supplied enough energy to run fifteen hundred homes. "It costs a fortune to look this trashy," Bono quipped to the one hundred journalists in attendance. And he wasn't exaggerating. The LED screen required an investment of $7 million to develop, while operating costs came in at $250,000 a day—gig or no gig.

U2—with the help of stage designer Willie Williams and architect Mark Fisher—conceived the PopMart Tour as a satire on consumerism, influenced by pop artists such as Roy Lichtenstein and Andy Warhol and their all-embracing stance toward commercial culture. "The show is really trying to reinforce the point that commercialism is just part and parcel of the process of being in a big band," Edge told *Guitar World*. "I suppose the Pop Art movement really touched on that, pointing out that commercialism is part of this era and that art and music shouldn't see it as the Big Bad Wolf, but to learn that it is possible to have a sense of the commercial world and still be true to your work."

In a highly irregular move—but one made unavoidable because of the *Pop* delays—tickets for the PopMart Tour were put on sale in mid-February, two weeks before the release of the album it was designed to promote. Regardless, early sales were encouraging—everywhere but North America, that is. Fewer extra shows were required in major cities like New York and Chicago than predicted, while markets such as Los Angeles, San Diego, and Arizona were having trouble selling out altogether. Many in the industry blamed the inflation in ticket prices. Others suggested that the fact that U2 was playing fifty-thousand-capacity stadiums from the get-go lessened the urgency to snap up a ticket. But the lack of general excitement ran deeper than that. "Discothèque" had put U2 in a precarious position stateside, far from the musical tolerance of their older fans and out of step with the younger sneakers-and-short-pants rock crowd.

To make matters worse, U2, nervous and under-rehearsed, bombed in spectacular fashion at the star-studded PopMart premiere in Las Vegas in April. "It was like watching a car crash in slow motion with your friends in the car," recalls Marc Marot. "We were all under enormous pressure. They had this massive tour to sell and I as a managing director of Island was under pressure, not only from the band and Paul but also from my bosses, in terms of promoting the tour. So I then passed on the pressure to all the worldwide managing directors that Island worked with and virtually every territory sent maybe the three best or biggest journalists from their country—so as you can imagine we sent *Q* magazine, *The Times,* and *NME* from the UK and that was multiplied around the world with the best writers from each major country in attendance. So we had fifty of the top reviewers and journalists watching a car crash, where the band stopped halfway through 'Staring at the Sun' because they couldn't play it. It was really difficult."

"It was the worst U2 show I've ever seen," says Carter Alan. "They just didn't have it together and there was mistake after mistake. They set themselves up. It was a massive plan by McGuinness and it could have been fine. But by their own admission they didn't leave themselves enough time to finish the album until finally it's, 'We gotta start rehearsing!' If it had just been like a regular show, a Joshua Tree–type show with the band in a big place, they could have pulled it off easily, but it was a complicated show and they couldn't do it. Now, by the time the first leg ended in Boston it was pretty good at that point. Even though I didn't like some of the material from that album, I did like the concert. And the lemon was just ridiculous; that was such a send-up of Kiss and all those bands. But I remember sitting in the audience going, 'I hope people get the joke.'"

But Boston was all too little, too late for U2. Following the Las Vegas debacle, PopMart had a new name and it was "FlopMart." "U2 are feeling the cool wind of rejection for the first time," reported *The Guardian*. "PopMart is open for business, but the shoppers aren't exactly cluttering the aisles—time for a clearance sale," mocked *The Irish Times*. While *The Observer* sneered, "If Hubris has a sound it is the hiss of air leaking out of the giant inflatable olive that is key prop on the world's most expensive rock tour."

Although the tour was received more favorably in Europe—highlights of which included U2 setting a new world record for the highest attendance at a one-act concert when they performed to 150,000-plus Italians at Reggio Emilia and a historic night in war-battered Sarajevo in which they were credited with bringing formerly warring factions together for the first major spectacle in the city since the 1984 Winter Olympics—U2's commercial appeal in the United States had only decreased when they returned for the third leg of the trek. In Tampa, Florida, for example, only twenty thousand people came out to see them perform, while in neighboring Jacksonville as few as fifteen thousand showed up. And in true U2 tradition, when the chips were down, the band and McGuinness turned on one another—and on anyone else associated with them.

"That tour did terrible business," Barry Fey later told the author. "Michael [Cohl] I don't think ever ended up paying what he was supposed to, but they gave him a break. And they blamed the promoters, [that because] we were only getting a fee we didn't try that hard. That's absurd. I would never do anything like that with U2. I just think that project was such a departure in their music that the people said, 'No, we don't want to go see this.' One kid in the Corps record store came up to me and said, 'I've supported U2 from the beginning. They've gotten plenty of my money, but they're not going to get this.' They shouldn't have done the album or the tour. What happened was they tried to be cutting edge. They wanted to be U2 the leader instead of just being U2. People couldn't give a shit about their placing, they just wanted to see U2."

The PopMart Tour came to a stop in Johannesburg in March 1998, screen full of dents, olive deflated, and lemon well and truly gone sour. Bono, who craved adulation and relevance, put on a brave public face, but privately he was inconsolable.

15

Billion-Dollar Dreams

Bono and Edge, exerting influence afforded them by a society increasingly shaped by the cult of celebrity, made a surprise appearance alongside the Northern Irish band Ash at a free concert held on May 19, 1998, at the Waterfront Hall in Belfast to promote the "Yes" vote in the upcoming referendum on the Good Friday Agreement and bring an end to The Troubles. The benefit gig came at a crucial point in the "Yes" campaign as some early polls suggested that just over 52 percent of voters were in favor of the peace agreement, with a quarter of the remaining voters still undecided. A monumental moment occurred during the set, when Bono invited Ulster Unionist leader David Trimble and his counterpart in the nationalist Social Democratic and Labour Party John Hume on stage and raised their arms aloft in a symbolic gesture of unity reminiscent of the Bob Marley One Love Peace Concert in Jamaica in 1978 when Marley joined the hands of opposing party leaders Michael Manley and Edward Seaga. Hume, deeply moved by the whole experience, left the stage in tears.

Bono recalled: "I spoke to David Trimble and John Hume backstage and I said to them, 'I'm going to ask you to do something that's almost impossible for politicians to do. I'm going to ask you to go out on stage and not say anything.' And they were kind of looking around and going 'What?' I said, 'This is a photograph, that's what this is, and we need to stage-manage it. You walk from this side and you walk from that.'

"It was an amazing moment, one of the great, great moments to be a part of. And to see the courage of both of those men. I suppose compromise is a word that has connotations of weakness, but I think it's one of the great strengths of human beings."

Three days later, the agreement passed by votes of 94.4 percent in favor in Ireland and 71.1 percent in favor in Northern Ireland. "It was an incredibly humbling feeling to realize that without that concert, without that moment captured by the media, the vote could have easily gone the other way," Edge said.

Later that year, Trimble and Hume shared the Nobel Peace Prize "for their efforts to find a peaceful solution to the conflict in Northern Ireland." Bono, meanwhile, became convinced his charisma and powers of persuasion made him an ideal candidate for a major political position should the opportunity arise.

McGuinness had reason to breathe a deep sigh of relief in July when U2 finally granted him permission to show his friend-turned-nemesis Ossie Kilkenny the door after years of poor investments and what McGuinness allies characterized as nefarious attempts to wrest control of the band. In September 1996, McGuinness had recruited Trevor Bowen, a former senior partner at KPMG specializing in banking and finance, as a financial director of Principle Management to help him reverse U2's declining fortunes. A source close to the band told *The Sunday Times* in 1998: "Bowen looked at the series of investments made for the band and you could say none of them had performed particularly well. If the money had been put into Allied Irish Bank Shares over a ten-year period instead, they would have had a better return." It was an extremely messy divorce between McGuinness and Kilkenny, who also shared major interests in Ardmore Studios and the independent television station TV3. One source likened it to a warring couple "fighting over the kids."

McGuinness would never discuss in detail what happened between the pair—not then, not ever. But without fail the mere mention of Kilkenny's name would blacken his mood. In an interview with the *Financial Times* in 2001, he said: "I don't know what to say about Ossie. My mother used to say, if you can't think of anything good to say about a person, say nothing at all and I think I'll take her advice. It was certainly a very big falling out."

Eager to recoup their losses, U2 vowed to take a more active role in their business affairs and set about restructuring their empire with the aid of Bowen. As part of a new seven-year plan, they negotiated a lucrative contract with PolyGram's Island Records for the release of three "best of" compilations. Even though the figure of $50 million was publicized and printed in the *Financial Times,* Island insiders speak of a deal that was almost twice that amount, making it the biggest of its kind in music history.

Released in November, the first set of songs, entitled *U2: The Best of 1980–1990 & B-sides,* included well-known chart hits such as "New Year's Day" and "With or Without You," as well as a radio-friendly reworking of an old B-side, "Sweetest Thing," which became the band's fourth-biggest-selling single of all time in the UK. "I'm not saying I found 'Sweetest Thing,' but it was my idea to put it out as a single," says Marc Marot. "Bono said to me, 'It's not even going to make it into the top twenty-five. It's not good enough.' And I said, 'It's a top-five single, Bono.' We went back and forth and eventually he bet me that it wouldn't get in the top five and of course it went in at number three and went on to be absolutely massive. The single helped us to sell 14 million copies of the compilation album, which is just unbelievable. As a single, it really helped put them back on the map. It was a bit more 'ordinary,' if that's the right word, from some of the things that they'd been releasing. They'd been getting a little esoteric, a little out there for certain fans, and 'Sweetest Thing' was kind of a return to song form. I was really proud of that campaign and my goodness didn't it sell well."

As the compilation topped the album charts in twenty-one countries (with the exception of America, where it charted at number two, albeit with record first-week sales for a greatest hits package), reminding everyone of U2's past glories, the band was once again planting the seeds for their future. Bolstered by the infallible production partnership of Brian Eno and Daniel Lanois for the first time since *Achtung Baby,* and this time working without a deadline, they had begun sketching new ideas in their rehearsal room at Hanover Quay. "Edge seems to have rediscovered the electric guitar after falling out with it for most of the '90s," Bono told *Q.* "Anyway they've kissed and made up in a spectacular way, a way that makes me want to go to work in '99."

However, Bono's vox was in bad shape, real bad shape. He was unable to hit the high notes the songs demanded and the pain in his throat at the end of each recording day was unbearable. The singer had had his fair share of vocal problems in the late 1980s, mostly as a result of poor technique and one or two nasty habits. A vocal coach had taught him how to get the best out of his voice without destroying it, resulting in less screaming and more measured vocals in the high baritone range, as heard on *Achtung Baby* and *Zooropa.* The coach also helped him develop that haunting falsetto. But Bono's fondness for alcohol and a smoking habit he picked up during the *Joshua Tree* era ensured it was all for naught, and by the PopMart Tour his voice was noticeably weak, even with the band tuning songs down to a lower key to compensate. "Everyone was saying it was my lifestyle, on the phone all the time, never going to bed, smoking, drinking too much, so I was making changes but I was just not able to really get there," he later told *The Telegraph.*

And Bono paid the price for his lifestyle choices. In February 1999 he underwent an emergency operation at Dublin's exclusive Blackrock Clinic after experiencing episodes of shortness of breath and rapid heartbeat. Surgeons operated on his nose, throat, and ears to clear a blockage caused by severe sinus problems. They discovered that his condition was aggravated by an allergy to certain salicylates present in cigarettes and alcohol (particularly in his beloved red wine) and advised him to give up both for good—alas, medical advice he ultimately ignored, leaving him with a much thinner and raspier voice. "You have to pace yourself," says Paul Gambaccini, "but most pop singers haven't had the sufficient vocal training that classical singers have had to know when to stop, to know when they're going into injury time. But I'm glad Bono can at least still sing to a certain level after surgery. Look at Julie Andrews. She had a bad operation and couldn't do it anymore."

■

Fame and fortune in the music business were not enough for the enormously ambitious Bono. He longed for power on a major scale and harbored political aspirations. At the suggestion of Marc Marot, he lent his name and services to Jubilee 2000, an international coalition of church organizations and development NGOs calling for western creditors to cancel the unpayable debts of the world's poorest countries and thus release funds for health care and education projects by the new millennium, inspired by the biblical concept of the Year of Jubilee in which all debts are forgiven and slaves are set free. The fifty-two identified countries in need of debt relief owed a total of $375 billion to OECD member nations, the International Monetary Fund (IMF), and the World Bank, to be repaid over time periods of up to forty years. Jubilee 2000 estimated that around $300 billion of the total debt amount was "unpayable."

Marot recalls: "Jamie Drummond [global strategist for Jubilee 2000] approached me in 1998 to see if there was anything that I could do to help the coalition to, in his words, 'pull itself out of the pulpit and into the real world.' My family are Mauritian, so the whole concept of Third World debt had a resonance for me personally. So I sent a handwritten letter to Bono, among others, and explained what I wanted from him was for him to put his signature on a petition which we would then use to go in *NME, Melody Maker,* and *Music Week* to begin to publicize it." Marot listed a number of facts to communicate the scale of the crisis to Bono, such as Live Aid raised around $250 million with the U2 singer's help, yet Sub-Saharan Africa owed this much in debt repayments every five days. Bono's response two days later was more than Marot could have hoped for. "He called me saying, 'Marc, I love this concept and I'm going to dedicate the rest of my life to this. I knew I needed to do something and this is it.' And I just sat there at my desk gobsmacked."

Bono asked Marot to round up all the people that were pivotal to the campaign and bring them over to Dublin where they could strategize. "I got Ann Pettifor, the economist, and Jamie Drummond," recalls Marot. "By this time I'd also enlisted Richard Constant, who was the top lawyer at Universal [the parent company that owned PolyGram], and Bob Geldof, and we flew out to Dublin and met Bono and talked it through and decided this was not a Live Aid, you didn't need to raise money for this, you needed to raise awareness. I came backward and forward to Dublin quite a few times with various people until Bono was completely familiar [with Jubilee 2000]. He didn't talk about this at all until he absolutely understood every single reason for it and every single reason that would be thrown at him against it. And then he went to work. And my god did he go to work."

Bono's first notable action was on February 16, 1999, when he wrote an editorial piece for *The Guardian* newspaper entitled "World Debt Angers Me" and attended the annual televised pop shindig the Brit Awards in London, where he accepted the Freddie Mercury Award for "outstanding social engagement" on behalf of the coalition and brought the award down to Muhammad Ali in the VIP section for a stage-managed photo op. Within twenty-four hours, Bono had introduced the Jubilee 2000 concept to an audience of over 100 million across Europe and turned it into a bona fide movement.

One month later, Gordon Brown, the British chancellor of the exchequer, reiterated an earlier commitment to review the much-maligned Heavily Indebted Poor Countries (HIPC) Initiative administered by the IMF and World Bank after over half a million letters and postcards asking for full debt cancellation landed on the doorsteps of 10 Downing Street and the treasury, including one from Brown's own mother.

Jubilee 2000's momentum was building rapidly in the public and political domain, powered by Bono's celebrity stardust and the campaign's sense of urgency. But the coalition recognized that they would ultimately fail without gaining the support of Washington, D.C., where it had fallen on deaf ears despite a number of religious groups beating the drum. Even the U.S. media weren't touching the issue, with their attention directed toward a refugee crisis in Kosovo. Thus, Bono called on an old acquaintance, President Bill Clinton, to get some traction stateside. Bono visited the outgoing president at the Oval Office in April and asked him if the coalition could count on his support. Clinton said yes, although Bono suspected that the man journalists had nicknamed "Elvis" on account of his early populist style also had his own Colonel Parker to answer to (namely, the money men in Congress and various specialist interest groups).

Stepping up his efforts, Bono needed a Washington guide and reached out to Kennedy clan member Bobby Shriver, who he came to know in 1987 when U2 contributed a cover version of Phil Spector's "Christmas (Baby Please Come Home)" to the Shriver-organized benefit album *A Very Special Christmas* to help fund the Special Olympics. Shriver had a direct line to the Democratic elite on Capitol Hill, as well as one or two strong Republican connections via his brother-in-law Arnold Schwarzenegger, and suggested that, instead of building political support by collecting signatures, they directly lobby Congress, the World Bank, and Wall Street to "get the check" required to push Jubilee 2000 over the finishing line.

To that end, Shriver introduced Bono and Bob Geldof to his old friend James D. Wolfensohn, the president of the World Bank and chief architect of the HIPC Initiative, with whom he had worked in the venture capital business in the 1980s. Shriver also arranged for himself and Bono to take a two-day crash course in economics at Harvard University under the private tutelage of the controversial professor Jeffrey Sachs, whose one-time reputation as the heroic "Indiana Jones of economics" had been tarnished by a disastrous spell as an advisor to the Yeltsin government in Russia from 1991 to 1994 in which he advocated rapid mass privatization of state industries along with Western assistance, otherwise known as neoliberal "shock therapy." Russia's implementation of shock therapy, without taking into consideration the lawless command system and inadequate infrastructure in place, resulted in appalling living conditions and an unprecedented decline in life expectancy for a nation not at war or experiencing a major famine in the twentieth century, according to the medical journal *The Lancet* and other published data. Yet Sachs, who refused to shoulder any of the blame for the devastation in Russia, arguing that Russia did not listen to his advice and the necessary aid was not forthcoming, was a natural go-to guy for Bono and Shriver. He was a notorious spotlight chaser, and welcomed the opportunity to work alongside the world's biggest rock star and Kennedy descendant, teaching them about capital markets and debt instruments as well as putting his entire department at their disposal. Soon enough, Sachs was Bono's official traveling companion through the corridors of power.

A number of meetings with high-level officials followed in quick succession, including appointments with Les Gelb, president of the Council on Foreign Relations; David Rockefeller, the Wall Street veteran and former chairman of Chase Manhattan Bank; and Paul Volcker, the influential former chairman of the Federal Reserve—the latter of whom roared with laughter when Bono first raised the topic of debt cancellation, before finally agreeing to pull a few strings behind the scenes. No one, it seemed, could resist the U2 singer's charms and passion for the subject. It should be noted that most of the officials, or, in some cases, their younger staff members and children, were part of the Baby Boom generation, which grew up idolizing rock-and-roll musicians. The sight of politicians and bankers lining up for an autograph or adorning their office walls with framed pictures of themselves with the singer was not uncommon. "I actually had a reception for him at my home on the outskirts of Iowa City," says Jim Leach, a moderate Republican and then-chairman of the House Committee on Banking and Financial Services, who had in fact already introduced a bill in the House in an attempt to advance the rebalancing of international debt relations. "My fifteen- or sixteen-year-old daughter was there and she asked for his autograph and Bono took his paper plate and drew a cartoon picture of her and signed it. We promptly framed the plate and it's kind of a prized family possession."

But it was the White House trio of Gene Sperling, Clinton's national economic advisor; Larry Summers, the incoming secretary of the treasury; and Sheryl Sandberg, Summers's chief of staff, that proved the most valuable of Washington allies, at least in the short term. Summers was the surprise package; one, because he was, to the amusement of Clinton and his staff, culturally challenged and one of the few people who had no idea who Bono was, and two, because he had signed a private memo when serving as chief economist for the World Bank in 1991 that advocated the dumping of toxic waste in LDCs (less developed countries), particularly "underpopulated countries in Africa," described as "vastly UNDER-polluted," on the basis that it was cost effective and poor people rarely live long enough to develop prostate cancer. (After the memo became public, Summers claimed that he hadn't carefully read what he signed, while the author of the document said it was meant to be a sarcastic critique of trade liberalization.) Summers—who, incidentally, would later resign as the president of Harvard University amid allegations that he used his position to protect his close friend and fellow faculty member Andrei Shleifer from the consequences of his nefarious role in the implosion of a Harvard advisory program in Russia in the mid-1990s—drummed his fingers on a sheet of blotting paper as Bono tried to convince him that full debt cancellation was "good value for America." Summers shrugged, remarking that all G8 finance ministers would have to be singing from the same sheet for it to happen. Bono appealed to his ego; according to Sperling, he looked the secretary directly in the eye and said: "I have been all over the world. I've met with all the finance ministers. They've all said if I can get Larry Summers, this can get done." Shortly after the meeting, Summers told Clinton: "You know, some guy just came in to see me in jeans and a T-shirt, and he just had one name, but he sure was smart."

Bono next showed up at the G8 summit in Cologne, Germany, where fifty thousand demonstrators formed a human chain around the city to protest creditors' resistance to debt relief and the structural adjustment conditions associated with the HIPC Initiative. Bono crossed through the police barricade and up the steps of Museum Ludwig in Dom Platz to hand Chancellor Gerhard Schröder, who was hosting the summit, the 17 million signatures the coalition had collected demanding full debt forgiveness. But the response from the government leaders and financial institutions flattered to deceive. They pledged a headline-grabbing figure of $100 billion of debt cancellation to forty-two countries, $50 billion of which was through an "enhanced" HIPC framework, $30 billion from traditional debt relief such as that distributed through the Paris Club, and $20 billion from cancellation of aid debts by bilateral creditors. But, as many campaigners noted, a large proportion of the debt cancellation was a rehash of previous proposals and was applied to unpayable loans that had in effect already been written off by creditors. Few countries initially qualified for significant cancellation under the HIPC program, and those that did faced more structural adjustments that ensured they remained forever enslaved to the G8, the World Bank, and IMF. Jubilee South, the Asia-Pacific wing of the coalition, called the G8 announcement a "cruel hoax" and later demanded that the World Bank and IMF be "decommissioned." Bono, for his part, was apoplectic and threatened to call off a planned get-together with British prime minister Tony Blair and his trusted spin doctor Alastair Campbell at the summit. He eventually yielded, only for his cantankerous companion Geldof—with whom he had adopted a good-cop, bad-cop routine—to launch into an expletive-laden tirade against the PM during the meeting, telling him that he hadn't done enough. Blair, an expert at deflecting and outmaneuvering criticism, appeared to empathize with Geldof, then swiftly turned to Bono and asked, "How's the *Best Of* doing?"

Bono kept the pressure on creditors to go further. In September, a Jubilee 2000 delegation that included the U2 front man, Sachs, and Geldof visited Pope John Paul II at his summer palace in Castel Gandolfo to drum up more global media attention. "You're a great showman as well as a great holy man," Bono told the pope, before handing him his powder-blue wraparound sunglasses (which the frail seventy-nine-year-old tried on) in exchange for a set of rosary beads. In a press conference after the closed-door meeting, Bono described John Paul II, who was an athlete, actor, and playwright in his youth, as the world's "first funky pontiff." Incidentally, since Zoo TV, Bono was rarely seen in public without a pair of wraparound sunglasses. He claimed that he wore them because he suffered from a form of photophobia, although U2 sources suggest it was more a conscious effort to establish an instantly recognizable trademark.

Later that month, the bug-eyed singer persuaded Gene Sperling to get President Clinton to use his speech at the Annual Meetings of the IMF and World Bank to pledge to cancel 100 percent of HIPC bilateral debt owed to the United States, estimated at around $5.6 billion. Clinton agreed, and also challenged the other G8 leaders to do the same, receiving a standing ovation from those in the auditorium. Blair and Brown were the first to follow his example, followed one by one by the other heads of state of the principal donor countries. Bono was ecstatic, until he learned that the leaders' promises amounted to nothing more than a series of empty gestures unless approved by their respective legislative bodies and parliaments. Consequently, Bono turned the spotlight on the biggest political obstacle of all: the Republican-controlled Congress, whose House members had earlier voted to impeach Clinton on charges of perjury and obstructing justice in the Monica Lewinsky affair and opposed foreign aid in general. It wasn't going to be easy to get them on board.

Meanwhile, in October, the dogged and ubiquitous Bono helped launch NetAid, a joint online venture between the networking giant Cisco Systems and the United Nations Development Program to raise money and awareness for antipoverty projects such as Jubilee 2000 through the power of the Internet. But the public response was surprisingly apathetic. Billed as the largest webcast ever, with a potential audience of over one billion, NetAid was comprised of three star-studded concerts staged simultaneously in Geneva, London, and New Jersey, with Bono and rap artist Wyclef Jean opening the latter show with a live performance of their official theme song "New Day," itself a chart flop, in front of a near-empty Giants Stadium and fewer Web users than the media and some campaigners anticipated. "The New Jersey show left some fans wondering if the concert should have been dubbed Sleep-Aid rather than NetAid," mocked the online music site *Launch*. NetAid raised only $12 million in total; $1 million from online donations and the rest from two corporate sponsors. Bono blamed the antipoverty initiative's low numbers on charity fatigue and a lack of focus, although promoter Harvey Goldsmith maintains that it hit all its realistic targets. "The truth we got from the actual operators was about 144,000 [people logged on to netaid.org]. So the numbers that we got we were pretty proud of. There wasn't a cat's chance in hell that there was enough bandwidth at that time to even get close to a billion, let alone if there were a billion people who could actually log on. So all these figures are just nonsense."

Bono was fully committed to his new life in politics, much to the annoyance of his bandmates who were in the throes of recording their tenth studio album, *All That You Can't Leave Behind*. The suit-and-ties at U2's record label weren't exactly thrilled either, and blamed the record's long gestation on Marot for encouraging Bono to get involved with Jubilee 2000 in the first place. "There were people at Universal who absolutely hated the Jubilee campaign because it was distracting U2 from finishing *All That You Can't Leave Behind*," recalls Marot. "Bono was putting so much effort in elsewhere, and my bosses knew that it was my fault."

Another unwelcome distraction for the label was the Wim Wenders–directed film *The Million Dollar Hotel*. Based on a concept story cowritten by Bono, who also served as its producer, the L.A.-set film juggled three fables (an art scam, murder mystery, and love story) with absurdist humor and biting commentary on post-Reagan America. "It was initially going to be a play about a leap of faith," Bono explained in *The Guardian*, "but then it mutated into something bigger and darker. I'd call it a dark fable about the redemptive power of love. And love, of course, is the ultimate leap of faith."

Bono wrote three songs with members of the Million Dollar Hotel Band (an all-star group comprising producers Brian Eno and Daniel Lanois, guitarist Bill Frisell, trumpeter Jon Hassell, and others) for the moody soundtrack, which they recorded in just ten days in Dublin by playing to images of the film on a screen in the same way Miles Davis had for *Ascenseur Pour L'échafaud.* In addition to the MDH Band cuts, U2 contributed two leftovers from their forthcoming album, "Stateless" and "The Ground Beneath Her Feet," the latter of which was built around lyrics taken from Salman Rushdie's rock-and-roll novel of the same name, itself inspired by the world of U2. "It was very easy to put music to," Bono said of the rock ballad. "It took us about two minutes, and you may say it sounds like that. It's a beautiful melody and came out of the words." Writing in *Newsday,* critic Steve Matteo described it as "a haunting track of rousing, visceral majesty that can stand alongside anything U2 has recorded."

Bono planned to release "The Ground Beneath Her Feet" as a single to promote *The Million Dollar Hotel,* but was eventually talked out of it by Marot. "I was invited to Dublin to watch the film with Bono and Paul [McGuinness] and I was embarrassed, as I felt that the film was poor," recalls the former Island president. "I went back to Principle Management and I sat with Paul and I said, 'Do you want my real feelings? You shouldn't go anywhere near this. If you want me to put out the soundtrack album, I will; however, I don't think we should release a single. Don't do anything to draw attention to the film.' And then I had to meet with Bono and give him my view and he went quiet for about ten seconds and then he pinched me on the arm gently and said, 'Okay.' And that was it. We never discussed it again. But it was a very awkward moment because the project was such a labor of love for him."

Marot's advice proved to be spot-on. Despite starring box office names such as Mel Gibson and Milla Jovovich, as well as containing a brief cameo appearance by Bono himself, *The Million Dollar Hotel* was both a commercial and critical flop when released sporadically over the next two years. In the crucial U.S. market, for example, it recouped just $59,989 of its estimated budget of $8 million, while poor reviews saw it obtain only a 25 percent approval rating on the Rotten Tomatoes Web site (although it did take home the Silver Bear at the Berlin International Film Festival where it premiered). The film's fate was sealed when Gibson, who also produced it through his company Icon Productions, called it "as boring as a dog's ass" at an Australian press conference. In response, Bono accused Gibson of neglecting to support the film and leaving Wenders in the lurch. He told the *New York Post*: "Wim has made two, maybe more, of the top thirty films ever made. Has Mel? In the end, is it about box office over being great? Wim is a great filmmaker and I think he should be treated with respect. Wim will never talk like this. I can, so I am."

In March 2000, Bono had cause to smile when Mick Jagger presented him with the Free Your Mind award at the MTV European Music Awards in Dublin, the first of many high-profile accolades he accepted in person on behalf of his antipoverty work. "It's the Devil giving God an award, is it?" he joked with the audience. During his speech, Bono thanked Marot for introducing him to Jubilee 2000 and altering the course of his life forever, which prompted the Island man to make a few life-changing decisions himself. "I hit my midlife crisis," he says. "I decided that everything I was doing was so ephemeral and meaningless, and it crystalized at that moment. I had to walk out of the MTV Awards—I couldn't get my head together. Ultimately it ended up with me splitting up with my family, unfortunately, and quitting Island Records and remaking my life. It was all part of the same maneuver."

Faced with losing one of their most trusted associates in the music business, U2 hired Marot to oversee the development and launch of their official Web site U2.com, despite Universal enforcing a restrictive covenant prohibiting him from working in the industry for a year for breaking his contract. Marot recalls: "Paul and the boys stepped in and said, 'Okay. You might not want Marc to work for a year, but we're your biggest client and we want to carry on working with him.'" Adam's brother Sebastian, who ran the Dublin-based new media company Digital: CC, was also involved in the creation of U2.com, but according to insiders, the band didn't feel he was experienced enough at the time to build it or to direct it. "We worked closely together on it," says Marot, "but I used a company called Good Technology that had built Island.co.uk for me. So Good Technology designed it and built it and Sebastian and I split responsibility for different sections with me as the producer. It won so many awards it was fantastic. The team we put together in 2000 are still running the site today."

By mid-2000 the HIPC process was no further forward, with the deeply Christian, Republican-dominated Congress reluctant to contribute to debt relief despite the conditionalities that weighed heavily in the creditors' favor. The Jubilee 2000 USA coalition eventually came up with the idea of convincing the controversial Nigerian president and born-again Christian Olusegun Obasanjo to write a letter to the leadership of the Southern Baptist Convention, the largest Protestant denomination in America, calling for Southern Baptists to contact their congressmen to urge support for debt cancellation. They also enlisted the help of Reverend Billy Graham, the television evangelist who for almost fifty years had served as a spiritual advisor to U.S. presidents and impressionable couch potatoes. Graham was a friend of Eunice Shriver's and agreed to record a video statement endorsing Bono and the Jubilee 2000 effort, which was then sent out to impenetrable congressmen. And just like that, Bono, who had also won the backing of frugal House Budget Committee chairman John Kasich, had the ears of the American far right.

In September, Bono was granted a meeting with the ultraconservative Republican senator from North Carolina and head of the Foreign Relations Committee Jesse Helms, viewed by many liberals as a bigot, a racist, and a homophobe. Helms had once claimed in a 1981 interview with *The New York Times* that "crime rates and irresponsibility among Negroes are a fact of life which must be faced" and had continuously opposed civil rights legislation. What's more, for almost two decades he had led the fight in the Senate against increased federal funding for AIDS research (AIDS victims, he told *The New York Times* in 1995, contracted the disease through "deliberate, disgusting, revolting conduct") and had repeatedly slashed the international aid budget, likening such assistance to "pouring money down foreign rat holes."

However, Helms was such an admirer of Billy Graham's that he had lined his office with photos of himself with the evangelist and a plaque commemorating his financial support of the Ruth and Billy Graham Children's Health Center, and had quietly signaled a softening in his attitude toward foreign aid after taking calls from Graham, his son Reverend Franklin Graham, and other Christian conservatives prior to Bono's arrival. Adopting a creation-care tactic, Bono spoke Helms's language during the meeting; he reminded him that 2,103 verses of scripture refer to the poor, and quoted Matthew chapter 25: "I was naked and you clothed me." He also told him stories about African children and married couples dying of AIDS and equated it with biblical leprosy. Helms told *The Hill* newspaper that he was deeply moved by Bono, telling him: "If I can find some way that the Lord would show me how to really help these people, I'd quit the Senate and try to do it." Bono later claimed that the seventy-nine-year-old Helms also wept.

The last policy gatekeeper to put up a fight was Sonny Callahan, the chairman of the House Subcommittee on Foreign Operations, Export Financing, and Related Programs. In June, Callahan had recommended to the House of Representatives that Congress actually reduce foreign aid, placing the entire debt cancellation movement in jeopardy. However, he eventually bowed to pressure from his peers and the Christian community in his district. And in October, Congress approved the additional $435 million needed for 100 percent bilateral debt relief under the HIPC Initiative. As the Jubilee year drew to a close, Bono and other members of the coalition could claim a small victory, although they had ultimately failed to achieve their two other goals: getting the World Bank and IMF to forgive the HIPC debt owed them and structural legislative change.

In urging God-fearing Republicans to look at debt cancellation as a moral and religious obligation, Bono's approach—often regarded as idealistic, albeit deeply versed in the issues—had generated some surprising results. Along with his partner, Bob Geldof (who, incidentally, would also carve out a lucrative sideline gig on the speakers' circuit, demanding anywhere between fifty thousand and one hundred thousand dollars and first-class pampering to share his knowledge about world poverty), Bono had, in the words of *The Guardian,* "pioneered a new kind of celebrity activism: he is a lobbyist, not a fundraiser." The same mainstream media who openly mocked and ridiculed the U2 singer throughout the PopMart trek now lauded him for his heroic selflessness and ability to put aside his own political and religious views to break bread with anyone who could be of assistance to the antipoverty campaign. In January 2000, the cover of *Newsweek* had asked: "Can Bono Save the Third World?" Barely two years later, *Time* would go one step further by posing the question: "Can Bono Save the World?" The magazine's answer was an emphatic yes. "[H]e has grown even larger over the past three years, molding himself into a shrewd, dedicated political advocate, transforming himself into the most secular of saints, becoming a worldwide symbol of rock-'n'-roll activism," gushed writer Josh Tyrangiel.

"I think in the history of celebrity no one has advocated deeper, wiser causes than Bono," says Jim Leach, "and he's dealt with it in a way that is unique. First, as a persona, he's made a point of coming over as the common man with no effort to look pretty. The other thing that is unique is Bono has an extraordinarily high intellect—I consider him to be an underappreciated intellectual and classically so smart that he doesn't want people to think of him as smart. Toward the end of the Clinton administration a group of those of us who had been interested in the debt issue were invited to the White House to meet with the president in the Cabinet Room. There were about twenty of us, and I nudged the individual next to me and I said, 'I will tell you in this room with the president and the vice president, easily the highest IQ is that guy sitting over there.' And we look across the table and then he turns to me. 'Who is that scruffy guy?' I said, 'His name is Bono.' And of everyone that spoke, Bono's words were the most well phrased. He has a real capacity to communicate. His wording, in my experience, was always right on, always uniquely his. There's melody, but there's also poignancy. He knows what he's doing.

"Bono has also been what I would call 'diplomatically deft,'" continues Leach. "That is, very careful not to identify with a political party, to deal with people on all sides of the political spectrum and to be cautious of being critical of countries' policies when he might not totally agree with them. It's a difficult line to walk—to be a constructive advocate that is careful not to let feelings out that might damage a cause. I consider myself his greatest admirer in the world—and he has many."

However, some liberals questioned Bono's decision to assume the role of the nonpartisan, non-dissident "celebrity wonk" working through the established system. History, they argued, does not support the idea that working through the system achieves real change; on the contrary, it tends to achieve token change, as those trying to change it often end up being co-opted by it or at least forced to compromise significantly. Bono, who referred to himself as a "champagne socialist," felt it was a risk worth taking and even joked that he would have lunch with the devil if he thought it would lead to the possibility of more money for Africa. Besides, he had a newfound admiration for all politicians. He told *George*: "I have actually sat with people in bands who describe politicians as the anti-Christ and are sure that the Capitol is the domain for all anti-Christs. And I'm saying, 'You don't understand. These people get home really late. If they went into business, they'd be a lot wealthier. We should pay them more and expect more from them.' I have to confess, I've got a respect for them that I really didn't expect."

■

In October 2000, U2 released their new upbeat pop single "Beautiful Day." The song was as nostalgic as it was melodic, featuring Edge's vintage bell-like guitar sound not heard so brazenly since the band's '80s output. "Beautiful Day" was a phenomenal success for the band; it debuted at number one in the UK singles chart, while in the United States it reached number twenty-one on the *Billboard* Hot 100 on radio play alone.

Around that same time, news broke online that the Joshua tree that appeared on the cover of U2's 25 million–selling album of the same name had been found dead by a group of fans. It had simply collapsed under its own enormity and the weight of time, possibly two hundred years. For many, the Joshua tree had come to symbolize hope and longevity in the face of extreme diversity. Its very image was in tune with where U2 was in 1987. Painfully exposed, they stood in stark contrast to their environment. And yet, like the tree, they thrived. It was an achievement the band hoped to emulate in the current climate with *All That You Can't Leave Behind*. Set free into a fickle marketplace on October 30, where manufactured teen pop and misogynistic nu metal prevailed, the album debuted at number one in thirty-two markets, including the UK, Canada, and Australia. Meanwhile, in the States it entered the *Billboard* 200 at number three with opening-week sales of 428,000 copies, which at that point was a record for U2. "We've come to bite the arse of the pop charts," Bono warned their young rivals. "You're the boys, but we are the men. Move over."

16

The Goal Is $oul?

The back-to-basics *All That You Can't Leave Behind* was a resounding commercial and critical success. *Rolling Stone* hailed it as U2's "third masterpiece [alongside *The Joshua Tree* and *Achtung Baby*] . . . where tunefulness plays as central a role as on any Backstreet Boys hit." *USA Today* applauded its "simplicity and soul." And in a four-star review, *Billboard* welcomed the fact that "the chaotic electronic density of U2's last few efforts has been replaced by sticky, bite-size tunes—sporting candy-sweet choruses that are often underlined by unabashed words of love."

But as the critical establishment heaped praise upon it, a large section of U2 fans posting on Web sites dedicated to the group were left wondering what all the fuss was about. Indeed, the general consensus among online fans appeared to be that it was an album devoid of adventure, containing eleven painstakingly crafted arrangements infused with elements of "early U2," but watered down into an artificially positive, easily digestible pop radio format, combined with lyrics coated with syrupy religiosity and sentimentality, to appeal to the maximum number of consumers. Tom Moon of *The Philadelphia Inquirer* perhaps summed up their feelings best: "This is rock from a group that lusts for a hit, and will go through any contortion to get it. This is music of the market-research focus-group variety—not too harsh, not too outlandish, lots of melody, lots of empathy. Songs such as 'Walk On' and the deliriously sunny first single 'Beautiful Day' aren't driven by the fire of true believers; they are the result of bald calculation. . . ." Sources suggest that U2 hit the panic button after the less-than-stellar performance of *Pop* in America, resulting in a far more polished, accessible work aimed at the MTV demographic and MOR fans at the expense of intelligent songwriting and innovation. "It was simply to go in and write songs that would get on the radio and take what U2 does—take it out of the ghetto and compete with the Britneys and the Whitneys," Larry later confessed to Music.com. "We wanted to get on the radio, be on MTV or VH1 or compete on that level." But most importantly, the overwhelming commercial nature of the album marked the next phase of U2's seven-year corporate transformation and growth strategy, in which making music was no longer chiefly about artistic expression—it was about creating a greater revenue stream.

With the hands-on assistance of Interscope Records chief Jimmy Iovine, U2 and Principle Management meticulously put together a two-year plan for *All That You Can't Leave Behind* to win over the lucrative teen market, based around the false premise that the thirty-nine-to-forty-year-old U2 members were in fact a hip new band with no historical baggage. To that end, the Irish quartet hit the calculated charm offensive and made a succession of high-profile appearances on late-night talk shows, *Top of the Pops,* and even youth favorites *CD:UK* and MTV's *Total Request Live.* Bono was especially keen to endear the band to the key media gatekeepers and personalities, hosting many of them at his mausoleum-like penthouse in Manhattan's San Remo apartment complex, which he had recently bought for $14.5 million from Apple CEO Steve Jobs, or giving them the full VIP treatment at The Clarence Hotel in Dublin. The U2 camp also negotiated a deal with Paramount Pictures to tie in their Breeders-esque single "Elevation" with the 2001 summer blockbuster *Tomb Raider,* for which they filmed a $3 million action-packed music video with Britney Spears director Joseph Kahn.

U2's commercial rebirth was recognized by the Recording Academy with an impressive seven Grammy Awards over the next two years, including Song of the Year for "Beautiful Day," Best Pop Performance by a Duo or Group with Vocals for the gospel-tinged ballad "Stuck in a Moment You Can't Get Out Of," which Bono wrote as a fictitious conversation between himself and the late Michael Hutchence, who had committed suicide in 1997, and Record of the Year for the mid-tempo anthem "Walk On," which was dedicated to the Burmese pro-democracy leader Aung San Suu Kyi and sounded remarkably similar to "Here Comes Your Man" by the Pixies. In his acceptance speech during the first ceremony in February 2001, Bono proclaimed with typical (im)-modesty that U2 was "reapplying for the job. What job? The best band in the world job." Five days later at the Brit Awards in London, they also took home Best International Group and were presented with the Outstanding Contribution to Music Award by Oasis's Noel Gallagher.

With a string of awards for the album and chart-topping single "Beautiful Day" under their belt, U2 set off on the U.S. leg of the Elevation Tour, which marked a return to arenas and a stripped-down environment following a decade of stadium excess. The in-the-round stage setup—with a heart-shaped catwalk circling the main stage and an open center for three hundred early bird ticket holders—was designed to increase interaction with fans and maximize revenue. Tickets for the tour ranged from $40 for general-admission standing to $130 for reserved seating (the latter of which was geared toward "Mr. and Mrs. Wall Street," Bono joked) and sold out in record time, despite protest from U.S. concertgoers about the escalated prices and decision to use festival seating—the media, meanwhile, rarely broached either subject, having been advised by agents representing U2 that interviews with the band would be canceled should they attempt to do so.

In addition to his U2 responsibilities, Bono continued his political activities in Washington on behalf of Drop the Debt, the British-based pressure group formed after the disbanding of Jubilee 2000 to ensure the G8 fulfilled its commitment to the HIPC Initiative. On March 16, he began the process of formally introducing himself to members of the newly elected George W. Bush administration, starting with Secretary of State Colin Powell, with whom he also discussed the HIV/AIDS crisis in Africa. Powell told Bono that he was pleased the singer was using his celebrity status "to work on something good." Bono replied, "Our audience is smart and aware."

During that same period, Bono tried to come to the aid of an old American punk hero, Joey Ramone, after MTV VJ Kurt Loder phoned him to tell him that Ramone was dying of cancer at New York-Presbyterian Hospital in Manhattan. "Bono quickly called Joey in his hospital room," recalls Loder, "and he told Joey's family that he would write a check for any amount necessary to finance further treatment. Unfortunately, by then, it was too late. It was a very emotional gesture, I think—U2 had started out as a dinky little punk band covering Ramones tunes." It was reported that the last song Ramone heard was U2's "In a Little While" after his brother Mickey Leigh brought a copy of *All That You Can't Leave Behind* to the hospital and played it to him. "Just as the song finished, Joey finished," his mother Charlotte told New York *Daily News*. The gangly, leather-jacketed outcast-cum-icon was forty-nine. Following his death, U2 would frequently dedicate "In a Little While" to him on the Elevation Tour as well as perform an acoustic cover version of The Ramones' "I Remember You."

The month of June would be an eventful one for Bono. On the sixth, he delivered the commencement address at Harvard University at the invitation of Jeffrey Sachs. "My name is Bono, and I am a rock star," he told an excited audience of five thousand, including former vice president Al Gore. Taking the podium for around twenty minutes, Bono, wearing olive-green combat clothes, a camouflage cap backward, and his trademark wraparound sunglasses, spoke in grisly detail about the struggles and oppression of "the third of the world that lives on less than a dollar a day" and urged the graduating seniors to "follow through on your ideals." He said: "When I was a kid in Dublin, I watched in awe as America put a man on the moon and I thought, wow—this is mad! Nothing is impossible in America! America, they can do anything over there! Nothing was impossible, only human nature, and it followed because it was led. Is that still true? Tell me it's true. It is true isn't it? And if it isn't, you of all people can make it true again." After his speech, the class of 2001 presented Bono with an honorary degree, saying: "You too are now a member of our class."

Later that night, Bono faced an altogether tougher crowd when U2 shot concert footage for the *Elevation 2001: Live from Boston* DVD at the nearby Fleet Center. Die-hard fans—some of whom had traveled from around the world and waited for upward of twenty hours outside the venue to get a prized spot—were left visibly upset by U2's decision to instruct their security team to handpick people from the back of the GA line and usher them into the pit area before the venue doors swung open. Bono would later tell RTÉ 2fm that it was to ensure the band played to "the people of the town we're in, instead of the one that's following us," yet firsthand accounts from fans posting on *Wire,* the U2 Internet mailing list, painted a different story. They claimed that they heard straight from the production assistant's mouth that U2 explicitly wanted "good-looking, youthful" people in key camera positions up front and at the tip of the catwalk, with "Elevation" and "Where the Streets Have No Name" also set to be broadcast live on NBC during the opening game of the NBA Finals. As a result, around fifty of the scorned fans who eventually made it into the rear of the pit staged a protest throughout the show, first by turning their backs to the band members and then by sitting down in a circle to create a symbolic "hole in the heart." "Many of us were heartbroken that the band would intentionally screw us over like that," one fan wrote on *Wire,* adding that it seemed U2 had become "removed from even their most hard-core fans."

On the thirteenth, Bono was back in Washington, D.C., where once again he endeavored to impress upon the Bush administration the gravity of the debt situation. His main target, Secretary of the Treasury Paul O'Neill, had been reluctant to grant him a meeting but relented after some dicey prodding from his chief of staff, Tim Adams. "We were contacted by Drop the Debt [in May], saying that Bono wanted to come in and talk to Paul," recalls Adams. "I went to see Paul and I said to him, 'This is an important guy. You should probably think about it.' But I'm not sure Paul really knew who Bono was and he kept saying, 'I'm not interested.' And there were others in the building who were skeptical—skeptical of the concept of debt relief and skeptical of celebrities engaged in humanitarian issues. I told Paul at the time, 'I'll tell you what, I'll do a meeting with him just to screen him and make sure that he knows what he's talking about and then we'll get back together.' So we set up an appointment and Bono and others came in and obviously there was great excitement in the building and that created a bit of a stir. And what I found in spending an hour with him was that he really knew the substance. He had learned firsthand the challenges, opportunities, and complexities of the issues, with particular respect to Africa. It was a part of his DNA.

"And I went back to Paul and I said, 'Look, they want to come back and see you. Give him thirty minutes and if you're not impressed by the depth of his knowledge, I will resign. I will put my job on the line if you will simply sit down with him.' Because Paul is a no-nonsense, fact-oriented kind of guy and he just did not have time for someone who didn't know the facts. So he took me up on my bet and we brought Bono back and a thirty-minute meeting turned into probably an hour and a half to two hours. That's when they first talked about going to Africa together. And when Bono left Paul said, 'You were absolutely right. You don't have to resign. He really knows his stuff.' "

Meanwhile, Bono was welcomed with open arms by Senator Jesse Helms, who went to the trouble of throwing him a special lunch in the Senate Foreign Relations reception room of the Capitol, which was also attended by Republican senators Orrin Hatch of Utah, Rick Santorum of Pennsylvania, and Bill Frist of Tennessee. Bono called Helms a "brave and bold man" for inviting an "outsider" to lunch to discuss the African HIV/AIDS pandemic, to which Helms replied: "You'll never be an outsider. You'll always be a friend here." One day later, Bono returned the favor by hosting Helms backstage at U2's Washington gig as well as treating him and his grandchildren to a skybox. "When Bono shook his hips, that crowd shook their hips," marveled the right-wing senator, who that same week was pushing through an amendment to the education bill to strip federal funding from schools that discriminated against the Boy Scouts or similar groups that "prohibit the acceptance of homosexuals" and to combat "the organized lesbians and homosexuals in this country of ours." After the show, Bono sent Helms a note that said: "Hope you had fun at the concert. We are really confusing the cynics with our friendship and our action in Africa. You are blessed, [and] I am to know you. Love, Bono." Some months later, Helms, who was increasingly mindful of meeting his maker due to his ailing health, told Christian HIV/AIDS activists at a conference in Washington that he was "ashamed that I've done so little" about the HIV/AIDS pandemic and called for an additional $500 million in U.S. funding to eliminate mother-to-child transmission of the virus in Sub-Saharan Africa—although he was quick to clarify that his seemingly 180-degree turn on the issue did not apply to domestic victims or specifically gay and bisexual men, whom he cited as "the primary cause of the doubling and redoubling of AIDS cases in the United States." Helms's $500 million proposal was also contingent on being matched dollar for dollar by the private sector, an unusual requirement, according to aid experts.

Bono's performances on the Elevation Tour suffered as a direct result of his relentless politicking, leading some to question where his priorities lay. "I admire him for doing it, but it creates serious, serious difficulties," Larry said in *Q*. "He's running around trying to do everything and keep everybody happy. The reality is it's probably the most important thing he's going to do in his life, so my attitude would be, take a year out and do it properly."

The Elevation Tour was on occasion a family affair backstage, with U2's respective partners, children, and nannies joining them at certain stops on the road. Edge would spend time with Morleigh and their daughter Sian (b. 1997) and son Levi (b. 1999), and as much time as possible with his three daughters from his marriage to Aislinn, Hollie (b. 1984), Arran (b. 1985), and Blue Angel (b. 1989); Larry and Ann sought ways to entertain their three younglings, Aaron Elvis (b. 1995), Ava (b. 1998), and new arrival Ezra (b. 2001); Adam cozied up to McGuinness's personal assistant, Suzanne Smith; and Bono somehow managed to steal a few hours to hang out with Ali and their four children, Jordan (b. 1989), Memphis Eve (b. 1991), Elijah Bob Patricius Guggi Q (b. 1999), and newborn baby John Abraham (b. 2001), although nowhere near enough for his liking. "Cyberdad doesn't sit well with me," he told *Q*. "You know, I'm watching his [John's] progress on e-mail. There's something very sad about that."

But just three months after celebrating the latest addition to the family, the Hewsons found themselves grieving the loss of their seventy-five-year-old patriarch, Bob, who died in the early hours of August 21 at the Beaumont Hospital in Dublin after a long fight against cancer and Parkinson's disease. Later that night, Bono gave an emotional performance at U2's sell-out concert at London's Earls Court. "I want to thank my old man, my father, for giving me this voice," he told the audience. "He was a fine tenor and he always said if I had his voice who knows what might have happened." Bono had flown back to Dublin between U2's European gigs to be at his father's hospital bedside. There, he read a new translation of the Bible by Eugene H. Peterson to him and drew his portrait; things his tough, sharp-tongued father normally couldn't stomach. Bono, who was never particularly close to Bob, despite constantly seeking his approval, expressed a range of common emotions when his father shuffled off this mortal coil. But most of all, he mourned the relationship they never had.

"I would go down to the local pub on Sundays with my father. We would both drink whiskey, look at each other, and say nothing," Bono said later on RTÉ 2fm of the only man in the world to have always called him Paul. "My dad's whole thing with me was, 'My son, the fuckin' eejit.' No, no, the basic position was, 'It's great that it's happening for you. When it all completely unravels—which it's going to any second—I'm gonna sit in this chair and we can talk about it.' It was brilliant, the comedy of him. He was a real wind-up, that Irish male thing."

Bob was buried in the rain at Old Balgriffin Cemetery in County

Dublin after an hour-long mass at Howth Church of the Assumption, just twenty-four hours before the first of two huge homecoming shows for U2 on the grounds of Slane Castle. Bono and his brother Norman led the funeral-goers, which included ex-Boyzone singer Ronan Keating and Gerry Corr, father of The Corrs, as well as Edge and Larry, who helped the two Hewson siblings to carry the coffin which they had decorated with a bouquet of irises in memory of their late mother, Iris. In his address during the service, Father Jack Heaslip, U2's traveling chaplain, reasoned that Bob's deadpan cynicism and abrasiveness was all a front and that he cared deeply about Bono and was proud of his accomplishments. He told the congregation: "When Bono rang up his very ill father and told him he was sorry he couldn't be with him and that he felt useless being so far away, Bob said: 'Sure, if you were at home, you'd be useless anyway.' Translated: 'I know you have to do your job and it's all right.'" Bono also recalled his father's last words to him in his hospital room where the singer had nodded off during an all-night vigil. "He woke me up with a grumpy shout. I asked was he all right. Silence. I asked did he want to see a nurse. Silence. I got a nurse. Silence. Eventually, he motioned to us and we bent down to his ear. 'Are you all mad?' he said. 'This is a prison. I want to go home.' I thought he was delirious, that he was mad. Now I see he is out of the prison of his own body and he is going home."

■

Bono was enjoying a week's holiday in Venice with Elijah and his son's nanny, getting lost in the narrow, mazelike backstreets and canals, when he first learned about the September 11 terrorist attacks on the United States that killed nearly three thousand people and changed the world irrevocably. He recalled on CNN's *Larry King Weekend*: "I just saw a sign up saying, 'the American hotel' and I thought, well, they'll speak English. So, I went in there, and that's when it was on the TV, and there were a lot of Americans sort of just shell-shocked. . . . I mean, you immediately think of your friends in New York. I have a place in New York here. This is a second city for me. And I couldn't believe what I was seeing."

As the world mourned 9/11 and other acts canceled their U.S. shows, U2 announced another American leg of the tour via a Clear Channel Entertainment press release headlined: "Elevation Tour still a go!" Furthermore, Bono arranged for the proceeds from an all-star recording of Marvin Gaye's 1971 classic "What's Going On" which he'd executive produced to be split between HIV/AIDS programs in Africa and the United Way's September 11 Fund as well. The project had been created on September 5 and 7 in the Big Apple with the likes of Britney Spears, 'N Sync, and P. Diddy, under the name Artists Against AIDS Worldwide. The radio mix, one of nine different versions featured on the accompanying album of the same name, peaked at number twenty-seven on the *Billboard* Hot 100 and at number six in the UK. It was later given the dubious honor of being the second-worst song of the 2000s by *Village Voice*.

Shortly after the attacks, U.S. radio and television were regulated in such a way as to prevent any song that could be construed as anti-American or sympathetic to Muslims from making the airwaves. Clear Channel, for example, sent out a memo to its twelve hundred radio stations containing a long list of "lyrically questionable" songs, which included John Lennon's "Imagine." U2's sanguine *All That You Can't Leave Behind* was recognized as safe and inoffensive, and immediately tracks like "Walk On" and "Stuck in a Moment You Can't Get Out Of" were put on heavy rotation. Within days the album was rocketing back up the U.S. chart, having previously dropped out of the top one hundred altogether.

The Elevation Tour, meanwhile, was repackaged with chest-thumping American patriotism as U2 invited real-life police officers and firefighters to parade around the heart-shaped catwalk and scrolled the names of 9/11 victims on a huge backdrop during "One." Each night during "Sunday Bloody Sunday" Bono would also take a U.S. flag from an audience member at the front of the stage and then gently weep into it before handing it back. For many, the tour was an extremely cathartic experience. For others, it was contrived and exploitive. Some even described it as deeply distressing, as certain established antiviolence anthems were seemingly reinterpreted as post-traumatic revenge fantasies. "Hearing it ["Bullet the Blue Sky"] played in New York City became a disturbing experience: inside the arena, it felt like the audience was taking the song up as a battle cry, as a 'we want revenge' violence fantasy, losing themselves in the brutality of the music and not in its lyrics of condemnation for the exercise of force," wrote blogger Chris Conroy.

In the wake of 9/11 and the ongoing "war on terror," Bono adopted a far more pragmatic approach to lobbying in Washington, discussing Africa in financial and national security terms, inspired by Secretary of State Colin Powell's increased awareness of the link between poverty and terrorism. Bono recalled on BBC Radio 4: "It came out of a conversation I had with a senior White House official [Powell] who confessed to me that yes, there were potentially another ten Afghanistans in Africa, so suddenly we could make the argument, 'Look, it's cheaper to prevent the fires than to put them out.'"

In January 2002, Bono and fellow entrepreneur and activist Bobby Shriver co-founded DATA (Debt, AIDS, Trade, Africa), their own NGO calling for economic aid, lowered trade embargoes, and money to fight HIV/AIDS in Africa in return for African governments offering democracy, accountability, and transparency, with start-up funds from Microsoft billionaire Bill Gates, Hungarian-American business magnate George Soros, and Silicon Valley entrepreneur Edward W. Scott, Jr. (The U2 singer decided against pumping his own money into the organization for fear it would be viewed as a vanity project.) At the official launch of DATA at the World Economic Forum in New York, Bono, not for the last time, drew an analogy between the Marshall Plan, when the United States canceled debt and rebuilt Europe after World War II as a bulwark against communism, and the need for the G8 to agree on a similar plan for Africa to prevent the rise of terrorism. However, some critics argued that this was a false analogy: the Marshall Plan was directed at countries with an economic structure already in place. Bono conceded this point, but considered it a useful sales pitch, or "melody line," nevertheless.

In the post-9/11 climate, Bono and U2 were as popular and relevant as ever in the States. The seven-time Grammy Award–winning *All That You Can't Leave Behind* had gone platinum four times, while the Elevation Tour, which had ended in December 2001, had grossed a total of $109.7 million, making it the second-biggest grossing of all time in North America—a remarkable achievement in a year that saw fewer concert tickets sold. U2's importance was reflected in the NFL's decision to enlist the band as the sole halftime entertainment at the patriotic-themed Super Bowl XXXVI on February 3, playing to seventy-two thousand football fans at the Louisiana Superdome and 87 million television viewers in a performance that paid tribute to the victims of the atrocity and the spirit of a nation with a condensed reenactment of the remembrance segment from the Elevation Tour. Reviewing the show, the *San Francisco Chronicle* wrote that "U2's live breath of fresh air and dramatic, emotional spectacle that paid homage to the victims of Sept. 11 was both daringly bombastic and also pretty damn cool." New York *Daily News* said "U2 managed to strike the right mood of patriotism, pride, and solemnity in this first Super Bowl since the Sept. 11 tragedy. . . . It was theater, yes—but on a grand scale. Given the occasion, it was grand indeed." And *The Boston Globe* called U2's performance "the greatest halftime show in the history of sporting events. Hands down."

Yet there were some in the media who accused U2 of exploiting 9/11 for their own financial gain. *Chicago Sun-Times*, for example, remarked that "U2 has never seemed more like a band camouflaging salesmanship as sincerity, and cravenness for deep concern." Juan Rodriguez, veteran pop critic at *The Gazette*, took particular offense to Bono pulling open his leather jacket to reveal its stars-and-stripes lining to the cameras: "This gesture cemented his status as Honorary American, free, free at last to join the nauseatingly long list of 9/11 profiteers. It's cool to co-opt and sell out."

In March, President Bush pledged a three-year, $5 billion increase in foreign aid via the Millennium Challenge Account (MCA), a new U.S. bilateral development assistance program drafted to a certain extent in collaboration with DATA, which would provide funds to selected countries that demonstrated sound governance and deregulated their economies; however, looking to exploit Bono's celebrity currency, which was at a new high following *Time* magazine's aforementioned cover story, "Can Bono Save the World?," the Bush administration requested his public endorsement in return. Against the advice of his aides (and his bandmates), Bono agreed to accompany President Bush to make the announcement at the Inter-American Development Bank, and a photograph featuring the unlikely duo walking together across the White House lawn (with the singer flashing the peace sign to the press) received extensive media coverage around the world. Bush commended Bono in the speech for his willingness "to lead to achieve what his heart tells him, and that is nobody—nobody—should be living in poverty and hopelessness in the world." Afterward, Bono told reporters: "I am a pest, I am a stone in the shoe of a lot of people living here in this town, a squeaky wheel. It is much easier and hipper for me to be on the barricades with a handkerchief over my nose—it looks better on the resume of a rock 'n' roll star. But I can do better by just getting into the White House and talking to a man who I believe listens, wants to listen, on these subjects."

Bono escorted U.S. Treasury Secretary Paul O'Neill—who had taken upon himself the task of finding the best ways to allocate funds from the MCA—on an eleven-day tour of four Sub-Saharan African countries in May. With the press corps, *Rolling Stone*, and MTV in tow, the designer-scruffy U2 front man and silver-haired Republican statesman—dubbed "The Odd Couple," after the former doled out T-shirts printed with that ready-made slogan—swept through HIPC-funded HIV/AIDS clinics, hospitals, and orphanages, as well as a number of private-sector businesses at O'Neill's request, in Ghana, South Africa, Uganda, and Ethiopia. For Bono, the trip's agenda was to highlight the urgency of the HIV/AIDS pandemic, which claimed the lives of five thousand people every day, and to show the secretary that Africa put large-scale western aid and debt relief to good use as he pressed him for a significant increase in both. But his emotional appeals contrasted deeply with the "results-oriented" approach of O'Neill, who argued that private enterprise and better management of existing aid would enable Africa to help itself, without becoming an object of pity.

Tim Adams recalls: "We spent two weeks in Africa and it was one of the most amazing things I've done in public service, to spend time with two very different kind of individuals who both want to do the right thing and understand how to bring U.S. resources to bear in its greatest amount of good. I think that trip was a landmark in terms of the Bush administration really developing an internal compass for development assistance in general and with particular focus on Africa."

Although Bono and O'Neill bonded on the trip, each was bent on proving the other wrong. In the Soweto area of Johannesburg, South Africa, tired staff at the Chris Hani Baragwanath Hospital—the third-largest hospital in the world, with thirty-two hundred beds—told them that although they received $50 million annually for HIV/AIDS, nearly all of the two thousand HIV-positive mothers at the unit, who required just $2 million for treatment, remained untreated. "I am speechless," Bono conceded. O'Neill, who was visibly shaking with anger, told reporters: "Before we ask for more money, for God's sake what are we doing with what we've got?"

Upon visiting a water project that supplied clean water to a small village outside of Uganda's capital, O'Neill noted that it had cost $1,000 to build and calculated that the whole country could be provided with clean water for $25 million within a year. "Last year the World Bank lent $300 million to Uganda," he said later that day. "What was so important that there wasn't $25 million to $30 million to give everyone in Uganda clean water? Where did the money go?" O'Neill also voiced disbelief during a stop at a dirt-floor Wakiso primary school, when he was informed that for much of the year students had to carry water from four miles away, and he was even more outraged to learn that there was only one textbook to every six children. He suggested to Bono that rich people should "in effect, adopt children" by sending copies of children's books. "We need to make this into an individual people thing," he said, "and not some cosmic stuff about billions of dollars" of aid. Bono was furious, and told reporters that the school, which had been built with cash freed up by an "organized, government-to-government canceling of debts," was "an example of why we need big money for development. And it is absolutely not an example of why we don't. And if the secretary can't see that, we're going to have to get him a pair of glasses and a new set of ears." O'Neill cautioned that "there's a simplemindedness that goes with debt relief." Bono shot back: "If this country doesn't get help . . . if you come back in five years, they'll be throwing rocks at us."

Neither man budged during the trip, although O'Neill tried to ingrain in Bono that long-term growth in Africa would depend on domestic entrepreneurship and foreign investment, not official aid and debt forgiveness. Bono would later admit to learning a great deal from working alongside the pragmatic O'Neill, primarily that western governments justified a leadership role in demanding more value for their money. "Paul's message was an important one: you've got to show effectiveness," says Adams. "Paul used to say, 'I can't go to the plumbers and carpenters in Chicago and ask them to pay more taxes if I can't look them in the eye and tell them it's going to actually work.' So Paul's view was, 'We can't lose money to corruption. It has to be effective.' And I think Bono got the connection; if you want to increase aid either through additional financial resources or debt relief, you've got to be able to tell the voter that it's going to work and it's not going to be wasted and end up in a Swiss bank account."

O'Neill, for his part, returned to Washington as a man on a mission. He described the trip as the most intense experience of his life and vowed to push ahead with President Bush's reform agenda to boost African development. He was focused particularly on directing U.S. assistance toward the creation of wells and distribution of water in Ghana. But for all his enthusiasm and findings, O'Neill found himself at odds with the Iraq-obsessed administration. Furthermore, according to Ron Suskind's book *The Price of Loyalty,* written with O'Neill's cooperation, a series of off-the-cuff comments, including the promise of tangible results in Africa within three years, and his familiarity with the press had made him an old-fashioned moderate Republican operating on borrowed time, as evidenced when Bush welcomed him back from the trip to Africa thusly: "Hey, there, Big O. You know something? You're getting quite a reputation as a truth-teller. You've got yourself a real cult following, don't ya?" O'Neill waited for the president to crack a smile, but none was forthcoming. Soon after the Republican victory in the elections, O'Neill was unceremoniously fired by Vice President Dick Cheney, without even a phone call from Bush himself, and the MCA was put on the back burner. Bono, who was branded a political puppet by liberals, refused to acknowledge that he had been betrayed by the president and call him out. "Even aside from him saying it publicly, I'd just like him to say it to himself," Jeffrey Sachs later grumbled in *The New York Times*.

However, O'Neill's former chief of staff, Tim Adams, is at pains to stress that Bono's faith in the Bush administration was not in vain, and in time was duly rewarded. "In working with others like Mike Gerson, the president's speechwriter, and Josh Bolton, the deputy chief of staff, the administration really began to embrace some of the things that Bono was advocating: debt relief as well as spending money on HIV/AIDs in Africa which ultimately led to PEPFAR [the president's $15 billion HIV/AIDS relief program which was tied into U.S. economic interests and the spread of conservative religious doctrine], and the Millennium Challenge Corporation [the independent agency which administers the MCA, which slowly came into effect in 2004], which tried to set up a whole new and different pot of money to reward good behavior. So those series of meetings in 2001 and then a receptive West Wing and Bono's constant push I think lured the administration into really great programs, additional resources, debt relief, PEPFAR, all the things that we celebrate—many of which, to be honest with you, are now in peril because of financial constraints, [and] the Obama administration doesn't seem to embrace it as much as the previous one. But Bono, beginning at the treasury and working through the White House for all those years, working with West Wing officials, working with President Bush, I think brought about a real transformation in the way in which Washington and the U.S. government approached development and brought about hundreds of billions of dollars' worth of assistance to African development countries, and I don't know any other individual who could've pulled that off."

■

Already proud parents of two children together, Edge and Morleigh officially sealed their family status by tying the knot in a small civil service at a Dublin registry office on June 17, 2002, with Bono and Chantal O'Sullivan, a millionaire antiques dealer, sharing "best man" duties. Four days later, the newlyweds repeated their vows before two hundred A-list guests in a lavish hilltop celebration in the Exotic Garden located in the ancient ruins of the fortress of Èze, close to their beachside villa. Edge wore a cream jacket with a black shirt and tie, plus a black beanie, which had become his go-to headgear when out in public. Morleigh was dressed in a traditional wedding gown. Among those attending the wedding party—which combined both Christian and Jewish rituals—were his bandmates and McGuinness, the supermodels Christy Turlington and Helena Christensen, and Hollywood hell-raiser Dennis Hopper. Upon their return to Ireland, the Evans family moved into a €4 million Victorian house in upmarket Killiney called Fortlands, which was set on 1.25 acres of land with its own grass tennis court, orchard, and stables. Their celebrity neighbors included Bono and Ali, ethereal songstress Enya, and F1 driver Eddie Irvine.

Through strategic marketing, the pinnacle of which was the 12-million-selling *All That You Can't Leave Behind* album itself, U2 had succeeded in reestablishing themselves as one of the biggest music brands in the world, and they wasted little time in cashing in on this lucrative position by releasing their second greatest hits compilation, *The Best of 1990–2000,* in November. They recorded two new tracks for the set, "Electrical Storm" and "The Hands That Built America," the first of which was a top-ten hit single throughout Europe, while the latter featured on the soundtrack to the Martin Scorsese movie *Gangs of New York,* and was performed live at the Seventy-Fifth Academy Awards after it was nominated for Best Original Song. In addition, four tracks, "Discothèque," "Gone," "Numb," and "Staring at the Sun," were substantially reworked to give them a more radio-friendly sound akin to *All That You Can't Leave Behind,* which didn't go down well with some long-time fans. "[*The*] *Best of 1990–2000* was an absolute travesty," one forum member later blasted on the fan site interference.com. "Between omitting 'The Fly,' the 'new mixes,' the new songs, and tacking on BD ['Beautiful Day'], they watered down their bravest decade with a fire hose. U2 are really deeply, deeply insecure. They NEED love and acceptance and when they don't get it they will eat their children." Nevertheless, U2's latest piece of revisionist history certainly got the cash tills working overtime, with worldwide sales of more than 7 million.

17

Love and Money or Else

Bono hit the U.S. heartland by bus in December 2002 for the DATA-organized Heart of America speaking tour, spreading the word about his African AIDS crusade and looking to fuel an eclectic grassroots movement of churchgoers, professors, students, and soccer moms to keep the pressure on the Bush administration and Congress. The star-studded seven-day, seven-state road show went from Lincoln, Nebraska, to Nashville, Tennessee, with Hollywood actress Ashley Judd, billionaire investor Warren Buffett, and the cyclist Lance Armstrong also on board. "Don't appeal to the conscience of America," Buffett advised Bono. "Appeal to the greatness of America and I think you'll get the job done." Bono heeded the wise old man's advice, although he did challenge the American church to change its stance toward domestic HIV/AIDS victims.

"The subject of AIDS brings out the best in the church, like you see today in response to these children suffering HIV," Bono told pastors at an airlift of eighty thousand gift-filled shoeboxes to HIV-infected children in Africa, spearheaded by Franklin Graham's Operation Christmas

Child. "But if we're honest, it has also brought the worst out of the church. Judgmentalism, a kind of sense that people who have AIDS, well, they got it because they deserve it. Well, from my studies of the Scriptures, I don't see a hierarchy to sin. I don't see sexual immorality registering higher up on the list than institutional greed (or greed of any kind, actually), problems we suffer from in the West. . . . This is a defining moment for us: for the church, for our values, for the culture that we live in."

With Bono absent for weeks at a time due to his political work (which earned him the first of three Nobel Peace Prize nominations), U2's new studio album was very much Edge's baby. Going into the project, he had made a conscious decision to leave his minimalist approach behind to explore the primal colors of rock guitar. The result, captured and embellished by legendary Sex Pistols producer Chris Thomas, was pedal to the metal rock and roll with huge riffs and piercing solos. Lyrically, the material was also some of the band's most political to date, dealing with the war in Iraq, American gun laws, and Africa. However, by the end of 2003, U2 had backtracked on the original concept after Larry and Adam argued that the songs lacked commercial appeal, while Bono, for his part, had, as he explained to *Time* magazine earlier, become resigned to the fact that "U2 is about the impossible. Politics is about the art of the possible." The album's release date was postponed and Chris Thomas was replaced by Steve Lillywhite at the production desk.

Throughout this period, Bono was in agony because of a slipped disc in his back that forced him to cancel a number of public engagements, including the induction of The Clash into the Rock and Roll Hall of Fame, with Edge agreeing to take his place at the last minute. "It's so bad that he's had to literally lie on the floor giving direction on what he wants done [in the recording studio]," a friend of the singer told *People*. "But you know Bono, nothing will stop him from making music. Once he gets going there's no stopping him—he'd come to work in an ambulance if he had to." Meanwhile, the impact his strictly nonpartisan and inclusive lobbying was having on U2's public image remained a touchy subject within the group. Edge confessed in *Vanity Fair*: "It doesn't necessarily help our band that Bono is so well known now as a political activist. It's great on one level, but being photographed with George W. Bush and the Pope—I don't like it particularly and he knows it. . . . I just worry that with political work it's a murky business. You never really know if the deal you're getting is the deal you think you're getting. He's had to make certain compromises I'm not sure I would be comfortable making."

In June 2004, Bono completed what many critics considered to be his transformation from would-be global healer to cannibal arch-capitalist by becoming a cofounder and managing director of Elevation Partners, a $1.9 billion Silicon Valley private-equity firm "seeking to profit from turmoil" in media, entertainment, and consumer-related companies—some of which, *Bloomberg* noted, "clash with his ideals," including a stake in L.A.-based video game developer Pandemic Studios, which was a subcontractor for the U.S. military- and CIA-funded Institute for Creative Technologies. Pandemic went on to create a video game called *Mercenaries 2: World in Flames*, depicting guns for hire invading oil-rich Venezuela, which led the Venezuelan Solidarity Network to accuse it of being "a justification for an imperialist aggression." The developer stated that as a partner in Elevation Partners, Bono "has visibility into all projects at Pandemic. . . ."

Just a few months later, Bono and U2 also announced a landmark alliance with Apple Computer, Inc., which yielded a signature U2 iPod model and the first-ever digital box set, with a total of 446 songs, sold exclusively on iTunes. As part of the deal, the band shot a television commercial plugging the availability of their forthcoming single "Vertigo" on the online store. U2 and Apple's cross-branding caused a stir, with fans and critics divided between those who saluted the band for becoming the new face of the digital download revolution and those who viewed it as one more nail in the coffin for indie retailers. Bono said that U2 was meeting the New Media age head on; where Metallica sued, they were embracing it, promoting it, and entering uncharted territory. He also revealed that no money had changed hands between the two companies. "It's a horizontal relationship rather than a vertical one," he said at the official launch. "We will make [money] on the products that we put out together. If they don't sell, we won't."

The U2-iTunes television spot, which was a cross between a traditional music video and Apple's catchy silhouette ad campaign, went on heavy rotation on prime-time television. U2 benefited enormously from the exposure. "Vertigo," built around a guitar riff reminiscent of Sonic Youth's "Dirty Boots," spent twenty weeks on the *Billboard* Hot 100 chart and nine weeks in the UK Top 40, where it also debuted at number one, when it was unleashed in November.

Later that month, following a number of headline-grabbing promotional events, which included throwing a free gig under the blue-steel silhouette of New York's Brooklyn Bridge, U2 released their eleventh studio album, *How to Dismantle an Atomic Bomb,* named that as a tribute to Bono's father (in fact, Bono frequently joked that the album should really have been called *How to Dismantle an Atomic Bob*). Their turbulent relationship was the focus of the album's centerpiece ballad and second single, "Sometimes You Can't Make It on Your Own," which Bono and Edge had first performed live at Bob's funeral. "He just loved opera, so in the song, I hit one of those big tenor notes that he would have loved so much," Bono told U2.com. "I think he would have loved it, I hope so."

Betraying its earlier hard-rock sound, U2's *How to Dismantle an Atomic Bomb* found them, in the opinion of Chicago music critic Greg Kot and online fans, in full cover-band mode once again, rehashing their best moves from the '80s but with the liberal-minded political anger replaced by vague self-help bromides to broaden its appeal. "The point with Bono is that bigger is better, and that U2 craves the worldwide stage, or there's no point to doing it at all," concludes Kot, who became engaged in a heated debate with the singer over the collision of art and commerce during an interview. "He also makes no bones about wanting a cross-generational audience, to draw newer, younger fans into the U2 fold. If that means doing iPod ads, so be it. He's absolutely proud to be in the vanguard of the new corporate rock. U2 are The Rolling Stones disguised as philanthropists. Bono suggests that his brand of corporate rock is more enlightened than the '70s and '80s version, that it can help transform the world. But who's kidding whom? The foundation of this approach is Bono's need to be at the center of it all. He is unapologetic about his bald ambition, and I applaud him for it. But ambition needs to be backed up by substance, and U2 is slipping. . . . [*How to Dismantle an Atomic Bomb*] in particular sounds like it was put together by committee at a Jimmy Iovine board meeting in the Interscope offices. It's a shame, because for me the U2 of *Achtung Baby, Zooropa,* and *Pop* was the band at its best: influenced by new wave, but at heart a very European art-rock band. Those albums are all flawed, but they're weirdly personal statements that perfectly reflect the dissonance of the era in which they were made. It's clear that U2 retreated from that approach after *Pop* stiffed commercially, and reached back for a sound that initially made them successful twenty years ago. The back-to-basics album is one of rock's hoariest clichés. Every dinosaur act has done it, and it was disappointing but perhaps inevitable to see U2 follow suit—twice."

U2's strategy clearly worked: *How to Dismantle an Atomic Bomb* outdid the opening-week success of *All That You Can't Leave Behind* stateside, knocking rap star Eminem off the top spot with 840,000 copies sold. In all, like its predecessor, it debuted at number one in thirty-two countries. The album was hailed by the critical establishment as a grand artistic success. In his top-star review, Robert Hilburn of the *Los Angeles Times* said that "the CD stands with *The Joshua Tree* and *Achtung Baby* as one of the Irish quartet's essential works." Peter Murphy of *Hot Press* found it "positively Spector-esque in its ambition." And *NME*—to which Bono had agreed to contribute a piece about his last twelve months in politics—called it "a classic U2 album, but also a breathtakingly modern heavy fucker," and urged its readers to "[b]uy the new U2 album and keep rock's premiere political pest in work." At the Grammy Awards, the album even outperformed *All That You Can't Leave Behind* and Michael Jackson's landmark *Thriller,* bagging all nine awards for which it was nominated, including Album of the Year, Best Rock Song for "Vertigo," and Best Song for "Sometimes You Can't Make It on Your Own."

The discrepancy between what U2 fans thought of *How to Dismantle an Atomic Bomb* and how the critical establishment responded to it was there for all to see, with the album regularly battling it out with *October* for the dubious title of worst U2 album in online fan polls. Therefore, given the extraordinary amount of critical acclaim and industry awards their post-2000 output received, it could be surmised that the band had reached a stage in their career where they were largely beyond criticism in the eyes of the establishment and were regarded as cultural pop icons that ought to be celebrated and cherished, not questioned or challenged. "It's true that an artist gets to a certain point with the Grammys, for example, where the voters want to throw awards at them," nods Paul Gambaccini. "I mean, Aretha Franklin won the R&B category year after year. Sting would get every conceivable award. Alison Krauss is another one. It's like The Rolling Stones. There's no question that The Stones were absolutely vital at their peak. The Stones of 1968 were thrilling, they were terrifying—'Street Fighting Man,' 'Sympathy for the Devil.' They were of the time, of the moment. Well, fast forward forty years and of course that no longer applies, but people with an eye on the history book are just thankful that they once were. That's where we're at with U2. The way we defer to them now is because of what they werc doing late '80s, early '90s. We turn up because we want to hear those songs performed by the people who did them, not because we expect that in 2014 there's going to be a classic album."

"I think [U2 is] very badly served by the critical establishment," says John Waters. "They either get mindlessly praised or mindlessly slagged off. But the band must also take responsibility because they cultivate tame 'critics' in many markets who prepare the way for each new release and more or less tell everyone what to think about it. They claim to welcome criticism, but they don't really, not even when it's obviously based on goodwill toward them and toward their past work."

U2 was once again the toast of the establishment when the band was inducted into both the UK Music Hall of Fame and U.S. Rock and Roll Hall of Fame, respectively. But not everyone in the band was uncorking the champagne bottles. Larry, tired of U2's mind-numbing business chores and the lack of respect accorded to him by Bono, confided to close friends that he intended to quit the group after the release of two more albums. The original U2 lineup, it seemed, would also be a thing of the past.

■

It was December 13, 2004. U2 was busy filming the music promo for "Sometimes You Can't Make It on Your Own" at Dublin's Gaiety Theatre when Edge received the kind of call that every father dreads. His seven-year-old daughter, Sian, was seriously ill and he needed to come home immediately. He and Morleigh were informed by doctors that their daughter had a form of aggressive leukemia, but curable. The following three weeks were tough on everyone, going back and forth from the hospital for treatment, meeting specialists, weighing up options, more treatment. But Sian was a courageous young girl, blessed with her mother's soothing serenity and her father's unassuming self-confidence, and they found great comfort in this once the initial shock had passed. As Sian's condition began responding to treatment, Edge was able to mull over what 2005 had in store for U2. His bandmates had been nothing but supportive throughout the ordeal, postponing the announcement of their worldwide Vertigo Tour indefinitely and canceling all other commitments. It was a gesture of solidarity, but one it was eventually decided was not required. Edge and Morleigh were advised to maintain some semblance of normality for the sake of their own sanity and their daughter's, and it was agreed that the guitarist would return to his day job with a revised tour plan scheduled around Sian's needs.

"It was a difficult decision and it was not taken lightly," Edge recalled on NewsTalk 106. "And really it boiled down to everybody in my own family feeling that we as a family could take it on and that it could work for us." He added: "One of the turning points for me was her reaction which was go for it—quite an unexpected reaction and I was pretty blown away as you can imagine."

However, chaos ensued when tickets for the Vertigo Tour finally went on sale. In line with U2's corporate ethos, the band had begun charging their fans forty dollars to join U2.com, with the guarantee that they would provide subscribers "with an advance window when they can buy

U2 tickets at all venues before they are offered to the general public." The Web site also sweetened the deal by assuring fans that they had "secured some of the best available tickets for U2.com subscribers." But when most fans tried to access the club-only presale, five days before tickets went on general release, the coveted $49.50 standing tickets in front of the stage had mysteriously vanished and they had to settle for the more expensive $95–$165 seats high up in the nosebleed sections or risk losing out entirely. Adding insult to injury, third-party profiteers—many of whom were, according to Kate Fettig, a publicist representing TicketsNow which catered to ticket brokers, "people close to the band with connections trying to make a buck"—had already pounced and were offering prime tickets for more than $1,000 apiece on eBay and online ticket broker services.

It soon emerged that U2 had sold far too many memberships to fulfill their promise and had also failed to rank fan club members accordingly (despite making yet another guarantee that subscribers to their now-defunct official fanzine *Propaganda* would "go straight to the front of the line"); incredibly, they had implemented a lottery system, which allowed scalpers to join U2.com and gate-crash the presale. Many incensed fans talked of boycotting the tour altogether, while others contemplated class-action suits against the band and Ticketmaster, which carried out the presale in partnership with San Francisco music branding and merchandising company Signatures Network, Inc. As the world's media picked up the story, Larry, in full damage-control mode, posted an open letter addressed to fans on the official Web site. "Some of it was beyond our control, but some of it wasn't," he acknowledged, before assuring everyone affected that he was personally devising a plan to avoid a similar snafu during future presales. The drummer signed off thusly: "By the way, a note to those so-called U2 fans who are quick to accuse U2 of unseemly behavior, I've only got two words for you . . ."

During the Elevation Tour, fans had encountered similar problems with presale orders, but back then they hadn't been asked to cough up a subscription fee in advance. But presales through official Web sites had become increasingly fashionable among major artists who regarded fan clubs as ready-made revenue streams, including the likes of Christina Aguilera, The Who, and The Rolling Stones (in 2002, The Stones had charged fans sixty dollars to gain access to tickets before Joe Public). It's big business. Take U2, for example: with an estimated one hundred thousand fans signing up to the 2005 presale, this amounted to an extra $4 million in revenue.

"Every artist has to ultimately make their own decisions on how they want to financially exploit their art and be viewed by their fans," says Gary Bongiovanni, editor of the concert industry trade publication *Pollstar*. "From the artist's perspective, if they are going to charge a premium membership to their fan club, the most important perk they can give is some form of priority access to tickets. The problem we have seen is that there are now so many presales, that the initial on-sale has become anticlimactic because huge chunks of tickets are already sold. And of course the scalpers are the first to join the fan club if that gets them priority tickets. Initially most fan clubs were free or only a nominal fee to join and the artists were happy just to have that direct connection to fans. In today's world, everyone seems to be looking at every possible new revenue stream to replace the decline in physical recorded music sales."

The Vertigo Tour commenced on March 28 at the iPayOne Center in San Diego, California. It was an intensely cathartic experience for Edge, yet again turning to sound and appliance to vent his internal pain. However, fans who managed to get tickets complained that the tour, which used a similar set design as Elevation, lacked a sense of danger and aesthetic originality (with the exception of a shimmering curtain of LED lights that served as an all-encompassing backdrop during indoor shows in the United States). Bono's lengthy lectures on the importance of participating in the ONE Campaign, a new effort run by DATA lobbying governments to donate more federal aid to developing countries, also sucked the life out of many shows. Holding the audience in complete silence, Bono urged them to take out their cell phones and sign up to the initiative via the text message number advertised on the screens. "We are more extraordinary and more powerful when we act together as one," he would then whisper over the poignant opening synth strings of "One." Needless to say, punters could be excused for thinking they were attending a political rally, not a rock concert.

U2 blurred the line further by marching into antiwar staples "Sunday Bloody Sunday" and "Bullet the Blue Sky," during which Bono donned a white headband decorated with the Star of David, the Christian cross, and Islamic crescent, while chanting, "Jesus, Jew, Mohammed, it's true . . . all sons of Abraham" as the symbols appeared on the screens to spell out the word "CoeXisT" in blood red. Then the singer pulled the headband down over his eyes and fell to his knees, his hands crossed and seemingly bound above his head as images of fighter planes whizzed by in the background. He repeatedly mouthed "peace," then rose to his feet. "These are the hands that built America," he crooned mournfully, recasting another U2 song in the band's condemnation of the U.S.-led invasion of Iraq and the mistreatment of prisoners at Abu Ghraib prison. But like a slippery political figure well aware of the consequences of alienating even a small fraction of his supporters, Bono, clad in leather jacket with stars and stripes down one arm, then removed the sting by dedicating somber junkie tale now turned anti-persecution paean "Running to Stand Still" to "the brave men and women of the U.S. military" as the articles of the Universal Declaration of Human Rights, adopted by the UN in 1948, scrolled by on a screen to appreciative applause. For the encore, Bono sang "Where the Streets Have No Name" with the altered lyric: "I want to tear down the walls that hold freedom tonight." "Martin Luther King's dream was bigger than America," he'd proclaim. "It was big enough to fit the whole world. It was a dream where everyone was equal. Asian. European. African. Let's sing it for Africa!" The 1987 anthem also saw its iconic red backdrop traded in for digital flags of African countries.

In the spring of 2005, Bono and Ali, merging philanthropy with consumerism, launched EDUN, a for-profit fashion brand which aimed to "raise awareness of the possibilities in Africa and encourage the industry to do business there" by sourcing garments made in Africa with African-grown cotton. With its emphasis on Christianity, civilization, and commerce, Bono's political work was nicknamed "the white band's burden" in aid circles, after the 1899 poem by the Victorian imperialist Rudyard Kipling, which urged Americans to "Take up the White Man's burden . . . To serve your captives' need . . . To veil the threat of terror . . . To seek another's profit."

But Bono's primary focus was on the G8 summit in July at Gleneagles, Scotland, where the cancellation of $40 billion of debt owed by developing nations to the World Bank, the IMF, and other multilateral institutions was to be a central item on the agenda. In May, the Gleneagles movement gained impetus when European Union development ministers, led by British prime minister Tony Blair as summit host, vowed to increase global aid from $60 billion to $120 billion by 2010, while Paul Wolfowitz, President Bush's former deputy secretary of defense and the newly appointed head of the World Bank, welcomed the UN's recommended aid target of 0.7 percent of rich countries' gross national income.

But while American and British treasury officials reached a compromise with regard to multilateral debt (with DATA acting as an unofficial liaison, according to Bono), the Bush administration firmly opposed Blair's proposal to double aid to Sub-Saharan Africa; as per reports, the White House believed that they hadn't been given the sort of credit they deserved for establishing PEPFAR and the MCC, and were quite content to keep the door closed until treated otherwise. Left distraught by the Bush administration's obstinacy, Bono flew into Washington on his private plane in late May to meet Joshua Bolten, director of the Office of Management and Budget; Karl Rove, senior advisor and deputy chief of staff; and Condoleezza Rice, who had been appointed secretary of state since their last get-together. Over lunch, Bono told them: "I know that important programs are being cut, but this kind of momentum doesn't come along every year." He also proposed two major initiatives on malaria and girls' education.

As the summit fast approached, it dawned on Bono that the campaigners needed to create a sense of occasion, a defining moment, to ensure all eyes and ears would be on Gleneagles. "Politicians are performers of a kind," he told *Time,* "but they're not great at dramatizing a situation." Realizing that the summit would take place around the twentieth anniversary of Live Aid, his solution was to persuade Bob Geldof to stage a massive concert to coincide with the date and illustrate the progress made on debt relief since 1985. Geldof was reluctant at first, but came on board when Bono scrapped the original one-gig concept for a series of free concerts held almost simultaneously in G8 states and South Africa instead and told him that they would go ahead with or without his assistance. In a flurry of activity and emotional blackmail, venues were booked, sponsors signed up, and pop acts told to drop everything and lend their name to the cause.

In what he described as his proudest moment in the weeks leading up to Gleneagles, Bono also found the time to make full use of his access to Blair, whom he had hosted at his Dublin home and considered himself a great admirer of, by interrupting a meeting between "sherpas," the uncompromising personal representatives of the G8 heads of state, at 10 Downing Street. Bono strolled in like an old friend dropping by for a quick drink as they were squabbling over how to fund the PM's proposed aid package. "First I tried to get them to laugh," he recalled to James Traub of *The New York Times.* "And I did get them to laugh. Then I tried to inspire them. I think I inspired them." Blair looked on in amazement. "These are all pretty hard-bitten people who have worked in international relations a long time," he said later, "but they were very, very enthused by that spirit."

Dubbed Live 8, the star-studded benefit concerts took place on July 2 with more than one thousand musicians performing live, including Madonna, Neil Young, and the classic lineup of Pink Floyd, and were broadcast on almost two hundred television networks around the globe. U2 opened the show at London's Hyde Park with a four-song set, the highlight of which was a duet with Paul McCartney on "Sgt. Pepper's Lonely Hearts Club Band," the first time the former Beatle had performed the song since the original recording sessions in 1967. "This is our moment, this is our time, this is our chance to stand up for what is right. We are not looking for charity, we are looking for justice," Bono told the two-hundred-thousand-strong audience, before jetting off to Vienna to resume the Vertigo Tour later that evening.

But with few African-born or black artists performing at the main concerts, Live 8 was accused of further marginalizing Africa and reinforcing white dominance. "They [the critics] said the same thing about Live Aid," says Harvey Goldsmith, who produced both charity events. "The truth of the matter is, is that we wanted to raise as much attention to the cause as possible, and the way you do that is by working with the biggest names in the industry who are selling the most records. And anyway, the black artists we did ask didn't want to do it. It's as simple as that."

Then, when it was leaked to the media that performers looking to "make poverty history" were given three-thousand-dollar gift bags for participating in the Philadelphia show, it only seemed to confirm suspicions that Live 8 was a self-serving PR exercise for rich middle-aged pop stars, many of whom benefited further by enjoying an enormous increase in record sales following their appearance (Pink Floyd's David Gilmour, to his credit, declared he would donate all resulting profits to charities that reflected the goals of Live 8, and urged other artists to do the same).

At the summit itself four days later, Bono, with Geldof and advisors in tow, took the opportunity to bend the ears of diplomats and five of the eight heads of state: German chancellor Gerhard Schröder, with whom he discussed trade reform and vowed to endorse in the upcoming general election at every stop on the German leg of the Vertigo Tour ("It will be a seriously uncool thing for a rock star to do," he told the chancellor); Tony Blair, whom he convinced to hold, in a departure from summit protocol, an official document signing ceremony; Canadian prime minister Paul Martin; French president Jacques Chirac; and American president George Bush. Meeting Bush in his luxurious nineteen-hundred-pounds-a-night suite at the Gleneagles Hotel, Bono tried to reverse his stance on doubling aid by once again appealing to his religiosity. "On so many issues it's difficult to know what God wants from us," Bono told him. "But on this issue, helping the desperately poor, we know God will bless it." As he later boasted to DATA's Erin Thornton, "Sometimes you just have to listen to the poetry."

On July 8, the G8 leaders formally pledged $50 billion in aid to developing countries by 2010, of which $25 billion would go to Africa, in addition to universal access to anti-HIV drugs and full debt cancellation for the poorest eighteen nations, fourteen of them African. Bono was euphoric at the post-summit press conference. "Six hundred thousand people will be alive to remember this G8 in Gleneagles who would have lost their lives to a mosquito bite. If an Irish rock star can quote Churchill, this is not the end of extreme poverty, but it is the beginning of the end." He added later, trembling with pride: "The world spoke and politicians listened."

Geldof agreed. "This has been the most important summit there ever has been for Africa. On aid, ten out of ten. On debt, eight out of ten. On trade . . . it is quite clear that this summit, uniquely, decided that enforced liberalization must no longer take place. That is a serious, excellent result on trade."

The mob of journalists and trigger-happy photographers on hand burst into rapturous applause and jumped to their feet, and subsequent mainstream media coverage focused on the two celebrity campaigners' ringing endorsement. "It's hard to imagine much of it would have been done without him," Paul Martin told reporters, referring specifically to the U2 vocalist.

But few African leaders or activists shared Bono and Geldof's "mission accomplished" sentiment, and with good reason. It soon emerged that most of the G8's pledges—already deemed "grossly inadequate" by the Global Call to Action Against Poverty (GCAP) coalition—were quickly shelved or bogus in the first place. For example, the debt and aid money that were thought to be separate transpired to be one and the same and ensured Africa would receive as little as half the amount that had been announced with such fanfare. And as reported by *Red Pepper,* although assurances were made that debt relief would be "unconditional," the eighteen countries chosen had in fact been force-fed structural adjustment under the HIPC Initiative, while the twenty other nations penciled in for future debt cancellation would also have to meet the HIPC's "specific policy criteria," which meant, in the words of Eric Toussaint of the Belgium-based Committee for the Abolition of the Third World Debt, "more long years of privatization and liberalization. . . . For Geldof to stand there and say that conditionality is over was a lie." According to Africa Action, African countries still owed over $200 billion and were required to pay $14 billion annually in debt service. "This is barely a modest improvement from the $15 billion annual payment that existed before the G8 deal," the nonprofit organization lamented. "Most African countries continue to spend more on debt repayment than on health and education for their populations."

The list of disappointments was endless, and both Bono and Geldof were informed of this by the GCAP prior to delivering an endorsement at the press conference that ensured the African agenda vanished from the news just days after the summit came to an end. Consequently, Bono was criticized for sugarcoating the G8's pledge and legitimizing its role in Africa rather than challenging it.

"Criticism of the deal was blunted by the celebrities," says Charles Abugre, whose observations relate to his former role as head of the Global Advocacy and Policy Division of Christian Aid, UK. "You had Bono and Geldof basically positioning themselves as the spokespersons for civil society and scoring the deal very high, and this put campaigners in a very embarrassing position of having a public fallout."

Says Dr. Kumi Naidoo, the international executive director of Greenpeace and one of the founders of the GCAP: "Bono and particularly Geldof were more enthusiastic at what was put on the table than the GCAP, which I was the chair of. Our one-line assessment was, 'The people roared and the G8 whispered.' But Geldof said at the press conference that this will raise so much money and this could save so many lives, and then he turned to me and said, 'And anybody who says saving so many lives is a whisper is a total damn disgrace!'

"After July 2005 there was a big debate within the GCAP about whether we should work with celebrities at all given the way things happened at the G8," reveals Dr. Naidoo. "Lots of people were quite upset with Bob's depiction of us being a disgrace and also how the public disagreement took the media focus off the real issues."

Without question, Bono had truly altered the political power of celebrity. He had made, as he had originally set out to do, foreign aid and debt cancellation, particularly in Africa, something "sexy" in the eyes of the mainstream media. But at what cost? In addition to the aforementioned criticisms thrown his way, his highly publicized efforts had inspired a wave of less-equipped celebrities to follow his lead and gate-crash the world of politics, each with an African cause close to their hearts to sell; but in doing so, the spotlight was rarely directed toward the cause itself in any meaningful way, only the star promoting it, with the fawning, celeb-obsessed media looking to give tough subjects a sexy twist in dumbed-down, non-investigative, non-challenging reports. According to critics, the result was complex issues reduced to oversimplistic celebrity sound bites and generalizations detrimental to the overall image and development of Africa.

"The reality is if we have a press conference with Bono in it, we're able to get significantly more media interest and media capacity than when we try to do it on our own. So celebrities have a distinctive value in terms of what they can actually contribute," says Dr. Naidoo. "However, I think that because the media is so celebrity obsessed, if he and I did a press conference somewhere—and we've done several around G8, for example—inadvertently he will be the one that will get quoted rather than me. And I understand that, but there are people within the movement who say, 'Kumi, this is something you are working on on a 24/7 basis. You understand it more than most people and certainly more than Bono. Surely your perspective is more valid than his?' So yeah, I think the problem of what some have called 'celebrocracy,' which is the domination of public space and political life by celebrity, has been the way in which the media's obsession with celebrity has actually constructed this challenge for us."

And nowhere was this more evident than at the G8 summit. Says Abugre: "The celebrities, having helped to mobilize public sentiment through their music, actually undermined the process by drawing attention to themselves and being the judge and jury of the Gleneagles deal. And as it turned out, the whole process of Africa's involvement becomes reduced to other people's charitable action—whether it's charitable action on debt or aid. In fact, it did quite a lot in undermining public confidence in Africa for aid, which is why there's been a string of books recently, mainly from Africa, that have become very anti-aid. So the whole imagery of the way the continent is presented simply as a basket case with other people's largesse is more suited and it undermines development assistance as instrumental solidarity between peoples and as a progressive instrument for development. So inadvertently the whole Gleneagles agenda has done the aid industry more harm than it probably has done it good. But hopefully if that translates as it is doing to increasing skepticism by African leaders and civil society on the aid agenda, that might just move the development process forward."

The very notion that Bono, a strong proponent of aid, had unintentionally breathed new life into the anti-aid movement was of great annoyance and embarrassment to him. "Whenever you see Africans saying they don't want aid it's pretty clear it's not their sisters, brothers, cousins who are dying for lack of the few cents a day for the two little pills that would keep them alive," he seethed in *The Independent*. In the aftermath of Gleneagles, he forged ahead relentlessly with his crusade to end extreme poverty and the HIV/AIDS crisis, his faith in the G8's commitments and desire to see them fully implemented stronger than ever before. "People need to know that by marching on Gleneagles they made the world a better place," he said. "Naysayers who belittle that take the wind out of the sails of momentum. We mustn't lose momentum."

"We've got others coming through now: Angelina Jolie, George Clooney, Brad Pitt, football players, hip-hop stars, NASCAR stars," he told *The Sunday Times*. "It's the [ONE Campaign] movement that will stop the tin-cupping [and] give us real political muscle."

18

The Ecstasy of Gold

It had been a hectic year for Bono, even by his standards. He put on a buoyant front, but dark circles and puffy tissue were clearly visible behind his flash-pink designer sunglasses—the result of a grueling schedule, sleep deprivation, and middle age snapping at his heels as a reminder of his own mortality. The prolapsed disc in his back remained a painful nuisance, halting his daily workout sessions, which in turn caused him to gain a considerable amount of weight. Moreover, his relationship with the three business partners he valued most had become strained. U2 continued, for the most part, to support his political work, but agonized over whether it overshadowed the music product. "The band has survived," Adam remarked in *The New York Times,* "but there's been a price in terms of relationships."

Bono and Larry, whose long-term animosity for each other was only outweighed by their mutual love of power and money, were also in constant disagreement over the precise nature of the singer's relationships with government officials. Larry respected Bono's nonpartisan approach, but felt on a personal level he had become far too close to the Bushes and the Blairs of the world, and he was strongly against these "war criminals" using the U2 brand name for their own political gain. His frustrations were likely compounded when Democratic Senator Hillary Clinton (whose spouse, Bill, remained a good friend of Bono's) hired a private suite at U2's Vertigo gig in Washington, D.C., in October and offered to host eighteen people at twenty-five hundred dollars a head to help fund her political action committee, while Republican Senator—and alleged homophobe—Rick Santorum picked up sixty-six tickets and invited supporters to repurchase them for a thousand dollars each. "The senator has a very warm and deep relationship with Bono," Santorum's chief spokesman, Robert Traynham, told *The New York Times*. (As criticism mounted, DATA's Jamie Drummond issued a statement, claiming: "If any political fund-raising events take place at a U2 concert, it is without the involvement or knowledge of DATA, U2, or Bono.")

Larry, who was resigned to leaving the group in the not-so-distant future, longed for the days when it was just four Dublin boys against the world; when the aftershow party would be filled with great music and genuine laughter; and when he didn't feel like a stranger in his own mobile home. But those days had long since passed, replaced by tedious small talk and closed-door negotiations as U2's VIP area was regularly commandeered by the most influential pen wielders in politics and finance, including House Minority Leader Nancy Pelosi, Secretary of State Condoleezza Rice, National Security Adviser Stephen Hadley, Microsoft's Bill Gates, Apple's Steve Jobs, and Senator John Kerry (former Senator Jesse Helms also put in a preshow cafeteria appearance in Charlotte, but didn't stick around for the gig). Larry would see Bono cozying up to these political and financial big shots, like old pals planning a fishing trip, and his blood would boil. His frustration spilled over into U2's Washington, D.C., gig when, to the astonishment of Bono and the various suit-and-ties of Capitol Hill watching from the wings, he put down his drumsticks during Bono's lengthy sales pitch for the ONE Campaign and began timing it on his watch in protest. "U2 is a democracy, to an extent, and you have to be allowed to express your views, and I have to, it's my duty," Larry said later. "You have to meet and do deals with people you don't particularly like—that's life. It's when they feel that it's basically a friendship and it crosses that line between business and pleasure."

Bono, in what U2 sources describe as a typically condescending manner, countered, "Larry's views are something I really need to hear and he keeps me on the straight and narrow. [But] what I've learned from my job as an activist is the politics is often moved by personal chemistry. It shouldn't be, but it is. So I do tend to go that extra mile."

In January 2006, Bono expanded his political efforts by launching (PRODUCT)^{RED}, a simultaneously for-profit and philanthropic brand licensed to partner companies such as American Express, Apple Inc., Gap, Giorgio Armani, and Motorola to raise money for the Global Fund to Fight AIDS, Tuberculosis, and Malaria, at the World Economic Forum in Davos. In this initiative, the brainchild of Bono and Bobby Shriver of DATA, each corporate partner created a line of products inscribed with the (RED) logo and, in return for the opportunity to market themselves as socially conscious and boost their own revenue, paid a licensing fee up front to (RED) and donated a portion of the profits to the Global Fund. The initiative drew praise for its consumer-driven approach, but also came under fire for a lack of transparency and accountability with the legal entity behind the brand—the limited liability company co-owned by Bono and Shriver and incorporated in the state of Delaware, which is known as a corporate haven, under the name of the Persuaders LLC—disclosing nothing about its earnings, licensing fee structure, or overheads and salaries, including the amount Shriver was "compensated" for serving as CEO and chairman; but more importantly, the exact dollar figure each partner donated by year was undisclosed, which, in the words of William Easterly, professor of economics at New York University, resulted in a "Byzantine structure . . . in which the consumer never knows who is paying how much to whom."

Inger Stole, communications professor at the University of Illinois, also noted in *The New York Times* that (RED) advertisements "seem to be more about promoting the [partner] companies and how good they are than the issue" of HIV/AIDS. Mark Rosenman, a professor of public service at the Union Institute & University in Cincinnati, expressed growing concern in *Advertising Age* that "business marketing is taking on the patina of philanthropy and crowding out philanthropic activity and even substituting for it," while Trent Stamp, president of Charity Navigator, America's largest independent charity evaluator, pondered "whether this edgy, innovative campaign inspires young people to be better citizens or just gives them an excuse to feel good about themselves while they buy an overpriced item they don't really need." Tamsin Smith, president of (PRODUCT)^{RED}, claimed such criticism failed to comprehend the campaign's objective. "We're not encouraging people to buy more, but if they're going to buy a pair of Armani sunglasses, we're trying to get a cut of that for a good cause," she told *The New York Times*. But (RED) critics accused Smith of painting a misleading picture of a business model designed primarily to create a "sustainable flow of money" and contradicting Bono and Shriver's initial pitch to corporate partners who, according to an article later published in *Advertising Age*, in the first year collectively spent as much as $100 million on marketing their (RED)-branded products—in which the public were urged to "Buy (RED). Save lives"—while contributing only $18 million to the Global Fund.

It was a testament to how far up the political ladder Bono had climbed and his value to those firmly entrenched in power when, after wrapping up (RED) commitments at the World Economic Forum, he next showed up on the media radar as the keynote speaker at the National Prayer Breakfast in Washington, D.C. An annual event organized by a shadowy evangelical Christian network called the Fellowship Foundation, a.k.a. "The Family," the breakfast had long been regarded by the political left as a thinly veiled excuse for congressional figures, business leaders, and evangelists to gather together in a luxury ballroom and partake in superficial, photo-opportunistic solemnity and false goodwill and perhaps even equate the president with Jesus Christ; to all hold hands and pray for the downtrodden while being served lavish food by impoverished black and Hispanic waiters; and to facilitate the worldwide funding and growth of the Fellowship's religion-based bigotry. "If you're wondering what I'm doing here, at a prayer breakfast, well so am I," Bono quipped from the podium during his twenty-minute sermon. Quoting the Bible, the Koran, and defunct British rockers Dire Straits, he called for "an additional 1 percent of the federal budget" to aid the world's poor—this coming, incidentally, just one day after the House approved a $40 billion budget-cutting bill that imposed "substantial changes on programs including Medicaid, welfare, child support, and student lending."

"I've gotten to know Bono," President Bush said to laughter and applause from the attendees. "He's a doer. The thing about this good citizen of the world is he's used his position to get things done. You're an amazing guy, Bono. God bless you."

■

Adam was once again on the verge of destroying his reputation as the eternal bachelor of U2 when he proposed to his on-off Canadian girlfriend of ten years, Suzanne Smith, on St. Valentine's Day at a private soiree in London. For years, the bass guitarist had lived a selfish existence by traditional standards. He had become so accustomed to the independence provided by unimaginable wealth that it had been impossible for him to compromise his lifestyle for the benefit of a serious relationship with a woman. For as long as he could remember, he alone had been his number-one concern.

Then he met Suzanne. According to friends, the newly engaged couple had their stormy moments, but on the whole Suzanne was the antithesis of Adam's previous partner, the part-time supermodel, full-time drama queen Naomi Campbell, in that she brought a semblance of normality to the former wild man's life, while he in turn introduced a little fun and excitement to hers. They divided their time between London, where Suzanne worked as a record company executive, having left her post as assistant to Paul McGuinness, and Adam's Georgian mansion in Rathfarnham, where they pottered around the stunning forty-four-acre grounds and entertained guests. It was a simple life, and an intensely private one.

Not so private was the fact that U2 and their accountants were laughing all the way to an offshore financial center in June when, just days after Bono returned from a six-nation, ten-day tour of the African continent with executives from Gap and Motorola to examine debt and foreign aid progress, they shifted their highly lucrative music publishing arm, U2 Ltd., from Ireland to the Netherlands to avoid paying tax—just six months before the Irish government amended the Artists' Tax Exemption Scheme established in 1969 to help struggling artists, which multimillionaires U2 had gladly exploited, and capped tax-free earnings for artists at €250,000. Yet again, they were following the business model of The Rolling Stones, who had fled to the very same Dutch holding company, Promogroup, in 1972 and had paid only 1.6 percent tax on earnings of $450 million since 1986, according to Dutch documents. Jan Favie, a reclusive Dutch accountant who masterminded Promogroup, was appointed the principal director of U2 Ltd.

Needless to say, Irish taxpayers were not amused by U2's decision to jump ship. The move, while completely legal, raised all kinds of questions with regard to the band's economic, social, and moral obligations. Bono, in particular, was singled out as a hypocrite—someone who was avoiding tax in his own backyard while asking the Irish government and others around the world to spend more tax revenue on causes he so passionately espoused. Upon learning the news, Joan Burton, Irish Labour's finance spokesperson, said, "Having listened to Bono on the necessity for the Irish government to give more money to Ireland Aid, of which I approve, I am surprised that U2 are not prepared to contribute to the Exchequer on a fair basis along with the bulk of Irish taxpayers." Indeed, many observers concluded that by shifting one-third of their business empire—which alone raked in $30 million-plus in royalty payments in 2006, according to documents obtained by the Associated Press—to another country, Bono and the rest of U2 had ultimately lost the right to a full voice in Irish society. (Later, when Bono publicly chastised the Irish government for not meeting the DATA-endorsed target of 0.7 percent of GDP, Minister of State Conor Lenihan suggested that if the singer paid all his taxes then the government would already be halfway to meeting the proposed figure.)

"Why are they escaping normal Irish taxation, especially at a time when the country needs tax money?" ponders Dick Molenaar, owner of All Arts Tax Advisers, a Rotterdam-based tax consulting firm for musicians and cultural institutions. "Everybody needs to pay their fair share of taxation to the government to finance education, health care, roads, national security, antipoverty programs and so on. This is not the way well-known artists who are an example for people living in the country should behave."

Although Bono initially refused to discuss the move offshore, an under-fire Edge told reporters, "Our business is a very complex business. Of course we're trying to be tax-efficient. Who doesn't want to be tax-efficient?" Writing in *The Observer,* Nick Cohen remarked that the guitarist "sounded as edgy as a plump accountant in the nineteenth hole." Bono's silence was perhaps unsurprising, given that the entire tax-shelter arrangement was at odds with his previous comments in 1988 that U2 had "no problem paying taxes" and they were in fact "very proud to pay taxes in Ireland." He had even reiterated their commitment to the Irish taxation system on Dave Fanning's RTÉ 2fm show in June 2005. "You know, we pay a lot of tax, enormous, millions of tax. Our publishing, which is about one-third of our income, we have tax breaks on, and that's great and that's encouraged us to stay in Ireland. And if that changes, it's not going to affect anything for U2; but young U2s might leave, and that would be a shame."

But what criticism Bono had to endure on home soil was relatively innocuous compared to that expressed by various international charity organizations with whom he had worked closely over the years, which seriously undermined his credibility as a Third World crusader. According to a 2007 Christian Aid report, entitled "Death and Taxes: The True Toll of Tax Dodging," developing nations were being cheated out of at least $160 billion every year as a result of tax avoidance and tax evasion—much more than the $40–$60 billion the World Bank estimated was needed to fund the UN's Millennium Development Goals—and the lives of 350,000 children under the age of five could have been saved every year if tax dodging was abolished. Christian Aid, which named Bono as one of the main "dissenters" responsible, concluded that the extent of tax abuse "is so widespread and damaging that it is tantamount to a new slavery."

Bono finally broke his silence in an interview with *The Irish Times* in 2009. "The thing that stung us [about the criticism] was the accusation of hypocrisy for my work as an activist," he said. "I can understand how people outside the country wouldn't understand how Ireland got to its prosperity, but everybody in Ireland knows that there are some very clever people in the Government and in the Revenue who created a financial architecture that prospered the entire nation—it was a way of attracting people to this country who wouldn't normally do business here. . . . What's actually hypocritical is the idea that then you couldn't use a financial services center in Holland."

Critics were quick to point out that Bono failed to mention that the same so-called Celtic Tiger that had roared so loudly, so cleverly for over a decade had now been shot, skinned, and gutted by a property market crash, government spending cuts and, in the words of Irish journalist and civil rights activist Eamonn McCann, "a banking scandal which, proportionately, dwarfs the crimes of the bankster class in the U.S." Another article printed in the same edition as Bono's defense stated: "After a decade of a credit-fueled property bubble, the [Irish] economy is not so much crumbling as vaporizing: were we the size of Britain, January's rise in unemployment would have been over half a million."

"This, unfortunately, puts Bono's truly astonishing comments in perspective," says Richard Murphy, a founder of the Tax Justice Network and director of Tax Research LLP. "The reality was that U2's royalty income was not taxed for many years in Ireland and when Ireland proposed taxing that income at a ludicrously low rate of 12.5 percent, they fled to the Netherlands—which is recognized as a tax haven—where the rate might be no more than 5 percent. Now, he defends this sort of tax engineering as being the normal part of Irish life. Well, it may be, but it's highly abusive and has been shown to suck money out of developing countries into developed states. He is defending a structure which works completely against the principles that he says he stands for.

"Not only is he dodging tax, he is also endorsing the tax dodging system. So there's a two-stage process here: one, he does it, and two, he says it's quite acceptable to do it. And yet we know that that is not true. We, the Tax Justice Network, have tried to engage Bono and DATA, his development agency, on this issue and get it onto their policy debate, but they have refused to do so and appear to resent us doing so.

"DATA," Murphy continues, "are now completely out of step with the rest of the world of development. If you look at Christian Aid, Action Aid, Oxfam, etc., you will find that they are saying tax is absolutely fundamental to development. And the reason is this: you can give aid to a country for as long as you like, but at the end of the day they are only developed when they are independent of you, and they can't do that until they have governments that we support to collect the tax that is owing to them. In other words, we must help them to collect tax within their economies so that they can provide education, health care, and build welfare systems for their own people because that's what they need. But instead of that, Bono is part of the old aid culture where people remain dependent upon us in the West. He is now part of the problem of maintaining these peoples' dependency, not part of the solution, which is creating a world where they can stand up on their own two feet with democratic governments—held accountable by the taxpaying electorate—which have it within their power to tax the multinational corporations based within them. Without tax that is not possible. But that's not what Bono seems to understand. He has his head firmly in the sand, no doubt for his own personal reasons."

In August, Bono added another notch to his money belt when he and Elevation Partners paid a reported $300 million for a 40 percent stake in Forbes Media, the parent company of *Forbes* magazine and Forbes.com. Like the tax avoidance move, Bono's multimillion-dollar investment in an American business magazine that had for eighty-nine years celebrated wealth and capitalist consumption was considered at variance with U2's purported brand values. Editor in chief Steve Forbes, who was on record as saying that Bono's "emphasis on giving more money to benighted countries is misbegotten," even blurted out that Bono was an avid reader of the self-styled "capitalist tool" and scourge of the left, while Roger McNamee, an Elevation partner, revealed that the singer was drawn to *Forbes* because it "has a point of view" and that he "drove this part of the discussion and likes the fact that there has been a consistent philosophy throughout its history." Incidentally, soon after Elevation's investment in Forbes, the company froze its employee pension plan and carried out mass layoffs.

Increasing Bono and U2's cash flow even more was the November release of *U218 Singles,* their third greatest hits package in as little as eight years. This cash cow included two new tracks recorded with U.S. producer Rick Rubin at Abbey Road Studios: the Beatles-inspired "Window in the Skies," and a rendition of the Skids' punk rock classic "The Saints Are Coming" in collaboration with Green Day; the latter of which was also in aid of Music Rising, a New Orleans–focused charity cofounded by Edge to help replace the musical instruments lost during Hurricane Katrina, and later performed live at the first American football game played at the infamous Louisiana Superdome since Katrina struck.

▪

That same month, the band resumed the Vertigo Tour in Brisbane, Australia, after an eight-month postponement engineered to give Edge and his family breathing space while Sian continued to receive treatment under Dr. William Li, the president of the Massachusetts-based Angiogenesis Foundation, who Edge credited with saving his daughter's life. They set up base at the exclusive four-grand-a-night Palazzo Versace resort on the Gold Coast and commuted via private jet and helicopter. But as well as fulfilling contractual obligations, the tour afforded Bono the opportunity to "invite" Australian prime minister John Howard to meet him to discuss the nation's foreign aid budget, which he felt was insufficient. "If he's not serious [about committing 0.7 percent of GDP],

I don't want to meet him," Bono warned. "I think the prime minister is looking on it, but you Australians have to give him permission to spend your money. I wouldn't dare to tell Australians what to do. I can only say what other countries are doing."

Howard, unfazed by Bono's celebrity status, declined the offer. "I don't accept preconditions from anybody," he told reporters. "I don't commit in advance to businessmen in this country and I certainly don't do it to—much and all that he is high grade—Irish entertainers." For Bono, accustomed to world leaders offering him a seat at their table, Howard's snub was terribly perplexing, and he criticized him on state-owned television. "[The PM] has led your country to the bottom of the league table in terms of engagement with the world's poor," he said, "and I don't think that's an Australia people want to live in."

Meanwhile, back in Dublin, Bono did get his own way when a High Court judge ruled in favor of U2 in a protracted legal battle with their former stylist Lola Cashman to establish ownership of £3,400 worth of band memorabilia, which included a *Joshua Tree*–era Stetson hat, a pair of hooped earrings, a pair of black trousers, and a green sweatshirt. "They sound like trivial items, they're really not," Bono told the court at one stage. "They are important items to the group and we take them seriously." Likewise, observers noted that there was nothing trivial about the main motivation behind a trial that was described by the media as "the most bizarre high-profile—and increasingly vicious—case ever seen in the Four Courts" and the consequences it had on the major players involved.

The legal dispute began in 2002 when Cashman, who maintained throughout that she was legitimately gifted the items by U2 during private moments on the Joshua Tree Tour, put them up for auction at Christie's in London after her trusted financial advisor "absconded with her life savings" while she was out of the country. The band, however, claimed she had taken them without their permission and instructed their lawyers to send two letters to the auction house querying her right to ownership and seeking their return. Cashman countered with a defamation writ in July 2004. The letters, she said, had "made it impossible to work in my industry" and she was subsequently "frozen out" of her chosen profession. It was at this point proceedings turned into a game of chess. Upon being served the legal documents by Cashman's representatives, U2's lawyers filed an application with the London High Court of Justice seeking a declaration that the court had no jurisdiction with regard to the claim and also issued proceedings in Ireland over ownership of the memorabilia—effectively hijacking Cashman's lawsuit.

The trial, which heard evidence from Bono, Paul McGuinness, and Cashman, first came before Judge Matthew Deery at Dublin's Circuit Court in July 2005. It was a highly irregular affair, with the world's paparazzi camped outside, while inside star-struck barristers in wigs and gowns climbed over each other to get Bono's autograph during breaks in proceedings. Taking the stand, Bono, the scripture-quoting, rosary-wearing philanthropist, chose not to swear on the Bible but affirm the oath instead. Between wisecracks he told the packed courtroom that the Stetson hat had taken on "iconic" status and giving it away "would be like the Edge giving away his guitar. It just wouldn't happen." Judge Deery concurred, stating U2's version of events seemed "more likely to have happened" due to their strict archiving policy, and he ordered the stylist to return the items to the band within seven days. He also instructed her to hand over a cardboard Christmas decoration, two chipped souvenir mugs, and a collection of photographs (which originally were not part of the proceedings) that he was satisfied she had shot on film purchased by the band. Regarding claims U2 had taken action in Ireland to hamper the defamation proceedings, Deery acknowledged that "the outcome of these present proceedings in Ireland will substantially determine the outcome of the issue in the English courts," but added that, given that they were extremely successful musicians, "it would seem odd if the group were to make a provision to pursue a claim of this nature if the subject was not of importance to the band."

Cashman, who was adamant that she had been wronged, launched an appeal at Dublin's High Court, to which U2, conscious of the fact that her lack of finances had momentarily halted proceedings in the middle of the Circuit Court case, responded by offering her what she now describes as "a huge amount of money" to drop the appeal and quietly disappear. Her family and friends, most of whom thought she was foolish and running on emotions, begged her to take the cash as legal expenses had spiraled out of control, including a court order to pay one thousand pounds a month to the band in costs pending the outcome of the appeal. But Cashman says the original lawsuit was never about money; it was about justice and protecting her reputation, which is why she told the band in no uncertain terms where they could stick their proposition. "All I wanted was a letter of apology," she says, "because I didn't do what they accused me of."

The plot thickened when, just two weeks before the High Court appeal was set to be heard, Cashman's senior counsel, Hugh Hartnett, decided he could no longer represent her, for reasons known only to himself. The stylist, who had gone on to work with George Michael and the Pet Shop Boys following her spell with the Irish quartet, also found help within the music industry scarce. Onetime colleagues were genuinely terrified of the corporate behemoth known as Not Us Ltd. U2 and McGuinness, it was understood, ruled not with love and peace, but with an iron fist. Silence was rewarded, while speaking one's mind, regardless of how unpopular it would be received, led to being blacklisted and cast out of the industry like a leper. "If you say a word against them," says a former U2 employee, "the work dries up."

Cashman, now faced with the daunting prospect of going it alone in court, breathed a small sigh of relief when her distress signal was picked up by none other than the former attorney general of Ireland, John Rogers SC. Rogers, perhaps intrigued by the David vs. Goliath scenario, agreed to be in her corner despite being of the opinion that, unlike the archetypal biblical underdog, they would emerge defeated, at least in the eyes of the court. "You'll never win," he told Cashman, "because what judge in the land would bring Bono's reputation into question? But we'll give them a good hiding anyway."

U2's own counsel, the equally lauded Paul Sreenan SC, adopted a measured and pedantic approach throughout the trial. Cross-examining

Cashman for over three hours, he repeatedly turned to a copy of the stylist's 2003 book, *Inside the Zoo with U2*, in which she revealed the problems Bono had with his height and weight, to trip her up. He inquired, for example, as to why had she taken bags of the band's "stuff" with her on a flight home in December 1987, to which she replied she was putting the finishing touches to a style project for the band and was under contract for a further four months. Sreenan, who could barely contain his glee, returned to the book and read aloud a passage in which she said she had quit U2 duty that fateful December, even though Bono and McGuinness urged her to stay on permanently.

Questioned by Sreenan, Bono, who avoided making eye contact with Cashman throughout the court battle, portrayed the stylist as an eccentric magpie who regularly wore his and the other band members' clothes and quarreled with management. The U2 front man appeared "calm, composed, and in control," noted Jason O'Brien of the *Irish Independent*. "He was center stage. He was Bono, he was enjoying the attention."

But then up stepped Rogers, who called attention to his client's defamation case against the band and how "because they are international rock stars they [think] they can simply lie," which immediately unsettled Bono. He poured scorn over the singer's claims that U2 publicist Regine Moylett had seen "an Aladdin's Cave" of memorabilia and video equipment in Cashman's apartment in 1992. "Just a second, now, this is the first we've heard of it, yet it was twelve years later that you demanded to bring a case?" he said incredulously. Rogers "scored heavily," according to O'Brien, when, after Bono spoke of the band's stringent policy of archiving items, he pointed out that their archive had in fact not been established until 1998 and that Cashman had made it known she had various items as opposed to U2 even being aware that they were "missing."

"That's a fair criticism," Bono conceded, beads of sweat on his forehead.

Rogers accused Bono of trying to "put a vile view" of Cashman across and presented video evidence of him on stage saying, "Lola, come back. I love you!" The singer's answers became shorter, his speech low and mumbled. He had, in the words of another eyewitness, been "torn to shreds" by the formidable barrister, who at this point had removed his wig and was standing with one leg up on a chair like John Wayne. This was Rogers's domain, and Bono clearly wanted out, according to O'Brien.

Larissa Nolan of the *Sunday Independent* stated that while "Sreenan methodically picked away at Cashman, Rogers went straight for the jugular and treated us to pure theater . . . he made the U2 front man—who seemed a lot less rock-starish without his trademark glasses—look like a spoiled child who wanted his ball back. At one point, he even drove Bono to admit that he 'felt like a fool' for being there."

How fascinating it was for those present to see the charismatic rock star and activist, who did not seem to be intimidated by anyone or anything, suddenly reduced in stature. One question arose from such a singular occurrence: why would a man who appeared to have everything invite so much ridicule upon himself for something that was, at least on the surface, relatively nothing? Pressed, Bono revealed why: Cashman's book. "That book was reprehensible," he said. "That is why I am here. She took advantage of the band." The silence in the courtroom was deafening.

Thus, the general consensus among the Irish journalists in attendance was that the case was never about a few measly trinkets for U2; it was about power and revenge. Cashman was the first person to provide a window into their carefully guarded inner sanctum, to leave the door of deception ajar, and now they were punishing her for it. Furthermore, it was the potentially brand-damaging details she left out of the book, such as "who was sleeping with who," that gave them restless nights, and she needed to be discredited and silenced in a preemptive strike. Brendan O'Connor of the *Irish Independent* noted that "some lawyers will tell you that every court case is about either money or sex and clearly U2 don't need money." McGuinness was, unquestionably, the most eager and purposeful in his character assassination when, completely unrelated to the discussion in progress, he described Cashman as "one of the most difficult people I've ever had to deal with in my life," "utterly disloyal," and "a traitor." "It was his last comment that gave the clearest insight into the psyche of U2—nobody messes with the Dublin rock 'family,'" concluded Larissa Nolan.

"It all comes back to power," says Cashman, "and how they want to control everything that is said about them. Bono himself told the court that he had never been as close to an employee as he was with me, and it's absolutely right that I know a lot of personal things about him and the others. But *Inside the Zoo* wasn't a 'rock and roll' kind of book—it was quite respectful and affectionate, all things considered. But ultimately they were afraid of the things I didn't say more than the things I did. They're power mad."

Nevertheless, despite Bono's admitted motive, Rogers's prediction came true when in November 2006 Justice Michael Peart ruled that "on the balance of probability" the items were not given to Cashman and affirmed the order made by the Circuit Court. He stated that the case rested on the credibility of Bono and Cashman, and he chose to side with the former. "There are many instances where her evidence lacks credibility, plausibility, or probability," he said, before acknowledging these instances related to matters peripheral to the central issues. In his thirty-eight-page judgment, Justice Peart did, however, accept that a pair of black Converse All Star boots worn by Larry were in fact given to Cashman, as well as other gifts such as rosary beads and a Bible signed, "To Lola, with real love, Larry," despite Bono's assertion that the band never gave away parts of their wardrobe to personnel. What Cashman found most frustrating about the return of the boots in particular was that the Christie's auction was stopped due primarily to the fact that Larry claimed the footwear had never belonged to him. "It came out in court that in fact he did own them and he did give them to me. I was proven to be telling the truth about the one item that had started off the whole thing," she says.

U2 declared publicly that they would not be pursuing the stylist for their legal fees, although they had the power to do so. But this was of little comfort to Cashman, who was forced to declare bankruptcy with debts in excess of £350,000.

"How magnanimous of them," says Cashman. "They'd already bankrupted me. I'd taken out loan after loan for the court case and I'm still struggling to this day. I don't want to play the victim here, but it was a disgrace what they did to me, to actually try to ruin me twenty years later because I had written this little book and they had no control over it. But I feel so good about myself because I wasn't a coward and I took them on and the world can judge for itself."

In December, while their onetime stylist and friend came to terms with the reality of losing the keys to her home and car, U2 wrapped up their highly profitable Vertigo Tour in sun-kissed Hawaii. Generating $389 million in ticket sales, the tour was the second-highest grossing of all time, but only one source of income for the U2 empire in a two-year consumer assault which saw the release of two albums, the 10 million–selling *How to Dismantle an Atomic Bomb* and 4.5 million–selling *U218 Singles*; the launch of a remodeled U2 iPod; an ESPN tie-in ("nothing extraordinary," McGuinness said, "but we did get paid"); and a best-selling coffee-table tome, entitled *U2 by U2* (HarperCollins), for which they received a $3 million advance. Vast sums of revenue also poured in via a complex network of companies and trusts structured to minimize their tax liability, including concert-booking agency Target Tours Inc., U2 Clothing Co., and Ravencrest Ltd., as well as Bono's personal investment in private equity firm Elevation Partners.

All told, it was Bono and U2's most lucrative period yet. "I've not been famously profit-oriented," the self-described "traveling salesman" said. "I believe that brilliance brings a better bottom line. Always."

19

The Wrong Compromise

With U2 business taken care of for the time being, Bono was able to focus on what had become his real full-time job, that of the shrewd political lobbyist and venture capitalist. He was incredibly adept at his dual role and knew just what buttons to push to get results—for example, Christian guilt trips for Jesse Helms and his God-fearing ilk, good old, hard facts for Paul O'Neill and other briefcase-carrying number crunchers, and rock-star mystique for Tony Blair and his celebrity-obsessed New Labour Party. And it was the effectiveness of such methods that enabled him to again steal the show at the World Economic Forum in Davos in January 2007, despite sharing the panel with Blair, Bill Gates, Dr. Kumi Naidoo, and Ellen Johnson Sirleaf, Africa's first female president. With the forum hanging on his every word, there was little doubt about who the headline act was. (In subsequent annual visits, Bono would use the stage to urge world leaders to honor their commitments to the Millennium Development Goals, as well as highlight the value of his and Gates's campaign for increased aid and market-based social change, or "creative capitalism," as demonstrated with (RED) and EDUN, to alleviate the problems in developing nations.)

Bono was once more handsomely rewarded by members of the establishment, both new and old, for his efforts on behalf of Africa. In March, he received the NAACP Chairman's Award and got a repeated standing ovation for his acceptance speech, in which he evoked the spirit of Martin Luther King, Jr. "The poor are where God lives. God is in the slums, in the cardboard boxes where the poor play house. God is where the opportunity is lost and lives are shattered. God is with the mother who has infected her child with the virus that will take both their lives. God is under the rubble and the cries we hear during wartime. God, my friends, is with the poor. And God is with us, if we are with them."

That same month, he accepted an honorary knighthood—the Status of Honorary Knight Commander of the Most Excellent Order of the British Empire (KBE)—in a ceremony at the British embassy in Dublin. As an Irish citizen, he was not permitted to adopt the title "Sir" (although that hadn't exactly stopped Bob Geldof from doing so). Accompanied by Ali and their children, as well as Edge and Adam, Bono suggested two alternatives: "Lord of lords [or] your demigodness," he quipped. Tony Blair didn't attend the ceremony, but he did send a letter thanking him for his commitment to tackling extreme poverty in Africa. Blair wrote: "I want personally to thank you for the invaluable role you played in the run up to the Gleneagles G8 Summit. Without your personal contribution, we could not have achieved the results we did. So thank you and I look forward to continuing to work together to maintain momentum on Africa, and ensure leaders around the world meet the promises they have made."

His bandmates were also active throughout this period. Edge forked out $15 million for a 120-acre parcel in Malibu with a cottage and a creek on it. Adam was a bachelor again after splitting up with his fiancée Suzanne Smith. Associates claimed that the couple separated "amicably" and hoped to remain good friends. Larry, meanwhile, was planning his exit strategy from U2, with long-harbored ambitions of becoming an actor looking the most practical route to take. The painfully shy drummer boy of old had long since matured into a quietly self-confident man, with a deadpan sense of humor and zero tolerance for bullshit. He was told by friends that his ageless, James Dean–like features made him ideal for the big screen, and in time he met the Irish director Mary McGuckian over a drink to discuss the likelihood of him making the leap from music to acting. McGuckian advised him to pick up a copy of the French crime drama *Man on the Train*. "You have to see Johnny Hallyday [France's version of Elvis Presley] and his transition into making a good film," she told him. "He's really believable." And with that, Larry's acting career slowly began to take shape behind the scenes, with his partner Ann and McGuckian eventually securing the rights to remake the aforementioned film. Their English-language version, which starred Larry in the lead role as a mysterious criminal alongside a typically hammy Donald Sutherland, would go on limited release in 2011 to modest acclaim.

In May, U2 regrouped at the Cannes Film Festival for the unveiling of their first digital 3-D concert film *U2: 3D*, put together by longtime collaborators Catherine Owens and Mark Pellington from over one hundred hours of concert footage shot on the Latin America leg of the Vertigo Tour, with the majority sourced from two shows in front of seventy-five thousand fans in Buenos Aires. Prior to the screening, the band played a brief live set on the famous red-carpeted steps of the Palais des Festivals. Afterward, they attended a party hosted by *Vanity Fair* magazine, for which Bono had been hired to guest-edit a "historic" celebrity-driven Africa edition. Upon its commercial release in 2008, *U2: 3D* would rake in over $26 million at the international box office, making it one of the highest-grossing concert films of all time.

Following the *Vanity Fair* bash, U2 flew out to Morocco for two weeks to lay the groundwork for their next recording venture, *No Line on the Horizon*. With Eno and Lanois on board as songwriters, they saw it as an opportunity to rediscover the experimental edge that had shaped their mid-'80s and -'90s work. Eno's official songwriting credit was the result of a dispute he and the band had had after the release of *All That You*

Can't Leave Behind when its liner notes read "Music by U2," without mentioning Eno's own contribution. The band's reluctance to give him his due had almost destroyed their relationship.

The U2 camp set up a makeshift studio in the courtyard of a converted Riad in Fez, the so-called spiritual capital of the kingdom. The annual Festival of World Sacred Music was a major draw for the band and Eno, who had expressed an interest in Arabic music for many years. One particular performance that made an impression on them was by the Persian vocalist Parīsā, accompanied by the musically dextrous Dastan ensemble, in the grounds of the Batha Museum. The seventy-five-minute set was comprised of two songs that were forty-five minutes and thirty minutes in length respectively and eschewed the traditional verse-chorus-verse pop structure altogether. "Can you believe this?" Bono enthused. "Isn't that something else?"

The group, at times working with an oud player and local percussionists, started to incorporate elements of Sufi singing and Joujouka drum patterns, which Eno prepared in advance for Larry, as well as Hindu and Jewish music, in an attempt to fashion "future hymns—spiritual songs for the future," Lanois explained later to Canadian DJ Alan Cross. It was a liberating experience, the kind that reminded everyone why they got into music in the first place. They recorded around ten songs, each in one live take, during the Fez sessions, including "Moment of Surrender" and "Unknown Caller," and talked about releasing them before the end of the year. But all urgency was lost as soon as U2 returned home to Dublin and France, and the album took a backseat to numerous other business projects.

According to associates, U2 had become obsessed with ensuring their legacy lives on long after the music has stopped, and pushed through plans via Geranger—a consortium of property developers and band members—to build a €200 million skyscraper at the mouth of Dublin Bay as part of a radical redevelopment of the area. Dubbed U2 Tower, the 180-meter landmark structure would be the tallest building in Ireland, and it would house €1–1.5 million luxury apartments and a two-floor recording studio for the band at its peak. (As of late 2008, the project was put on hold because of the financial crisis, although whispers persist of a revised proposal.)

Bono and Edge were also granted planning permission by Dublin City Council for a controversial €150 million revamp of The Clarence Hotel, transforming their loss-making property into an eight-story, 141-bedroom five-star hotel and spa, complete with a futuristic floodlit glass roof atrium nicknamed "the flying saucer," but at the expense of gutting six listed buildings, including The Clarence itself. Conservationists and environmentalists expressed outrage, with the council's own city conservation architect advising a refusal in her report because the planned development did not meet legal requirements. Michael Smith, former head of the national heritage trust An Taisce, told *Bloomberg* that the hotel demolition was "an old-fashioned, money-driven, anti-environmental exploit. Bono is behaving like just another private jet–addicted property speculator feeding on Ireland's greedy zeitgeist."

In March 2008, U2 struck a twelve-year global deal with Live Nation, allowing the corporate concert behemoth to handle all merchandising, digital, and branding rights as well as touring for the band. The deal came on the heels of the radical $120 million recording and touring contract Madonna had signed with the Clear Channel spin-off in 2007. However, unlike the Material Girl, U2 would continue to release records through Universal Music. "The opportunity to integrate U2 and Live Nation's vision of the future is a great extension of our established business," McGuinness announced. U2 received $80 million up front and 1.6 million shares, which they soon cashed in for $25 million under the terms of their contract, even though the stock's market value had dropped to just $6.1 million. For many, the sight of the biggest band in the world jumping into bed with Live Nation in such an eager fashion only spelled trouble for the music industry, even more so in the wake of the company's controversial merger with Ticketmaster in 2010, which led to claims that it had an unfair near-monopoly on live music.

"U2 are cowards, charlatans, and frauds in the narrow sense of the music business," says acclaimed music critic Jim DeRogatis. "I interviewed Bono backstage [at a radio promo event in Chicago in March 2009] and he lied to my face. I asked him, 'What is your opinion on the Ticketmaster-Live Nation merger?' and he said, 'I haven't really spent any time thinking about it. I'm not really following it.' Who are you kidding? You guys are making millions of dollars from this corporation which many people in America and throughout the world say is a great force of negativity in the music business. And not only that, he later did an introduction when Michael Rapino and Irving Azoff had their meeting with stockholders. I mean, save the Third World, feed Africa. But conscientious politics begin at home, and the way U2 operate in the music business is as despicable as any act you could care to name, whether that's Britney Spears, Jay Z, or Madonna. U2 don't operate any differently, and they should, because they mean more. They're a band with a moral compass, and yet their business dealings are not reflecting that."

■

Recording on U2's long-gestating *No Line on the Horizon* was completed in December 2008 after additional writing sessions in Dublin, New York, and, finally, around a month at London's Olympic Studios. The end product was barely recognizable from the material recorded in Morocco eighteen months earlier. As the sessions developed, home and abroad, a clash of philosophies had emerged between Eno and Lanois, believers of enduring art arising from remaining true to your vision and creating music for one's self with the understanding that it will ultimately find its own audience, and U2, determined to manufacture easily digestible forty-fives to reach as wide an audience as possible. The album was gradually stripped of its Moroccan identity and much of its experimental spirit in general, with Steve Lillywhite called in to give it the same pedestrian production sound as the previous two hit albums. Bono, much like the in-house tunesmiths and instant sloganeers of the '50s and '60s, also wrote the three tracks "I'll Go Crazy If I Don't Go Crazy Tonight," "Get on Your Boots," and "Stand Up Comedy" with the sole intent of scoring a hit single. Lanois, who had gone on record as saying that the album was "fantastically innovative" in the weeks leading up to its completion, was so disheartened by U2's U-turn that he and the band were barely on speaking terms by the end of the mixing stage, according to a source.

The U2 publicity machine was fired up in January 2009, beginning with the publication of Bono's first of nine op-ed columns for *The New York Times* as well as the band's appearance at U.S. president Barack Obama's inauguration ceremony. They opened both the Fifty-first Grammy Awards and the 2009 BRIT Awards with *No Line on the Horizon*'s first single "Get on Your Boots," even though neither the song nor the album was in contention for a prize. They did an unprecedented five-night residency on the *Late Show with David Letterman*. Michael Bloomberg, mayor of New York City, marked the occasion by renaming part of West Fifty-third Street "U2 Way" for one week. And they received blanket coverage across the BBC, culminating with a concert on the roof of Broadcasting House. Tory MP Nigel Evans, who sat on the culture, media, and sport select committee, complained that it was "the sort of publicity money can't buy," adding: "Why should license fee-payers shoulder the cost of U2's publicity?" Experts calculated the cost at €1 million. The BBC, which critics branded the "Big Bono Corporation," later acknowledged that coverage of the U2 album launch breached guidelines, and that use of the onscreen logo "U2 = BBC" gave "an inappropriate impression of endorsement."

No Line on the Horizon garnered a mostly positive reception from music critics when it was released on February 27. In a five-star review, David Fricke of *Rolling Stone* enthused that it was U2's "best [album], in its textural exploration and tenacious melodic grip, since 1991's *Achtung Baby*." In another perfect score, *Q* magazine's Paul Rees suggested that in time "it may prove to be better still" than U2's Berlin-set opus. *Pitchfork Media* reviewer Ryan Dombal, on the other hand, graded it 4.2 out of 10, concluding that "the album's ballyhooed experimentation is either terribly misguided or hidden underneath a wash of shameless U2-isms." Encouraged by many of the early reviews, Bono announced in interviews that U2 would release a follow-up album provisionally titled

Songs of Ascent, consisting primarily of the more esoteric, meditative songs left over from the sessions in Morocco, by the end of the year.

However, the idea would be shelved following *No Line on the Horizon*'s underwhelming commercial performance. Although it debuted at number one in thirty countries, including the UK and America, sales of the album dropped at an alarming rate. In the end, U2 moved just 5 million copies of it worldwide. McGuinness blamed the disappointing sales figures on illegal downloading, and pointed out that it was still the seventh biggest-selling album of 2009. Bono, to the dismay of online fans, claimed that it was too challenging for people and that in the future the band would do well to avoid the "disease" of so-called progressive rock. He also said that their audience weren't "groovy" enough to appreciate "Get on Your Boots," which only made number thirty-seven on the *Billboard* Hot 100 and number twelve in the UK. He told *Rolling Stone*: "Look, sometimes our audience isn't as groovy as we'd like. 'Get on Your Boots,' as it was released, is a sort of crossover, half-club, half-indie-rock record.... They [our audience] want 'Vertigo.' And when we did this the last time—with 'Discothèque,' from *Pop,* they didn't like it either." For many, Bono's comments were confirmation that U2 was completely out of touch with their fan base.

"What a pile of crap," replied one fan on the @U2 forum. "Bono, the song isn't very good, plain & simple. Being 'groovy' has nothing to do with it. We were all able to groove to 'Mysterious Ways.'" Another chimed in: "He [Bono] sounds almost bitter, not willing to accept that fans simply do not think 'Boots' is a good song. Hopefully, the failure of these awful NLOTH [*No Line on the Horizon*] singles will push the band to make better songs next time round."

Says Paul Gambaccini: "The last album was such a disappointment. They've gotten into this record industry habit of only releasing a record every four or five years, and this is so different from their early days when they were productive. It's like an athlete—if you don't train, you lose fitness, and why should that be any different in the performing arts? When artists take a couple of years out, who's to say that when they return they'll be writing as well? The Beatles' entire recording career was in seven years, and they just kept getting better and better because they were doing. And when you don't do, you get worse. I know Bono once said to me that he's gotten into a routine of one year writing, one year recording, one year touring. But that has stretched recently. And what it says is a) they don't have that much to say anymore and b) they don't say it as well. When the first single ['Get on Your Boots'] came out sounding like their version of 'Subterranean Homesick Blues' I just thought, 'Whoever thought this was good?' And, unfortunately, they crossed over the line from believability to sellouts, because they used their power to achieve one of the most publicized album launches of all time. It was like they were streaking. They were in public, and they were naked. That was very embarrassing."

The Blackberry-sponsored U2 360° Tour was deemed equally frustrating. Its gargantuan four-legged steel structure—which Bono conceptually designed using a set of forks over dinner one day during the Vertigo Tour—was truly a sight to behold. Dubbed "the Claw," the 164-foot-tall structure supported over two hundred tons of state-of-the art equipment, including 250 speakers and a cylindrical LED video screen. Three separate structures were built for around $25 million each, and cost in the region of $750,000 a day to run. It was, all told, the largest and most expensive concert stage ever constructed. Every one of the 110 dates on the stadium tour sold out, typically within minutes of tickets going on general sale. However, U2's pedestrian-like performances, as well as the exorbitant ticket prices, left longtime fans feeling cold and disconnected.

Ahead of playing three nights at Croke Park in July, U2 announced a pledge of €5 million to help fund Music Generation, a music education initiative for Ireland's youth, to be rolled out between 2010 and 2015. The news came on the back of government spending cuts on education in a bid to save €6 billion, which was part of the terms of the country's economic bailout package. Batt O'Keeffe TD, minister for education and science, welcomed the U2 donation, although some critics questioned the timing of it. They viewed it as the band's calculated attempt to pacify the anti-U2 movement in Ireland in time for their first gigs in Dublin since moving their lucrative publishing arm to a Dutch tax shelter. It didn't work. "Irish people have a strong love-hate relationship with U2," says Colm Henry. "They admire what they've done for their pride of country thing, but they don't warm to the guys . . . A lot of the thing with U2 is that the Irish who go to their concerts are not necessarily hugely into U2's music, but it's the biggest event in the country and they have to see it and be part of it."

"I think their popularity in Ireland is nowadays more than ever a reflection of their international status," adds John Waters. "Their fans are not much heard in public, and mainly what's heard is the media hostility toward them, mainly on account of the tax issue and Bono's campaigning, which tend not to endear themselves to journalists. As for the band themselves, they care less. In fact they seem to be semidetached from Ireland in more sense than one. After their gigs in Dublin, they apparently hightailed it to the airport on the final night without even dropping in on the post-gig party. I don't blame them. It's been pretty toxic for the past couple of years."

U2 faced more criticism when environmentalists noted that the first leg of the 360° Tour was on course to create the equivalent carbon footprint of a return trip to Mars in a passenger plane. "Put another way," *The Guardian* chimed in, "U2's CO2 emissions are reportedly the equivalent to the average annual waste produced by 6,500 British people, or the same as leaving a lightbulb running for 159,000 years." It was said that the construction and transportation of U2's stage emitted three times more carbon than Madonna's 2006 world tour. Even Talking Heads' David Byrne weighed in on the U2 carbon debate, saying that their concert production was "overkill" and "looks a wee bit out of balance given all the starving people in Africa and all." In an interview with BBC 6 Music, Edge dismissed the criticism, which came just a few years after Bono had warned that "[c]limate change will most affect the poorest people: the people who do not have the resources to deal with the coming changes" at a TED conference, as "unfair" and insisted that the band would "offset whatever carbon footprint we have." Helen

Roberts, an environmental consultant for carbonfootprint.com, said that they would need to plant over twenty thousand trees a year to do so. In the end, U2 and Live Nation's solution was to encourage fans to carpool to their shows as well as pay an extra $1.89 on top of regular concert ticket prices to help raise $450,000 for various environmentally conscious power plants.

By late autumn, the U2 360° Tour juggernaut had swallowed up whole stadiums in Spain, England, Germany, North America, Canada, and other key markets as well. The band took a long break over the winter and spring months before preparing themselves for another sixteen tour dates in the United States and their first-ever headlining performance at the UK's Glastonbury Festival in June 2010. However, U2 was forced to postpone all their commitments after their leader sustained a devastating back injury. It happened in New York on May 11, just twenty-four hours after celebrating his fiftieth birthday. During a training session for the forthcoming third leg of the tour, Bono slipped a disc in his back which punctured a ligament and broke into two pieces, traveling into his spinal canal. He experienced partial paralysis in his lower right leg and had to walk around with a cane for several days until an MRI scan revealed the extent of the damage. On the recommendation of celebrity healer Dr. Hans-Wilhelm Müller-Wohlfahrt, he underwent emergency spinal surgery at Munich's LMU University Hospital. "This surgery was the only course of treatment for full recovery and to avoid further paralysis," said his surgeon, Professor Jörg Christian Tonn, in a press statement. "Bono is now much better, with complete recovery of his motor deficit. The prognosis is excellent but to obtain a sustainable result, he must now enter a period of rehabilitation." U2 lost around $15 million as a result of the delayed shows, half of which was covered by insurance.

Following an eight-week, three-hour-per-day rehabilitation program, Bono made a triumphant return to the stage on August 6 at the Stadio Olimpico in Turin, Italy. He showed no signs of his injuries as he strutted and shadowboxed around the circular stage like a man half his age. During the show, he thanked fans for their support after receiving thousands of get-well wishes on the group's Web site. "This band is like a family. It's a family business, U2. I am the prodigal son. I would like to thank my brothers for their patience," he also said, pointing to his bandmates. In interviews, he described himself as "Bono 2.0."

U2 closed the LED curtain on the 360° Tour in Moncton, Canada, in July 2011, by which time they had performed 110 dates around the world, as well as a rearranged headline slot at the Glastonbury Festival, in which they did their best to overcome the rainy conditions and a heated protest against their tax status. Despite all the trials and tribulations that they had faced both on and off stage, the U2 360° Tour had ended up dethroning The Rolling Stones' 2005–07 A Bigger Bang Tour for the title of the highest-grossing concert trek in history, with approximately $736 million in ticket sales. McGuinness said the tour's success represented the culmination of over more than three decades' worth of hard graft and military-like planning. "We were always very conscious that we had two parallel careers, as recording artists and as live performers, and each was absolutely vitally important," he told *Billboard*. "In our own kind of quiet way we were all somewhat military about it. We would talk about territories and conquering them, and if there was somewhere that was slower to come along, we would go back there and work it again. Bono is kind of a closet General Patton. So, for us, this is a real victory."

■

The U2 quartet spent the next two years as busy as ever, just not necessarily with the band itself. Bono and Edge focused more of their energies on their problem-plagued Broadway musical *Spider-Man: Turn Off the Dark,* for which they had composed both lyrics and music. The duo's involvement in the $75 million production, the most expensive in Broadway history, stretched back to 2002, when its veteran producer Tony Adams approached them to write the score. But the production seemed to be cursed from the outset. In 2005, Edge and Adams met in the guitarist's New York penthouse to sign the official partnership agreement, but as Edge left the room to fetch a pen, Adams suffered a stroke. Two days later, he passed away, at the age of fifty-two. Adams's business partner, David Garfinkle, stepped in as producer, but the entertainment lawyer was soon found out of his depth, preferring to entrust director Julie Taymor, as well as Bono and Edge, with the creative aspects of the musical. By early 2009, the show was $25 million in the red and still without a completed book or score. With the production in limbo, Bono convinced Michael Cohl and Jeremiah J. Harris to take over as co-lead producers, and the pair raised a further $30 million for the project.

Taymor, a Tony Award winner for *The Lion King,* was ousted in March 2011 after a series of further setbacks—including multiple cast member injuries and scathing preview reviews—had seen the musical reduced to a punchline on late-night television. *New York Times* critic Ben Brantley wrote: "*Spider-Man* is not only the most expensive musical ever to hit Broadway; it may also rank among the worst." Bono and Edge cited concerns for Taymor's well-being and a reluctance to approve key script changes as grounds for her dismissal. Taymor, who had given Bono a brief role as an antiwar shaman in her 2007 big-screen musical *Across the Universe,* accused the U2 pair of being absent from critical development stages, delivering an unsuitable score, and plotting to undermine her vision. Taymor filed a lawsuit against the producers for violating her "creative rights as an author" of the musical, which was eventually settled out of court in her favor. The settlement potentially saved Bono from another embarrassing high-profile court appearance. A private e-mail composed by Taymor's writing partner, Glen Berger, and highlighted in the legal papers, alleged that the singer had disrupted a scheduled meeting intended to address the show's problems when he "showed up in our room with Christy Turlington and a couple other supermodels, and he had already had a few beers, rendering him useless." The producers agreed to hold off the meeting until the following afternoon, but it never took place. By January 2012, the critically panned *Spider-Man: Turn Off the Dark* had become an unlikely tourist attraction, although a slow decline in box office in recent months would suggest that the musical may never recoup its $75 million capitalization.

Elsewhere, Bono continued to make interesting friends and enemies in the world of politics, often in the unlikeliest of places. (PRODUCT) RED had itself become an iconic global brand, and claimed to have contributed over $150 million for HIV/AIDS programs in Africa via the Global Fund. EDUN, which Bono and Ali had sunk $20 million of their money into, had demonstrated the potential of ethical trade after a rocky start, even though less than 40 percent of the collection was actually made in Africa. And the celebrity-packaged ONE Campaign, which had merged with DATA, kept the spotlight on Africa, although its methods and overall message remained a point of contention among aid experts. The names and backgrounds of its board members, including Larry Summers and Condoleezza Rice, were reason enough to become suspicious of its motives. George Monbiot of *The Guardian* wrote: "It claims to work on behalf of the extremely poor. But its board is largely composed of multimillionaires, corporate aristocrats, and U.S. enforcers. . . . If, as ONE does, an organization keeps telling you that it's a 'grassroots campaign,' it's a fair bet that it is nothing of the kind. This collaboration of multimillionaires and technocrats looks to me more like a projection of U.S. and corporate power." The shit hit the proverbial fan when it emerged that Bono and ONE had endorsed the G8's New Alliance for Food Security and Nutrition, an initiative to mobilize private capital for investment in Africa's agricultural sector. Or, as Rady Ananda of *Activist Post* explained, "a euphemism for monocultured, genetically modified crops and toxic agrochemicals aimed at making poor farmers debt slaves to corporations, while destroying the ecosphere for profit." When Bono, in a speech to students at Georgetown University in November 2012, declared that only capitalism can end poverty, few people questioned his zeal.

Edge came under fire from environmental groups and neighboring residents for his attempts to build five eco-luxury homes on a rugged ridgeline above Malibu. In August 2011, he and three associates filed lawsuits in the Superior Court looking to overturn the California Coastal Commission's vote of eight to four against the proposal, which was described by the commission's executive director, the late

Peter Douglas, as "one of the three worst projects that I've seen in terms of environmental devastation [in thirty-eight years]." Edge had tried to get around the various rules and regulations limiting mega-developments in the coastal area by submitting five separate applications, each under a different corporate name, but the commission still identified them as a single project. He'd even donated $1 million to the Santa Monica Mountains Conservancy. But as of yet, no progress. Edge would have to keep his Zen-like cool.

Adam was again involved in his own highly publicized courtroom drama—only this time he wasn't the one standing trial. His former personal assistant Carol Hawkins was sentenced to seven years in prison in July 2012 for the embezzlement of €2.8 million of his money. She was convicted at Dublin Circuit Criminal Court on 181 counts of theft from the bassist's bank accounts between 2005 and 2008. Hawkins, originally hired as a housekeeper at Adam's Rathfarnham mansion in 1992, had gained his "absolute trust" over the years, the court heard. She was appointed a signatory on two of his bank accounts, from which she deposited 181 checks into her own personal account. Adam's money was splashed on twenty-two horses, exotic holidays, and a $465,000 pad in New York, among other extravagances. Straight after her sentencing, Hawkins was driven off to jail in a police van marked with, of all things, the security number U2.

It was also announced that Adam had fathered a son in 2010, although the French mother's identity would remain a mystery. And he again entered uncharted territory on September 4, 2013, when he tied the knot with his Brazilian girlfriend, Mariana Teixeira de Carvalho, in a civil ceremony in Dublin, with Edge and Morleigh on hand to take a few snaps. The silver-haired bassist and youthful art gallery director, who had been dating for around eighteen months, later celebrated their union in regal fashion with a second ceremony at the fourteenth-century Château de la Napoule on the French Riviera.

Larry, meanwhile, appeared opposite French actress Juliette Binoche in his second feature-length film, *A Thousand Times Good Night*. The film premiered on August 31, 2013, at the Thirty-seventh Montreal World

Film Festival, where it was received by standing applause from the fifteen hundred audience members and won the Special Grand Prix of the jury. The dream was still very much alive.

As for the business of U2, Paul McGuinness announced on November 13, 2013, his intention to step down from his role as full-time manager of the band after thirty-five years, as part of a $30 million deal that would see Live Nation buy Principle Management and Maverick, Madonna's management company run by Guy Oseary. Under the new arrangement, Oseary, who was forty-one years old at the time, would take over the day-to-day running of the U2 empire itself, with McGuinness assuming the title of "chairman" at Principle. *The New York Times* quoted McGuinness as saying: "It could be seen as slightly poor etiquette for a manager to consider retiring before his artist has split, quit, or died, but U2 have never subscribed to the rock 'n' roll code of conduct. As I approach the musically relevant age of sixty-four I have resolved to take a less hands-on role as the band embarks on the next cycle of their extraordinary career."

Although news of McGuinness's imminent departure came as a shock to U2 fans worldwide, it was perhaps less surprising to friends of the portly impresario who had harbored concerns about his health in recent years. The band themselves also hoped that the addition of the new- and social-media savvy Oseary would aid their recruitment of high-profile brand partners to help promote the release of their next studio album, tentatively due in spring 2014. The quartet had been working sporadically on two projects, according to Bono: a "club-sounding album" with will.i.am, RedOne, and David Guetta, and a "rock album" with super-producer Danger Mouse. At the time *U2: The Definitive Biography* was written, neither project had been officially confirmed as the new album, although Bono was at pains to reiterate the aging band's desire and need to remain relevant by writing songs custom-made for the radio.

But what of U2's legacy?

"What their legacy will be is what it was at their high point, which was to reintroduce social relevance into rock, to be the conscience of the industry (which they were), to have a new kind of mix of hard rock and experimental sound, and to be one of the few bands whose every member is known by millions for a distinctive way of performing. You have The Beatles and The Stones, and then you have U2," says Paul Gambaccini, adding: "I don't want to sound heretical, but I doubt that they're going to substantially add to their legacy. They just seem to be out of sync at the moment. I only note the disappointments of U2 with regret because I love them so much, but there is this problem that they've lost their exceptionalism."

Indeed. Many firmly believe that what was once a yearning for acceptance and a global platform to bring about positive change has mutated into a lust for money and power, and that absolutely nothing will stand in the way of U2 achieving their corporate goals. The band members are both victims of the rock-and-roll machine and the architects of their own moral downfall.

"Young bands view U2 with a lot of skepticism," says Greg Kot. "They may admire them for their money and fame, but U2 is no longer the model of how to succeed in a vile business without selling your soul. That job is better filled by people like Neil Young."

"They are the '80s generation, the post-punk generation, Rolling Stones or Eagles," states Jim DeRogatis. "They've become this giant megacorporation that needs to sustain itself. If you look at the ticket prices on the last tour, it's absurd. I've interviewed Larry and I know it makes him sore to think of any U2 fan not being able to afford a ticket, being mistreated, being subject to scams by Ticketmaster, etc. There are elements of the band that genuinely care for their fans, but I'm sorry, you play these enormous stadiums with a company like you're working with, Live Nation, and people get screwed. Could Radiohead successfully tour without a giant promoter? I don't know. But U2 could do what it wants. U2 could become its own record company. It could become its own global touring company. It's got the money, it's got the clout, it's got the name, and yet it does business the old-fashioned way with the worst elements of the music business. How much more money do you need?

"[Musically] had the band ended at *Pop,* they still would have been perceived as going out on top, because they were at least challenging themselves up to the end. [*No Line on the Horizon*] was a bit of a bounce back, but it wasn't as sonically exciting.

"It is the end of the U2 story," concludes DeRogatis. "But we're probably doomed to ten more years of them because of Live Nation. If it didn't matter, it wouldn't be so heartbreaking. But to see bands like U2 become what they once hated and operated in opposition to, it really is heartbreaking."

Bibliography

Books

Alan, Carter. *U2: The Road to Pop*. Boston: Faber and Faber, 1997.

Bono and Michka Assayas. *Bono: In Conversation with Michka Assayas with a Foreword by Bono*. London: Hodder & Stoughton, 2005.

Cashman, Lola. *Inside the Zoo with U2: My Life with the World's Biggest Rock Band*. London: John Blake, 2003.

Chatterton, Mark. *U2: The Ultimate Encyclopedia*. London: Firefly Pub., 2004.

Clayton-Lea, Tony. *Chris De Burgh: The Authorized Biography*. London: Sidgwick & Jackson, 1996.

Coleman, Ray. *Sinatra, A Portrait of the Artist*. London: Pavilion, 1998.

Dunphy, Eamon. *Unforgettable Fire: Past, Present, and the Future—The Definitive Biography of U2*. New York: Warner Books, Inc., 1987.

Flanagan, Bill. *U2 at the End of the World*. New York: Delacorte, 1995.

Graham, Bill, and Amy Garvey. *U2, the Early Days*. New York: Delta, 1989.

Hertz, Noreena. *The Debt Threat: How Debt Is Destroying the Developing World*. New York: HarperBusiness, 2004.

McCormick, Neil. *I Was Bono's Doppelganger*. London: Penguin, 2005.

———*U2 by U2*. New York: HarperCollins, 2006.

McGee, Matt. *U2: A Diary*. London: Omnibus, 2011.

Negus, Keith. *Producing Pop: Culture and Conflict in the Popular Music Industry*. London: Edward Arnold, 1992.

Polman, Linda. *War Games: The Story of Aid and War in Modern Times*. London: Viking, 2010.

Rushdie, Salman. *The Ground Beneath Her Feet: A Novel*. New York: Henry Holt, 1999.

Sachs, Jeffrey. *The End of Poverty: Economic Possibilities for Our Time*. New York: Penguin, 2005.

Scrimgeour, Diana. *U2 Show*. New York: Riverhead, 2004.

Stokes, Niall. *U2: The Stories Behind Every U2 Song*. London: Carlton, 2009.

The Complete Guide to the Music of U2. London: Omnibus, 2004.

U2 Live: A Concert Documentary. London: Omnibus, 2003.

U2: The Best of Propaganda: 20 Years of the Official U2 Magazine. New York: Thunder's Mouth, 2003.

Waters, John. *Race of Angels: Ireland and the Genesis of U2*. Belfast: Blackstaff, 1994.

Williams, Peter, and Steve Turner. *U2: Rattle & Hum: The Official Book of the U2 Movie: A Journey into the Heartland of Two Americas*. New York: Harmony, 1988.

Articles

"A Day With Bono: 'We Have to Make Africa an Adventure.'" *The Guardian*, June 2005.

"Africa: IMF, World Bank Are a Major Cause of Poverty." *allAfrica*, March 2007.

Baer, Susan. "U2's Bono in Washington." *Washingtonian*, March 2006.

"Blair, Bono Win One for Africa." *The Christian Science Monitor*, June 2005.

Block, Adam. "Bono Bites Back." *Mother Jones*, May 1989.

"Bono Kicks Off 'Wardrobe Tour.'" *Irish Independent*, June 2005.

Bono. "World Debt Angers Me." *The Guardian*, February 1999.

Brainbridge, Luke. "This Much I Know." *The Observer*, August 2009.

Burns, John. "Out of Control." *The Sunday Times*, July 1998

Bush, Dana. "U2 Singer, Jesse Helms Discuss AIDS." *CNN*, June 2001.

"Can Bono Save the Third World?" *Newsweek*, January 2000.

"Can Bono Save the World?" *Time,* March 2003.

Cameron, Keith. "U2 at the Crossroads." *Mojo,* July 2005.

"Cashman Will Not Have to Pay Band's Costs." *The Independent,* November 2006.

Clymer, Adam. "Helms Reverses Opposition to Help on AIDS." *The New York Times,* March 2002.

Cocks, Jay. "U2 Soars with a Top Album, a Hot Tour and Songs of Spirit and Conscience." *Time,* April 1987.

Dalton, Stephen. "How the West Was Won." *Uncut,* October 2003.

——— "U2 and the Making of Achtung Baby." *Uncut,* November 2004.

——— "U2: In the Name of Love." *Uncut,* November 1999.

Donnelly, John. "Helms's Reversal on U.S. Aid Reverberates: Senator Seeks $500M to Help Stamp Out AIDS Transmission in Africa." *The Boston Globe,* March 2002.

Doyle, Tom. "10 Years of Turmoil Inside U2." *Q,* October 2002.

———"U2 People #2: Brian Eno." *Q,* February 2007.

Easterly, William. "Cui Bono? The Murky Finances of Project (RED)™." *Aidwatch,* December 2009.

"Edge Wedding Is a French Connection." *Ireland on Sunday,* June 2002.

"Evidence Points to Only One Winner: The Lawyers." *The Independent,* October 2006.

Fay, Liam. "The Verdict." *Hot Press,* September 1989.

Fitzgerald, Garret. "King of Rock 'n' Roll Deals Has Regal Air." *The Irish Times,* September 1998.

Flanagan, Bill. "Soul Revelation and the Baptism of Fire." *Musician,* February 1984.

Fletcher, Tony. "U2: The Pride of Lions." *Jamming!,* October 1984.

Friedman, Wayne. "Iovine Learns U2's All about El-e-va-tion to a New Demographic." *Advertising Age,* March 2002.

Gorman, John. "Radio and the Labels: Outlandish Accusations and Propositions." *GormanMedia,* August 2007.

Graham, Bill. "U2 Could Be a Headline." *Hot Press,* March 1979.

"Guggi Knights." *The Sunday Times,* May 2000.

"Gwenda More than Just a Famous Mother." *Fingal-Independent.ie,* November 2008.

Hayes, Dermott. "Do You Know This Man?" *Select,* June 1993.

"Heart of America Tour: Africa's Future and Ours' Kicks Off on World AIDS Day." DATA Press Release, November 2002.

"Heavily Indebted Poor Countries (HIPC) Initiative—Status of Implementation." Prepared by the Staffs of the IMF and World Bank, August 2005.

Hodkinson, Stuart. "G8 - Africa Nil." *Red Pepper,* November 2005.

Iley, Chrissy. "U2 Interview: Group Therapy." *The Sunday Times,* November 2004.

Jolson-Colburn, Jeffrey. "U2, Cohl to Take $100 Mil Tour." *The Hollywood Reporter,* March 1996.

Kent, Nick. "Dreamer in the Real World." *The Face,* May 1985.

Kim, Jae-Ha. "An In Depth History: R U2 4 Real?" *VRS* magazine, July 1985.

Kot, Greg. "U2 Apologizes for Site's Ticket Sale Debacle." *Chicago Tribune,* January 2006.

Mackey, Liam. "Articulate Speech of the Heart." *Hot Press,* July 1983.

Martin, Gavin. "Kings of the Celtic Fringe." *NME,* February 1981.

McDonagh, Patricia. "Planners Backed U2 Bid out of Deference." *Irish Independent,* November 2007.

McElhatton, Shane. "U-2." *Imprint,* October 1979.

McNally, Frank. "The Man Who Made Sure U2 Did the Business." *The Irish Times,* August 1997.

McWeeney, Myles. "Naomi: When the Glam Goes." *Independent.ie,* February 2002.

Morley, Paul. "Boy's Own Weepies." *NME,* October 1980.

Nolan, Larissa. "Bono May Be a Big Star But All Else about Him Is Little: Lola." *The Sunday Independent,* December 2006.

——— "Why Lola Just Won't Take Her Stetson Off to U2." *The Sunday Independent,* October 2006.

Nolan, Tom & Jas Obrecht. "The Edge of U2." *Guitar Player,* June 1985.

O'Brien, Jason. "Master Legal Eagle Finally Sweeps Bono from Centre Stage." *Irish Independent,* October 2006.

O'Doherty, Caroline. "Bono Bids His Father Fond Farewell: 'He's Going Home.'" *Irish Examiner,* August 2001.

O'Hagan, Sean. "The Observer Profile: Bono." *The Observer,* September 2004.

O'Loughlin, Ann. "Bono Completely Paranoid about His Appearance." *The Independent,* October 2006.

O'Morain, Paidraig. "He made his mark in a ravaged, grim Dublin." *The Evening Herald*, January 2009.

Smith, Ethan. "For U2, Live Nation Deal Rocks." *The Wall Street Journal*, December 2008.

Stoute, Lenny. "Looking for the Soul of America." *Rock Express*, April 1987.

Sutton, Rich. "Exclusive Interview with U2." *Song Hits*, September 1983.

"The Modern Drummer." *Propaganda*, January 1996.

"The World According to Guggi." *Independent.ie*, July 2013.

Tomlinson, Richard. "Bono, Who Preaches Charity, Profits from Buyouts, Tax Breaks." *Bloomberg*, January 2007.

Traub, James. "The Statesman." *The New York Times Magazine*, September 2005.

Tyrangiel, Josh. "The Constant Charmer." *Time*, December 2005.

"U2 Member Guilty of Drunken Driving." *The Irish Times*, 1984.

Weissman, Robert. "The IMF on the Run: The International Monetary Fund Tries to Outrun Its Critics." *Multinational Monitor*, April 2000.

Wenner, Jann. "Bono: The Rolling Stone Interview." *Rolling Stone*, November 2005.

William, Chris. "U2: Anthems Away." *BAM*, December 1984.

Acknowledgments

The author would like to thank the interviewees and real stars of this book. Those who did not request anonymity include: Adriana Kaegi, Annie Roseberry, Barry Fey, Bob Vogt, Carter Alan, Charles Abugre, Chas de Whalley, Cheryl Poirier, Chris Spedding, Colm Henry, Dave Meegan, Dave Robinson, David Batstone, David Petrie, David Rieff, Dick Molenaar, Don Knox, Don Law, Fachtna O'Ceallaigh, Francis Kennedy, Greg Kot, Harvey Goldsmith, Jack Dublin, Janice Bearman, Jas Obrecht, Jerry Mickelson, Jim DeRogatis, Jim Leach, John Hilary, John Leslie, John Waters, Kevin Moloney, Kurt Loder, Dr. Kumi Naidoo, Lola Cashman, Lou Maglia, Marc Marot, Mark Evans, Mark Sinker, Mark Wallis, Meiert Avis, Neil Storey, Nick Stewart, Paolo Hewitt, Patrick Pfeiffer, Paul Gambaccini, Paul Slattery, Paul Williams, Randy Ezratty, Richard Murphy, Simon Osborne, Stephen Rainford, Terry Elcock, Tim Adams, Tim Devine, Tom Sheehan, Tony Michaelides.

Thank you to the following people who helped directly in the making of this book: Alan Godden, Ben Lavelle, Chris Gibbon, Christina MacDonald, Christopher Collins, David Gibbon, Diana and Laurie

Jobling, Dion Simte, Elaine and Rodney Joyce, Erik Hersman, Glenn Shambrook, Jennifer Letwack, Kieran Frost, Lauren Jobling, Marjorie and Alan Jackson, Michael Gloyne, Neil Morganstein, Nicole Sohl, Otto Kitsinger, Paul Gibbon, Peter McAviney, Phil Romans, René Imre, Steve Kalinsky, Steven Clarkson, Vern Evans.

The author would like to extend his heartfelt gratitude to his tireless and supportive agent, Andrew Lownie, and diligent editor, Rob Kirkpatrick. Thanks for sticking by the project through its ups and downs.

Finally, the author would especially like to thank his mother, Mary Jobling, for her constant support and guidance throughout his life.

Index

Index

Index

Index

Index